Family Tree Maker

™

USER'S TUTORIAL AND REFERENCE MANUAL

CREDITS

Family Members
Thanks to our family members: Joane and Ross Anderson; Debi Bodenheimer; Gary Corda; John Costello; Stephanie Duiven; Marjorie and James Ewart; Ryan and Kyle Fineran; Lori Glantz; Jocelyn Goldfein, Tani, Braden, and Davis Holstege; Connie and Amber Hess; Michelle Javier; Andrew Johnson; David and Judy Johnson; Amy King; Doug Kraft; Jun, Tae, and Ellice Lee; Ivonne Merrin; Charlie Mullin; Paul Paternoster; Elizabeth, Christie, and Jennifer Paz; Kelley and Kayla Powers; Terry, Sandy, Sara, and Barney Rudy; Herb and Elaine Schoech; Bob, Nancy, and Taryn Stanko; Sheng, Ming, and Ken Tang; and Dennis and Cynthia Vanata. They were supportive and understanding during the months it took to complete these projects.

Program Design, Coding, and Management
Doug Anderson, Randy Eike, Cathi Fineran, Nolan Glantz, Dan Handalian II, Kenneth L. Hess, Eric Holstege, Bryan Johnson, Courtney Kermeen, Dave King, Daniel Kraft, Jeff Levinsky, Kimberly Mullin, Kim Paternoster, Gary Quigg, Hugo Paz, Teri Schoech, Steve Stanko, Danielle Sunshine, Harvey Tang, Cathy Thompson, and Michael Vanata

Research, Technical Assistance, and Data Entry
Jennifer Bjork, Paul Burchfield, Courtney Chandler, Kimberly Mullin, Dalit Muzzarelli, Tina C. Nomura, Brenda Plant, Terry Rudy, and Danielle Sunshine

Proofing, Testing, and Critiquing
Shagufta Ahmad, Paul Arthur, Sylvia Costello, Dave Fox, Todd Funasaki, Lisa Graves, Dan Handalian II, Denis Khoo, Joab Kong, Claire LaBeaux, Scott Leavitt, Allen Lee, Ted Lee, Derek Lin, Kristian Ljungqvist, Tim Markley, Charles Merrin, Tina C. Nomura, Brenda Plant, Bruce Powers, Terry Rudy, Joy Zhao, and Gwen Zierdt

Documentation
Kimberly Mullin and Cathi Fineran, with assistance from Sylvia Costello

Packaging
Woods and Woods, Kate Anderson, Courtney Kermeen, and Andria Strelow

About Your Family Tree Maker Software and Manual

Brøderbund Software, Incorporated encourages you to make a backup copy of Family Tree Maker for your own use. However, the software and manual are protected by United States and International copyright laws. Except for backup purposes, it is a Federal Crime to make copies of the software for any purpose, including for use by another person.

It is a Federal Crime to copy the manual in whole or in part without Brøderbund's prior written consent.

Trademarks

Avery is a registered trademark of the Avery Dennison Corporation.
Microsoft is a registered trademark and Windows is a trademark of Microsoft Corporation.
Automated Archives Incorporated is a trademark of Brøderbund Software.
Photo CD portions © the Eastman Kodak Company.
All other brands or products are trademarks or registered trademarks of their respective holders and should be treated as such.

TABLE OF CONTENTS

Introduction... 3
    Viewing Your Information 4
    Print Several Kinds of Trees 4
    Enter Any Type of Information 6
    Research Your Family History at Home... 6
    Windows 95 Users 8
    System Requirements.. 8
    Technical Support 9
    We Want to Hear from You!...10
    Ordering Products 10
    Customer Registration 10
    About Mailing Lists 10
    Family Tree Maker Product Upgrade Plan 10

Chapter 1: Program Setup...13
    Installing Family Tree Maker 13
        Windows 95 Users...13
        Storing Your Family Tree Maker Diskette(s)..............................13
        Installing a Diskette Version of Family Tree Maker 14
        Installing a CD-ROM Version of Family Tree Maker..................15
        Installing a Diskette Version Under Windows 95 16
        Installing a CD-ROM Version Under Windows 95......................16
    Starting Family Tree Maker..17
        If You've Never Used a Family Tree Maker Product 18
        If You Have Family Tree Maker for DOS Files...........................19
    Where to Go from Here 20
    Windows Basics and Family Tree Maker 20
    Getting Help..25
    Preferences — Customizing Family Tree Maker....................................26
        Selecting Startup Preferences 26
        Selecting Help System Preferences 28

Chapter 2: Tutorial..33
    Before You Start 33
    Starting Family Tree Maker..34
    Part I: Entering Family Information..35
    Part II: The More About Dialog Boxes...50

Part III: Scrapbooks 59
Part IV: Printing a Family Tree 66
    What to Do Next...72

Chapter 3: Entering Basic Information **75**
  A Quick Overview...75
  The Family Page 76
    Entering Family Information..77

Chapter 4: Moving Around...**105**
  Moving Between Closely-Related Individuals 105
    Parents' Family Page...107
    Child's Family Page 108
    Sibling's Family Page 108
    Other Spouses...110
    Other Parents 113
  Moving to Anyone in Your Family File 117
    Opening the Index of Individuals 117
    Moving Around in the Index of Individuals 118
    Rearranging the Index of Individuals 120
    Moving to Other Views from the Index of Individuals 121
  Locating Individuals in Your Family File.............................122

Chapter 5: Entering Detailed Information **129**
  Entering Brief Biographical Facts.......................................130
  Entering Addresses 132
  Entering Medical Information...133
  Entering Nicknames, Titles, and Parental Relationship Information 134
  Entering Stories and Notes...137
    Moving Around in the Notes Dialog Box.........................139
    Editing Text in the Notes Dialog Box 140
    Moving or Copying Text from One Notes Dialog Box
      to Another...140
    Finding Text in the Notes Dialog Box.............................141
    Formatting Text in the Notes Dialog Box 142
    Copying Text from Another Windows Program into a
      Notes Dialog Box 142
    Importing Text from Another Program into a Notes Dialog Box...143
    Exporting Text from the Notes Dialog Box into
      Another Program 144

Entering Details About a Marriage 145
    Entering Brief Marriage Facts 145
    Entering Marriage Stories and Notes 146
Scrapbooks: The Basics 147
    Opening a Scrapbook for an Individual or Marriage 148
    What Goes into a Scrapbook? 149
    Setting Defaults for Picture Resolution and Compression 152
Scrapbooks: Inserting Items 153
    Picture/Object: Insert Photo CD Picture 154
    Picture/Object: Insert Picture from File 157
    Picture/Object: Insert Object 159
    Edit: Paste and Edit: Paste Special 161
Scrapbooks: Working with Picture/Objects 164
    Recording Important Picture/Object Information 164
    Finding Picture/Objects in a Scrapbook 167
    Moving Around in a Scrapbook 168
    Viewing Pictures at Full Size 168
    Playing OLE Objects 170
    Playing a Scrapbook 170
    Sorting a Scrapbook 171
    Editing Picture/Objects 172
    Controlling Picture/Object Brightness and Contrast 177
    Controlling Picture Resolution and Compression 178
    Moving or Copying Picture/Objects Between Scrapbooks 180
    Removing Picture/Objects from a Scrapbook 181

Chapter 6: Fixing Relationship Mistakes **185**
Removing an Individual from Your Family File 185
Detaching a Child from the Wrong Parents 186
Detaching Incorrect Spouses from Each Other 187
Linking Children to Their Parents 188
Linking Individuals by Marriage 189

Chapter 7: Searching Archives at Home **193**
How Can Family Tree Maker Help with Family Research? 193
How Do the Family Archives and FamilyFinder Index Work? 193
What Can I Do with Information from Family Archives? 194
Why Use Family Archives and the FamilyFinder Index? 194

Opening Family Archives and the FamilyFinder Index.......................195
    Moving Around in Family Archives and the
       FamilyFinder Index 195
    Where to Go from Here..195
All About Introduction Pages 196
All About Contents Pages..197
All About Index Pages...198
    Scrolling Through an Index..199
All About Family Archive Information Pages 200
    Scrolling Through the Information Pages...201
Locating Names with the Search Expert..202
    Preferences for Searching...202
    Searching in the FamilyFinder Index 203
    Searching in Family Archives 208
    Copying Information from Family Archives to Your
       Family File 210
    Searching in World Family Tree Archives.......................................214
What if I Can't Find My Ancestor's Name?.......................................218
Purchasing Family Archives 219
The "How-To" Guide 220
Using Family Archives Responsibly..223
    Acceptable Use..223
    Why are Family Archives Copyrighted?..224
    Abuse of Copyright 224
    Frequently Asked Questions...225

Chapter 8: Creating and Printing Trees.......................................229
Types of Trees 229
    Fit to Page Ancestor Trees 229
    Custom Ancestor Trees 230
    Descendant Trees 232
    Direct Descendant Trees..232
    Outline Descendant Trees..234
    Outline Direct Descendant Trees...234
Creating Ancestor Trees 237
Creating All Types of Descendant Trees 238
Customizing Trees 239
    Zooming 240
    Showing Page Lines 241
    Using Your Mouse in Trees 241

Choosing the Number of Generations 242
Selecting Information to Include in Your Tree...............................243
Formatting the Information in Your Tree......................................247
Formatting Text...253
Choosing Styles for Boxes, Lines, & Tree Borders.......................254
Adding a Title and Footnote..254
Selecting the Layout for Box-Style Trees 255
Selecting the Layout for Outline-Style Trees 256
Limiting the Width of Boxes and Picture/Objects..........................258
Other Printing Options 259
Controlling the Size of Your Tree...261
If Your Tree Is Too Tall..261
If Your Tree Is Too Wide..262
Printing Your Tree 263
Creating a Set of Trees...264
Print Setup 266

Chapter 9: Printing Detailed Information 271
The Basics of Printing..271
All About Labels and Cards..272
Creating Labels and Cards..272
Customizing Labels and Cards..273
All About Family Group Sheets...273
Creating a Family Group Sheet 273
Customizing a Family Group Sheet..274
All About Reports 275
Creating a Report...275
Customizing a Report...278
All About Printed Scrapbook Pages...278
Displaying Scrapbook Pages 279
Customizing Scrapbook Pages 279
Customizing Your Documents...280
Zooming 280
Showing Page Lines 281
Using Your Mouse in Reports and Labels and Cards....................281
Label/Card Size and Print Setup..282
Selecting Individuals to Include in Your Document 283
Finding Individuals in Reports 291
Choosing the Number of Generations for Kinship Reports...........292
Selecting Information to Include in Your Document 293

Formatting the Information in Your Document.............................297
Formatting Text...308
Adding a Title and Footnote...310
Choosing the Layout for Scrapbooks 312
Choosing Borders and Line Styles 313
Limiting the Width of Picture/Objects 314
Choosing Column Widths and Spacing in Reports 315
Choosing the Family Group Sheet Format 316
Setting Other Printing Options 316
Choosing the Sorting Order..318
Printing Your Document 319

Chapter 10: Other Printing...323
Calendars 323
Creating a Calendar 323
Customizing a Calendar 324
Selecting Individuals to Include in Your Calendar................324
Selecting Information to Include in Your Calendar................331
Formatting Text...332
Adding a Subtitle and Footnote..332
Borders, Background Colors, and Fill Colors 333
Printing a Calendar..333
Family Pages and More About Dialog Boxes.............................335
Printing Family Page Information 335
Printing More About Information...336
Batch Printing 338
Selecting and Setting Up the Document Type........................338
Selecting a Print Order and Individuals to Print...................339
Selecting Print Settings 346
Special Uses for Batch Printing..347
Creating Family Books 348
Copying Items to Other Applications...................................348

Chapter 11: Managing Your Files...351
Creating New Family Files 351
Opening Existing Files..351
Opening PAF Files..352
GEDCOM Import and Export..353
Importing GEDCOM Files into Family Tree Maker 353
Exporting GEDCOM Files from Family Tree Maker 359

The World Family Tree Project 362
    Details of Participation 362
    Your Participation is Important 364
    How to Submit Your File 365
Checking Your File for Errors 367
    Data Entry Checking 368
    The Find Error Command 370
    Data Errors Reports 371
    Error Types...371
Backing Up Your Family File...376
Opening Backup Files...378
Combining Files...379
    Opening the Files..379
    Mapping Information Between the Source and Destination Files ..380
    Selecting Individuals to Include 382
    Appending and Merging Information...383
Merging Duplicate Individuals 387
Copying and Exporting Files 389
Exporting and Deleting Groups of Individuals 390
Finding Files 392
Deleting Files 393
Getting Information About Your Environment..393
Family File Status 394

Appendix A: Researching Families **397**

Appendix B: LDS Ordinance Information **405**

Appendix C: Kodak Photo CD-ROM Discs......................................**407**

Appendix D: Accessories **415**

Appendix E: Troubleshooting...**417**
System Requirements...418
Installation Problems 419
Printing Problems 421
Error Messages 425
Display Problems 426
Computer Problems 427
CD-ROM Problems 428
Disk Type...428
Disk Space 429
Memory and Resources..430

Playing Videos in Scrapbooks 431
Reinstalling DLLs...431
Print Setup 432
Doing a Clean Boot..434
   Editing Your Files 435
Working with Share 438
   Removing SHARE.EXE..439
   Removing VSHARE.386 439

INTRODUCTION

The maternal grandmother of Dan Handalian, one of Family Tree Maker's designers, was quite a card in her younger years. Here she is playfully posing in an old clamming bucket during the summer of 1938, in Wareham, Massachusetts. A year later she was married, and to this day remains youthful, spirited, and lots of fun.

INTRODUCTION

FAMILY TREE MAKER for Windows can store any kind of family information, from names and birth dates to priceless family stories, pictures, and videos.

Family Tree Maker is quick and easy to use. You enter basic family information just as if you were filling out a form. Optional screens let you enter more extensive information and store pictures, sounds, and OLE objects. From the information you enter, Family Tree Maker can automatically create trees, calendars, and more. You only enter information once — Family Tree Maker does the rest of the work for you.

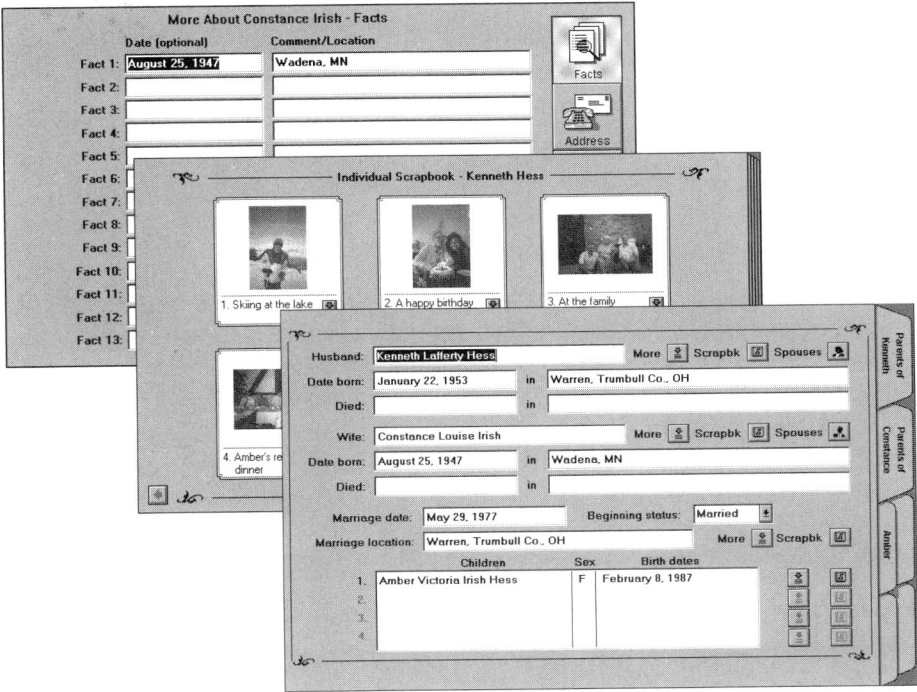

Figure I-1. A few of the places where you can enter information

VIEWING YOUR INFORMATION

You may wonder how Family Tree Maker can create several different documents from information that you only have to enter once. Family Tree Maker creates all of these different items by using **views**. Views are different ways of looking at the information that you enter.

For example, if you want to print an Ancestor tree, Family Tree Maker shows you an Ancestor Tree view of your information. Or, if you want a calendar filled with family birthdays and anniversaries, Family Tree Maker shows you a Calendar view of your information.

PRINT SEVERAL KINDS OF TREES

When you are ready to print family trees, Family Tree Maker will create them for you. You can choose from Ancestor trees, Descendant trees, Direct Descendant trees, Outline Descendant trees, and Outline Direct Descendant trees.

Ancestor trees (sometimes called "pedigree" trees) make great gifts for family members because they show an individual's roots. Two parents, four grandparents, eight great-grandparents, and more are printed with perfect spacing. You can choose a Fit to Page Ancestor tree to get a one-page tree or a Custom Ancestor tree to get a multiple-page tree.

Descendant trees are ideal for family gatherings and reunions because they show where everyone fits in the family. Starting with a relative in the distant past, a Descendant tree shows children, grandchildren, great-grandchildren and so on. Outline Descendant trees contain the same information as Descendant trees, but they are much more compact because they don't use boxes to organize each individual's information. Direct Descendant trees and Outline Direct Descendant trees are even more compact because they include fewer individuals.

Your printed trees can contain any type of information that Family Tree Maker holds, including photos. Family Tree Maker prints them right in your tree. If you don't have electronic photographs, you can leave space in the boxes to attach photos by hand. You can also have video and sound in your trees. This can be especially fun at family gatherings!

You can print as many different family trees as you like from the family information that you enter just once. The resulting trees are wonderful heirlooms that your family will treasure for years to come.

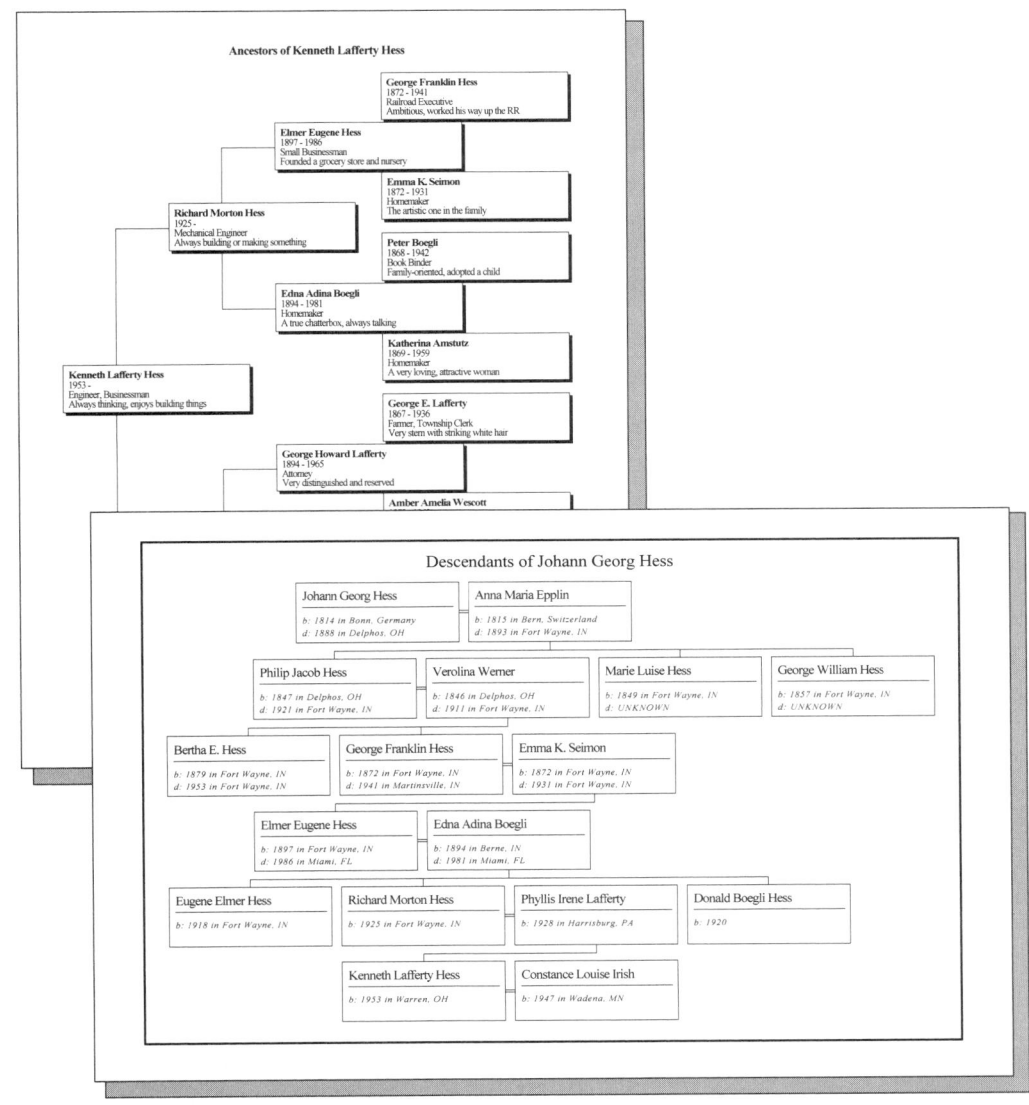

Ancestors of Kenneth Lafferty Hess

George Franklin Hess
1872 - 1941
Railroad Executive
Ambitious, worked his way up the RR

Elmer Eugene Hess
1897 - 1986
Small Businessman
Founded a grocery store and nursery

Emma K. Seimon
1872 - 1931
Homemaker
The artistic one in the family

Richard Morton Hess
1925 -
Mechanical Engineer
Always building or making something

Peter Boegli
1868 - 1942
Book Binder
Family-oriented, adopted a child

Edna Adina Boegli
1894 - 1981
Homemaker
A true chatterbox, always talking

Katherina Amstutz
1869 - 1959
Homemaker
A very loving, attractive woman

Kenneth Lafferty Hess
1953 -
Engineer, Businessman
Always thinking, enjoys building things

George E. Lafferty
1867 - 1936
Farmer, Township Clerk
Very stern with striking white hair

George Howard Lafferty
1894 - 1965
Attorney
Very distinguished and reserved

Amber Amelia Wescott

Descendants of Johann Georg Hess

Johann Georg Hess
b: 1814 in Bonn, Germany
d: 1888 in Delphos, OH

Anna Maria Epplin
b: 1815 in Bern, Switzerland
d: 1893 in Fort Wayne, IN

Philip Jacob Hess
b: 1847 in Delphos, OH
d: 1921 in Fort Wayne, IN

Verolina Werner
b: 1846 in Delphos, OH
d: 1911 in Fort Wayne, IN

Marie Luise Hess
b: 1849 in Fort Wayne, IN
d: UNKNOWN

George William Hess
b: 1857 in Fort Wayne, IN
d: UNKNOWN

Bertha E. Hess
b: 1879 in Fort Wayne, IN
d: 1953 in Fort Wayne, IN

George Franklin Hess
b: 1872 in Fort Wayne, IN
d: 1941 in Martinsville, IN

Emma K. Seimon
b: 1872 in Fort Wayne, IN
d: 1931 in Fort Wayne, IN

Elmer Eugene Hess
b: 1897 in Fort Wayne, IN
d: 1986 in Miami, FL

Edna Adina Boegli
b: 1894 in Berne, IN
d: 1981 in Miami, FL

Eugene Elmer Hess
b: 1918 in Fort Wayne, IN

Richard Morton Hess
b: 1925 in Fort Wayne, IN

Phyllis Irene Lafferty
b: 1928 in Harrisburg, PA

Donald Boegli Hess
b: 1920

Kenneth Lafferty Hess
b: 1953 in Warren, OH

Constance Louise Irish
b: 1947 in Wadena, MN

Figure I-2. Two types of family trees

ENTER ANY TYPE OF INFORMATION

Beyond the basic names and dates, you can extend your family research to include military service, occupations, and even characteristics like height, weight, and personality. You can track an individual's medical history or write several pages of stories, habits, jokes, and favorite recipes. It's nice to know an individual's name and birth date, but the extra information really makes an individual come to life.

In addition, Family Tree Maker's Scrapbook feature lets you add multimedia elements to your collection of family information. Scrapbooks can store almost any type of information, including Kodak Photo CD pictures; OLE objects such as sound, video, and text files; and pictures, such as bitmaps and TIFF files. Each individual and each marriage has a Scrapbook, so you can use your creativity to put together a wonderfully complete collection of family information to pass from generation to generation.

RESEARCH YOUR FAMILY HISTORY AT HOME

Family Tree Maker's specialties have always been organizing family information and creating family trees. Now, however, Family Tree Maker can also help you with your family research!

If you have a CD-ROM drive, you can use the FamilyFinder view to read **Family Archives** and the **FamilyFinder Index**. Family Archives are CDs containing information from a variety of records, such as census records, marriage records, Social Security death benefits records, and linked pedigrees. You can print the information from the Family Archives, or even copy information from them directly into your Family File. The FamilyFinder Index is the index to all of the Family Archives. It helps you find the information that you need.

If you own the Deluxe Edition of Family Tree Maker, you already have the FamilyFinder Index — it came on the same CD as your Family Tree Maker program. Both the FamilyFinder Index and Family Archives can be purchased from Brøderbund, or you may find them in selected libraries.

The Genealogy "How-To" Guide is also part of the Deluxe Edition. This step-by-step guide tells you what questions to ask, where to go, and how to find important facts about your ancestors, using sources both in the United States and abroad. With this interactive guide, you can go straight to the information regarding your heritage and bypass any information that isn't useful to you.

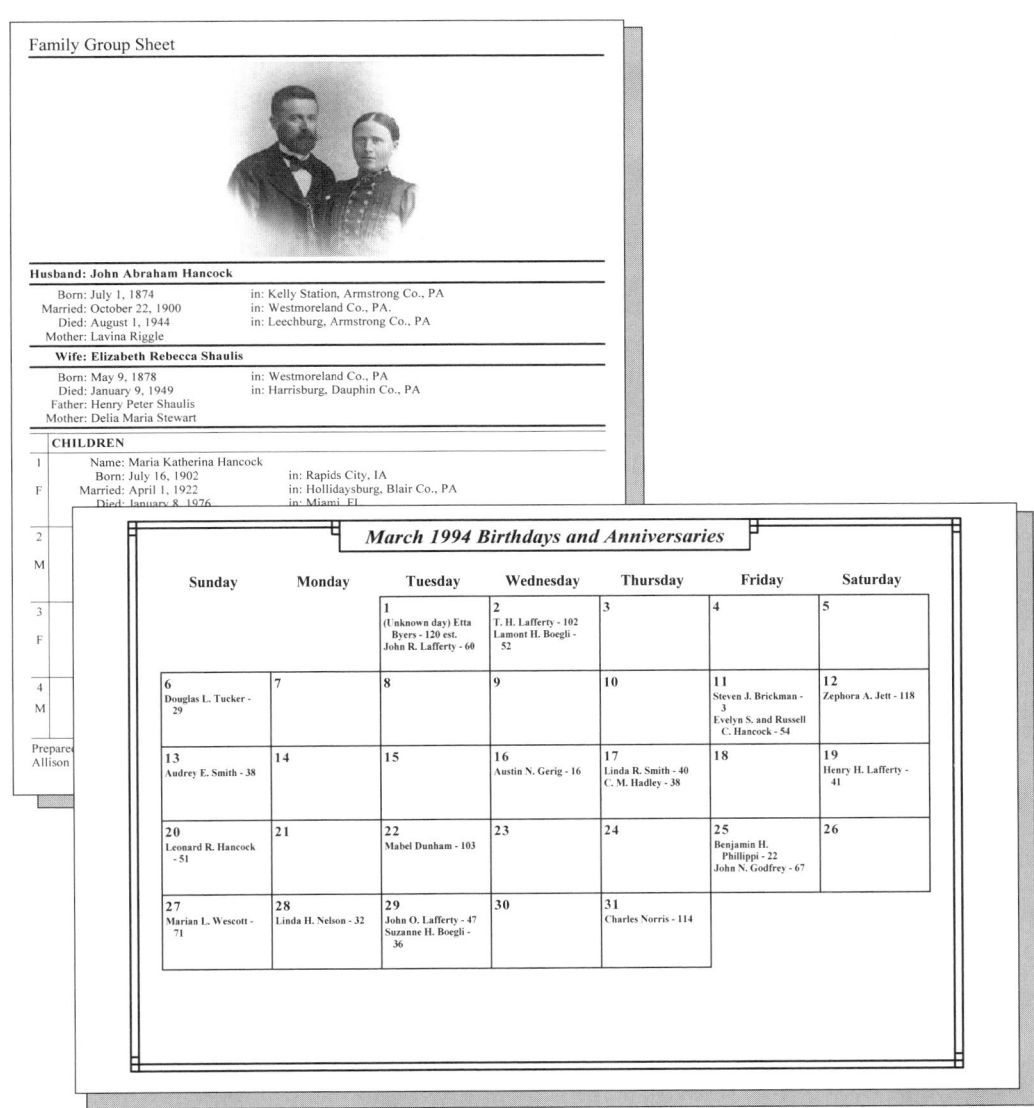

Figure I-3. A Family Group Sheet and calendar

WINDOWS 95 USERS

Family Tree Maker is now compatible with Windows 95. Although this manual was written with the Windows 3.1 interface in mind, the instructions it contains do apply to the Windows 95 interface, except where noted. For additional instructions pertaining to Windows 95, check Family Tree Maker's ReadMe file. To see the ReadMe file, go to Program Manager and double-click the **FTW ReadMe** icon. For now, please be aware of the following:

- To install under Windows 95, see the separate instructions on page 16.

- The section titled "Windows Basics and Family Tree Maker" on page 20 does not apply to Windows 95 users.

- Windows 95 users can use long file names instead of the standard file name of eight characters plus a three-letter extension.

- Most figures in this manual will look slightly different than what Windows 95 users will see on screen. For example, Windows 95 dialog boxes have a more "chiseled" look. However, the important elements of the figures, such as field names, will be the same.

SYSTEM REQUIREMENTS

Family Tree Maker for Windows requires an IBM PC or compatible, 386 CPU (486 or higher recommended), Windows 3.1 or higher running in enhanced mode, a hard disk with *at least* 9 megabytes free space, *at least* 4 megabytes of physical RAM (8 megabytes highly recommended), a VGA monitor running in at least 16 colors, and a Microsoft compatible mouse. Please note that these are the minimum requirements — the more family information you enter, the more free hard disk space and available RAM you will need. If you plan to include many pictures, sounds, and videos in your Family Tree Maker Scrapbooks, you will need a substantial amount of hard disk space. In addition, a scanner, a Kodak Photo CD compatible CD-ROM drive, a sound card, and a video capture card are optional.

The Deluxe Edition of Family Tree maker has the same system requirements, with the addition of a CD-ROM drive. The CD-ROM drive does not need to be Kodak compatible unless you want to insert Kodak Photo CD pictures into your Family Tree Maker Scrapbooks.

To run Family Tree Maker under Windows 95, you must have Windows 95. In this case, 8 megabytes of RAM are highly recommended.

TECHNICAL SUPPORT

If you have any problems with Family Tree Maker, take the following steps in the order listed:

1. From the **Prefs** menu, select **Help Tools**, and make sure that all of the **Show Cue Cards in** and **Show Bubble Help in** check boxes are selected. This will ensure that Bubble Help and Cue Cards are available in all parts of Family Tree Maker. Then, go to the place in Family Tree Maker where you are having difficulties; Family Tree Maker will display help that may provide you with a solution.

2. Check the index of this manual for the subject you need help with and then read the appropriate pages. Also check the contents of the on-line Help system by pressing **F1** and clicking **Contents**.

3. Consult Appendix E, "Troubleshooting." This section describes how to solve common problems.

4. Call Brøderbund's Banner Blue Division Technical Support.

    Make sure to call while you are at your computer. It's also useful if you have information about your printer and monitor handy, as well as the release date of your software. To find the release date, from the **Help** menu, select **About Family Tree Maker**.

    The Banner Blue Technical Support phone number is 510-794-6850. You can speak directly to a technical support representative Monday through Friday, 8:00 AM to 5:00 PM, Pacific time.

    In addition, Banner Blue's Technical Support Department now has an **interactive automated help system**, which consists of pre-recorded voice instructions and the ability to fax back written instructions. It is available 24 hours a day, seven days a week by calling 510-794-6850.

The Technical Support phone number is for questions specifically about Family Tree Maker. The person you speak to cannot tell you about Microsoft Windows or genealogical research. For help with Windows, consult your Windows manual. For help with genealogical research, consult Appendix A of this manual or your local library, historical society, or genealogical society. If you have the Deluxe Edition of Family Tree Maker, it contains extensive information about conducting family research. In addition, several genealogical resources are listed in the Help system topic "Genealogy Information Sources."

WE WANT TO HEAR FROM YOU!

Banner Blue is committed to improving our products. We encourage you to write to us and share your ideas about improving Family Tree Maker.

Banner Blue Software   510-794-6850 Phone
Technical Support   510-795-4488 Fax
P.O. Box 7865
Fremont, CA 94537-7865

ORDERING PRODUCTS

When you would like more information about a product or want to place an order, contact Brøderbund's Customer Support. Lines are open Monday through Thursday, 6 AM to 4:45 PM, and Friday, 6 AM to 3:45 PM, Pacific time. You can also write to the address below (please include your address and phone number so that we can contact you).

Brøderbund Customer Support   415-382-4770 Phone
P.O. Box 6125   415-382-4419 Fax
Novato, CA 94948-6125

CUSTOMER REGISTRATION

Please fill out and return the registration card now. We offer registered users the following special benefits: free telephone assistance with Family Tree Maker, the Family Tree Maker Product Upgrade Plan, and information about Family Tree Maker accessory programs and services.

ABOUT MAILING LISTS

We currently don't sell our registration lists to other companies and have no intention of doing so. You can be assured that your name will be kept completely confidential.

FAMILY TREE MAKER PRODUCT UPGRADE PLAN

Periodically we make new versions of our software available to registered users at substantial discounts. If you return your registration card, we'll notify you about new versions as they become available.

Chapter 1

PROGRAM SETUP

Michelle Shinn, one of the manual's writers, was just under a year when her parents took this picture—she seems to be showing an early interest in technology.

PROGRAM SETUP

This chapter tells you how to install Family Tree Maker on your computer, how to start your first new Family File, and also gives you a quick introduction to the on-screen Help system. Whenever you have to type something into your computer, the letters are shown in **bold like this**. If you have any problems installing Family Tree Maker, please consult Appendix E for troubleshooting tips.

INSTALLING FAMILY TREE MAKER

To use Family Tree Maker, you must install it on your hard disk. You *cannot* run it directly from the original program diskettes, CD-ROM disc, or backup floppy diskettes.

Several different versions of Family Tree Maker are available. Each version adds more features to the program. The features of each version are outlined in Figure 1-1 on the next page.

Windows 95 Users

Family Tree Maker is now compatible with Windows 95. To install Family Tree Maker under Windows 95, see "Installing a Diskette Version Under Windows 95" or "Installing a CD-ROM Version Under Windows 95" on page 16.

Although this manual was written with the Windows 3.1 interface in mind, the instructions it contains apply to the Windows 95 interface except where noted. Be sure to read "Windows 95 Users" on page 8.

Storing Your Family Tree Maker Diskette(s)

When you are finished installing Family Tree Maker, please store the program diskette(s) in a safe place. This way you will be able to reinstall the program if the files on your hard disk are ever damaged or deleted.

If you have a CD-ROM version, keep the CD-ROM disc handy when you are running the program. You will occasionally have to insert the disc into your CD-ROM drive so that Family Tree Maker can access files.

Program Name	Added Features
Family Tree Maker for Windows, version 1.0	Basic program
Family Tree Maker Deluxe Edition, version 1.0	The FamilyFinder Index and Genealogy "How-To" Guide
Family Tree Maker for Windows, version 2.0	Scrapbooks, batch print, labels and cards, and other features
Family Tree Maker Deluxe Edition, version 2.0	Improved search capabilities in the FamilyFinder Index
Family Tree Maker for Windows, version 3.0	Error checking, PAF file import, multiple sets of parents, FamilyFinder capabilities
Family Tree Maker Deluxe Edition, version 3.0	Now reads and searches all Family Archives

Figure 1-1. Features of different versions of Family Tree Maker

Installing a Diskette Version of Family Tree Maker

If you already have a CD-ROM version of Family Tree Maker on your computer, we *do not* recommend that you install a diskette version over it. If you install a diskette version over version 1.0 or 2.0 of the CD-ROM version, you will lose some FamilyFinder capabilities. You can either install the diskette version in a different directory or upgrade to the latest CD-ROM version. If you have Windows 95, see "Installing a Diskette Version Under Windows 95" on page 16.

To install Family Tree Maker for Windows on your hard disk:

1. Start Microsoft Windows and go to Program Manager.

2. Insert the Family Tree Maker program diskette into your diskette drive.

3. From the **File** menu in Program Manager, select **Run**.

4. In the **Command Line** field, type **A:SETUP**

    The "A" in "A:SETUP" stands for drive A. If you are installing from a drive other than drive A, type that letter instead. For example, to install from drive B, type **B:SETUP**

5. Click **OK** to continue.

   Family Tree Maker displays the Family Tree Maker Installation dialog box. To continue installing Family Tree Maker, follow the instructions on the screen. The defaults supplied by Family Tree Maker are the best choices, so if you come to a screen that you are unsure about, it is best to choose **OK**. You only want to change the settings if you know something special about your computer's setup.

   Note: As you are installing Family Tree Maker, you will be asked into which directory you want Family Tree Maker installed. We strongly suggest installing into the directory "C:\FTW". Using this directory will help ensure that all program features function correctly.

6. Once Family Tree Maker has finished installing, you will need to exit Windows and restart your computer.

   Note: You *will not* be able to use Family Tree Maker until your computer has been restarted!

Installing a CD-ROM Version

To install a CD-ROM version of Family Tree Maker, see the instructions on the back side of the plastic CD-ROM holder. If you have Windows 95, see "Installing a CD-ROM Version Under Windows 95" on the next page. If you already have a version of Family Tree Maker installed on your hard drive, just install the new CD-ROM version over the old version. It doesn't matter whether the old version was a diskette version or a CD-ROM version.

Note: As you are installing Family Tree Maker, you will be asked into which directory you want Family Tree Maker installed. We strongly suggest installing into the directory "C:\FTW" This is especially important when you are installing a CD-ROM version of the program. Using this directory will help ensure that all program features function correctly.

After you've installed Family Tree Maker, keep the CD-ROM disc handy when you are running the program. You will occasionally have to insert the disc into your CD-ROM drive so that Family Tree Maker can access files.

Installing a Diskette Version Under Windows 95

If you have a diskette version of Family Tree Maker, use these instructions:

1. Start Windows.

2. Insert the first program diskette into your diskette drive.

3. Click **Start**.

4. Select the **Settings** menu.

5. Select **Control Panel**.

6. Double-click the **Add/Remove Programs** icon.

7. Select the **Install/Uninstall** tab.

8. Click **Install**.

9. Click **Next**.

10. Click **Finish**.

    Family Tree Maker displays the Family Tree Maker Installation dialog box. To continue installing Family Tree Maker, follow the instructions on the screen. The defaults supplied by Family Tree Maker are the best choices, so if you come to a screen that you are unsure about, it is best to choose **OK**. You only want to change the settings if you know something special about your computer's setup.

    Note: As you are installing Family Tree Maker, you will be asked into which directory you want Family Tree Maker installed. We strongly suggest installing into the directory "C:\FTW" Using this directory will help ensure that all program features function correctly.

Installing a CD-ROM Version Under Windows 95

If you have a CD-ROM version of Family Tree Maker, simply insert the CD-ROM into your CD-ROM drive. Windows 95 will ask if you want to install the program. Click **OK** and then follow the instructions on the screen. The defaults supplied by Family Tree Maker are the best choices, so if you come to a screen that you are unsure about, it is best to choose **OK**. As mentioned in the note above this paragraph, it is best to install the program in your "C:\FTW" directory.

STARTING FAMILY TREE MAKER

Once you've finished installing Family Tree Maker, the fun begins! Just start Family Tree Maker, and then you can either open an existing file or create a new file. You'll be ready to start entering your family information in no time.

To start Family Tree Maker after you have installed it to your hard disk:

1. Make sure you're in Program Manager.

2. In Program Manager, double-click the **Family Tree Maker** program icon.

    Family Tree Maker displays the title screen and then the Open Family File dialog box.

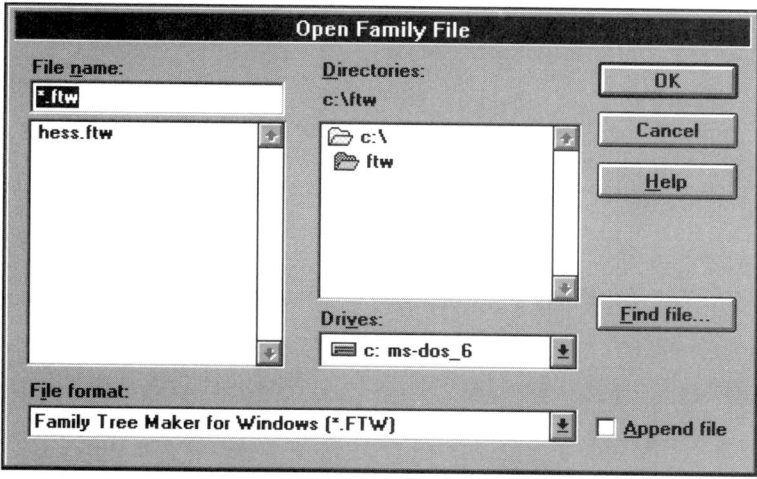

Figure 1-2. The Open Family File dialog box

- If you had a previous version of Family Tree Maker for Windows and you installed Family Tree Maker for Windows 3.0 into the same directory, your previous .FTW file will open automatically. You can begin working with the file immediately.

- If you are new to Family Tree Maker products, follow the instructions in "If You've Never Used a Family Tree Maker Product" on the next page.

- If you have files from a DOS version of Family Tree Maker, proceed to "If You Have Family Tree Maker for DOS Files" on page 19.

- If you have PAF files from PAF version 2.1 or later, see "Opening PAF Files" on page 352.

- Finally, if you have files from another genealogy software program that supports GEDCOM, see "GEDCOM Import and Export" on page 353.

If You've Never Used a Family Tree Maker Product

To begin working with Family Tree Maker, follow the instructions below:

1. Since this is the first time you've used Family Tree Maker, click **New** in the Open Family File dialog box.

   Family Tree Maker displays the New Family File dialog box. This is where you'll create a name for your new Family File.

2. Type a name in the **File name** field.

   The name of your file must be eight letters or less, plus the extension .FTW For example, you could type **smith.ftw**

3. Click **OK** when you've entered a name for your new Family File.

   Family Tree Maker creates the new Family File for you and then displays the **Family Page**. This is where you'll begin entering information about your family. Skip to "Where to Go From Here" on page 20.

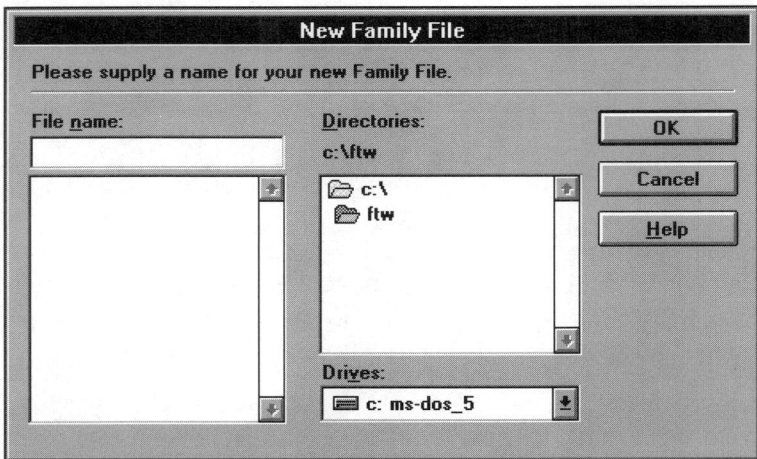

Figure 1-3. The New Family File dialog box

If You Have Family Tree Maker for DOS Files

1. In the Open Family File dialog box (see Figure 1-2 on page 17), click the **Drives** field and select the drive where your Family Tree Maker for DOS file is located.

   For example, if your file is on a diskette in drive A:, select **a:**

2. If your file is located in a specific directory on that drive, double-click that directory in the **Directories** field.

   If you are unsure where your file is, click **Find file** and follow the instructions in "Finding Files" on page 392.

3. Click the **File format** field and select **Family Tree Maker (*.ftw, *.ftm, *. fbk, *.ged, indiv2.dat)**.

4. Click the name of your file in the **File name** field and then click **OK**.

   Family Tree Maker displays the New Family File dialog box. In the "File name" field, Family Tree Maker suggests a name for your new Family File.

5. Click **OK** to accept the name for your new file, or type in a different name.

   The name must be eight letters or less, and must have the extension .FTW For example, you could type **myfamily.ftw** or **smith.ftw**

6. In the **Directories** field, select the directory where you installed Family Tree Maker for Windows. Usually, this is C:\FTW.

7. Click **OK**.

   Family Tree Maker creates the new Family File for you and then displays the **Family Page**. This is where you'll begin entering your family information.

   Note: If you have several Family Tree Maker for DOS files that you wish to join together into one large file, see "Combining Files" on page 379.

WHERE TO GO FROM HERE

When you have installed and started Family Tree Maker, you're ready to begin entering your family information. You should go through the tutorial first because it shows you how to use the main features of the program. The tutorial starts on page 31. Also, if the Windows environment is new to you, look through your Windows manual and the section below to learn the basics. Once you've gone through this information, you can move on to Chapter 3, "Entering Basic Information," beginning on page 75. You may also want to glance through the last five pages of this chapter, beginning with "Getting Help" on page 25. You'll find information about using Help and customizing Family Tree Maker.

WINDOWS BASICS AND FAMILY TREE MAKER

To use Family Tree Maker, you should be familiar with basic Windows concepts such as clicking, double-clicking, dragging, and using menus. Please note that this section does not apply to Windows 95 users.

A standard Windows feature that you may also want to use is the **secondary mouse button menu**. The secondary mouse button menu is a floating menu that Family Tree Maker displays when you click an item with the secondary mouse button. The **secondary mouse button** is the button on your mouse that you do not normally use to select menu commands. Most often, the right mouse button is the secondary button, although left-handed individuals sometimes use the left mouse button as the secondary button.

The secondary mouse button menu is available everywhere except in the Family Page, the More About dialog boxes, the Index of Individuals, and the FamilyFinder view. The menu usually contains the most commonly-used commands for the current view, although the menu contents will vary according to what you click in the view. All of the commands that are on the secondary mouse button menus can be accessed using the regular menu bar at the top of the window.

To display the secondary mouse button menu, click the secondary mouse button. To select a command on the secondary mouse button menu, place the mouse pointer on the command and click with the primary mouse button. When you click outside of the secondary mouse button menu, the menu will disappear.

The rest of this section points out some of the important features on several Family Tree Maker for Windows screens.

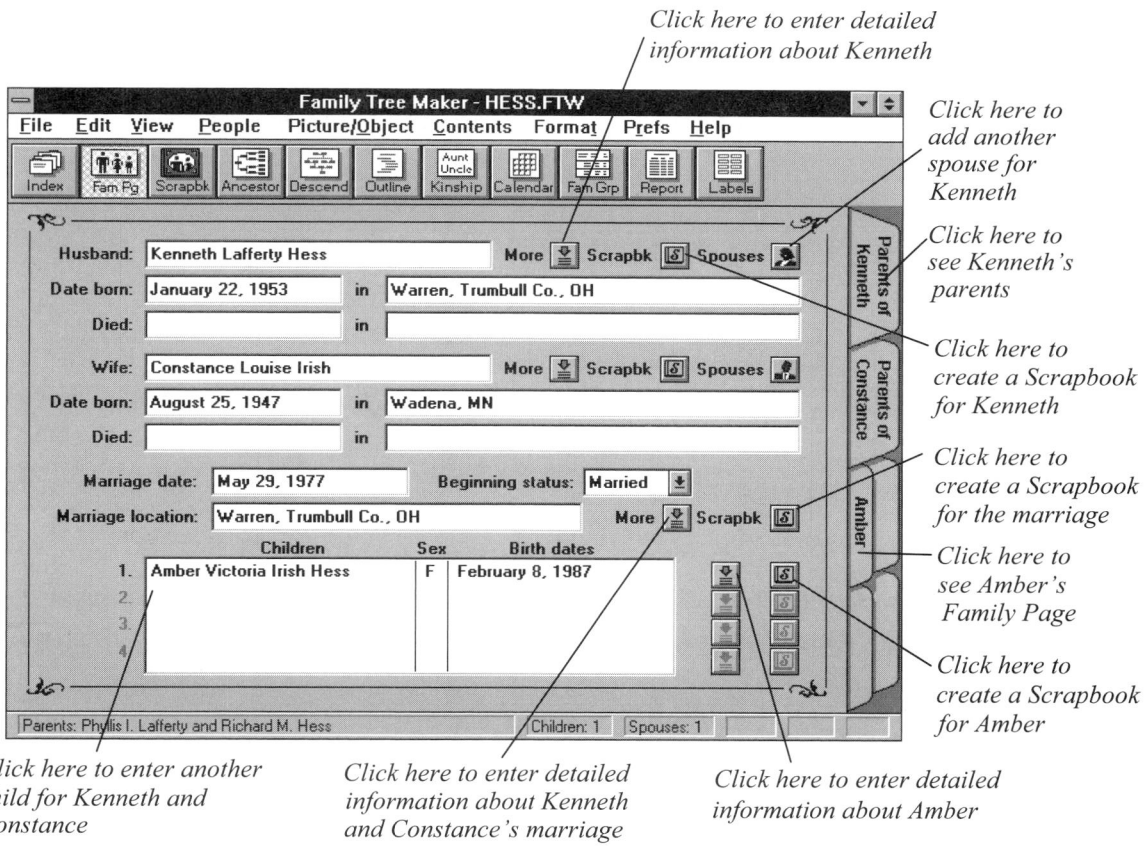

Click here to enter detailed information about Kenneth

Click here to add another spouse for Kenneth

Click here to see Kenneth's parents

Click here to create a Scrapbook for Kenneth

Click here to create a Scrapbook for the marriage

Click here to see Amber's Family Page

Click here to create a Scrapbook for Amber

Click here to enter another child for Kenneth and Constance

Click here to enter detailed information about Kenneth and Constance's marriage

Click here to enter detailed information about Amber

Figure 1-4. Some elements of the Family Page

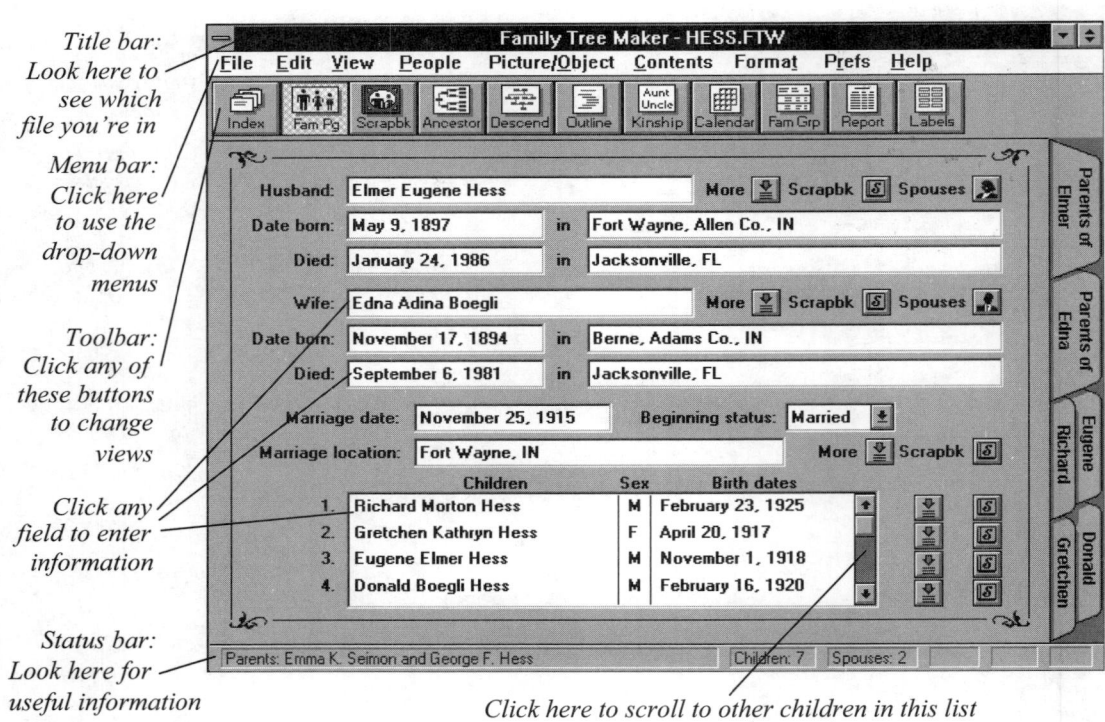

Title bar:
Look here to
see which
file you're in

Menu bar:
Click here
to use the
drop-down
menus

Toolbar:
Click any of
these buttons
to change
views

Click any
field to enter
information

Status bar:
Look here for
useful information

Click here to scroll to other children in this list

Figure 1-5. More elements of the Family Page

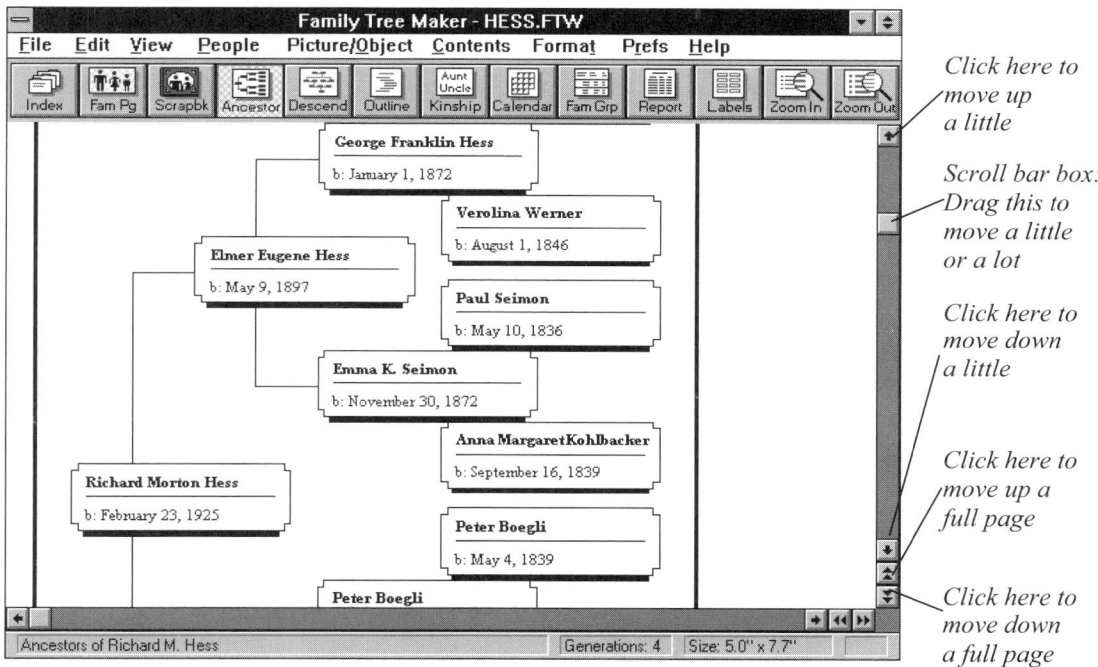

Click here to
move up
a little

Scroll bar box:
Drag this to
move a little
or a lot

Click here to
move down
a little

Click here to
move up a
full page

Click here to
move down
a full page

Figure 1-6. Scroll bars

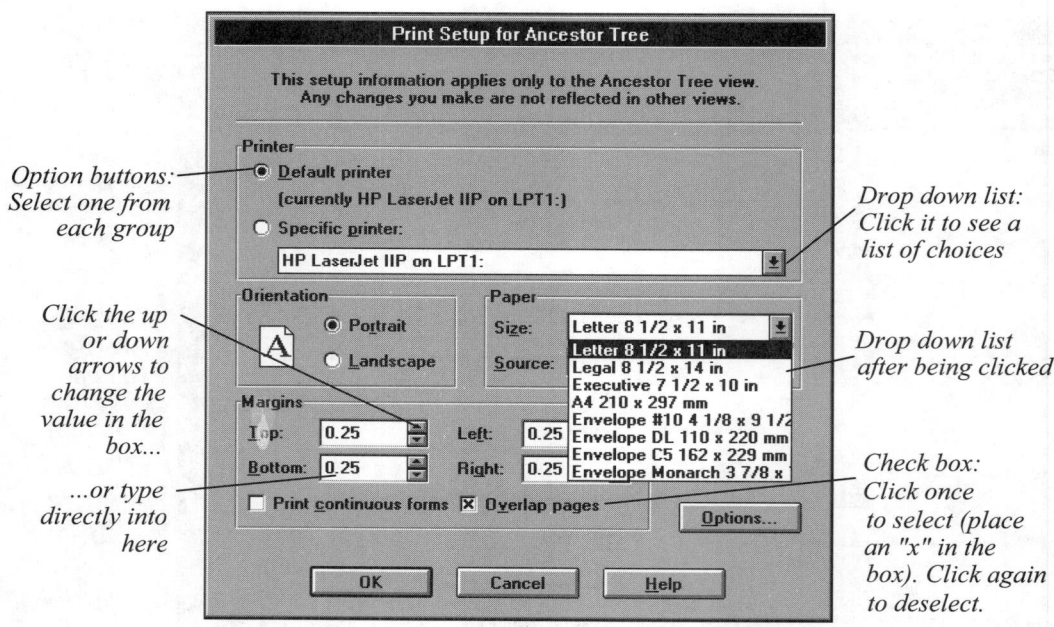

Option buttons:
Select one from
each group

Click the up
or down
arrows to
change the
value in the
box...

...or type
directly into
here

Drop down list:
Click it to see a
list of choices

Drop down list
after being clicked

Check box:
Click once
to select (place
an "x" in the
box). Click again
to deselect.

Figure 1-7. Basic dialog box elements

GETTING HELP

Like most other Windows products, Family Tree Maker has an on-screen Help system. An on-screen Help system is just like your paper manual, except it is on your computer's hard disk. It can tell you how to do things and will help you out when you get stuck.

Opening the Help system is simple: from the **Help** menu, select **Contents**. Or, you can press [FI]. To get help about a particular menu command, first click the menu, next use the arrow keys to highlight the command, and then press [FI]. To get help in a dialog box, press [FI] while you are in the dialog box. The Help system will take you directly to help related to that command or dialog box.

Family Tree Maker has two other types of help: **Cue Cards** and **Bubble Help**. (See "Selecting Help System Preferences" on page 28.) Cue Cards appear automatically when you enter a view. They give you tips about what you can do in that view. Click **OK** to close a Cue Card when you are finished reading it.

Bubble Help pops up when you hold your mouse pointer over things like buttons and fields for more than two seconds. It gives you instructions related to the item under your mouse pointer. When you move your mouse pointer away from a Bubble Help window, it will close.

You can prevent Cue Cards or Bubble Help windows from appearing in a view by deselecting the check box for that view in the Help Tools dialog box. See "Selecting Help System Preferences" on page 28.

If you have a CD-ROM version of Family Tree Maker, you have access to another Help system: the Genealogy "How-To" Guide. This Help system is all about how to find your ancestors. It tells you how to begin, who to contact, and how to trace your relatives. There are even tips for researching in foreign countries. For a complete description of how to use a Help system, from the **Help** menu, select **How to use Help**.

PREFERENCES — CUSTOMIZING FAMILY TREE MAKER

Using the **Prefs** menu, you can customize different parts of Family Tree Maker. For example, you can choose default date formats, change field labels, and select when Bubble Help and Cue Cards appear.

In this section you will learn how to set Startup preferences, and Help System preferences. We'll describe the other items on the **Prefs** menu in later chapters.

Selecting Startup Preferences

To set your Startup preferences:

1. From the **Prefs** menu, select **Startup**.

   Family Tree Maker displays the Startup dialog box (see Figure 1-8). Each of your options is described below.

   Editing Mode — Selecting **Overtype** lets you type over old text. The old text is lost forever, and the new text is put in its place. Selecting **Insert** mode places new text in front of the old text.

   Automatically backup Family File — Normally, Family Tree Maker saves a copy of your Family File when you exit the program. The backup file has the same name as the original file, but with the extension .FBK. You can use this backup file if your original file is ever lost or damaged. However, since the backup file takes up space on your computer's hard drive, you may want to deselect this option if your computer's hard drive space is limited.

   To help save space on your hard drive, you can also make your own compressed backup files to store on diskettes or in other directories. These backup copies that you create manually will have the extension **.FBC**. See "Backing Up Your Family File" on page 376. Making regular backup copies of your Family File can help ensure that you won't lose all of your genealogical information if something ever happens to the Family File that you work with regularly.

   Allow replacing existing files — Normally, Family Tree Maker does not allow you to replace an old file with a new file of the same name. If you select this option, Family Tree Maker will only give you a warning message before it writes over an existing file. Any files that you choose to overwrite will be lost permanently.

To protect your Family Files as much as possible, make sure that "Automatically backup Family Files" is selected and "Allow replacing existing files" is not selected.

Figure 1-8. The Startup dialog box

Cache size — The cache is the memory where Family Tree Maker stores recently used information. The program will run more efficiently if you make the optimum amount of cache available to Family Tree Maker. If you have large Family Files, you should have a larger cache, but if you have small Family Files, you should have a smaller cache. With larger Family Files, a good rule of thumb for the cache size is about one-fourth of your computer's available memory. The maximum cache size is four megabytes.

2. Click **OK** when you've made your selections.

   Some Startup preferences do not take effect until you exit Family Tree Maker and then restart the program.

Selecting Help System Preferences

Cue Cards and Bubble Help windows contain helpful hints and tips to keep you on track while you work with Family Tree Maker.

To turn Cue Cards and Bubble Help windows on or off:

1. From the **Prefs** menu, select **Help Tools**.

   Family Tree Maker displays the Help Tools dialog box. Each of your options is described below.

   Show Bubble Help in — Select the check boxes for the views in which you want Bubble Help to appear while you are working. If you don't want the Bubble Help to appear in a particular view, deselect the check box for that view.

   > Note: The **Family Page** check box includes the Bubble Help that appears in More About dialog boxes.

   Show Cue Cards in — Select the check boxes for the views in which you want Cue Cards to appear while you are working. If you don't want the Cue Cards to appear in a particular view, deselect the check box for that view.

   All — Click this button to select all of the check boxes.

   None — Click this button to deselect all of the check boxes.

2. Click **OK** when you've made your selections.

   Family Tree Maker closes the dialog box and saves your changes.

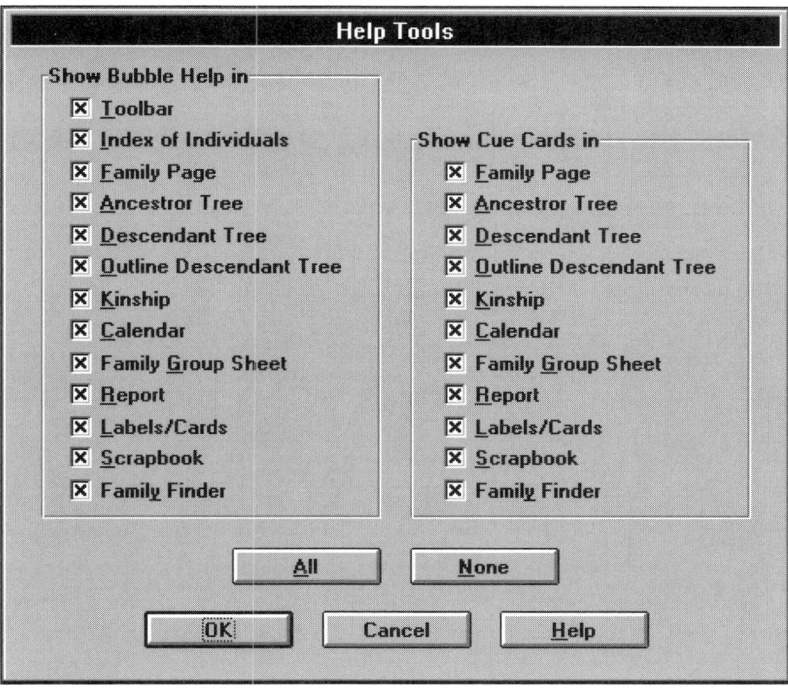

Figure 1-9. The Help Tools dialog box

Chapter 2

TUTORIAL

Harvey Tang, one of Family Tree Maker's programmers, poses here with his family on graduation day. This picture, which includes his mother Ming, father Sheng, and younger brother Ken, was taken on the University of California's Berkeley campus in May 1989.

TUTORIAL

This tutorial shows you how easy it is to use Family Tree Maker by leading you step-by-step through the main features of the program. It uses as its example the ancestry of Abraham Lincoln, the 16th president of the United States.

First, you will enter information about Abraham Lincoln's family, back through his parents and grandparents. Then, you'll enter a brief story about Abraham. Finally, you'll print a Custom Ancestor tree, just one type of tree you can create with Family Tree Maker. All together, this should take about an hour, but don't feel that you have to do it all at once.

In the process, you will learn about many of Family Tree Maker's most useful commands and options, but don't put the manual away once you've done this tutorial! Read the other chapters as you work with Family Tree Maker — you'll find out about even more features and become a Family Tree Maker expert.

BEFORE YOU START

This chapter assumes a few things:

- You know how to use a typewriter or computer keyboard. (Hunt-and-peck typing is fine!)

- You've already read Chapter 1, "Program Setup."

- Family Tree Maker is installed and set up on your computer.

- Your printer is correctly installed and configured under Windows.

If you haven't done these things, go back and follow the instructions in Chapter 1. Consult your Windows manual if your printer is not properly configured. When you've completed the items listed above, you'll be ready to begin this tutorial.

STARTING FAMILY TREE MAKER

Once Family Tree Maker is running, you can begin the tutorial.

To start Family Tree Maker:

1. Turn your computer on and start Windows.

    If you're unsure how to start Windows, refer to your Windows manual.

2. In the Program Manager, double-click the **Family Tree Maker** icon.

    Family Tree Maker appears in a few moments. Unless you've previously worked with Family Tree Maker for Windows, the Open Family File dialog box appears. (If the Open Family File dialog box doesn't appear, from the **File** menu, select **New Family File** and skip to step 4.)

3. Click **New**.

    Family Tree Maker displays the New Family File dialog box

4. Type a name for the new Family File in the **File name** field.

    All the information that you enter about all of your relatives is stored in a Family File. Family Tree Maker uses the information in this file to create special documents for you, such as family trees and calendars.

    Since we're going to enter information about Abraham Lincoln's family in this tutorial, type **LINCOLN.FTW** in the **File name** field. File names must be eight letters or less, plus a three letter extension.

    Note: If you want to store your Family File on a drive or directory other than the default, you should make that selection in this dialog box. However, you will not be able to select a floppy diskette drive (or other removable media). The Family File you're currently working on **must** be on your hard disk. You can keep a backup copy on a floppy diskette, but you must transfer it to your hard disk before you can use it.

5. Click **OK**.

    Family Tree Maker creates the new Family File and then displays an empty Family Page. You are now ready to start entering information about the Lincoln family.

PART I: ENTERING FAMILY INFORMATION

In this section you'll enter information about several generations of the Lincoln family. Follow all the steps exactly and within an hour or so you will be printing your first family tree!

The **Family Page** is where you enter information about the individuals in your family. It is made up of a series of **labels** and **fields**. A field is a place for you to type information. A label tells the purpose of a field.

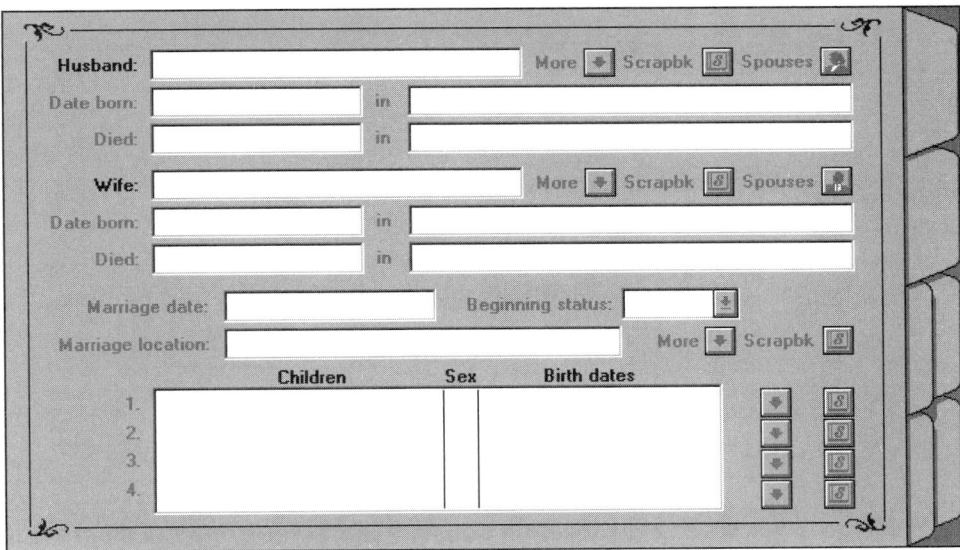

Figure 2-1. An empty Family Page

The row of words across the top of the screen is the set of menus that you'll be using. This is called the **menu bar**. When you click one of the words on the menu bar, such as "Edit," a list of commands appears below it. This list is called a **pull-down menu**. You will choose items from the menu bar and pull-down menus to do things such as edit your information and print family trees.

The tabs along the right side of the Family Page are for going to other Family Pages. (These tabs are blank now, since you haven't entered any names yet.) Buttons placed throughout the Family Page will take you to other parts of the program. We'll tell you more about these buttons and tabs later.

Filling Out the Family Page

On this Family Page you'll enter some facts about Abraham Lincoln's immediate family (his "nuclear" family), starting with Abraham Lincoln himself.

Figure 2-2 shows what the completed Family Page will look like. The steps that follow tell you how to get your computer screen to look like the figure.

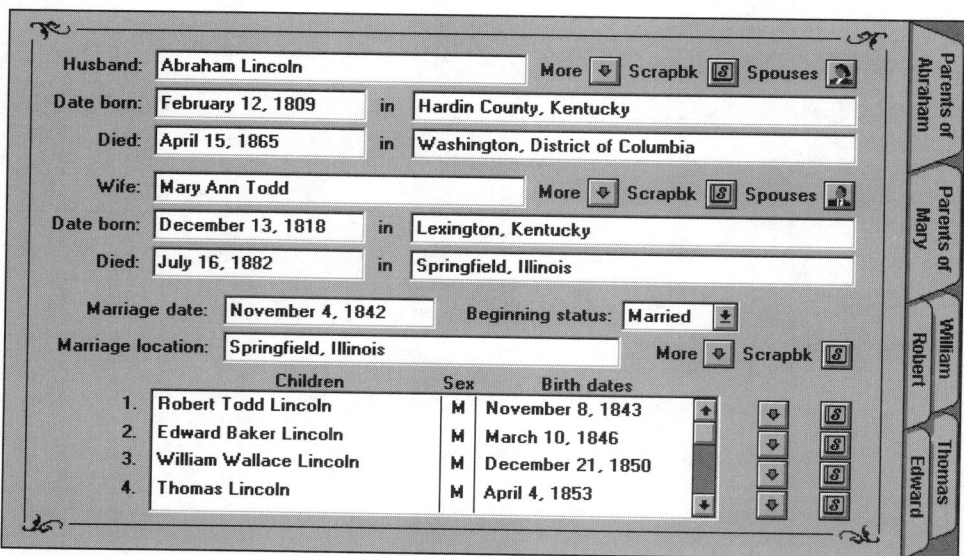

Figure 2-2. Abraham Lincoln's Family Page, completely filled out

The cursor is already in the "Husband" field. (The cursor is the blinking vertical line. It marks where the next character you type will appear.) In this tutorial, any letters that you should type are shown in **bold letters like this**.

1. Type **Abraham Lincoln** in the **Husband** field.

   If you make a mistake, use ⬅ to move the cursor back to the left, and use Backspace ⬅BkSp to delete the incorrect characters. The Backspace ⬅BkSp key deletes characters as it moves the cursor to the left. If you need to move the cursor back to the right, press ➡.

   The ⬅ and ➡ arrow keys are usually on the right side of the keyboard; sometimes they're part of the numeric keypad (the rectangular arrangement of number keys — not the ones across the top of your keyboard). If you press the arrow keys but you get numbers on the screen, press Num Lock [num lock] to put the numeric keypad into cursor-moving mode.

You can also fix mistakes by simply typing over them with the correct information. To do so, press Insert [ins] to turn on overwrite mode. (Because Family Tree Maker defaults to insert mode, pressing insert now turns insert mode off and overwrite mode on.) You know when you're in overwrite mode, because the **status bar** displays the letters "OVER." The status bar is at the very bottom of your screen. Pressing Insert [ins] a second time turns overwrite mode off.

2. Click the **Date born** field and watch the tabs on the right side of the screen.

   As soon as you have provided the husband's name, Family Tree Maker creates a Family Page for Abraham's parents. The tab on the right side of the page labeled "Parents of Abraham" can take you to their Family Page. You will enter information on that page later in this tutorial.

   You can also move between fields by using Tab [⇥] or [Enter↵].

   If you notice a mistake in the "Husband" field after you have moved the cursor out of it, click in the field with your mouse pointer, and then use [←] or [→] to move to your mistake. Use Backspace [←BkSp] to delete the incorrect characters, then type in the correct ones.

3. Type **Feb 12 1809** in the **Date born** field.

4. Click the **in** field and watch what happens.

   When you leave a date field, Family Tree Maker automatically converts what you've typed to a standard date format. You can type the date almost any way that you would like; Family Tree Maker can usually figure out what you mean. If Family Tree Maker cannot understand your date, it will ask you for clarification. Simply retype the date in a more standard format.

5. Type the name of Lincoln's birthplace — **Hardin County, Kentucky** — in the **in** field.

6. Fill out the next two fields with the following information: **15 Apr 1865** for the date of his death, and **Washington, District of Columbia** for the location.

   Don't be afraid of making mistakes. This is just a tutorial, nobody's keeping score, and you can't hurt the computer by typing something wrong.

7. Type the following information for Lincoln's wife into the proper fields (refer to Figure 2-2 on page 36 if you need help):

Mary Ann Todd

| born | **Dec 13, 1818** | in | **Lexington, Kentucky** |
| died | **July 16, 1882** | in | **Springfield, Illinois** |

You fill in the information for a wife the same way you do for a husband, being especially careful to use the wife's maiden name (her last name before she was married).

Remember to click in the next field when you've filled in the information for a particular field — don't try to type all that information into the same field! There are five fields' worth of information: "Wife," "Date born," "in" (for birth location), "died," and "in" (for death location).

As with Abraham, Family Tree Maker automatically creates a Family Page for Mary's parents and reformats dates as you exit the date fields.

8. The Lincolns were wed on **November 4, 1842**, so type that into the **Marriage date** field.

9. Click the **Beginning status** field when you've typed in the marriage date.

Family Tree Maker displays a drop-down list of relationship codes when you click this field. The **default** for the "Beginning status" field is "Married," so you don't need to change anything in this field. A default is what's already in a field when you come to it. Family Tree Maker uses defaults in several places to make your work quicker and easier.

If they had never been married, you'd be able to select a different relationship code, such as "Unknown." Since the Lincolns don't fall into this category, move on to the next step.

10. Click the **Marriage location** field and type **Springfield, Illinois**

Notice that Family Tree Maker automatically filled in the rest of "Springfield, Illinois" as you typed it. This is thanks to the Fastfields feature, described on page 40.

You're now finished entering basic information about Abraham Lincoln and his wife, Mary, so we'll move on to their children.

11. Click the first row in the **Children** list.

This list is where you record the names, sexes, and birth dates of a couple's children. Be sure to always record the full name, including the last name.

12. In the field where the cursor now lies (the first row in the **Children** list), type **Robert Todd Lincoln** and press ⏎.

You will notice that Family Tree Maker automatically fills in the name "Lincoln" for you. Again, this is Fastfields at work.

13. As soon as the cursor moves to the **Sex** field, an "F" appears. Type **M** over the "F" and then press ⏎ to go on to the **Birth dates** field.

"F" for "Female" is the default value for the "Sex" field.

14. Type **8 Nov 1843** into the **Birth dates** field and press ⏎.

Family Tree Maker converts the date you type into a standard date format.

15. Type the following information into the appropriate fields for the Lincolns' other four sons:

William Wallace Lincoln, sex **M**, born **Dec 21, 1850**
Edward Baker Lincoln, sex **M**, born **March 10, 1846**
Thomas Lincoln, sex **M**, born **April 4, 1853**
Tad Lincoln, sex **M**, born **UNKNOWN**

Be sure to enter their full names, last name included. As you can see, the information for the children isn't as extensive as the information for the parents — at least not on this page. Later in this tutorial, you'll see that each child has his or her own Family Page where he or she appears as a (potential) husband or wife.

Even though the Family Page only displays four children at a time, you can enter up to ninety-nine children for each marriage. Use the scroll bar on the right side of the "Children" list to display the other children.

Fastfields

You may have noticed that as you began to type "Springfield, Illinois" in step 10, Family Tree Maker automatically filled it in for you. The same happened with the name "Lincoln." This is because name and location fields, in addition to a few other fields, are Fastfields.

Location Fastfields remember the names of the last 50 locations that you've entered into any location field. This means that when you move the cursor into a location field and start typing the name of a town that you've previously entered into Family Tree Maker, Fastfields automatically tries to fill it in for you. You don't need to do anything special, just keep typing the name of the town until Family Tree Maker gets it right or runs out of guesses. You may save time this way, but if Fastfields doesn't have the correct location name, you certainly won't lose any time. Other Fastfields work in the same way. For more information, see "Fastfields" on page 90.

Sorting Children

If you entered the children in the order that we listed them, they're not in birth order. It's generally a good idea to have the children in birth order, so Family Tree Maker has a special command that will sort the children for you.

To sort the children on a Family Page:

1. From the **People** menu, select **Sort children**.

    Family Tree Maker displays a message asking you to confirm that you want to sort the children.

2. Click **OK**.

3. Look at the list of children.

    If the children weren't in birth order before, you'll notice that they are now.

Congratulations! You've just finished filling out your first Family Page. To make sure all of the information is correct, compare your Family Page to Figure 2-2 on page 36.

If any of the information is different, go back and change it. Just click the fields whose information you need to change and use ← and → to move around within a field. See Figure 3-3 on page 83 for a complete list of editing and cursor-moving keys.

Filling Out Other Family Pages

Look at the right side of the screen — the tabs now say "Parents of Mary," "Parents of Abraham." There are also tabs for each child, labeled "Robert," "Edward," "William," and "Thomas." You can click these tabs to go to other Family Pages in your Family File.

Note: The fifth child, Tad, is still on this page. You can see him by using the scroll bar on the right side of the "Children" list.

Each Family Page holds two generations — parents and their children. As you work on your own Family File, you'll fill out many Family Pages, moving both forward and backwards in time. Your Family File will be like an album filled with pages of information about your family.

For the purposes of this tutorial, you'll only go backwards in time and fill out the Family Pages for Abraham Lincoln's parents and grandparents. To go forward in time, you would fill out Family Pages for his children, grandchildren, great-grandchildren, and so on. In your personal Family File you'll do both.

On the next page, we'll begin going backwards in time by filling out the Family Page for Abraham's parents.

Lincoln's Parents' Family Page

Fill out the Family Page for Lincoln's parents:

1. Click the **Parents of Abraham** tab to go to Lincoln's parents' Family Page.

   Family Tree Maker displays Lincoln's parents' Family Page.

   This Family Page is already partially filled out — one of the lines in the "Children" list contains Abraham Lincoln's information. This is because Family Tree Maker copied the information from Lincoln's Family Page to his parents' Family Page.

2. Enter the following information for Lincoln's father, Thomas Lincoln, his mother, Nancy Hanks, and their marriage:

   Thomas Lincoln
   born **Jan 6 1778**   in **Rockingham County, Virginia**

   Nancy Hanks
   born **Feb 5 1784**   in **Campbell County, Virginia**
   died **Oct 5 1818**   in **Spencer County, Indiana**

   Married **12 June 1806**

You don't have the information for the death of Thomas Lincoln, nor for the location of Thomas and Nancy's wedding, so you could either leave those fields blank or enter a question mark (?) in them. For now, just leave them blank. They were married, so you do not need to change the "Beginning status" field. For this tutorial, you don't need to enter any more information about their children. Check what you've typed against Figure 2-3, on the next page.

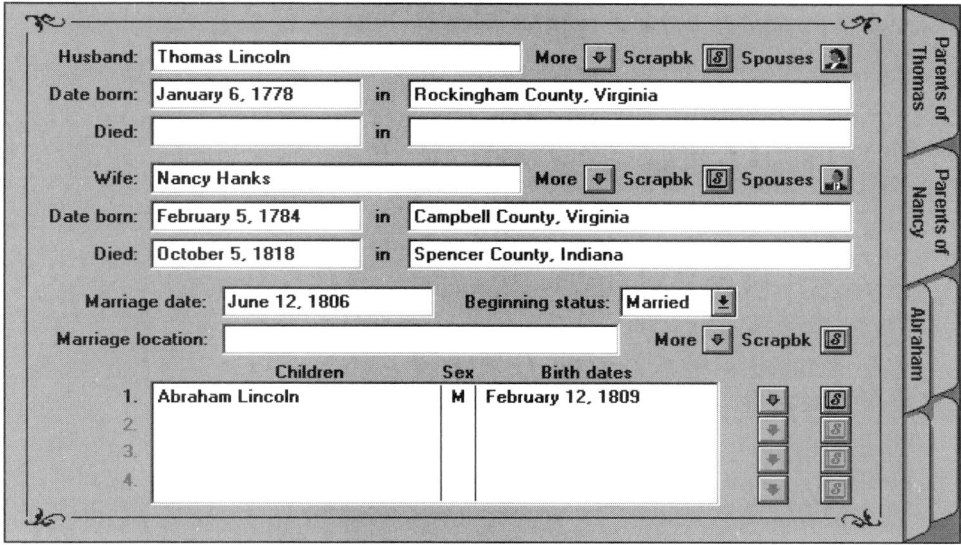

Figure 2-3. Completed Family Page for Thomas and Nancy

You now need to go back one more generation to fill out two more Family Pages — one for Abraham Lincoln's paternal grandparents (the parents of his father, Thomas), and one for his maternal grandparents (the parents of his mother, Nancy).

Don't skip this part of the tutorial. You won't have to enter a lot of information, and you will see some things that you haven't seen yet.

Lincoln's Paternal Grandparents' Family Page

In this section you'll learn how to add information if either the husband or wife has been married more than once.

1. On the Family Page that shows Thomas and Nancy as husband and wife, click the **Parents of Thomas** tab.

   Family Tree Maker displays the Family Page of Thomas' parents.

2. Enter the following information about Lincoln's grandparents.

   Lincoln's paternal grandfather was also named **Abraham Lincoln**, and was also born in **Kentucky**. His paternal grandmother was **Bathsheba Herring**. That's all of the available information.

   Check what you've typed against Figure 2-4 to make sure it's accurate. If necessary, go back and make changes.

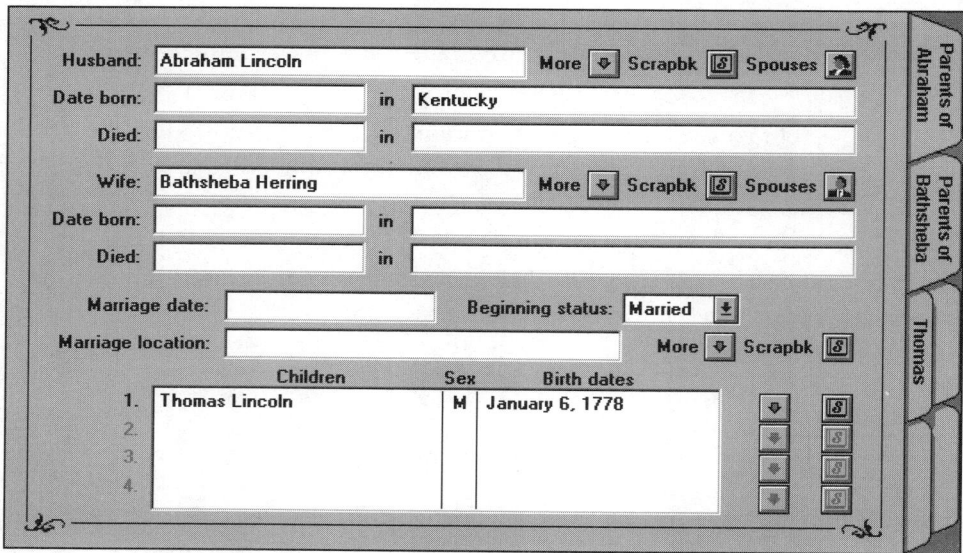

Figure 2-4. Completed Family Page for Abraham and Bathsheba

Note: Ordinarily, when you don't know the date of an individual's death, you should enter a question mark (?) in the date of death field. For the purposes of this tutorial, however, you can leave these fields blank.

3. It turns out that Grandfather Abraham was married to another woman before he married Bathsheba Herring. To the right of Grandfather Abraham's name, there is a button labeled "Spouses." Click this button to add information about Grandfather Abraham's other wife.

Family Tree Maker displays the Spouses dialog box. See Figure 2-5. You have the choice of going to an existing spouse or creating a new spouse. Each individual in Family Tree Maker can have up to 99 spouses.

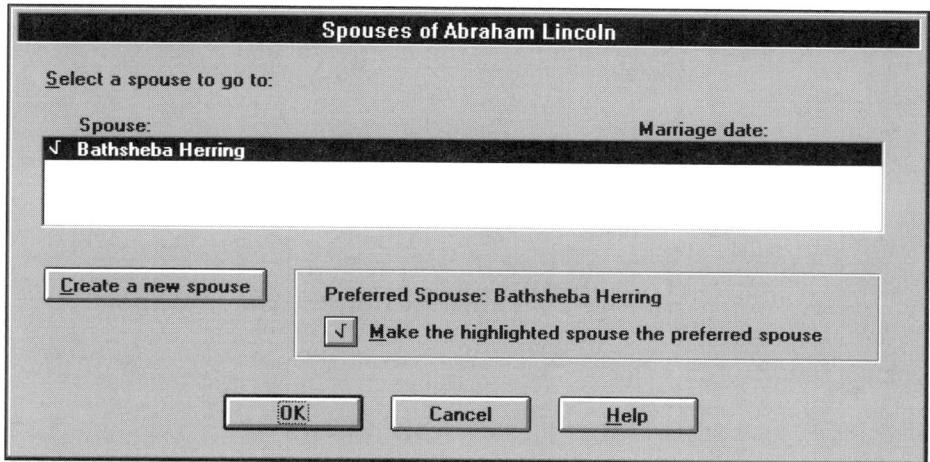

Figure 2-5. Spouses dialog box

4. Click **Create a new spouse**.

Family Tree Maker displays another Family Page containing Grandfather Abraham in the "Husband" field, but the "Wife" field is empty.

5. Type the name of Grandfather Abraham's first wife, **Mary Shipley** in the **Wife** field. See Figure 2-6 on the next page.

There are no children to list on this Family Page because Thomas was the child of Abraham and Bathsheba, not of Abraham and Mary.

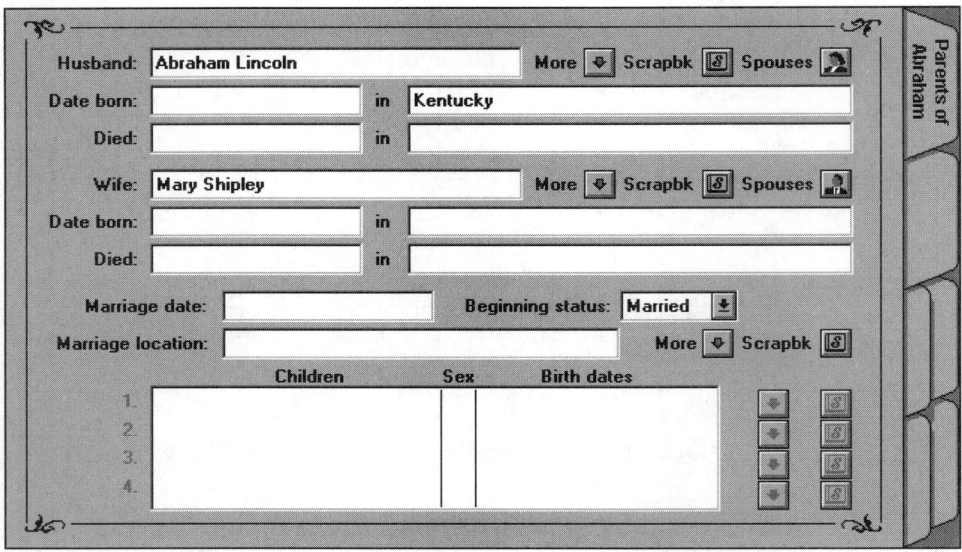

Figure 2-6. Completed Family Page with Abraham and Mary

6. Click Grandfather Abraham's **Spouses** button again.

   Family Tree Maker displays the Spouses dialog box, which now shows both of Grandfather Abraham's wives.

   Note: There is a check mark next to Bathsheba's name. This indicates that she is the preferred spouse of Abraham. This tells Family Tree Maker that you want Bathsheba to be shown when you display Abraham's Family Page, not Mary.

7. In the list of names, click **Bathsheba Herring**.

8. Click **OK**.

   Family Tree Maker returns you to Abraham's and Bathsheba's Family Page.

Lincoln's Maternal Grandparents' Family Page

In this section you'll fill in information about President Lincoln's maternal grandparents. You'll also learn a quick way to move between Family Pages.

To enter information about Lincoln's maternal grandparents, you first need to display the Family Page of his mother, Nancy Hanks. This is because Nancy is the closest relative who is already in the Family File.

To find Nancy's Family Page, you'll use the Index of Individuals:

1. From the **View** menu, select **Index of Individuals**.

   Family Tree Maker displays the Index of Individuals. It lists all of the names that you've entered into this Family File.

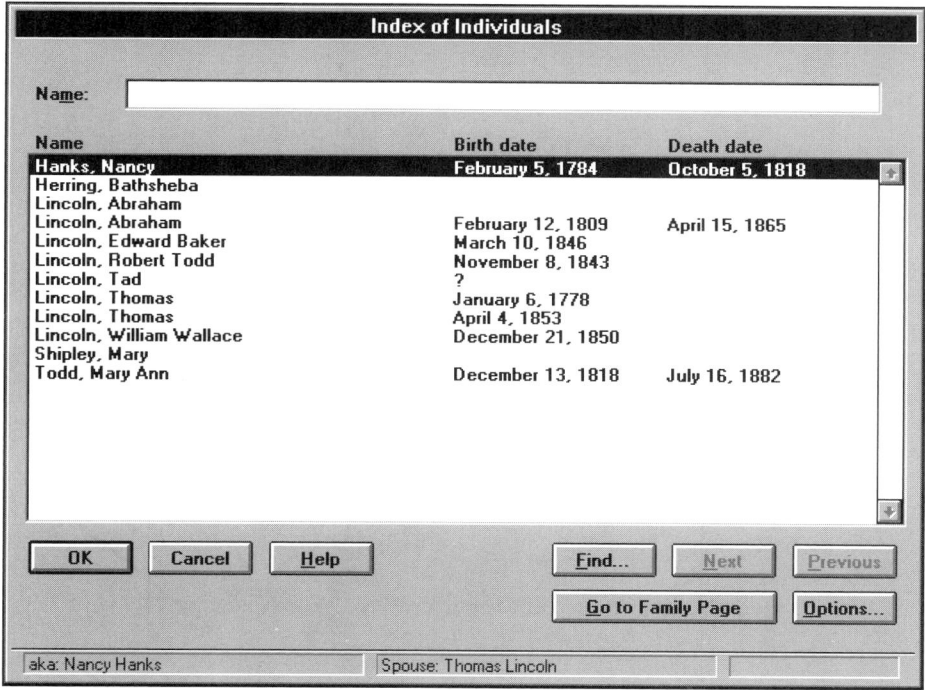

Figure 2-7. The Index of Individuals

2. Click **Hanks, Nancy** so that it is highlighted.

3. Click **Go to Family Page**.

   Family Tree Maker displays Thomas's and Nancy's Family Page (see Figure 2-3 on page 43).

Now you're ready to fill in information about the President's maternal grandparents. The only information you have is the name of his maternal grandfather — Joseph Hanks.

1. Click the **Parents of Nancy** tab on the right side of Thomas and Nancy's Family Page.

   Family Tree Maker displays the Family Page of Nancy's parents.

2. Type **Joseph Hanks** in the **Husband** field.

That's all there is to enter for Nancy's parents. Now we want to return to President Lincoln's Family Page. We'll use a different feature in the Index of Individuals to do this.

1. From the **View** menu, select **Index of Individuals**.

   Family Tree Maker displays the Index of Individuals. You can see that Abraham Lincoln is listed twice in the Index of Individuals. President Lincoln is the one who was born in 1809. However, this is a good chance to practice using the Find command.

2. Click **Find** at the bottom of the Index of Individuals.

   Family Tree Maker displays the Find Name dialog box.

3. Type **Abraham** in the **Name** field.

4. Click **OK**.

   Family Tree Maker closes the Find Name dialog box and highlights the first "Abraham Lincoln" listed in the Index of Individuals. That's President Lincoln's grandfather, so it's not the individual that you want.

5. Click **Next**.

   Family Tree Maker highlights the second "Abraham Lincoln" in the list. That's President Lincoln. You want to go to his Family Page.

6. Click **Go to Family Page**.

   Family Tree Maker displays President Lincoln's Family Page.

Removing an Individual from Your File

It's always good practice to check your information from time to time. Sometimes you'll find that you have made a mistake. But don't worry — Family Tree Maker has commands that can help you find some types of errors automatically. See "Checking Your File for Errors" on page 367. In this case, we checked our records and found that Tad Lincoln was not a separate child, but in fact, "Tad" is Thomas's nickname. To correct this mistake, we'll delete Tad.

To remove Tad from the file:

1. Click the down arrow at the bottom of the scroll bar on the **Children** list so that Tad becomes visible.

2. Click Tad's name.

3. From the **People** menu, select **Delete Individual**.

   Family Tree Maker displays a dialog box asking you to confirm that you want to delete Tad.

4. Click **Yes**.

   Tad is now gone from your file. Family Tree Maker returns you to Tad's parents' Family Page.

Note: It's important to remember to use the Delete Individual command whenever you want to remove someone permanently from your file. Using the backspace or delete keys to remove someone only removes their name — it doesn't remove any of their other information or any of their relationships with other individuals.

PART II: THE MORE ABOUT DIALOG BOXES

Family Tree Maker provides five other dialog boxes for each individual in your Family File. These dialog boxes are collectively called More About dialog boxes because they let you enter more information about an individual.

Entering Brief Facts

Next, we will add a bit more information about President Abraham Lincoln — specifically, that he was a rail splitter in his youth.

1. Click **More** to the right of Lincoln's name.

   Family Tree Maker displays the Facts dialog box. It contains 13 fields where you can enter short comments about an individual, such as their occupation or interests. See Figure 2-8 on the next page.

   Note: Family Tree Maker remembers which More About dialog box you were using last. If the dialog box you see now is not the Facts dialog box, don't worry. It simply means you were exploring Family Tree Maker before doing this tutorial. To open the Facts dialog box, click the **Facts** button at the top right of the currently open More About dialog box.

2. Type **Rail splitter (in youth)** into the first **Comment/Location** field. Since this isn't something that happened on a specific date, leave the **Date** field blank.

   You could continue adding more facts in this dialog box, but for now, we'll just leave it at this one fact.

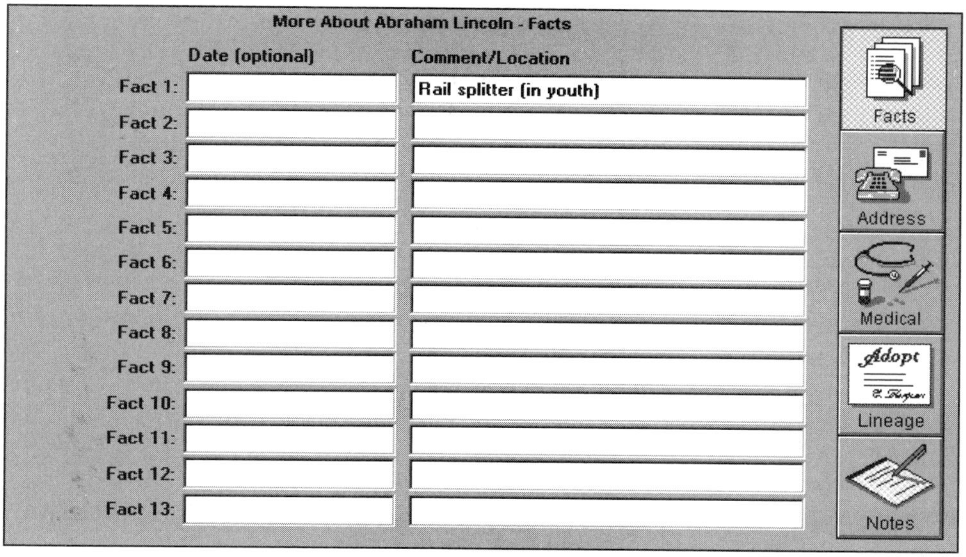

Figure 2-8. Facts dialog box

Changing Field Labels

Although the field label for the line we just entered says "Fact 1," we can change it to something that will remind us what "fact" goes in that field for the other individuals in Lincoln's family.

To change the "Fact 1" field label:

1. From the **Prefs** menu, select **Labels**.

2. Click the label which says "Fact 1."

3. Type `Occupation`

4. Click **OK**.

Family Tree Maker returns you to the Facts dialog box. Now the first fact field in everyone's Fact dialog box has the label "Occupation." This way, it is easy to remember which facts go where.

The Other More About Dialog Boxes

You'll notice that on the right side of the More About dialog boxes there are five buttons labeled "Facts," "Address," "Medical," "Lineage," and "Notes." You can click these buttons to take you to the other More About dialog boxes. We won't go through all of the More About dialog boxes now, but we'll give you a short description of each one.

In the Medical dialog box you can enter an individual's physical and medical information, such as height, weight, and cause of death. The Address dialog box is for entering an individual's address and phone number. This information would be handy if you wanted to print an address list for your family. In the Lineage dialog box you can record an individual's nickname and any special title that they use. You can also record special information about that individual's relationship with their parents, for example, you can indicate that they were adopted as a child. Finally, there is the Notes dialog box, which you can use to record several pages of stories and notes about an individual. We'll enter some information in the Lineage and Notes dialog boxes in the next few sections.

Entering Nicknames into the Lineage Dialog Box

People frequently have nicknames that they prefer to use. For example, earlier, we found that there was no Tad Lincoln, but that "Tad" was Thomas Lincoln's nickname. In addition, Abraham Lincoln was also known as "Honest Abe." You can record nicknames in the Lineage dialog box. This is also a good place to record name changes.

To enter a nickname for Abraham Lincoln:

1. Click **Lineage** on the right side of the Facts dialog box.

    Family Tree Maker displays the Lineage dialog box.

2. Click the **This person is also known as (aka)** field.

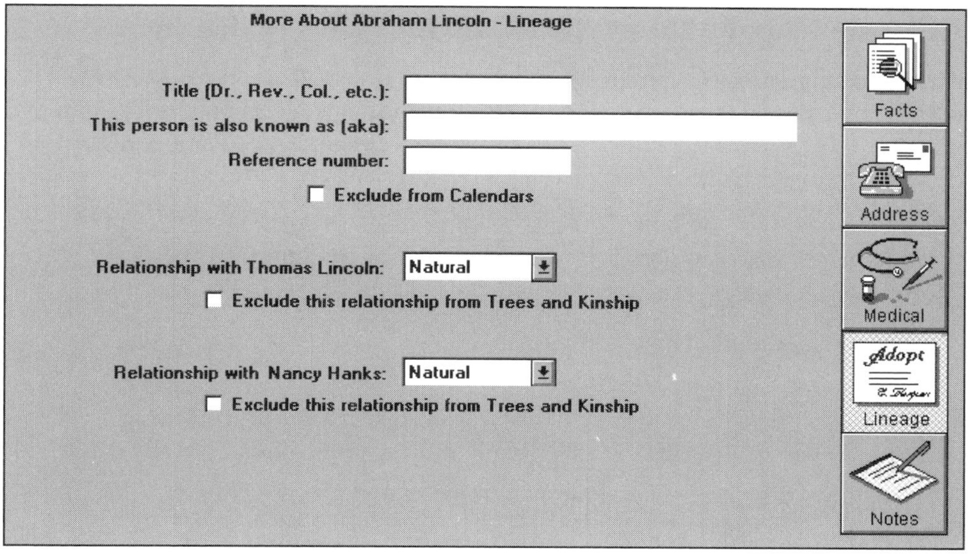

Figure 2-9. Lineage dialog box

3. Type **Honest Abe Lincoln**

Notice that you entered Abe's full name, instead of just entering "Honest Abe." This is because Family Tree Maker gives you the option of printing nicknames instead of given names. If you had only typed "Honest Abe," then it would always print as "Honest Abe," with no last name when you chose to print nicknames. Always enter the individual's *complete* name exactly as you wish it to print, not just the nickname.

Now let's look at the Notes dialog box.

Entering Lengthy Information into the Notes Dialog Box

The Notes dialog box is a mini word processor. In it you can record and organize virtually any information you like, including several pages of a family member's favorite recipes, jokes, or even short stories. If you want, you can print them for easy filing.

This section shows you how easy it is to enter notes by leading you step-by-step through the experience of creating the notes shown in Figure 2-10 on page 55. You'll learn how to:

- Enter text and make corrections
- Change the style of the text
- Rearrange the order of paragraphs

You're now ready to enter biographical information about Abraham Lincoln.

1. Click **Notes** at the right side of the **Lineage** dialog box.

   Family Tree Maker displays the Notes dialog box.

2. Type **He volunteered**

   If you make a mistake, use [←] to move the cursor back to the left and use Backspace [←BkSp] to delete the incorrect characters. The Backspace [←BkSp] key deletes characters as it moves the cursor to the left. If you need to move the cursor back to the right, press [→].

3. Continue typing on the same line: **and became a Captain in the Black Hawk War of 1832**.

4. Press the space bar twice.

   Do *not* press [Enter←]. If you do, press Backspace [←BkSp] to move the cursor back to the end of the sentence you typed in step 2.

5. Type **He commented afterwards that he saw no live, fighting Indians, but had a good many bloody struggles with the mosquitoes**.

   As you can see, if a word doesn't fit at the end of a line, Family Tree Maker automatically moves it to the beginning of the next line. You should only press [Enter←] when you reach the end of a paragraph.

6. Press ⌜Enter⏎⌝ to end the paragraph.

7. Press ⌜Enter⏎⌝ to create a blank line.

8. Type the second paragraph:

    **Abe Lincoln had a passion for learning. He only had
    one year of formal schooling, but he would walk for
    miles to borrow books to teach himself math,
    science, and law.**

Your screen should now look like the one shown in Figure 2-10. Different
monitors can fit different amounts of text on each line, so don't worry if your
screen doesn't look exactly like the figure.

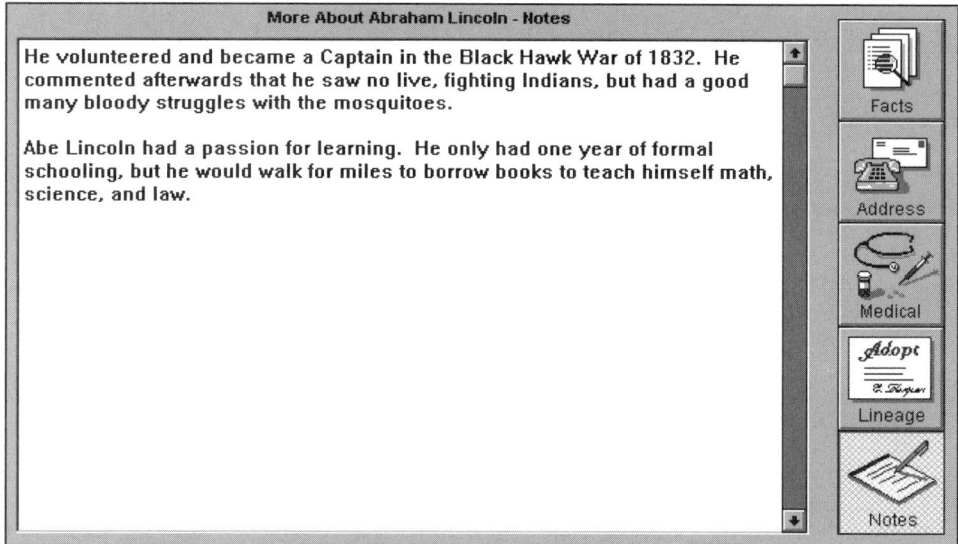

Figure 2-10. Notes for Abraham Lincoln

Changing Text

You may want to change your notes after entering them. In the following steps, you'll make a simple textual change and find that Family Tree Maker automatically reformats your notes for you.

1. Move the mouse pointer in front the of the "l" in "learning" and then click the primary mouse button so that the flashing cursor appears in front of the word "learning."

   The word "learning" is in the first line of the second paragraph.

2. Type **knowledge**

3. Press Delete ⌨delete⌨ until all of "learning" is deleted.

   Family Tree Maker reformats each paragraph for you automatically as you insert or delete words.

Moving Paragraphs

The paragraphs in our example are really in the wrong order. The next few steps show you how to rearrange them.

1. Move the mouse pointer to the beginning of the second paragraph, in front of the "A" in "Abe."

2. Press and hold your primary mouse button and then drag the mouse down to the end of the paragraph. This is called "clicking and dragging."

   Notice that characters are highlighted, or **selected**, as you drag over them.

3. Release the mouse button when you're at the end of the paragraph, being careful not to press another key.

   The second paragraph should be completely highlighted, as shown in Figure 2-11. If it isn't, start over from step 1.

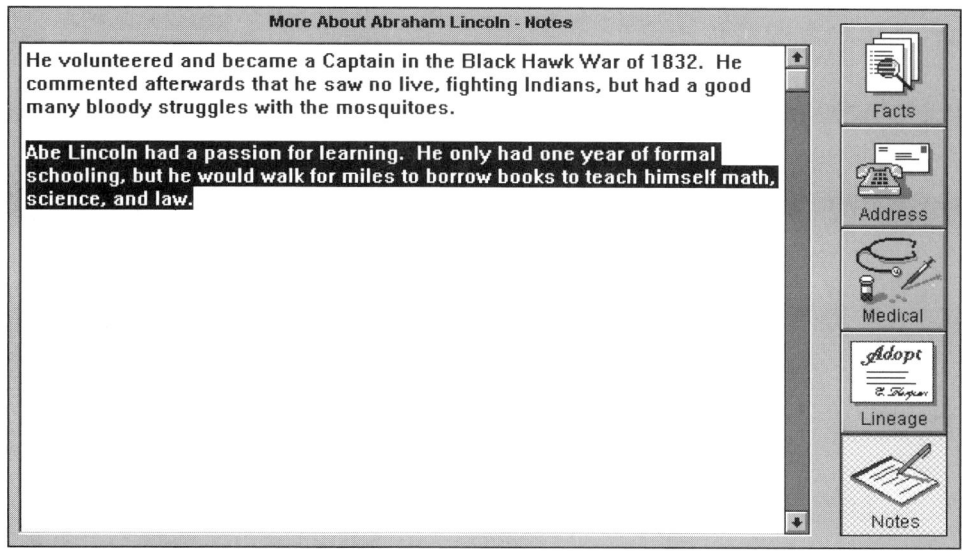

More About Abraham Lincoln - Notes

He volunteered and became a Captain in the Black Hawk War of 1832. He commented afterwards that he saw no live, fighting Indians, but had a good many bloody struggles with the mosquitoes.

Abe Lincoln had a passion for learning. He only had one year of formal schooling, but he would walk for miles to borrow books to teach himself math, science, and law.

Facts

Address

Medical

Adopt

Lineage

Notes

Figure 2-11. A highlighted, or *selected*, paragraph

4. From the **Edit** menu, select **Cut**.

   The paragraph disappears from the screen, but it's not gone. It's in a temporary storage place in memory called the **Clipboard**. Using **Paste**, you can insert the paragraph back into your notes wherever you like.

5. Move the cursor to the beginning of the first paragraph by clicking in front of the "H" in "He."

6. Press [Enter◄─┘] twice to make space for the paragraph you're about to paste in.

7. Press [↑] twice to move the cursor to the top of the screen.

8. From the **Edit** menu, select **Paste**.

   Family Tree Maker now pastes the paragraph from the Clipboard into your notes as shown in Figure 2-12 on the next page. In a few simple steps, you moved an entire paragraph from the end of your notes to the beginning.

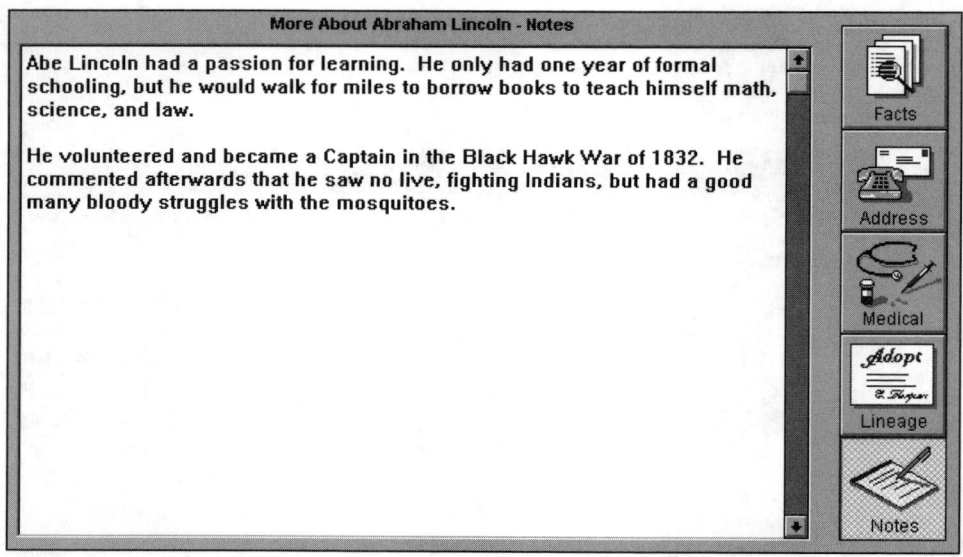

Figure 2-12. Abraham's newly arranged Notes dialog box

Printing Your Notes

1. Adjust the paper in your printer so that the print head is at the top of the page. (Ignore this step if you have a paper tray, sheet feeder, or plotter.)

2. Turn on your printer.

3. From the **File** menu, select **Print Notes**.

   Family Tree Maker displays the Print dialog box.

4. Click **OK** to begin printing your notes.

   The printer starts printing; in a few moments you'll have a printed copy of your notes about Abraham Lincoln. We're now done entering lengthy text for Abraham, so we will return to his Family Page.

5. From the **View** menu, select **Family Page**.

   Family Tree Maker returns you to the Family Page.

PART III: SCRAPBOOKS

Each individual and each marriage in your Family File has a **Scrapbook**. Scrapbooks are where you can store any type of electronic information, such as scanned pictures or other scanned memorabilia; sound clips, video clips, and OLE objects such as word processor documents; and even Kodak Photo CD pictures. Each item that you place into a Scrapbook is called a **Picture/Object**. With Scrapbooks, you can create a wonderful collection of information about each of your family members!

In this section you'll learn how to paste a picture into a Scrapbook. You'll also find out how to tell Family Tree Maker to print Picture/Objects in trees and other Family Tree Maker documents.

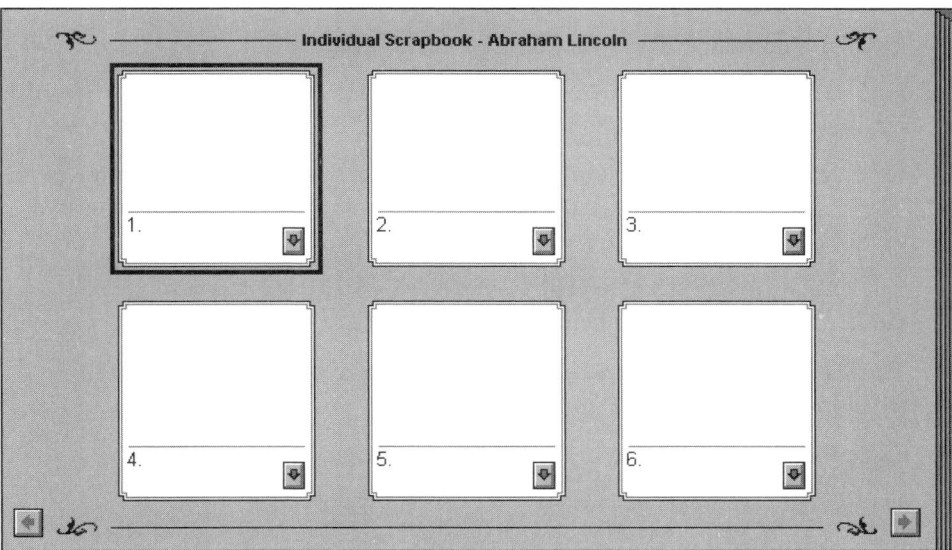

Figure 2-13. An empty Scrapbook page

Placing an Item in a Scrapbook

There are five different ways to place items into a Scrapbook. Each of these methods is described later in the manual, but for now, we'll just show you how to use the Insert Picture command to insert a picture of Abraham Lincoln that we have provided. Let's begin by opening Abraham Lincoln's Scrapbook. Make sure that you are on Abraham Lincoln's Family Page and that the cursor is on his name.

1. From the **View** menu, select **Scrapbook**.

    Family Tree Maker displays Abraham Lincoln's Scrapbook. No items have been placed in Abraham Lincoln's Scrapbook before, so the Scrapbook opens to the first page with the first empty Picture/Object area selected.

2. From the **Picture/Object** menu, select **Insert Picture from File**.

    Family Tree Maker displays the Insert Picture dialog box. See Figure 2-14.

3. In the **Drives** and **Directories** fields, select the drive and directory where the picture you want to insert is located.

    Since you'll be using the sample picture that we have provided, change to the "FTW" directory on the C:\ drive. If you installed Family Tree Maker to a directory other than "FTW," change to that directory.

4. Click the arrow next to the **List Files of Type** field and select the format of the file that you want to open.

    The sample picture we have provided is a bitmap file, so select **Windows Bitmap (*.bmp)**.

5. Click the name of the file in the **File Name** field.

    In this case, click **lincoln.bmp**.

    When a file name is selected, you have several options. You can try them out if you like:

    Preview Picture — Select this check box to view the picture at reduced size in the "Preview" window.

    View Picture — Use this button to display the picture at full size in the View Picture dialog box. In the View Picture dialog box you can use the scroll bars and the **Zoom** buttons to get a better look at your picture. Click **OK** in the View Picture dialog box to return to the Insert Picture dialog box.

Compression — Use this button to change the compression with which your picture will be stored in the Scrapbook. Click **OK** to return to the Insert Picture dialog box.

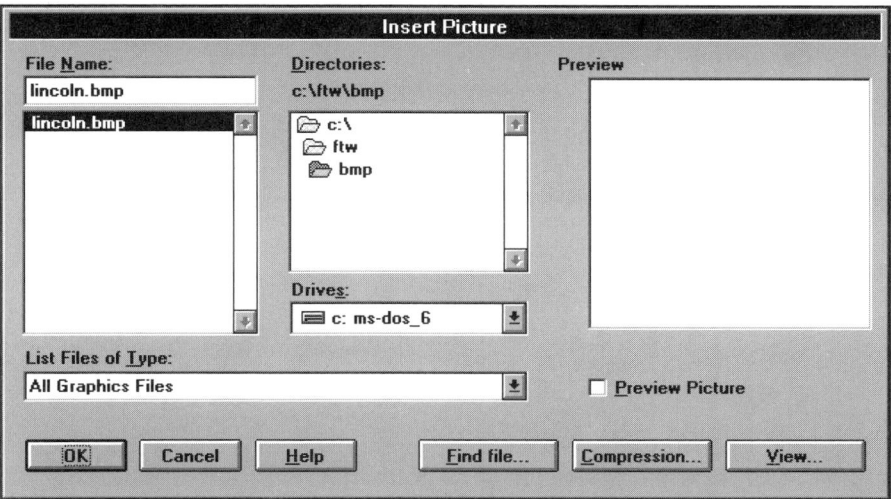

Figure 2-14. The Insert Picture dialog box

6. Click **OK** in the Insert Picture dialog box.

   Family Tree Maker displays the Edit Picture dialog box. See Figure 2-15. This allows you to rotate, flip, or crop your picture before it is compressed and placed into the Scrapbook.

   Note: If you want to edit a picture, this is the best time to do it. This is because Family Tree Maker compresses images for storage, unless you select 1:1 compression. Once you have placed a picture in the Scrapbook, it must be decompressed and recompressed each time you edit it again. Decompressing and recompressing a picture multiple times reduces the quality of the picture. (Family Tree Maker uses the industry standard JPEG compression method.) Please note that printing and viewing your picture at different sizes does not involve compression and will not reduce the quality of your picture.

Editing a Picture

You can rotate, flip, and crop pictures. Rotating a picture lets you turn it in the right direction when it is facing the wrong way. Flipping allows you to turn your picture around if it's backwards. Cropping lets you store select a portion of a picture to place in your Scrapbook. We'll rotate and crop the picture that you've just brought into Family Tree Maker.

Figure 2-15. The Edit Picture dialog box

1. Click **Rotate R**.

   Family Tree Maker rotates the picture ninety degrees to the right. Now that the picture is right side up, we'll crop it to remove the large background.

2. Position the cross-hair (large plus sign) over the exact spot where you want the top left corner of the cropped picture to be.

3. Press and hold the mouse button while you drag diagonally to the exact spot where you want the lower right corner of the cropped picture to be, then release the mouse button.

   The area of the picture that will remain after the picture is cropped will have a box around it. If you do not like the position of the box, simply repeat steps 2 and 3 to create a new box.

4. When you have a box around the area of the picture that you want to keep, click **Crop**.

   Family Tree Maker deletes the part of the picture that you chose to crop off, showing you what the cropped picture will look like. If you want to remove even more of the original picture, repeat steps 2, 3, and 4.

5. Click **OK**.

   Family Tree Maker permanently crops the picture and places the new cropped version in the Scrapbook.

As you can see, when you place a picture in a Scrapbook, Family Tree Maker displays a miniature (thumbnail) version of it. However, you can always view the picture at full size by double-clicking it. You can also print pictures in trees, Family Group Sheets, on labels and cards, and more. "The More About Picture/Object Dialog Box," below, explains more about printing pictures.

The More About Picture/Object Dialog Box

After you insert an item into the Scrapbook, you should use the More About Picture/Object dialog box to create a caption for it and to tell Family Tree Maker in which documents you want the picture to print. (An item that has been inserted into the Scrapbook is called a **Picture/Object**.)

1. Select the Picture/Object by clicking it once.

2. From the **Picture/Object** menu, select **More About**. You can also open the More About Picture/Object dialog box by pressing Ctrl + **M**.

   Family Tree Maker displays the More About Picture/Object dialog box.

3. Click the **Caption** field and type `Abraham Lincoln`

   This caption will appear on the Scrapbook page beneath the Picture/Object after you click **OK**. (But don't click **OK** yet.)

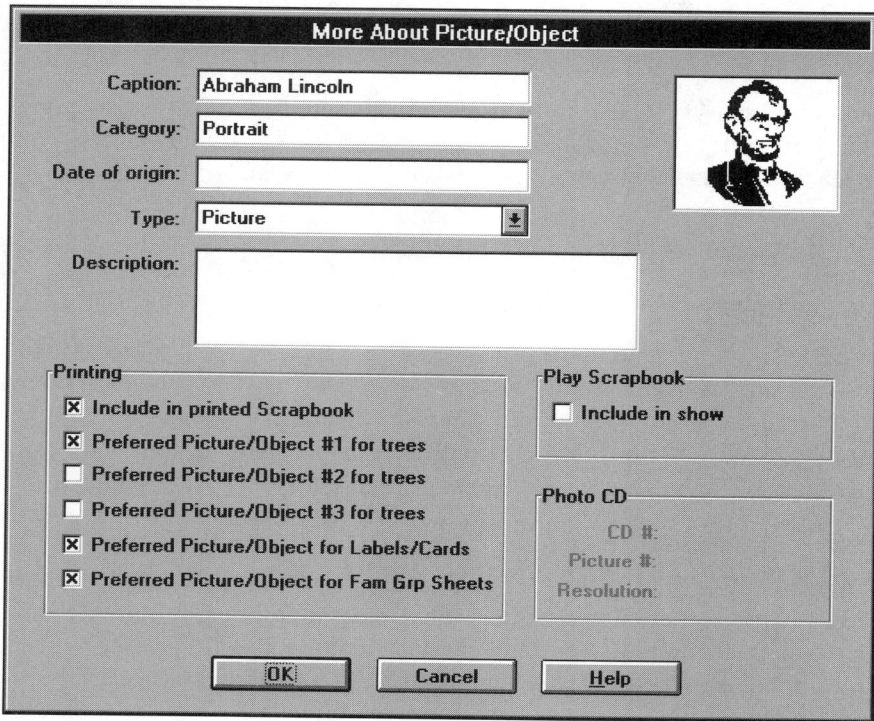

Figure 2-16. The More About Picture/Object dialog box

4. Click in the **Category** field and type `Portrait`

Make sure to fill in this field for each item that you place in the Scrapbook. You can create as many different categories as you like, but it is important to place similar photos in the same category. Categories are useful when it's time to print or search for a Picture/Object. For example, if you wanted to look at all of the Picture/Objects related to birthdays and you had given all of the family birthday Picture/Objects the category "Birthday," you'd be able to locate the birthday pictures easily.

When photos are in the same category, it's also easy to include them as a group in a document. For example, if you wanted to print a tree that contained each individual's picture and each individual had a picture in the "Portrait" category, you could easily print a tree that had a portrait in each individual's box.

5. In the **Type** field Family Tree Maker has already selected **Picture**.

   This field is used to identify what the Picture/Object is. For example, it could be a picture or sound clip. Family Tree Maker automatically identifies the items that it recognizes. Otherwise, it enters "Unknown" into the field and allows you to choose from the drop-down list.

   Make sure to fill in this field for each item that you place in Scrapbooks. You will need this information when you print or search for a Picture/Object.

6. Click the **Description** field and type the following: `Portrait of Abraham Lincoln.`

   You can use this field to describe your Picture/Objects more thoroughly than you can in the "Caption" field.

7. Notice that Family Tree Maker has already selected the **Include in Printed Scrapbook** check box.

   When this check box is selected, Family Tree Maker will include this Picture/Object in printed Scrapbooks. If you don't want a particular Picture/Object to appear in printed Scrapbooks, make sure this check box is not selected in its More About Picture/Object dialog box.

8. Select the **Include in Show** check box.

   Family Tree maker can display the items in a Scrapbook on the screen sequentially, similar to a slide show. When this check box is selected, Family Tree Maker will include this Picture/Object when you play the Scrapbook. See "Playing a Scrapbook" on page 170.

9. Make sure that the **Preferred Picture/Object #1 for trees** check box is already selected.

   To make it easier to select Picture/Objects to print in trees, Family Tree Maker allows you to select the three Picture/Objects that you are most likely to print for an individual. You can designate your three choices using the "Preferred Picture/Object for trees" check boxes.

   For example, if you picked each individual's birthday photo as the "Preferred Picture/Object #1 for trees" and told Family Tree Maker to include "Preferred Picture/Object #1 for trees" when you printed a tree, the tree would contain each individual's birthday photo.

   Please note that for each Scrapbook, you can only designate one Picture/Object as the "Preferred Picture/Object #1 for trees." The same holds for "Preferred Picture/Object #2 for trees" and so on. This means that if you already have selected one picture as the "Preferred Picture/Object #1 for trees" and then select it for a second picture, the first picture is no longer the "Preferred Picture/Object #1 for trees."

Although Family Tree Maker only allows you to designate three "preferred" Picture/Objects for trees, you can still include any other Picture/Object in a tree. You will simply use Categories, described in step four, when it is time to print.

10. Select both the **Preferred Picture/Object for Labels/Cards** check box and the **Preferred Picture/Object for Fam Grp Sheets** check box.

The same rules apply to "Preferred Picture/Object for Labels/Cards" and "Preferred Picture/Object for Fam Grp Sheets" as for "Preferred Picture/Object for trees," described on page 65. However, instead of designating three Picture/Objects, you can only designate one for each of them.

11. Click **OK**.

Family Tree Maker returns you to the Scrapbook view.

12. From the **View** menu, select **Family Page** to go to Lincoln's Family Page.

If you plan to use Scrapbooks, make sure to skim through the second half of Chapter 5 in this manual. These pages describe how to edit, play, and insert items into Scrapbooks. Printing Scrapbook pages is described in Chapter 9.

PART IV: PRINTING A FAMILY TREE

You've entered information about several of Abraham Lincoln's family members, so now you can print his family tree. If this were your own family tree, you'd probably want to add more information.

You may remember from the introduction to this manual that Family Tree Maker can print several types of trees: Ancestor trees, Descendant trees, Direct Descendant trees, Outline Descendant trees, and Outline Direct Descendant trees. Family Tree Maker creates these trees using **views**. You enter your family information once, and Family Tree Maker uses views to display your information in different ways. For example, when you want an Ancestor tree, Family Tree Maker displays your information in the Ancestor Tree view. Or, when you want a Descendant tree, Family Tree Maker displays your information in the Descendant Tree view. Most of the views are listed on the View menu.

Changing Views

In this section, we'll first look at a Descendant tree. This will give you more practice with changing views. Then, we'll look at an Ancestor tree and print it.

Right now you should be on the Family Page that shows Abraham Lincoln in the "Husband" field. If you are not currently on Abraham Lincoln's Family Page, go to the Index of Individuals, find Abraham Lincoln (the one that was born in 1809), and then go to his Family Page. If you aren't sure how to do this, see "Lincoln's Maternal Grandparents' Family Page" on page 47.

Make sure that the cursor is on Lincoln's name. By placing the cursor on Lincoln's name, you are making him the **primary individual**. The primary individual in a family tree is the main person in the tree. For example, if you are creating a Descendant tree, the primary individual is at the very top of the tree, and the tree shows the primary individual's descendants.

To view Abraham's Descendant tree:

1. From the **View** menu, select **Descendant Tree**.

   Family Tree Maker displays a Descendant tree on your screen. At the top of the tree there are boxes containing information about Abraham Lincoln and his wife, Mary. Beneath them are boxes containing information about each of their four children.

2. From the **View** menu, select **Zoom**, and then select the **Actual Size** option button from the dialog box that Family Tree Maker displays.

   Family Tree Maker shows Abraham's Descendant tree at Actual Size. Using the Zoom command does *not* change the size of your tree when you print.

   You can use the scroll bars that are along the bottom and right side of your tree to move around and look at different parts of the tree. When you're through looking at the tree, move on to the next step.

3. Now, to see someone else's Descendant tree, choose a different primary individual. From the **View** menu, select **Index of Individuals**.

   Family Tree Maker displays the Index of Individuals.

4. Click **Nancy Hanks**, and then click **OK**.

   Family Tree Maker displays a Descendant tree showing the descendants of Nancy Hanks and Thomas Lincoln. If you wanted to print the tree, you would do it from here, but let's print an Ancestor tree instead.

Printing an Ancestor Tree

We want to print an Ancestor tree for President Lincoln, so we need to make him the primary individual again and then switch to the Ancestor Tree view. We could find President Lincoln just by going to the Index of Individuals and clicking on his name, but this is a good opportunity to try out Quick Search.

To find someone with a Quick Search:

1. From the **View** menu, select **Index of Individuals**.

   Family Tree Maker displays the Index of Individuals. Notice that there is a flashing cursor in the "Name" field at the top of the screen. We'll use this field to do our search.

2. Type **Lincoln, Abraham**

   With each character you type, Family Tree Maker moves the highlight closer to the individual you're looking for. It stops on the first Abraham Lincoln, the President's grandfather. Notice also that we had you type his last name first. See Figure 2-18 below.

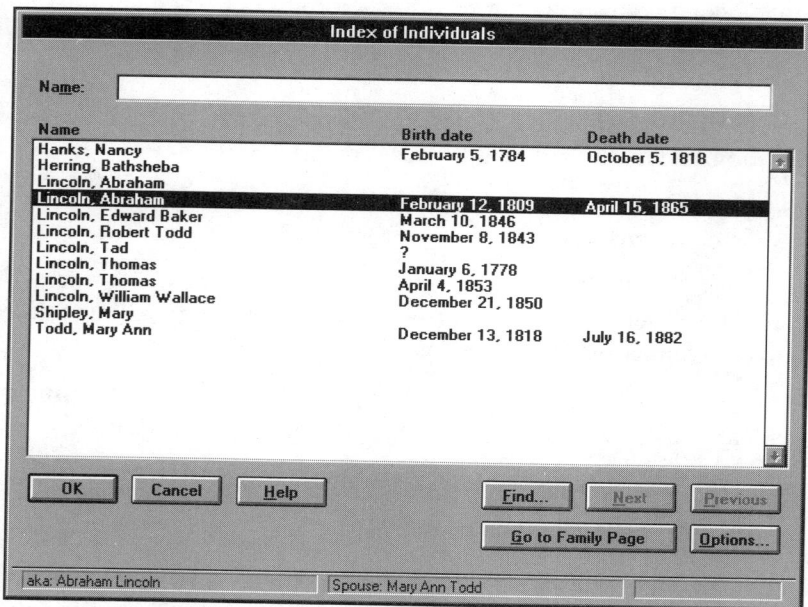

Figure 2-18. Quick searching in the Index of Individuals

3. Press ⬇ once to highlight the President.

4. Click **OK**.

   Family Tree Maker displays a Descendant tree with Abraham Lincoln as the primary individual. Why did it display a Descendant tree? Because the Descendant Tree view is the view that we were in before we changed to the Index of Individuals view. When you're in the Index of Individuals, clicking OK returns you to the view that you were in before you opened the Index of Individuals. The name that was highlighted in the Index of Individuals is the name that you will see when you return to the previous view.

5. Now you want to see an Ancestor tree, so from the **View** menu, select **Ancestor Tree**.

   Family Tree Maker displays an Ancestor tree containing Abraham Lincoln, his parents, and his grandparents. His children are not in this tree because they are his descendants, not his ancestors.

   Now that you have an Ancestor tree for Abraham, you can change the way it looks and the information it includes to create a tree you like. For now, we'll just show you how to control what information prints in the boxes, but feel free to experiment with the options on the **Contents** and **Format** menus!

Selecting Items to Include in the Boxes

1. From the **Contents** menu, select **Items to Include**.

   Family Tree Maker displays the Items to Include dialog box (see Figure 2-19 on the next page); it contains two lists. The list on the left is for selecting items to include in the tree's boxes and the list on the right shows which items are currently selected to be in the tree's boxes.

   The items that are currently selected are Name, Birth date and location, Marriage date and location, and Death date and location. Family Tree Maker uses examples to give you an idea of how the items will print. For example, the item that says "First Middle Last" tells you that individuals' complete names will print. If it just said "First Last," you would know that middle names wouldn't print. Family Tree Maker does the same thing with dates.

   Just for practice, we'll take some items out of the boxes of Abraham's tree.

2. Click the death date item in the list on the right. Unless a different format has been chosen previously, it will say **d: Date in Location**.

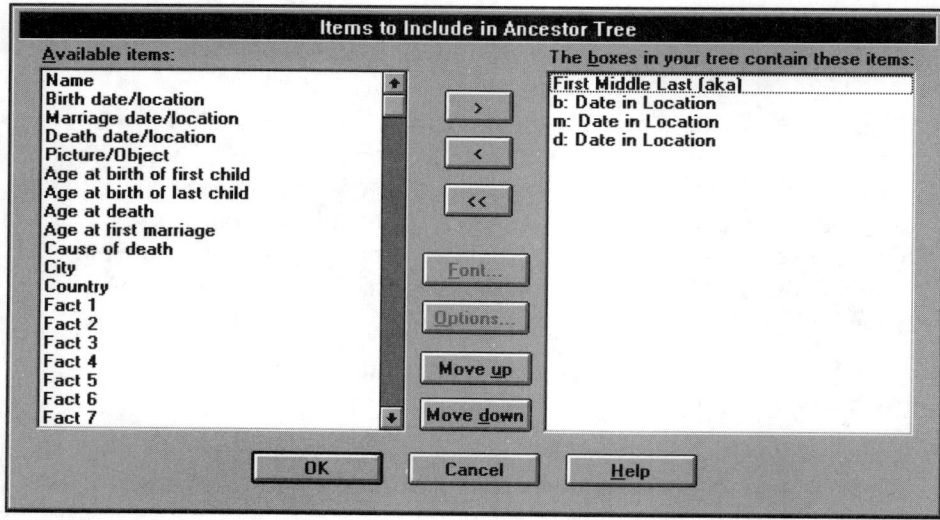

Figure 2-19. The Items to Include dialog box

3. Click the **Remove** button (the arrow that's pointing to the left).

   This will remove that item from *all* the boxes in the Ancestor tree. Now we want to select a new item to include: each individual's age at death.

4. In the list on the left, click **Age at death**.

5. Click the **Include** button (the arrow pointing to the right).

   Family Tree Maker displays the Options: Age at Death dialog box.

6. Make some formatting selections and then click **OK**.

   Family Tree Maker puts the "Age at death" item into the list on the right.

Now let's change the format of one of the items that we're already including in the boxes of Abraham's tree: each individual's name.

1. Click **First Middle Last (aka)** in the list on the right.

   Family Tree Maker highlights the item to show you it is selected.

2. Click **Options**.

   Family Tree Maker displays the Options: Name dialog box (Figure 2-20).

3. Click the **Format** drop-down list and select **First Last**.

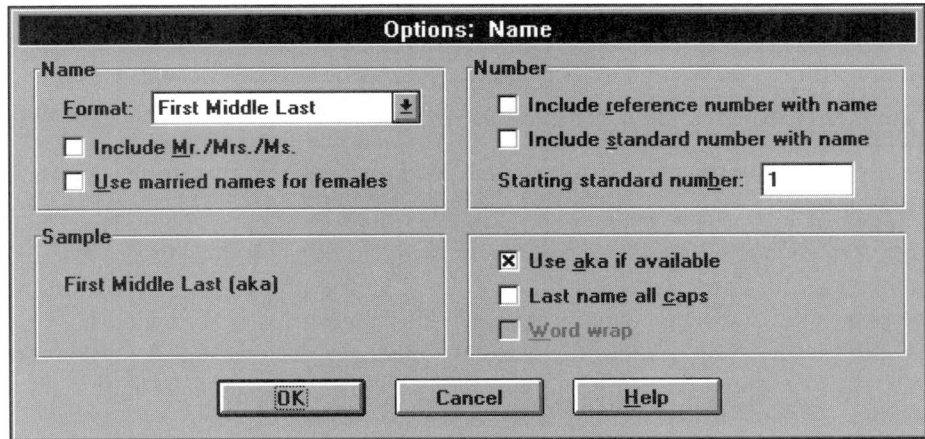

Figure 2-20. The Options: Name dialog box

As you can see, there are other options you can choose to format the Name item. For now, we'll just change this one.

4. Click **OK**.

    Family Tree Maker displays the Items to Include dialog box with the newly-selected name format displayed in the list on the right.

5. You can include many more items in a tree's boxes, but for now, click **OK**.

    Family Tree Maker returns to you the Ancestor Tree view with the items you just selected shown in your tree.

Printing a Tree

Now, to print Abraham's tree:

1. Adjust the paper so that the print head is at the top of the page.

    Ignore this step if you have a paper tray (as most laser printers do), sheet feeder, or plotter.

2. Turn on your printer.

3. From the **File** menu, select **Print Ancestor Tree**.

    Family Tree Maker displays the Print Ancestor Tree dialog box.

4. Click **OK** to begin printing your tree.

Saving Information in Family Tree Maker

You may think that it's about time to save your information, but with Family Tree Maker, you don't have to. Family Tree Maker is a database program, so it automatically saves your information while you are working. You won't even notice that it's happening. Family Tree Maker also saves your information right before you quit.

While Family Tree Maker doesn't have a Save command, it does have a Backup command. This command lets you make a copy of your Family File to store in a safe place You can also make second copy of your Family File on your hard disk, so it's easy to go back to this copy if something goes wrong. You'll want to use this command frequently — perhaps each time you use the program. The Backup command is described on page 376.

Quitting Family Tree Maker

Each time you're through using Family Tree Maker, you need to quit the program. Never shut off your machine before quitting Family Tree Maker and then quitting Windows.

To quit Family Tree Maker:

1. From the **File** menu, select **Exit**.

   Family Tree Maker saves your information and then closes the program.

2. If you're done using your computer, close Windows and then shut off the computer.

What to Do Next

To learn more about Family Tree Maker, skim through the rest of this manual. We encourage you to go through all the menus again, particularly the Format and Contents menus from within a tree view. There are many more options to choose from when creating and printing a tree.

Finally, start a new Family File — this time using information about your own family. Before you know it, you'll be creating beautiful family trees to use as gifts for everyone in your tree.

ENTERING BASIC INFORMATION

*This is George Franklin Hess, his son Franklin, and an unknown pilot sometime in the early 1900's. George was an executive with the Wabash Railroad. It was a Wabash passenger train, the **Banner Blue Limited**, that provided the name for the company that makes this program.*

ENTERING BASIC INFORMATION

Before you can print a tree or report, you need to enter information about your family. This chapter describes how to do that. (Chapters 8, 9, and 10 describe how to print the information you've entered.)

A QUICK OVERVIEW

To enter basic family information, such as names and birth dates, you fill out an electronic "page," called a **Family Page** (see Figure 3-1 on the next page). It is the first screen that you see after you open a Family File. Each nuclear family (two parents and their children) has its own Family Page.

You can add more details about each family member by filling out a series of **More About** dialog boxes. You can also store pictures, video clips, sound clips, and other OLE objects in each individual's **Scrapbook**. These are described in Chapter 5.

From time to time as you're entering information, Family Tree Maker will automatically save the information in your **Family File**. Your Family File is where all of the family information that you enter into Family Tree Maker is stored. You should not create a new Family File for every Family Page that you fill out.

Since Family Tree Maker saves your information automatically, you don't have to. However, you occasionally will want to make a backup copy of your Family File, perhaps to a floppy diskette that you store in a safe place. This way, if your Family Files are accidentally deleted or damaged, you won't have to rebuild your files from scratch. To learn how to backup your Family Files, see page 376.

While you're learning to use Family Tree Maker, don't be afraid to experiment. If you get lost, you can press ⌷ at any time to get on–screen help.

THE FAMILY PAGE

The **Family Page** is a view that shows all the members of a nuclear family: two parents and their children. This is the main **view** for entering information about your family. In Family Tree Maker, a "view" is a way of looking at information. For example, when you look at information on a Family Page, you are looking at the Family Page view. If you choose to see that same information in a Descendant tree, you are looking at the Descendant Tree view. We'll talk about moving between views later in the manual. In this chapter, we'll just describe how to enter information in the Family Page.

Family Tree Maker shows only one Family Page on the screen at a time, but your Family File can hold many Family Pages, just like a photo album can have many pages. In Chapter 4, "Moving Around," we'll show you how to move between different Family Pages.

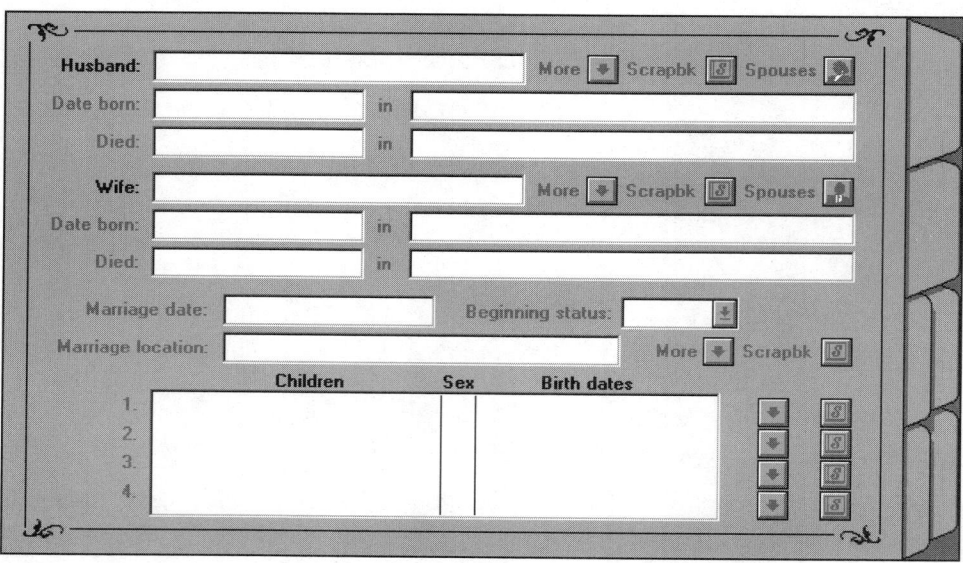

Figure 3-1. An empty Family Page

The row of words across the top of the screen is the set of menus that you'll be using. This is called the **menu bar**. When you click one of the words on the menu bar, such as "Edit," a list of commands appears below it. This list is called a **pull-down menu**. You will choose items from the menu bar and pull-down menus to do things such as edit your information and print family trees.

Below the menu bar is the **toolbar**. It contains buttons that you can click to display different views or to open dialog boxes, depending on which buttons are available.

Entering Family Information

When you start a new Family File, the Family Page appears blank as it does in Figure 3-1. It is ready for you to begin entering family information.

A Family Page is just like a paper form. It consists of labeled blanks to fill with information. The blanks are called **fields** and the labels that describe the blanks are called **field labels**. Right now, the fields have conventional labels, such as "Husband," "Wife," and "Children." You can change some of these labels if you want to. See "Preferences for Field Labels," on the next page.

You type information into the fields and then move from field to field using Tab `⬅|`, `Enter⏎`, the cursor keys `↓` and `↑`, or by clicking fields with your mouse pointer. To save typing time, you can also copy and paste information from one field to another. See "Cutting, Copying, and Pasting" on page 81 for more information.

Some fields only allow you to enter certain kinds of information. For example, sex fields only allow you to "M", "F", or a question mark. You can try to enter something else, but Family Tree Maker will catch it and ask you to fill in the field appropriately. Family Tree Maker can also catch any conflicting information that you enter. For example, you cannot give someone a marriage date that is prior to their birth date. To turn this type of error checking on and off, see "Data Entry Checking Preferences" on page 79.

Some fields are "Fastfields." Fastfields help you enter your information into Family Tree Maker more quickly by remembering the words that you type most often. We'll describe Fastfields in "Fastfields" on page 90.

Preferences for Field Labels

Changing field labels is useful if you want your Family Tree Maker records to match other genealogical records that you have. You can change a variety of labels on the Family Page and in the Facts and Marriage dialog boxes (see pages 130 and 145). You can also change the abbreviations for estimated dates (see page 87). If you want to conform to LDS standards, there is a special option that will change labels for you automatically.

Note: When you're changing field labels, remember that you're changing the label for each and every individual in your Family File. You cannot change a field label for only one individual.

To change field labels:

1.   From the **Prefs** menu, select **Labels**.

   Family Tree Maker displays the Labels dialog box.

2.   Type over the old labels with your new, preferred labels.

3.   If you want your field labels to conform to LDS standards, select **Use LDS format**. Selecting this option will affect the way Family Group Sheets are printed as well. For details, see Appendix B.

4.   Click **OK** when you've made your changes.

If you later decide that you want to restore the field labels to their default values, select **Reset labels to default**.

Data Entry Checking Preferences

Family Tree Maker can help you keep your Family File free of mistakes by examining information as you enter it in Family Pages. For example, Family Tree Maker will compare a child's birth date with its mother's death date to make sure that the child was born before his or her mother died. If Family Tree Maker finds questionable information, it will display a dialog box that gives you the option to correct it. For a complete list of the errors that Family Tree Maker can identify, see page 371.

Family Tree Maker can also examine the information that's already in your Family File. See "Checking Your File for Errors" on page 367 for more information about other methods of checking for errors.

To turn on the error checking options:

1. From the **Prefs** menu, select **Error Checking**.

    Family Tree Maker displays the Error Checking dialog box.

2. Select the check boxes for the types of errors that you want Family Tree Maker to look for.

3. Click **OK** when you've made your selections.

    Family Tree Maker closes the dialog box.

Moving the Cursor

The fastest way to move around the Family Page is to move the mouse pointer to the fields where you want to type and then click the primary mouse button. You can also use your computer keyboard to move the cursor around the Family Page. Figure 3-2 shows which keys work as navigational keys.

Press this key...	To do this...
↑	Move the cursor to the field above the current field
↓	Move the cursor to the field below the current field
←	Move the cursor one character to the left
→	Move the cursor one character to the right
⇥ (tab)	Move the cursor to the next field
⇧ Shift + ⇥	Move the cursor to the previous field
home	Move the cursor to the beginning of the current field
end	Move the cursor to the end of the current field
Enter ↵	Move the cursor to the next field
Ctrl + ←	Move the cursor to the previous word
Ctrl + →	Move the cursor to the next word
Ctrl + home	Move the cursor to the husband, or if in the "Children" list, move to the first child
Ctrl + end	Move to the first empty row in the "Children" list
PgUp	Move up through the list of children
PgDn	Move down through the list of children

Figure 3-2. Keys for moving the cursor on the Family Page

Editing Information

Family Tree Maker has the same basic editing commands that most other Windows programs have: Cut, Copy, Paste, and Undo. You can cut, copy, and paste any text in Family Tree Maker, including dates, locations, causes of death, notes, and telephone numbers. These commands make it easy to move information around and can help you avoid manual deleting and retyping.

Note: You should NOT cut and paste an individual's name. Cutting an individual's name DOES NOT delete that individual. To delete someone, use the Delete Individual command described on page 185. Cutting and pasting an individual's name DOES NOT move that individual to another location. To move an individual and all of the information associated with that individual, use the Detach and Attach commands, described in Chapter 6.

You can also copy and paste trees, Family Group Sheets, reports, and more. See "Copying Items to Other Applications" on page 348 for instructions.

Cutting, Copying, and Pasting

To cut and paste or copy and paste text in Family Tree Maker:

1. Highlight the text that you want to cut or copy.

   To highlight text with a mouse, place the mouse pointer in front of the first character you want to select. Press and hold the primary mouse button while you drag the mouse until the last character you want to select is highlighted. Then, release the mouse button.

2. From the **Edit** menu, select either **Cut** or **Copy**.

   The text (or a copy of it if you are copying the text) is placed in a temporary storage place called the **Clipboard**. You can use the Paste command to insert the contents of the Clipboard wherever you like.

3. Place the cursor where you want to paste the information. If you want to *replace* a section of existing text with the information that you've just copied or cut, highlight that text.

4. From the **Edit** menu, select **Paste**.

   Family Tree Maker inserts the text or pastes it over the selected text. Since the Clipboard is not erased until you use the Copy or Cut command again, you can paste the same text as many times as you like.

Reversing a Command

Using Undo, you can reverse the very last editing command that you performed. For example, if you cut some text, selecting Undo right away will restore it.

Note: To reverse an editing command, you must select Undo as the very next command. Otherwise, it will not reverse the correct command.

When you select the Edit menu, you will notice that the Undo command says different things at different times. For example, it may say "Undo Paste," or "Undo Copy," indicating what it will reverse.

To reverse an editing command:

1. Don't type any new text or perform any other editing commands. If you do, you won't be able to use Undo on the command that you want to reverse.

2. From the **Edit** menu, select **Undo**.

   It doesn't matter where your cursor is — Family Tree Maker will remember what it was that you did last and reverse it.

3. If you want to restore the editing command that you've just reversed, select **Redo** immediately.

   Note: If you accidentally deleted text using the **Cut** command, there is another way to restore it. Simply position your cursor where you wish to replace the text. Then, from the **Edit** menu, select **Paste**.

From time to time you may make a minor mistake when entering information about your family, for example, a spelling error. The following table shows you which keys you can use to edit the information in a field.

Press this key...	To do this...
[←BkSp] (backspace)	Back up and erase the previous character
[ins]	Switch back and forth between insert and overwrite modes
[delete]	Delete characters to the right, one by one
[alt] + [←BkSp]	Reverse your last editing command
[Ctrl] + [X]	Cut highlighted text and place it on the Clipboard
[Ctrl] + [C]	Copy highlighted text and place it on the Clipboard
[Ctrl] + [V]	Paste text from the Clipboard to your Family Page
[Ctrl] + [Z]	Undo/Redo the last editing command
[↹] (tab)	In the Notes dialog box, move the cursor to the next tab stop
[Enter←]	In the Notes dialog box, end a paragraph and move the cursor to the beginning of the next line

Figure 3-3. Editing keys

Entering Names

The "Husband," "Wife," and "Children" fields on the Family Page are where you enter names. The "Husband" and "Wife" fields work as Fastfields (see page 90) for last names. In addition, in the "Children" list, Family Tree Maker automatically inserts the husband's last name after the children's first and middle names. You can type over the name that Family Tree Maker inserts if the children have different last names.

It's always best to enter an individual's full given name, including the middle name. Also, be sure to enter names first-name-first and don't use initials. Nicknames should be entered in the Lineage dialog box (see page 134). In addition, when entering a woman's name, always use her maiden name (her name before she was married). "Name" fields can hold up to 48 characters.

Note: You can *print* names differently from the way you enter them. For example, you can print last names first or split names onto two lines. You also have the option of printing women with married names instead of maiden names or printing everyone's nicknames instead of given names. However, to print names in different ways, you must enter them completely (first, middle, and last name), with nicknames in the Lineage dialog box, and then let Family Tree Maker do the hard work for you.

First Middle Last

First M. Last

Last, First Middle

First Last

F. M. Last

F. Last

First Middle\\Last (split onto two lines)

Figure 3-4. Some of the name formats Family Tree Maker can create

Nicknames — It's quite acceptable to include nicknames in your Family File. However, enter them in the Lineage dialog box, described on page 134.

Name changes — Any name changes should also be entered in the Lineage dialog box, described on page 134. For example, if "Johann Smythe" changed his name to "John Smith," you could enter "Johann Smythe" as his name on the Family Page and record the fact that he was also known as "John Smith" in the Lineage dialog box.

Unusual last names — Family Tree Maker can usually tell the last name from other parts of an individual's name. However, if at some point you notice that it has incorrectly identified someone's last name, place the entire last name between backslash characters. The backslash characters will not appear in any printed documents. In the example below, Family Tree Maker interprets the last name as "Irish Hess."

`Connie \Irish Hess\`

Last names with suffixes — If a suffix is attached to the last name (for example, "Jr." or, "Ph.D.") be sure to separate it from the last name with a comma (John Smith, Jr.). The comma lets Family Tree Maker know that the suffix is not the last name. This way, the name will appear under the correct letter of the alphabet in the Index of Individuals and other alphabetized lists. You don't need to use commas with Roman numerals, unless the number is greater than eight.

Missing last names — In some cultures, last names aren't used. To show that an individual has no last name, place two backslash characters together without a space between them at the end of the name. The backslash characters will not appear in any printed documents. In this example, the individual "Running Bear" has no last name.

`Running Bear\\`

Titles — Do not enter titles such as "Mr.," "Mrs.," or "Dr." on the Family Page. You can use the Titles dialog box described in "Preferences for Titles," on the next page, to select titles such as "Mr." or "Mrs." for most of the individuals in your Family File. For anyone with a special title, such as "Dr." or "Reverend," see the description of the Lineage dialog box on page 134.

Preferences for Titles

With Family Tree Maker's Labels/Cards view, you can print address labels, name tags, rolling index cards, post cards, address book pages, and much more. When you print these items, you may want to use titles such as "Mr." and "Mrs." in front of people's names. The Title dialog box, where you can select default titles to use with most people in your Family File, is described below. If anyone in your Family File uses a more unique title, such as "Dr." or "Reverend," enter that title in the Lineage dialog box (see page 134.) For information about printing labels and cards, see Chapter 9, "Printing Detailed Information."

To change title preferences:

1. From the **Prefs** menu, select **Titles**.

    Family Tree Maker displays the Titles dialog box.

2. Make your changes in the Titles dialog box. Each of your options is described below.

    Married Males/Married Females — The title that you type here will appear on labels and cards for all men and women who are currently married or have ever been married. The defaults are "Mr." and "Mrs."

    Not married Males/Not married Females — The title that you type here will appear on labels and cards for all men and women who have never been married. The defaults are "Mr." and "Ms."

    Children Males/Children Females — The title that you type here will appear on labels and cards for all children. The default is to have no title.

    Children are individuals younger than X years old — All individuals under the age that you type in this field will appear on labels and cards with the "Children" title. All individuals this age and over will appear with either the "Married" or "Not married" title. The default age is 13.

    Use defaults — Use this button to reset the titles and the cutoff age to their default values.

3. Click **OK** when you've made your changes.

    Family Tree Maker saves your changes.

Entering Dates

The "Date" fields in Family Tree Maker are very smart and flexible and can handle any date after 1/1/100 A.D. You can enter a date almost any way you want, but when you move the cursor out of the field, Family Tree Maker automatically puts the date in a standard format. The first time you use Family Tree Maker, the standard format will be the same as the default format that's selected in your Windows Control Panel. You can change the standard format and even use European formats. See "Preferences for Dates and Measures" on page 88. "Date" fields can contain up to 49 characters.

There may be events for which you don't know an exact date. Or, you may be certain of the year, but not certain of the day and month. Figure 3-5, below, shows how you can record estimated and partial dates.

You type this...	You get this...
1776	1776
Jul 1776	July 1776
4 Jul	July 4
Est 7/4/1776	Abt July 4, 1776
Abt 7/4/1776	Abt July 4, 1776
About 7/4/1776	Abt July 4, 1776
Circa 7/4/1776	Abt July 4, 1776
Cir 7/4/1776	Abt July 4, 1776
Bef 7/4/1776	Bef July 4, 1776
Before 7/4/1776	Bef July 4, 1776
Aft 7/4/1776	Aft July 4, 1776
After 7/4/1776	Aft July 4, 1776
?	Unknown

Figure 3-5. How to enter estimated dates

In the table, you'll notice that "About" and "Abt" are used to indicate approximate dates. If you like, you can change these words. See "Preferences for Field Labels" on page 78 to change these labels.

Leaving a date field blank means the event hasn't happened. For example, if someone is not dead, leave the date field for that event blank. If they died, but you don't know the date of death, type a question mark. Entering a question mark means that you know the event happened, but aren't sure when. You can also type "Dead" or "Deceased" in death date fields.

If you merged information from the World Family Tree (see page 362), some date fields may contain the word "Private." This is to protect the privacy of individuals who are still living.

Family Tree Maker also understands date codes used by the Church of Jesus Christ of Latter–day Saints. See Appendix B, "LDS Ordinance Information," for details.

Double Dates — Family Tree Maker can display double dates to account for the crossover between the Julian and Gregorian calendars. If you enter a date that falls *between* December 31 and March 25 for any year before 1753, a double date will appear.

You can specify a double date by typing both of the years in the field. For example, you can type either Jan 1, 1493/4 or Jan 1, 1493/1494; both display as January 1, 1493/94. If you don't type in both of the years, Family Tree Maker assumes that the year you typed is the second year. For example, if you type January 1, 1494, it's displayed as January 1, 1493/94. See "Double Dates" in Appendix A for more information. If you would like to change the double date cutoff year to something other than 1752, see "Preferences for Dates and Measures," below.

Preferences for Dates and Measures

In the Dates & Measures dialog box, you can change the double date cutoff year and the standard date format for your date fields. You can also choose between the English and Metric measurement systems.

Figure 3-6, on the next page, lists possible date formats. Use the date format that you're most comfortable with, because it's important not to make mistakes with dates in your family information.

To choose a date format and to select a measurement system:

1. From the **Prefs** menu, select **Dates & Measures**.

    Family Tree Maker displays the Dates & Measures dialog box.

2. Select the date format that you want.

    If you don't want to use double dates, type **0** in the **Double date cutoff year** field.

```
July 4, 1776
Jul 4, 1776
4 July 1776
4 Jul 1776
07.04.1776
04.07.1776
07-4-1776
07/04/1776
```

Figure 3-6. Possible date formats

3. Choose between using the English (inches and feet) or Metric (centimeters and meters) measuring system.

4. Click **OK** when you've made your selections.

   Family Tree Maker saves your changes.

Entering Locations

"Location" fields are for entering an individual's place of birth, death, or marriage. (These fields are usually preceded by the field label "in.") Normally, you enter the city and state. You might want to enter the county if it's important.

To conserve space, enter the country name only if it's unusual. For example, if most family members were born in the United States, you would only enter the country for the few relatives who were born outside of the United States.

Note: Your trees will look better if you enter information in a consistent way. For example, either abbreviate states or spell them out. Don't abbreviate in some cases and spell them out in other cases.

Sometimes when Family Tree Maker prints single-page trees, it has limited space for the location fields. If Family Tree Maker needs to abbreviate a location, it will always try to keep the last word in the location field. This means that if you enter a state and a country in each location field, it may print the country, but drop the state. "Location" fields can contain up to 80 characters.

Be sure to put commas between the city, county, state, and country names. Correct punctuation allows Family Tree Maker to abbreviate correctly when it is necessary.

Fastfields

To help you save time when entering family information, Family Tree Maker has a special feature called **Fastfields**. Most of the Fastfields in Family Tree Maker are location fields, such as birth location, death location, and marriage location fields, so we'll use locations to explain how Fastfields work.

The Fastfields feature remembers the names of the last 50 locations that you've entered into any location field. This means that when you start typing the name of a town that you've previously typed in a location field, Fastfields automatically fills in the rest of the letters for you.

For example, say that you have typed the following two birth locations into Family Tree Maker: "Abilene, Louisiana" and "Arlington, Virginia." Then, you go to another birth location field and type the letter "A." Fastfields immediately looks for a location beginning with "A" that you've previously typed. Since "Abilene, Louisiana" is alphabetically the first location beginning with an "A," Fastfields automatically places "Abilene, Louisiana" into the field. If you then typed an "r" after the "A," Fastfields would replace "Abilene, Louisiana" with "Arlington, Virginia." If "Arlington, Virginia" wasn't the name that you wanted in that birth location field, you would just continue typing the name that you wanted, such as "Argyle, New York." In short, Fastfields refines its suggestions as you type and quits making suggestions when it no longer has any logical choices to offer.

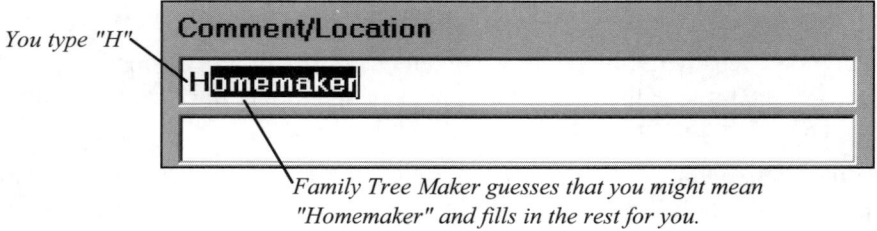

You type "H"

Family Tree Maker guesses that you might mean "Homemaker" and fills in the rest for you.

Figure 3-7. Fastfields help you fill some types of fields by guessing at what you are typing. When the guess is wrong, just keep typing.

In addition to location fields, Fastfields work with last names in the "Husband" and "Wife" fields. Also, the first time you type a name in a "Children" list on a Family Page, Family Tree Maker automatically inserts the husband's last name after the child's first name. If the child has a different last name, simply replace the name that Family Tree Maker inserted with the correct name. Any additional children will automatically get the same last name as the first child, although you can change those too, if necessary.

The other fields that work as Fastfields are "Cause of death," "Picture/Object category," "Comment/Location," and "Sources." You'll also find that Fastfields work in the Find Individual feature, described on page 122.

If you are not comfortable using Fastfields, you can turn them off. See "Preferences for Fastfields" below. You can also delete individual words from a Fastfield word list. You may want to do this if Family Tree Maker suggests a word that is misspelled. See "Deleting Words from a Fastfields Word List," on the next page.

Preferences for Fastfields

In the Fastfields dialog box, Family Tree Maker allows you to choose which fields work as Fastfields. This way, if you are not comfortable using Fastfields, you can turn them off.

To change Fastfields preferences:

1. From the **Prefs** menu, select **Fastfields**.

   Family Tree Maker displays the Fastfields dialog box.

2. Select the check boxes for the fields that you want to act as Fastfields or de-select the fields that you don't want to act as Fastfields. Click **All** to select all of the check boxes. Click **None** to de-select all of the check boxes.

3. Click **OK** when you've made your selections.

   Family Tree Maker closes the dialog box and saves your changes.

Deleting Words from a Fastfields Word List

You may want to delete a word from a Fastfield word list if it is misspelled or if you don't use it very often.

To delete a word from a Fastfield word list:

1. Go to a Fastfield for the type of word that you want to delete. For example, if you want to delete a last name, go to a name field.

2. Start typing the word.

3. When the word appears, click the trash can button that appears on the right side of the Fastfield.

Click here to delete "Mobile, Alabama"
from the Fastfield word list.

Figure 3-8. The trash can button

Family Tree Maker deletes the word from the Fastfield word list. The word remains deleted until you type it in a Fastfield again.

4. If necessary, re-type the correct information in the field where you just deleted the Fastfield word.

Entering Information About Marriages, Partnerships, and Friendships

The "Marriage" fields record the date and location of a couple's marriage. You can also record the status of their relationship in the relationship status fields. For example, if a couple was married, you would choose "Married" from the "Beginning status" drop-down list on the Family Page. Or, if it isn't certain that a couple was ever married, you would choose "Unknown."

Figure 3-9. The Beginning status field drop-down list

When both a husband and a wife are present, the default for the "Beginning status" field is "Married," but you can select any of the following terms from the drop-down list: Friends, Married, Other, Partners, Single, and Unknown. When you choose "Partner" or "Friend" in the "Beginning status" field, Family Tree Maker automatically substitutes "Meeting date" for "Marriage date" in the records you're keeping about those two individuals.

If you merged information from a World Family Tree (see page 362), some marriage fields may contain the word "Private." This is to protect the privacy of individuals who are still living.

Each marriage has its own set of More About dialog boxes for recording additional information about a marriage, including special marital events. The More About dialog boxes for a marriage are also where you'll find the "Ending status" field. For more information about the More About dialog boxes for a marriage, see "Entering Details About a Marriage" on page 145.

Entering Information About Children

The "Children" list at the bottom of the Family Page is for recording the names, sexes, and birth dates of the children of the parents on that Family Page. The date field in the "Children" list works just as it does for the husband and wife. The name field is a Fastfield (see page 90) for last names. Family Tree Maker automatically inserts the husband's last name after children's first and middle names. You can type over the name that Family Tree Maker inserts if the children have different last names.

	Children	Sex	Birth dates	
1	Robert Todd Lincoln	M	November 8, 1843	▲
2	Edward Baker Lincoln	M	March 10, 1846	
3	William Wallace Lincoln	M	December 21, 1850	
4	Thomas Lincoln	M	April 4, 1853	▼

Figure 3-10. The Children list

The "Sex" field accepts the letters "M" and "F" for "male" and "female," as well as "?" for cases where the sex is unknown. The default is female. Because the sex of a child determines where he or she appears in the construction of family trees, it's important that you fill in the sex correctly.

Note: You can change a child's sex at any time by typing over the current sex. If the child is married, the spouse's sex will not change automatically.

There are different ways that you can enter the names of children who were not born to their parents, such as stepchildren, foster children, or adopted children. Some people prefer only to record bloodline relationships in their family trees, while others just want to show who makes up the family.

If you are interested in tracing your family's bloodline, only enter the names of children born to the parents listed on a particular Family Page. In this case, you should enter stepchildren only as children of their birth parents. In addition, if you want to trace the family bloodline, you probably don't want to enter adopted and foster children.

If you want to record *everyone* who makes up the family, enter all children as you wish. You can enter adopted, foster, and stepchildren as children of their foster, adoptive, or stepparents and leave it at that, or you can use the Lineage dialog box to indicate the special nature of the relationship (see page 134). If children have more than two parents due to divorce and remarriage or other circumstances, you can enter those children on multiple Family Pages.

You can add up to 99 children on each Family Page. The Family Page appears to allow only 4, but when you press [Enter←] after the fourth child, the list scrolls up, revealing space to add more children.

When you enter children on a Family Page, it's good practice to list them in the order in which they were born. The oldest child goes first. If you are unsure of the exact birth date of a child, but know that the child was born before or after one of his siblings, give the child an approximate birth date using "Before," "After," "About," "Circa," or "Estimated." This way, the child will sort in the correct birth order. See "Entering Dates" on page 87.

Sometimes you'll uncover new children that need to be inserted between two children that are already listed. You may also find errors in children's birth dates so that you need to re-order them. Family Tree Maker provides commands such as Move Child, Insert Child, and Sort Children that let you rearrange children. See "Rearranging Children" on page 98 for details.

Caution: Never attempt to rearrange children by typing over names that are already there. Use the Sort Children command instead, described on page 99).

If you type over a name, all information associated with that name (that individual's spouse and children, More About dialog boxes, etc.) will then be associated with the *new* name you entered. You will quickly end up with brothers married to their sisters-in-law or brothers-in-law! See Figure 3-11 on page 96 and Figure 3-12 on page 97.

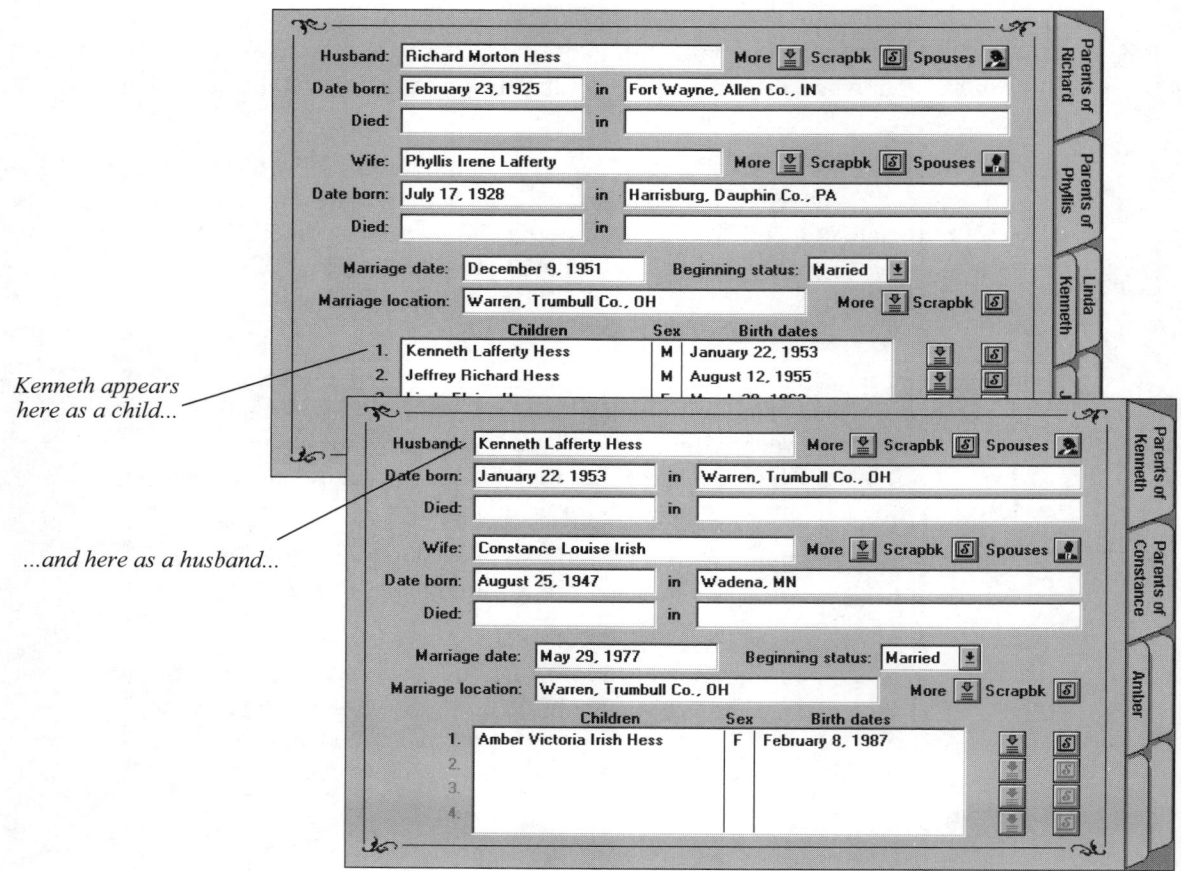

Kenneth appears here as a child...

...and here as a husband...

Figure 3-11. If you type over names...

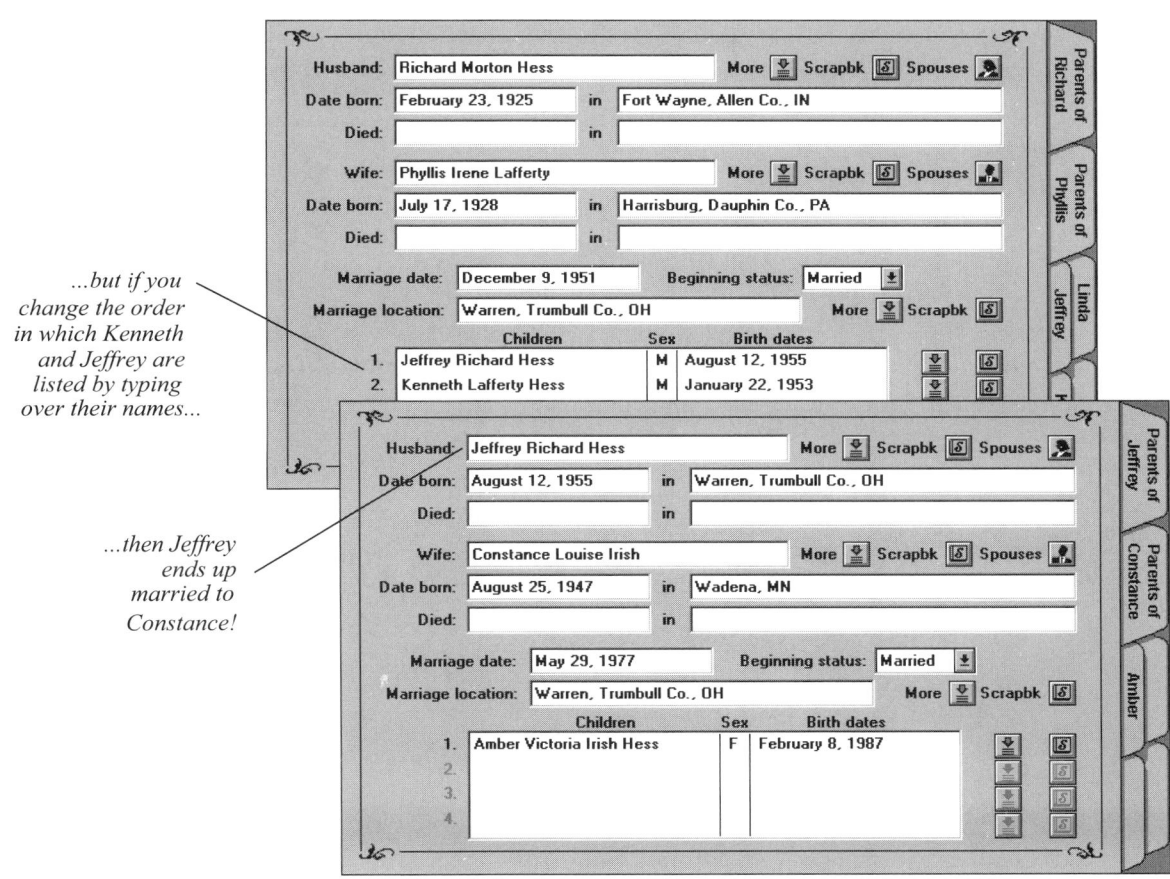

...but if you change the order in which Kenneth and Jeffrey are listed by typing over their names...

...then Jeffrey ends up married to Constance!

Figure 3-12. ... you might not like the results!

Rearranging Children

There are three commands you can use to rearrange the individuals in the "Children" list on a Family Page: Insert Child, Move Child, and Sort Children. Insert Child lets you add a new child between two existing children in a "Children" list. With Move Child you can move a child from one location to another within the same "Children" list. (If you need to move a child to a different Family Page, see "Detach Child" on page 186.) Sort Children lets you sort the children by birth order.

Inserting Children

To insert a new child:

1. Place the cursor on the row where you want the new child's name to appear.

2. From the **People** menu, select **Insert Child**.

   The child whose name the cursor is on moves down (as do the children below), leaving the cursor at the beginning of a new, empty line. You may now enter the new child's name, sex, and birth date on the empty line.

Moving Children

You cannot move a child to a different Family Page using the Move Child command. To move a child to another Family Page, use the Attach and Detach Child commands described in Chapter 6.

To move a child within a "Children" list:

1. In the **Children** list, place the cursor on the child you want to move.

   Note: To exchange two adjacent children in a "Children" list, select the lower child as the one to move, then move that child upward.

2. From the **People** menu, select **Move Child From**.

   Family Tree Maker displays a message asking you to confirm the move.

3. Click **OK**.

4. In the **Children** list on the same Family Page, place the cursor on the row where you want the child to end up.

5. From the **People** menu, select **Move Child To**.

   The other children on the list move down, and the individual you moved ends up in the row that you selected in step 4.

Sorting Children by Birth Order

To sort the children on a Family Page by birth order:

1. Go to the Family Page where you want to sort the children.

2. From the **People** menu, select **Sort Children**.

   Family Tree Maker tells you that it is sorting the children.

3. Click **OK** to continue.

   When the children are sorted, the oldest child's information appears at the top of the list, and the youngest child's information appears at the bottom. Twins or triplets stay in the order in which you entered them.

   Note: If a date field is blank, that child will sort at the top of the list. If a date field contains a question mark, that child will sort at the bottom of the list. If you don't know the exact birth date of a child, but know that the child was born before or after another child, use a "Before" or "After" date prefix so that the child sorts in the correct order. See Figure 3-5 on page 87 for information about entering estimated dates.

Entering Information About Other Relatives

Family Tree Maker automatically creates Family Pages for the parents and children of every individual you enter on the current Family Page. However, it doesn't automatically create Family Pages for the cousins, great-uncles, and so on. To enter family information about other relatives, you first must fill in the Family Pages of the individuals that link those relatives to the individuals that are already in your Family File.

For example, to enter information about your paternal uncle's family, you first fill in your father's Family Page, and then fill in his father's (your grandfather's) Family Page. On your grandfather's Family Page you'll enter your uncle as a child. You can then go directly to your uncle's page from your grandfather's page and enter his family information.

In other words, you can get to any relative's family by going through a parent, spouse, or child of someone already in your Family File. Once you have created a Family Page for a relative, you can go directly to their Family Page in other ways (see Chapter 4, "Moving Around").

Entering Intermarriages

You may find out that somewhere in your family two cousins got married or two brothers married two sisters. Family Tree Maker allows you to enter these individuals twice without duplicating all of their information. In these cases, Kinship reports will show multiple relationships between some individuals. In addition, these individuals may appear in trees more than once.

To enter an intermarriage:

1. On the Family Pages where each individual appears as a child, enter all of their information.

2. Go to the Family Page of one of the individuals. Enter only the name and birth date of their spouse. Don't enter the spouse's parents a second time!

   Make sure that the names and birth dates match the ones you entered in step 1 **exactly**. Family Tree Maker compares the information on the Family Pages to find out if you have the same individual entered more than once.

3. Family Tree Maker will ask if the two individuals are the same. If it doesn't ask, double-check that the names and birth dates are exactly the same.

4. Click **Yes**.

   Family Tree Maker "links" the two together.

Adding Individuals Whose Family Link is Unclear

You can use the Add Unrelated Individual command to add an individual to your Family File when you're not sure of their relationship to your family.

To use the Add Unrelated Individual command:

1. From the **People** menu, select **Add Unrelated Individual**.

2. Family Tree Maker displays a blank Family Page. Enter the individual's name and birth and death dates in the appropriate fields.

   Note: Because this individual is not currently related to anyone in your file, you will need to use the Index of Individuals to navigate to any other Family Page. See page 117 for instructions.

Unrelated individuals will *not* appear in trees or Kinship reports until you attach them to the rest of the family. When you find the link between the individual and the rest of your family, use the Attach Spouse or Attach Child command, described in Chapter 6, to connect them to the rest of your family.

Recording Sources for Your Information

One of the first commandments of genealogy is to thoroughly document the sources of your family information. That way you can return to the source if you need to, and you have a record of which sources you've already checked. A complete list of the fields for which you can record sources is below.

If you are not sure how to document your sources, check the genealogy books at your local library, or ask a local genealogy society for information. They should be able to offer you some tips.

If you are planning to submit your Family File to the World Family Tree (see page 362), we want to especially encourage you to document your sources. This way, others who use your file will have an easier time of verifying the information that it contains.

```
Birth date/location

Death date/location

Medical information

Each of the 13 Facts fields

Cause of death

Marriage date

Marriage ending date/location

Marriage fact date/location
```

Figure 3-13. Fields for which you can enter sources

To record source information for a field:

1. Place your cursor in the field for which you want to enter source information.

   Note: Each set of date and location fields (such as birth date and birth location) has one source field.

2. From the **View** menu, select **Source**.

   Family Tree Maker displays the Source dialog box.

3. Type the source information in the field.

For example, if your source of information was an individual, type that individual's name and the date in the field. If your source of information was a church record, you could enter the type of record used and name and location of the church.

4. When you're finished entering source information, click **OK.**

Family Tree Maker returns you to the field for which you recorded sources. There should be an "s" next to that field. If you want, you can print source information in your trees. See "Formatting the Information in Your Tree" on page 247.

Chapter 4

MOVING AROUND

Pictured here are Daniel Kraft, who designed the Family Tree Maker dialog boxes, and his two nephews, Neal and Curtis Luitjens in 1978. Daniel (right) and his nephews had just finished romping in a mud puddle on the Kraft family farm near Brewster, Minnesota.

MOVING AROUND

A complete family tree is, of course, made up of more than just one nuclear family on one Family Page. This means that once you've filled out your first Family Page, you need to fill out more Family Pages with information about other family members. Family Tree Maker makes it easy for you to move between different Family Pages so that you can quickly see and edit them.

Remember, don't be afraid to experiment. If you get lost, you can press F1 at any time to get on–screen help.

Note: Be sure that you're not creating a new Family File for each new Family Page. All of your Family Pages should be in the same Family File so that the information contained in them can be printed in the same family tree. The only exception to this is if you're creating a Family File for someone who is completely unrelated to your family, such as a neighbor.

MOVING BETWEEN CLOSELY-RELATED INDIVIDUALS

You can display the Family Pages of the parents and children of the husband and wife on the current Family Page by clicking the tabs on the right side of the screen. There's also an index of all the individuals in your Family File that you can use to find and display any Family Page instantly, no matter how many Family Pages you have.

Every individual appears on at least two Family Pages: as a child on his or her parents' Family Page and also as a husband or wife (or unmarried adult) on another Family Page. When you enter an individual on one page, Family Tree Maker automatically copies that individual onto the other page to make it easy for you to add new information to your Family File (see Figure 4-1 on page 106).

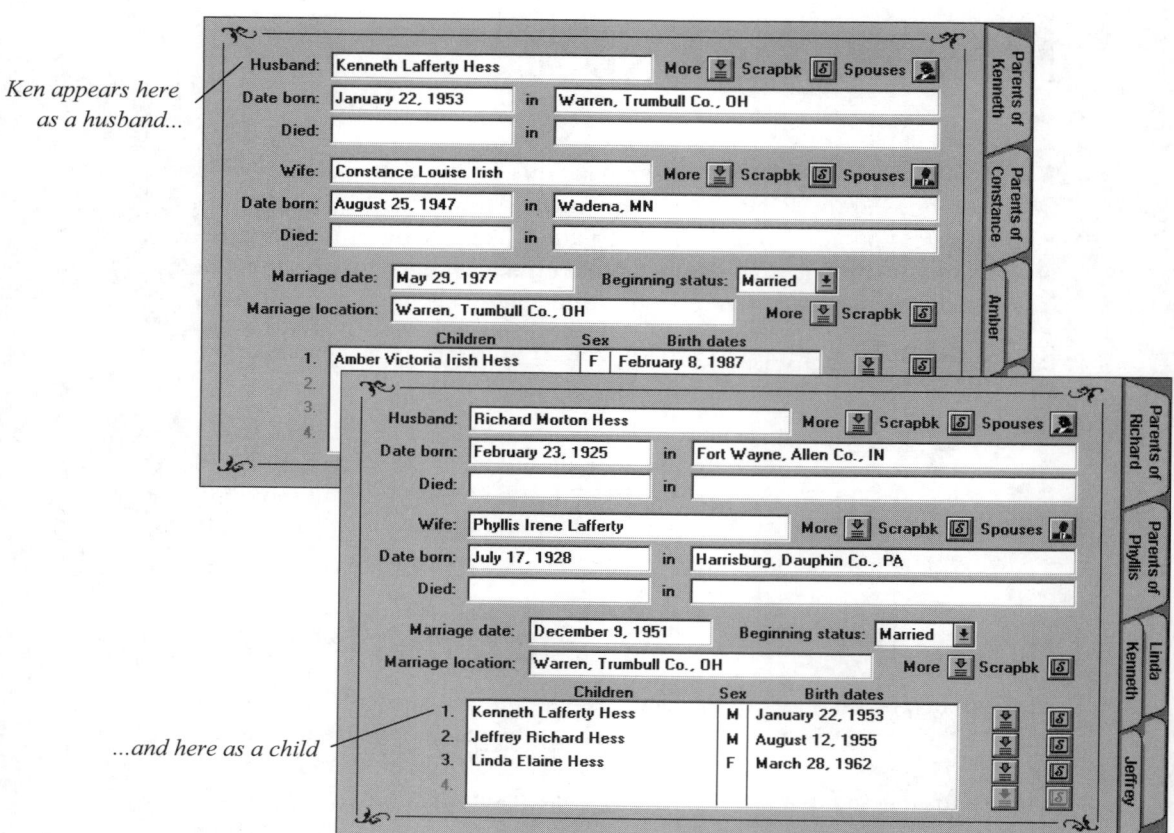

Ken appears here as a husband...

...and here as a child

Figure 4-1. An individual is on two Family Pages

An individual appears on more than two Family Pages if he or she has had more than one spouse or more than one set of parents. For each additional spouse, there is an additional Family Page where you can enter that spouse's name and the names of any children from that marriage. For information about creating additional marriages for an individual, see "Other Spouses" on page 110. For information about creating additional sets of parents for an individual, see "Other Parents" on page 113.

Parents' Family Page

If you are on a Family Page and you want to see the current wife's parents, click the tab on the right side of the screen that says "Parents of <wife>," as shown in Figure 4-2. You can also press F4. Family Tree Maker will display a Family Page with the wife listed as a child, and "Husband" and "Wife" fields where her parents should be.

If you are on a Family Page and you want to see the current husband's parents, click the tab on the right side of the screen that says "Parents of <husband>." You can also press F5. Family Tree Maker will display a Family Page with the husband listed as a child, and "Husband" and "Wife" fields where his parents should be.

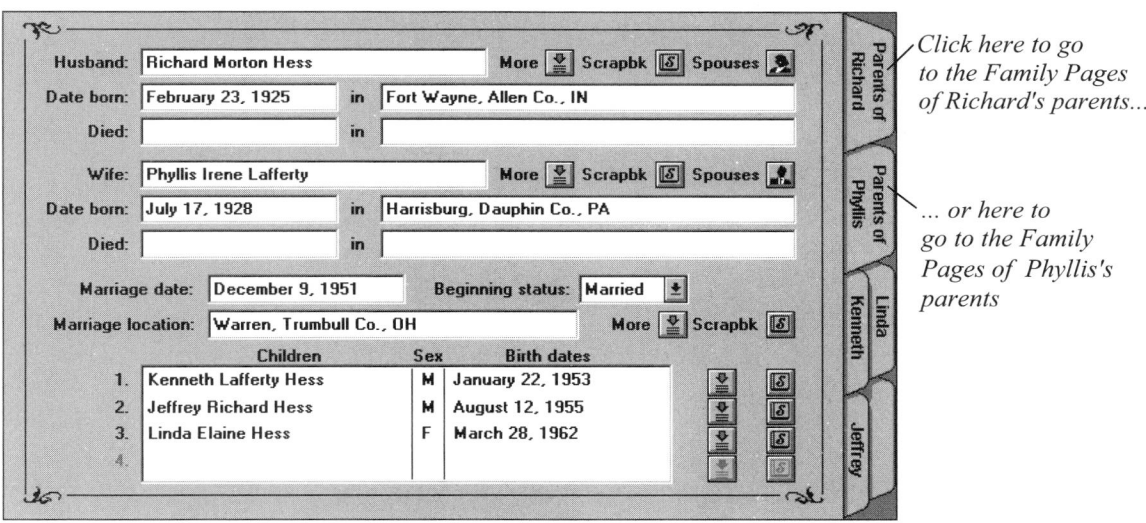

Figure 4-2. Moving to an individual's parents' Family Page

Child's Family Page

To see the Family Page of a child, click the tab on the right side of the screen labeled with that child's name. You can also click the child's name and press ⌨[F6]. Family Tree Maker will display a Family Page with the child listed either as a husband or wife, and a "Children" list where his or her children should be (see Figure 4-3).

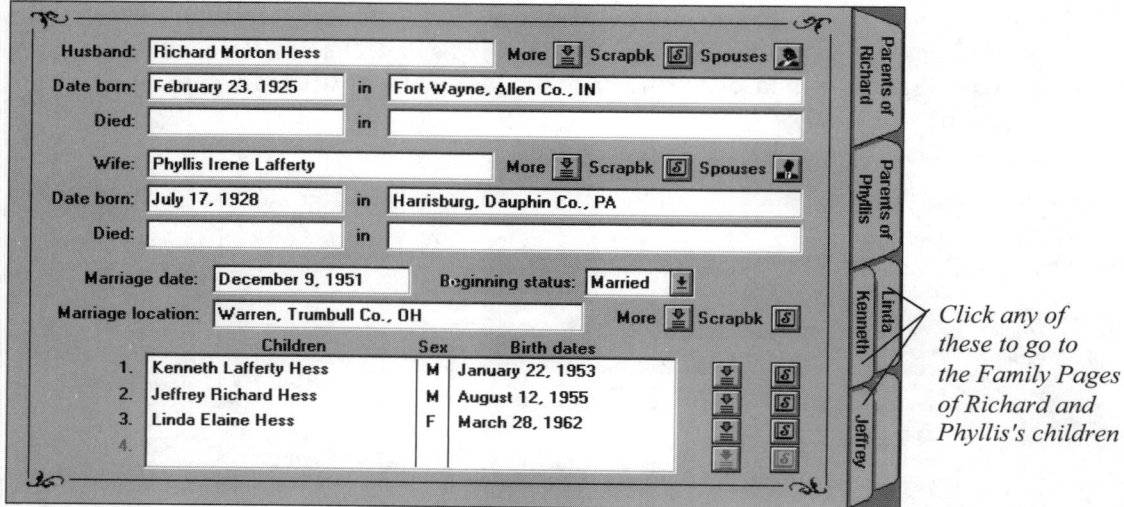

Click any of these to go to the Family Pages of Richard and Phyllis's children

Figure 4-3. Moving to a child's Family Page

Sibling's Family Page

A **sibling** is an individual's brother or sister. To see the Family Page of a husband's or wife's sibling:

1. Click the tab for the husband's or wife's parents.

    Family Tree Maker displays the Family Page of the parents.

2. On the parents' Family Page, click the tab labeled with the name of the child whose Family Page you want to see (see Figure 4-4).

    If the child whose Family Page you want to see is not visible in the "Children" list, use the scroll bar on the right side of the list to scroll through the children.

If you press [F3] when the cursor is in either the "Husband" or "Wife" field, Family Tree Maker goes to the Family Page of the husband's or wife's next sibling. (The "next" sibling is the sibling that is listed directly below the individual in the "Children" list on their parents' Family Page.)

If you press [alt] + [F3] when the cursor is in the "Husband" or "Wife" field, Family Tree Maker goes to the Family Page of the husband's or wife's previous sibling. (The "previous" sibling is the sibling that is listed directly above the individual in the "Children" list on their parents' Family Page.)

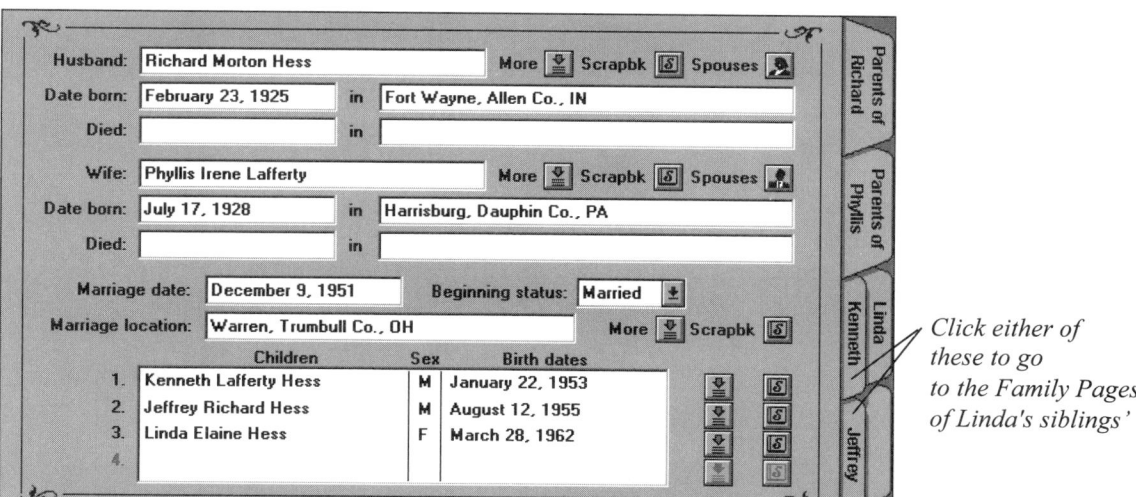

Figure 4-4. Moving to a sibling's Family Page

Other Spouses

When an individual has had more than one marriage, you must create a separate Family Page for each additional spouse. The individual with multiple spouses will then be on multiple Family Pages.

Creating Additional Spouses

To create another spouse for an individual:

1. Display the Family Page containing the individual for whom you want to create another spouse. If the individual has children that you want to appear on the new Family Page with the new spouse, be sure to display the Family Page containing those children.

   Many genealogists prefer to include children only on the Family Page of their birth parents. However, you may want multiple sets of parents for children if, for example, they were raised by parents other than their birth parents, or two sets of parents had joint custody. When you create multiple sets of parents for a child, you can note the nature of the relationship between the child and each parent. The child will then appear in trees and Kinship reports more than once, and will also appear in multiple Family Group Sheets.

2. Click **Spouses** next to the individual that you're creating a new spouse for. This button is to the right of that individual's name. Alternatively, from the **People** menu, select **Other Spouses**.

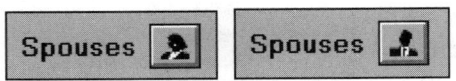

Figure 4-5. The Spouses buttons

Family Tree Maker displays the Spouses dialog box. See Figure 4-6 on the next page.

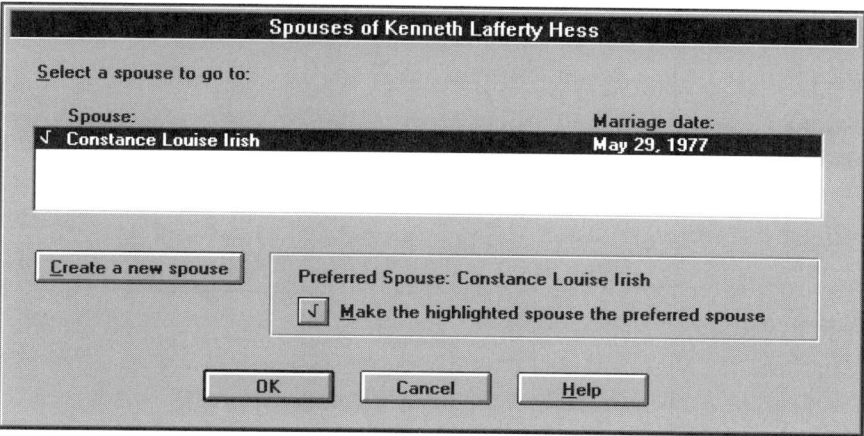

Figure 4-6. The Spouses dialog box

3. Click **Create a new spouse**.

4. If Family Page you displayed in step 1 contained children, Family Tree Maker asks if you want those children to appear on the new Family Page with the new spouse. Click either **Yes** or **No**.

    If you choose "Yes" the children will appear on the new Family Page and Family Tree Maker creates a step- relationship between the children and the new spouse. If the children actually have different relationships with the new spouse, you can go to each child's Lineage dialog box (see page 134) and choose the correct relationship.

5. Family Tree Maker takes you to a new Family Page. It contains the individual you selected in step 1 and any children that you chose to include. You can now enter information about the new spouse and any children that the couple had.

Displaying the Family Pages of Other Spouses

To see a Family Page containing another of an individual's spouses:

1. On the Family Page, click **Spouses** next to the individual whose Spouses dialog box you want to see. Or, click the name of the individual whose Spouses dialog box you want to see and then press ⌷F3⌷.

   Family Tree Maker displays the Spouses dialog box.

2. In the **Select a spouse to go to** list, click the name of the spouse whose Family Page you want to see and then click **OK**. Alternatively, you can double-click the spouse's name.

   Family Tree Maker displays the Family Page containing the other spouse.

Selecting the Preferred Spouse

When you go to an individual's Family Page, Family Tree Maker automatically displays the Family Page containing that individual's **preferred spouse**. For example, John has had two spouses, Susan and Mary. Mary is his preferred spouse. When you choose to see John's Family Page, you will see the Family Page that shows Mary as his wife.

Of course, you can still go to the Family Pages that contain an individual's other spouses, as described in "Displaying the Family Pages of Other Spouses" above.

To select an individual's preferred spouse:

1. On the Family Page, click **Spouses** next to the individual whose Spouses dialog box you want to see. Or, click the name of the individual whose Spouses dialog box you want to see and then press ⌷F3⌷.

   Family Tree Maker displays the Spouses dialog box.

2. In the **Select a spouse to go to** list, click the name of the spouse that you want to be the preferred spouse.

3. Click **Make the highlighted spouse the preferred spouse**.

4. Click **OK** when you've made your selection.

   Family Tree Maker displays the Family Page containing the individual and his or her preferred spouse.

You can change your preferred spouse selection at any time by repeating the four steps above.

Other Parents

When it comes to divorce, remarriage, and other types of special parent-child relationships, many genealogists prefer to include children only on the Family Page of their birth parents. However, with Family Tree Maker you can create multiple sets of parents for each child and then note the special nature of the relationships between the parents and the child. When you create multiple sets of parents for a child, the child will appear in trees and Kinship reports more than once, and will also appear in multiple Family Group Sheets.

Creating Additional Parents

To create an additional set of parents for a child:

1. Display the Family Page containing the child for whom you want to create another set of parents. The child must be displayed in the "Children" list, not in a "Husband" or "Wife" field.

    You can use either the Index of Individuals, described on page 117, or Find Individual, described on page 122, to quickly go to the correct Family Page.

2. Click the child's name, and then from the **People** menu, select **Other Parents**.

    Family Tree Maker displays the Other Parents dialog box.

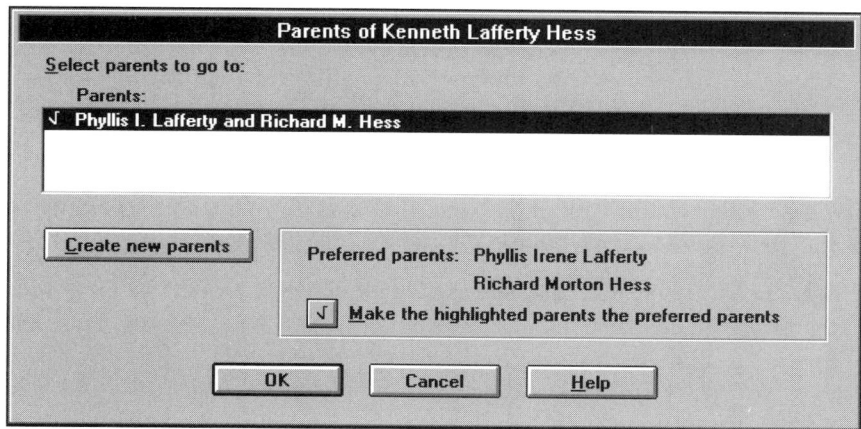

Figure 4-7. The Other Parents dialog box

3. Click **Create new parents**.

    Family Tree Maker displays the Create New Parents dialog box.

Figure 4-8. The Create New Parents dialog box

4. Select one of the three option buttons, **Two new parents**, **Another father**, or **Another mother**, depending on which parent(s) you need to create.

5. Click the **whose relationship with <child> is** drop-down list directly below the option button you selected in step 4 and choose the word that describes the relationship between the new parent(s) and the child.

    Please note that a child can only have one natural mother and one natural father. You must choose a different relationship for any additional parents.

6. Click **OK** after making your selections.

7. If the child has siblings, Family Tree Maker asks whether you want to associate those siblings with the new set of parents. Click either **Yes** or **No**.

    If you choose "Yes," Family Tree Maker adds any siblings that have the same preferred parents (see page 116). Family Tree Maker also gives the siblings the same relationship to the new parent(s), unless the siblings would then have too many natural parents. In this case Family Tree Maker gives them a step- relationship. If the children actually have different relationships, you can go to each child's Lineage dialog box (see page 134) and choose the correct relationship.

8. Family Tree Maker displays a new Family Page with children in the "Children" list. Depending on which option button you selected in step 4, either the "Husband" or the "Wife" field may be filled in already. Enter information about this set of parents in the **Husband**, **Wife**, and other fields.

    If either the husband or wife already exists elsewhere in your Family File, Family Tree Maker will ask you to verify the relationships.

Displaying the Family Pages of Other Parents

To see a Family Page containing another set of a child's parents:

1. On the Family Page, select the child whose Other Parents dialog box you want to see.

2. From the **People** menu, select **Other Parents**.

    Family Tree Maker displays the Other Parents dialog box.

3. In the **Parents** list, click the names of the parents whose Family Page you want to see and then click **OK**. Alternatively, you can just double-click the parents' names.

    To the right of the names of each set of parents are codes indicating the relationship between the parents and the child. This will help you distinguish between the different sets of parents.

    Family Tree Maker displays the Family Page containing those parents.

Selecting the Preferred Parents

An individual's **preferred parents** are the parents that Family Tree Maker will display in Ancestor trees.

To select an individual's preferred parents:

1. On the Family Page, select the child whose Other Parents dialog box you want to see.

2. From the **People** menu, select **Other Parents**.

   Family Tree Maker displays the Other Parents dialog box.

3. In the **Parents** list, click the names of the parents that you want to be the preferred parents.

4. Click **Make the highlighted parents the preferred parents**.

5. Click **OK** when you've made your selection.

   Family Tree Maker displays the Family Page containing the individual and his or her preferred parents.

You can change your preferred parents selection at any time by repeating the five steps above.

MOVING TO ANYONE IN YOUR FAMILY FILE

The **Index of Individuals** is a list of the names, birth dates, and death dates of every individual in your Family File. You can use this list to quickly see information about anyone in your Family File; instructions begin below. You can also move around your Family File by clicking in trees and other types of documents. See "Using Your Mouse in Trees" on page 241 and "Using Your Mouse in Reports and Labels/Cards" on page 281. Finally, you can use the Find command to search for any individual or information in your Family File. See "Locating Individuals in Your Family File" on page 122.

Opening the Index of Individuals

To view the Index of Individuals, from the **View** menu, select **Index of Individuals**. Alternatively, you can press ⌗F2. The individuals are listed alphabetically by last name, with birth and death dates on the right.

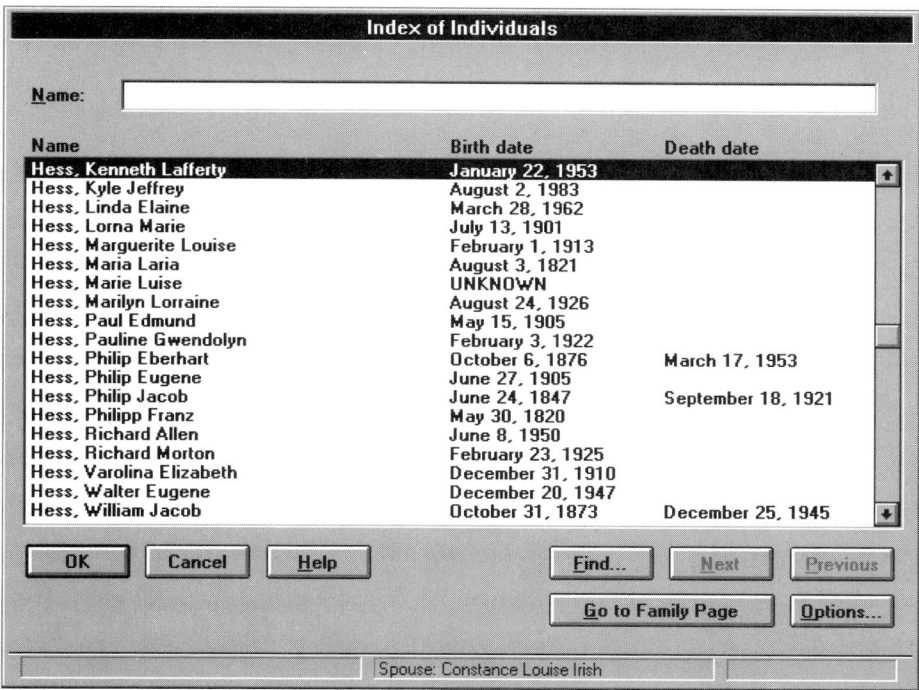

Figure 4-9. The Index of Individuals

Note: You'll see that individuals with nicknames (aka's) appear in the index twice, one entry for each of their names.

You cannot print the Index of Individuals itself, but you can create and print a report that contains the same information as the Index of Individuals. To create an print a report, see "All About Reports" on page 275.

Moving Around in the Index of Individuals

There are three ways to scroll up and down through the names in the Index of Individuals. Each of these methods is described below.

Using the Navigational Keys

You can use ↑, ↓, PgUp, and PgDn to move up and down through the Index of Individuals. If you press ↑ or ↓, the highlight will move up or down by one name. If you press PgUp or PgDn, the highlight will move up or down by a full screen's worth of names.

Doing a Quick Search

With a Quick Search, you can find an individual in the Index of Individuals just by typing their name.

Note: You cannot use this search feature when the Index of Individuals is arranged by birth dates rather than by last names, nor when it is sorted alphabetically from Z to A. To rearrange the names, see "Rearranging the Index of Individuals" on page 120.

To use the Quick Search feature:

1. Click in the **Name** field at the top of the Index of Individuals.

2. Start typing the last name of the individual that you want to find.

    With each character you type, you will get closer to the name you are looking for. You can type part or all of the name, as long as it is in the same format as the Index of Individuals (Last name, First name Middle name).

Using Find Name

To use the Find Name command in the Index of Individuals:

1. Click **Find**, located at the bottom of the Index of Individuals dialog box.

    Family Tree Maker displays the Find Name dialog box.

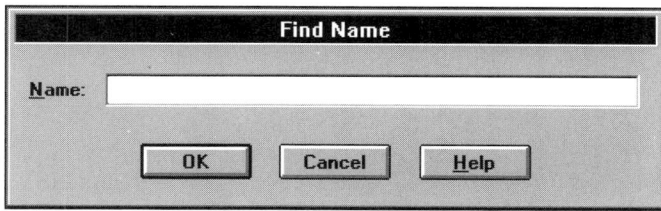

Figure 4-10. The Find Name dialog box

2. Type an individual's name.

    If you're not sure of the exact name, type any part of the name. Family Tree Maker will find any name containing those same letters. For example, if you type **hess**, Family Tree Maker will find "Kenneth Hess," "Hessel Smith," "George Chess, III," and so on.

3. Click **OK** to begin searching.

    Family Tree Maker highlights the name of the first individual meeting your request. If there are no matches, Family Tree Maker displays a message telling you this.

4. If you want to continue searching through the list of names, click **Next** to move to the next name that meets your request.

    Once you have moved past the first match in the list, you can also click **Previous** to go back to previous matches.

    Note: If you didn't find the name you were looking for, try typing a smaller portion of the name. You can search on any part of a name. For example, you could type **sm** to look for the last name "Smith."

Rearranging the Index of Individuals

To rearrange the list of names in the Index of Individuals:

1. Click **Options**, located at the bottom of the Index of Individuals dialog box.

    Family Tree Maker displays a dialog box with the following four sorting options: "Last name (A first)," "Last name (Z first)," "Birth date (oldest first)," and "Birth date (youngest first)."

Figure 4-11. Sorting Options dialog box

2. Select the option button for the type of sorting you prefer.

    Note: You can only use the Quick Search feature when "Last name (A first)" is selected.

3. Click **OK** when you've made your selection.

    Family Tree Maker sorts the Index of Individuals.

Moving to Other Views from the Index of Individuals

Once you find the name of the individual that you are looking for, you can do one of two things:

- Click **Go to Family Page** to see the Family Page containing the individual whose name is highlighted. That individual will be shown as a husband or wife on the Family Page.

  If the individual has been married more than once, Family Tree Maker shows you the Family Page containing the preferred spouse. (See "Selecting the Preferred Spouse" on page 112.)

- Click **OK** to go to the **current view** of the individual whose name is highlighted. The "current view" is the view that you were in before you opened the Index of Individuals. For example, if you were previously looking at an Ancestor tree, clicking **OK** in the Index of Individuals would take you to an Ancestor tree for the individual whose name is highlighted. Or, if you were previously looking at a Family Page, clicking **OK** in the Index of Individuals would take you to the Family Page containing the individual whose name is highlighted.

LOCATING INDIVIDUALS IN YOUR FAMILY FILE

Using **Find Individual**, you can quickly locate anyone in your Family File. You can search for individuals using almost any type of information, including names, dates, comments, items in Scrapbooks, and even phrases in the Notes dialog box. You can also search for individuals using parts of information. For example, you can type "jo" and find the name "Jonathan."

Find Individual is also useful for finding groups of individuals. For example, you could locate everyone in your Family File that has the same last name or birthplace. When Family Tree Maker finds an individual for you, you can edit that individual's information and then continue the search without needing to tell Family Tree Maker what to search for again.

Searching by Name

To search for an individual in your Family File by name, go to any Family Page and then:

1. From the **Edit** menu, select **Find Individual**.

    Family Tree Maker displays the Find Individual dialog box.

2. Click the **Search** drop-down list and select **Name**.

3. In the **for** field, type the name of the individual you wish to find.

    If you're not sure of the exact name, type any part of the name. Family Tree Maker will find any name containing those same letters. For example, if you type **hess**, Family Tree Maker will find "Kenneth Hess," "Hessel Smith," "George Chess, III," and so on.

4. Click **Find next** to start the search.

    Family Tree Maker displays the Family Page of the first individual who matches your request. If no matches are found, Family Tree Maker displays a message telling you so.

    If you like, you can edit this Family Page and then continue your search by reopening the Find Individual dialog box and clicking **Find next**. (To reopen the dialog box, from the **Edit** menu, select **Find Individual**.)

5. Click **Find next** to continue your search.

   Continue clicking **Find next** until you're done searching or until Family Tree Maker runs out of matches. To go back to previous matches, you can click **Find previous**.

6. To quit the search, click **Cancel**.

   If you didn't find the individual you wanted, try typing a smaller portion of their name. For example, type **sm** to look for the last name "Smith."

7. If you want to go through the same search again, click **Restart Search**.

   Family Tree Maker goes back to the beginning of the Family File and searches through it again.

Searching for Other Items

Family Tree Maker can search for dates, locations, sources, and comments — almost any information that you can enter into your Family File. In addition, you can locate parentless, childless individuals and individuals who were merged or who were not merged (see page 379).

To search for information other than a name, go to any Family Page and then:

1. From the **Edit** menu, select **Find Individual**.

   Family Tree Maker displays the Find Individual dialog box.

2. Click the **Search** drop-down list and choose the item you want to search for.

   For example, if you wanted to find an individual with a specific birth date, you would select "Birth date."

3. In the **for** field, type the information that you want to find.

   For example, if you were searching the "Birth date" field and wanted to find individuals born in October, you would type **October** Or, if you wanted to find individuals born before October of 1988, you would type **<October 1988** See Figure 4-12 on page 125 for more date searching tips.

   If the item you are searching for only has certain possible values (such as "male," "female," and "unknown"), Family Tree Maker will display a drop-down list in the "for" field. In this case, just click what you want to find.

   If the field that you are searching is a Fastfield, Family Tree Maker will help you fill in the "for" field.

4. Click **Find next** to start the search.

    Family Tree Maker displays the Family Page of the first individual who matches your request. If no matches are found, Family Tree Maker displays a message telling you so.

    If you like, you can edit this Family Page and then continue your search by reopening the Find Individual dialog box and clicking **Find next**. (To reopen the dialog box, from the **Edit** menu, select **Find Individual**.)

5. Click **Find next** to continue your search.

    Continue clicking **Find next** until you're done searching or until Family Tree Maker runs out of matches. To go back to previous matches, you can click **Find previous**.

6. To quit the search, click **Cancel**.

    If you didn't find the Family Page you were looking for, try typing a smaller portion of the information. For example, you could type **1988** to find "October, 1988."

7. If you want to go through the same search again, click **Restart Search**.

    Family Tree Maker goes back to the beginning of the Family File and searches through it again.

Searching Tips

-   Don't worry about punctuation when searching for names.

-   You can use any allowable date format. See page 87.

-   You can use Find Individual to find and fill in the empty fields in your Family File. Simply type **=** instead of a name, date, comment, etc. in the **for** field. For example, to find all empty marriage date fields, pick "Marriage date" from the **Search** field and type **=** in the **for** field.

-   If you want to search for a specific date, but not in any particular field, choose "Any and all date fields" from the **Search** field.

-   If you want to search for a specific set of words, but not in any particular field, choose "Any and all text fields" from the **Search** field.

-   If you want to search for numbers, you can use the operators >, <, >=, <=, and >X..<Y, just as they are used with dates in Figure 4-12.

You type this...	Family Tree Maker finds this...
=	All places where the field is empty
!=	All places where the field contains information
10/2/1988	All occurrences of October 2, 1988
<10/2/1988, or **BEFORE** 10/2/1988, or **BEF** 10/2/1988	All dates before October 2, 1988, including dates entered as "Before October 2, 1988"
<=10/2/1988	The date October 2, 1988 and all dates before it, including dates entered as "Before October 2, 1988"
>10/2/1988, or **AFTER** 10/2/1988, or **AFT** 10/2/1988	All dates after October 2, 1988, including dates entered as "After October 2, 1988"
>=10/2/1988	The date October 2, 1988 and all dates after it, including dates entered as "After October 2, 1988"
ABOUT 10/2/1988, or **CIRCA** 10/2/1988, or **EST** 10/2/1988	All dates entered as "About October 2, 1988," "Circa October 2, 1988," or "Est October 2, 1988"
10/2/1988..10/2/1990, or >=10/2/1988..<=10/2/1990	All dates between October 2, 1988 and October 2, 1990 including those two days
>10/2/1988..<10/2/1990	All dates between October 2, 1988 and October 2, 1990 not including those two days
UNKNOWN or ?	All dates entered as "Unknown" or "?"

Figure 4-12. Searching for dates

Chapter 5

ENTERING DETAILED INFORMATION

Showing an early interest in music, Steve Stanko, one of Family Tree Maker's programmers, is pictured here at the age of two. To this day, music is one of Steve's primary interests.

ENTERING DETAILED INFORMATION

The **More About** dialog boxes provide a place for you to record additional information about the individuals in your Family File. Each individual has five More About dialog boxes: the Facts dialog box, the Address dialog box, the Medical dialog box, the Lineage dialog box, and the Notes dialog box. With these dialog boxes, you can keep track of special events, such as baptism or immigration, track your family's medical history, and record all the details that paint a complete picture of an individual's life. Each marriage also has a Facts dialog box and a Notes dialog box so you can record special information about the marriage and the couple.

In addition, each individual and each marriage have a **Scrapbook**. In Scrapbooks, you can electronically store any type of information, including photos and other scanned images; video, sound, and text; and other OLE objects. With space for up to 16,000 items per individual and per marriage, you can create an unforgettable collection of family information — all stored neatly on your computer! Instructions for Scrapbooks begin on page 147.

Don't be afraid to experiment while using Family Tree Maker. Remember that if you get lost or have any difficulties, you can press [F1] at any time to get on-screen help.

To display an individual's or marriage's More About dialog boxes:

1. Go to the Family Page containing the individual or marriage whose More About dialog boxes you want to see.

2. On the Family Page, place the cursor either on the name of the individual or on the marriage whose More About dialog boxes you want to see.

3. From the **View** menu, select **More About**. From the submenu, select the name of a More About dialog box.

   Family Tree Maker displays the dialog box that you selected.

To display More About dialog boxes you can also click the **More** button on the Family Page next to the individual's name or next to the marriage.

Each More About dialog box has two parts:

- On the left, there's an area where you can record information about the individual or marriage.

- On the right, there are buttons that you can click to move to the four other More About dialog boxes. For example, to enter medical information, you would click **Medical**. These buttons appear on each of the More About dialog boxes, so it's easy to move from one dialog box to another. You can also move to the other More About dialog boxes using the **View** menu, as you did in step 3.

You'll always know whose More About dialog boxes you're working on because the top of the dialog box displays the individual's name.

To return to the Family Page from any More About dialog box, from the **View** menu, select **Family Page**.

Note: You can print the information in the More About dialog boxes. See Chapter 10, "Other Printing."

ENTERING BRIEF BIOGRAPHICAL FACTS

The **Facts** dialog box can show any 13 facts from an individual's life, such as special events, personal characteristics, or favorite activities. (See Figure 5-1.) Other information that you may want to record here includes christening dates and places, burial dates and places, and graduation dates and places. Enter this type of information in as many of the **Comment/Location** fields as you like. If there is a date related to the information, you can enter it in the **Date** field.

You can change the field labels in this dialog box (see "Preferences for Field Labels" on page 78), but keep in mind that the new field labels will appear in every individual's Facts dialog box.

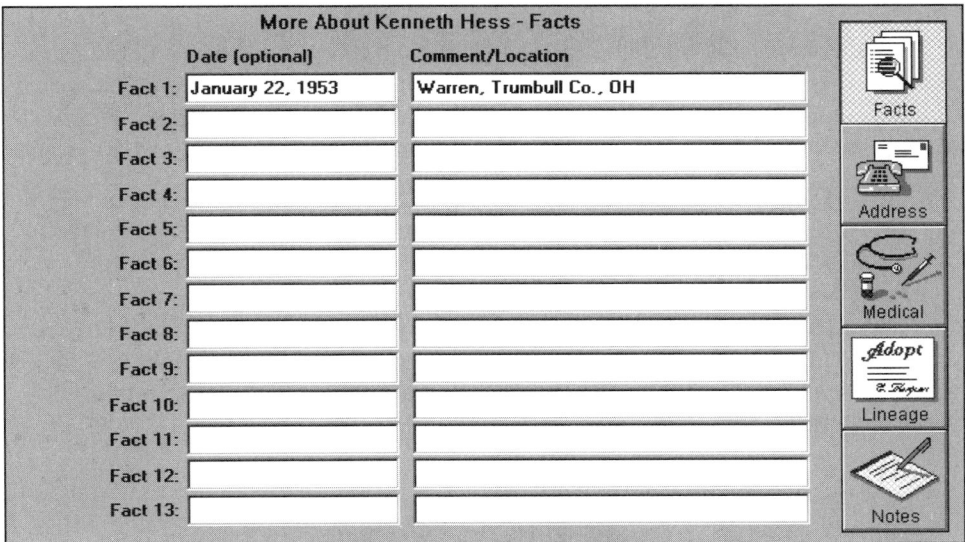

Figure 5-1. The Facts dialog box

Family Tree Maker can print information from the Facts dialog box in your trees and other documents. If Family Tree Maker needs to shorten these fields during printing, it will either abbreviate or truncate them. However, if you select the "Word wrap" option for a field in the Text Font, Style, & Size dialog box when you print, Family Tree Maker will not need to abbreviate or truncate the text in that field.

The "Comment/Location" fields can hold up to 80 characters. If you want to enter longer stories or biographical sketches to store separately from your trees, see "Entering Stories and Notes" on page 137.

ENTERING ADDRESSES

In the **Address** dialog box, you can record an individual's address and phone number. This information is handy if you're planning to send invitations to a family reunion or other family gathering, because this is where Family Tree Maker gets the addresses for printing mailing labels. See "All About Labels and Cards" on page 272.

For the purpose of mailing labels, you do not have to type an address into each individual's Address dialog box. This is because individuals can "inherit" addresses from their parents and spouses. If an individual does not have an address in his or her Address dialog box, Family Tree Maker first checks to see if the individual's spouse has an address. If the individual's spouse does not have an address, Family Tree Maker uses the address of the individual's parents. If the parents do not have an address either, the individual has no address.

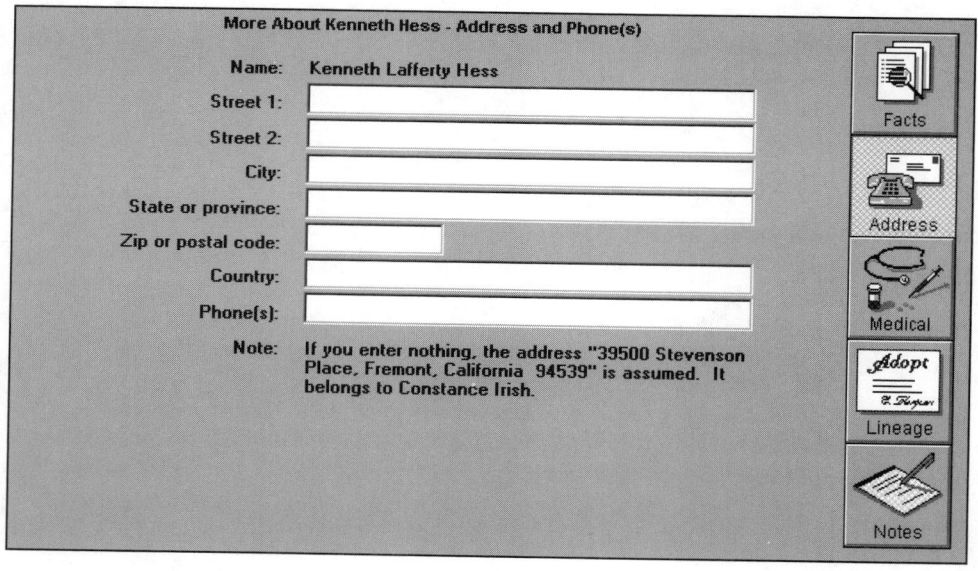

Figure 5-2. The Address dialog box

Street 1 *and* **Street 2** — Type the house or apartment number and street name in the "Street 1" field. You only need to use the "Street 2" field if the address is particularly long.

Phone(s) — You can enter more than one phone number in this field. Use whatever method you prefer to separate them, such as a comma, semicolon, or the word "or."

ENTERING MEDICAL INFORMATION

The **Medical** dialog box contains fields for recording physical and medical information about an individual, including height, weight, cause of death, and medical information. (See Figure 5-3.) If the individual has more information than will fit here, you can use the Notes dialog box to record additional medical information. You can also use the Facts dialog box if you want to record the dates of important medical events.

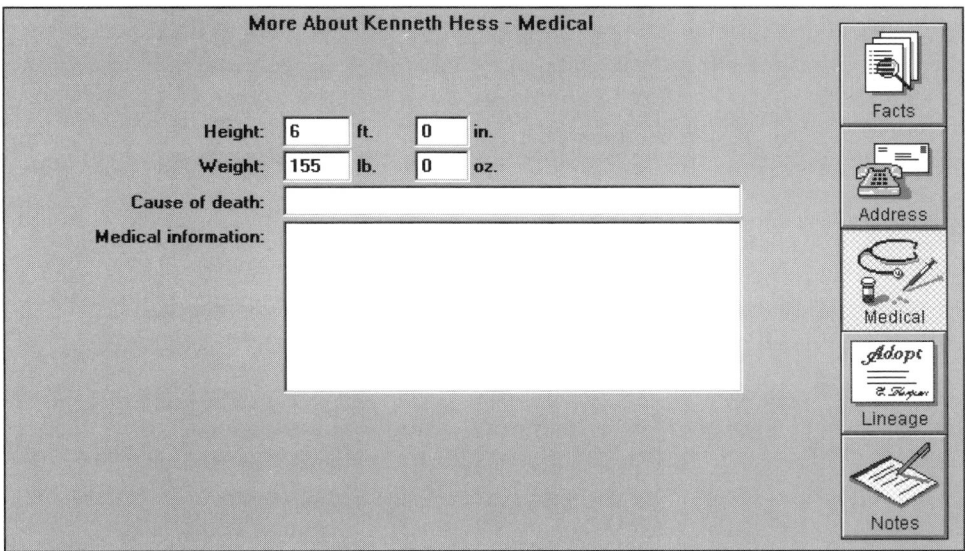

Figure 5-3. The Medical dialog box

Height — Use this field to record an individual's adult or current height. If your system is set for Metric units, enter the height in meters. If your system is set for English units, enter the height in feet and inches.

Note: For information about changing your system from Metric units to English units, see "Preferences for Dates and Measures" on page 88.

Weight — Use this field to record an individual's adult or current weight. If your system is set for Metric units, enter the weight in kilograms. If your system is set for English units, enter the weight in pounds and ounces.

Cause of death — Use this field to record the cause of an individual's death.

Medical information — You can enter any type of medical information about the individual in this field. You might want to record diseases, allergies, or serious illnesses that the individual had during his or her life.

ENTERING NICKNAMES, TITLES, AND PARENTAL RELATIONSHIP INFORMATION

The **Lineage** dialog box contains fields for recording special information about the relationship between an individual and their parents, such as an adoption or a step- relationship. When you open a husband's or wife's Lineage dialog box, the husband's or wife's Preferred Parents (see page 116) are shown. When you open a child's Lineage dialog box, the parents currently on the Family Page are shown. If you want to view other sets of parents, from the **People** menu, select **Other Parents**.

The Lineage dialog box is also where you enter nicknames (aka's) or special titles that people use (see Figure 5-4 on page 135). In addition, if you have a filing system, you can create reference numbers for each individual in the **Reference number** field.

Title (Dr., Rev., Col., etc.) — You can select default titles for everyone, such as "Mr.," "Mrs.," and "Ms.," using the Titles dialog box (see page 86). However, some individuals in your Family File may go by a special title, such as "Dr." or "Reverend." When an individual has a special title, enter it in the **Title** field in the Lineage dialog box. For all other individuals, leave this field blank.

This person is also known as (aka) — This field is where you enter an individual's nickname, if they had one. You can print nicknames in family trees and other documents, so it's important to use this field correctly. If an individual has had a nickname or a name change, you should record it as follows:

In the Family Page, make sure you enter the individual's full name. For example, you could enter `Gerald Charles Jansen`. Then in the Lineage dialog box you could enter the nickname `Bud Jansen`. You must enter both the nickname and the last name in the Lineage dialog box. If you only entered the nickname and then chose to print nicknames in trees, this individual would appear only as "Bud" without a last name.

This field is also good for indicating when individuals have hyphenated married names. For example, if John Smith and Alice Carson became John and Alice Carson-Smith, you would enter the couple's birth names on their Family Pages and their hyphenated married names in the Lineage dialog box.

If you want to use nicknames rather than given names in printed documents, you need to indicate this to Family Tree Maker. For more information about including nicknames in your trees, see "Formatting Information in Your Tree" on page 247. For information about including nicknames in your calendars, see "Selecting Information to Include in Your Calendar" on page 331. For information about including nicknames in labels and cards, see "Names on Labels and Cards" on page 298. For information about including nicknames in Custom reports, see "Selecting Information to Include in Your Document" on page 293.

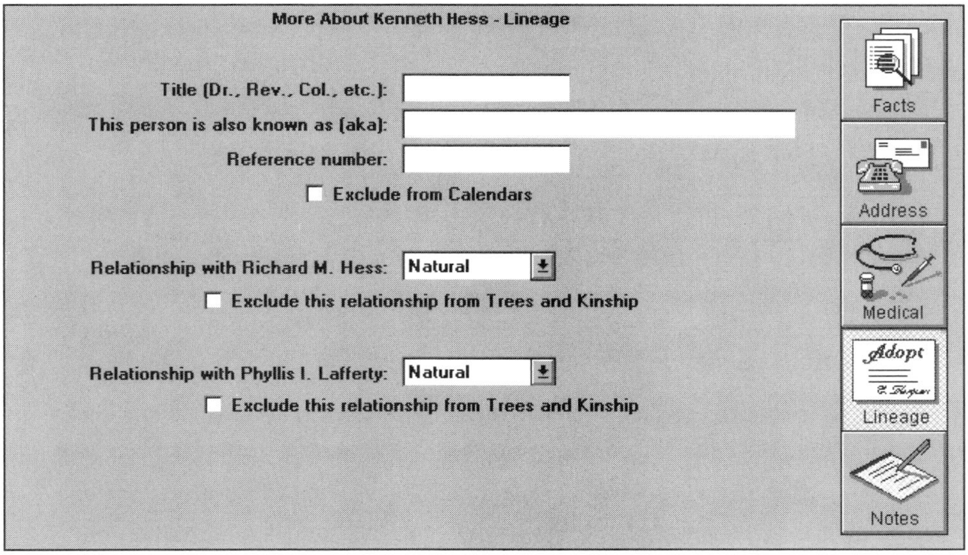

Figure 5-4. The Lineage dialog box

Reference number — This field can contain any numbers or letters that you choose. You might use this number as part of your own filing system. Its use is entirely optional.

Note: Family Tree Maker can create Ahnentafel (standard) numbers automatically when you print Ancestor trees. They have nothing to do with what you enter in the "Reference number" field. See page 245 for information about Ahnentafel numbering.

Exclude from Calendars — If you don't want this individual to appear in calendars, select this check box. Only this individual is affected; his or her ancestors and descendants *will* appear in calendars. If you want to exclude several individuals from a calendar, see "Selecting Individuals to Include in Your Calendar" on page 324, instead.

Relationship with Mother *and* **Relationship with Father** — Use these fields to record special parent/child relationships. If a special relationship exists with either parent, click the appropriate parent's drop-down list and select "Adopted," "Foster," "Unknown," "Step" or "Family member." Each child can only have one natural father and one natural mother.

If you imported information from a World Family Tree CD, the word "Private" may appear in this drop-down list in some cases. This is to protect the privacy of individuals who may still be living. For your own purposes, it's better not to use this term. If you submit your Family File to the World Family Tree Project (see page 362) "Private" will be selected automatically where necessary.

Exclude this relationship from Trees and Kinship — There may be occasions when you want to exclude certain relationships from a tree or Kinship report. If you select this check box for the relationship between a parent and a child, it means the following:

- In Ancestor trees, the child will appear in the tree, but the child's maternal and/or paternal ancestors will not appear in the tree, depending on which parent's check box(es) you select.

- In Descendant trees, checking either check box will exclude the child and any of the child's descendants. The child's siblings and their descendants will appear in the tree.

- In Kinship reports, the child will appear, but the child's maternal and/or paternal ancestors will not appear in the tree, depending on which parent's check box(es) you select.

ENTERING STORIES AND NOTES

The **Notes** dialog box is a mini-word processor. You can use it to enter and organize virtually any textual information, including a family member's favorite recipes, jokes, or even a short biography. You cannot print information from the Notes dialog box in your trees, but you can print your Notes on separate pages to include in a family book. See Figure 5-5 for an example. See Figure 5-6 on page 138 for a summary of what you can do in the Notes dialog box.

Note: If you're not familiar with word processors, you'll find it helpful to do Part II of the Tutorial, beginning on page 48.

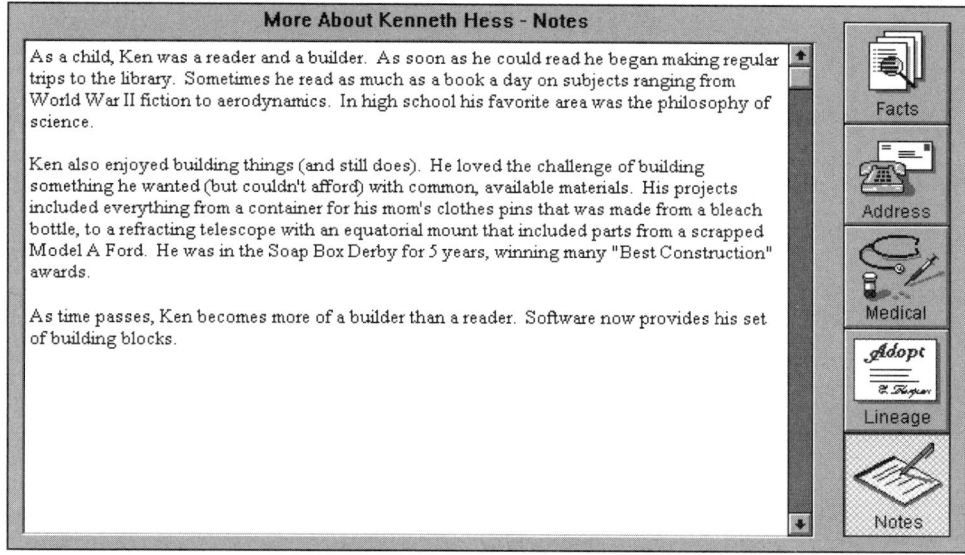

Figure 5-5. The Notes dialog box

Note: If you'd like help writing about an individual, see page 416 for information about *Biography Maker*, a program designed for Family Tree Maker customers who are interested in writing biographies about their relatives or autobiographies about themselves.

To do this...	Turn to this section...
Use your mouse or keyboard to move the cursor anywhere in your text	"Moving Around..." on page 139
Insert new text, delete old text, type over existing text, and reverse editing commands	"Editing Text in the Notes dialog box" on page 140
Rearrange text by **cutting** it from one place and **pasting** it to another	"Cutting, Copying, and Pasting" on page 81, and "Moving or Copying Text from One Notes Dialog to Another" on page 140
Avoid retyping information by **copying** it from one place and **pasting** it to another	"Cutting, Copying, and Pasting" on page 81
Change the text in the Notes dialog box to a different font, size, or style	"Formatting Text..." on page 142
Print the text in the Notes dialog box	"Printing More About Information" on page 336
Get information you've typed into another program and insert it directly into the Notes dialog box without retyping	"Importing Text..." on page 143
Take information you've typed in the Notes dialog box and export it to another program	"Exporting Text..." on page 144

Figure 5-6. A summary of what you can do in the Notes dialog box

Moving Around in the Notes Dialog Box

You can enter much more text into the Notes dialog box than can appear on the screen at any one time, so to edit your text you need to know how to move up and down through it. The scroll bar on the right side of the screen is the easiest way to do this. Just place the mouse pointer on the scroll box (that's the small square in the scroll bar), hold down your primary mouse button, and drag the scroll box up or down.

You can also use your keyboard to move through your text. Figure 5-7 shows which keys to use.

Press this key...	To do this...
⬅	Move the cursor one character to the left
➡	Move the cursor one character to the right
⬆	Move the cursor up one line
⬇	Move the cursor down one line
Ctrl + ⬅	Move the cursor one word to the left
Ctrl + ➡	Move the cursor one word to the right
PgUp	Move up a whole screen's worth of text
PgDn	Move down a whole screen's worth of text
home	Move the cursor to the beginning of the line
end	Move the cursor to the end of the line
Ctrl + home	Move the cursor to the beginning of the Notes
Ctrl + end	Move the cursor to the end of the Notes

Figure 5-7. How to move around in The Notes dialog box

Editing Text in the Notes Dialog Box

You can edit your Notes just like you can edit the text in any word processor. Pages 81-83 in Chapter 3 describe how to cut, copy, and paste text, delete information, reverse editing commands, and add extra lines and spaces.

Moving or Copying Text from One Notes Dialog Box to Another

You can move or copy sections of text from one individual's Notes dialog box to another individual's Notes dialog box.

To perform this operation, start with the individual who has the text you want to move or copy:

1. Display that individual's Notes dialog box.

2. Highlight the text you want to move or copy.

    To highlight text with a mouse, place the mouse pointer in front of the first character that want to select. Press and hold the primary mouse button while you drag the mouse until the last character you want to select is highlighted. Then, release the mouse button.

3. From the **Edit** menu, select **Cut** if you wish to move the text or select **Copy** if you wish to copy this text to another Notes dialog box.

4. From the **View** menu, select **Index of Individuals**.

    Family Tree Maker displays the Index of Individuals.

5. Select the individual to whom you want to transfer the text and then click **OK**.

    Family Tree Maker displays the Notes dialog box for that individual.

6. Position your cursor where you want to insert the text. If you want to use the new text to *replace* a section of existing text, highlight that section of text.

7. From the **Edit** menu, select **Paste**.

    Family Tree Maker pastes the text from the Clipboard into this individual's Notes and repositions any existing text, if necessary.

Since the Clipboard is not erased until you use the Copy or Cut command again, you can paste the same text as many times as you like.

Finding Text in the Notes Dialog Box

Using the Find command, you can locate any text in a Notes dialog box.

To find text in a Notes dialog box:

1. Make sure you are in the Notes dialog box that you want to search.

2. From the **Edit** menu, select **Find**.

3. In the **Find what** field, type the text that you want to locate.

   If you type the letters **the** Family Tree Maker will locate any word with "the" in it, including "there," "These," and "other," as well as "the." If you only want to find the whole word, and not pieces of other words, select the **Match whole word only** check box. If you only want to find words that are capitalized the same way as the text you typed in the "Find what" field, select the **Match case** check box.

4. Click **Find next** to start the search. Family Tree Maker scrolls down through the text to find what you're searching for.

   When Family Tree Maker locates the text, the cursor will stop on it. You can click **Find next** to look for additional occurrences of the text or **Cancel** to quit the search.

5. If you didn't start searching at the top of the Notes, Family Tree Maker will ask if you want to continue the search from the top. Click **Yes** to continue searching from the top or click **No** to quit the search. Click **Cancel** when you want to close the Search dialog box.

Formatting Text in the Notes Dialog Box

When you make formatting choices in the Notes dialog box, you are formatting all of the notes for this one individual. You cannot format individual words or lines. In addition, the formatting selections will only appear on printed copies of the notes, not on the screen.

To format text in a Notes dialog box:

1. From the **Format** menu, select **Text Font, Style, & Size**.

   Family Tree Maker displays the Text Font, Style, & Size dialog box.

2. Make your formatting selections from the drop-down lists on the right side of the dialog box.

   The "Sample" field shows what your choices will look like.

3. When you're finished making your selections, click **OK** to return to the Notes dialog box.

Copying Text from Another Windows Program into a Notes Dialog Box

If you have family stories in another Windows program, you can copy them to the Clipboard and then paste them into the appropriate Notes dialog boxes. If you want to transfer information from a DOS program into Family Tree Maker, see "Importing Text from Another Program into a Notes Dialog Box," on the next page.

To transfer information from another Windows program into Family Tree Maker:

1. In the other Windows program, copy the information to the Clipboard.

   If you need assistance with this, please consult the manual that came with the other program.

2. In Family Tree Maker, go to the Notes dialog box where you want to place the information.

3. Position your cursor where you want to insert the text. If you want to use the new text to *replace* a section of existing text, highlight that section of text.

4. From the **Edit** menu, select **Paste**.

Since the Clipboard is not erased until you use the Copy or Cut command again, you can paste the same information as many times as you like.

Importing Text from Another Program into a Notes Dialog Box

If you've written paragraphs of family information using another software program, such as a word processor, you may be able to import that information into the Notes dialog box to avoid retyping it. To do this, the other program must be able to export, or transfer, your information to an **ASCII** file. ASCII files are generic text files that many programs can read and create. DOS programs create "PC-8" ASCII files, while Windows programs create "ANSI" ASCII files. Check the manual of your other program to see if and how you can export your information to an ASCII file. Look under "ASCII," "PC-8," "ANSI," or "Export" in the index of the other program's manual.

Once you've created the ASCII file in the other program, you can import its contents into an individual's Notes dialog box. To do this:

1. Go to the Notes dialog box where you want to place the text.

2. Position the cursor where you want to insert the information.

3. From the **File** menu, select **Import Text File**.

    Family Tree Maker displays the Import Text File dialog box.

4. In the **Drives** and **Directories** fields, select the drive and directory where the file you want to import is located.

5. Select the correct file type from the **File format** drop-down list.

    In general, DOS programs create ASCII (PC-8) files, and Windows programs create ASCII (ANSI) files.

6. From the **File name** list, select the file that you want to import.

7. Click **OK**.

    Family Tree Maker inserts a copy of the text into the Notes dialog box.

    Note: To export your Notes to an ASCII file for use in *Biography Maker* or another program, see "Exporting Text from the Notes Dialog Box into Another Program," on the next page.

Exporting Text from the Notes Dialog Box into Another Program

You can export the text from a Notes dialog box and bring it into another program, such as a word processor. To do this, you create an ASCII text file with Family Tree Maker and then open or import it into the other program. ASCII files are generic text files that many programs can read and create. DOS programs create "PC-8" ASCII files, while Windows programs create "ANSI" ASCII files. Check the manual of your other program to see if it can read, or import, ASCII files. Look under "ASCII," "PC-8," "ANSI," or "Import" in the index.

To create an ASCII file containing the information in an individual's Notes dialog box:

1. Go to the Notes dialog box that has the text you want to export.

2. From the **File** menu, select **Export Notes**.

   Family Tree Maker displays the Export Notes dialog box.

3. In the **Drives** and **Directories** fields, select the drive and directory where you want to place the file you're creating.

4. Select the correct file type from the **File format** drop-down list.

   In general, DOS programs create ASCII (PC-8) files, and Windows programs create ASCII (ANSI) files.

5. Type a file name in the **File name** field.

6. Click **OK**.

   Family Tree Maker creates an ASCII file.

ENTERING DETAILS ABOUT A MARRIAGE

Each marriage in Family Tree Maker has its own set of More About dialog boxes: a Facts dialog box and a Notes dialog box. You can use these to record information about a marriage, such as a special anniversary or activities that the couple liked to share. If the status of the relationship has changed over time, you can also record the ending status of the marriage.

To display the More About dialog boxes for a marriage:

1. Go to the Family Page of the couple whose More About dialog boxes you want to see.

2. Place the cursor in one of the marriage fields.

3. From the **View** menu, select **More About**. From the submenu, select the name of the dialog box that you want to see.

   To display More About dialog boxes, you can also click the **More** button next to the marriage on the Family Page.

Entering Brief Marriage Facts

On the left side of the Facts dialog box, there are several fields for recording facts about the marriage. See Figure 5-8. On the right, there are two buttons that let you switch between the Facts dialog box and the Notes dialog box for the marriage. We'll describe the Marriage Facts dialog box first.

End date — If the relationship ended, type a date in this field.

Ending location — If the relationship ended, type a location in this field.

Ending status — You will want to record an ending status if the relationship changed over time. To select an ending status, click the **Ending status** field and then select a relationship code from the drop-down list. For example, if a couple divorced, you would choose "Divorce." If you imported information from a World Family Tree CD, "Private" may be selected in some cases. This is to protect the privacy of individuals who may still be living.

Marriage fact date/Marriage fact — If the marriage has another significant event or date associated with it, you can use these fields to record it. For example, you could record the date of the couple's engagement or of a special anniversary party.

Reference number — This field can contain any numbers or letters that you choose. You might use this number as part of your own filing system. Its use is entirely optional.

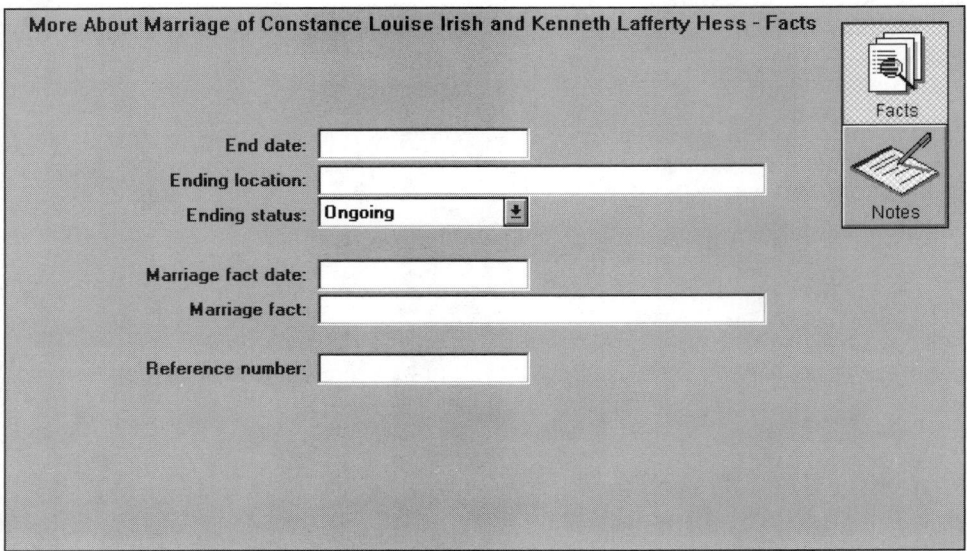

Figure 5-8. A sample More About Marriage Facts dialog box

Entering Marriage Stories and Notes

To display the Notes dialog box for a marriage, click the Notes button in the More About Marriage Facts dialog box.

A Notes dialog box for a marriage works exactly like a Notes dialog box for an individual. For instructions, see "Entering Stories and Notes" on page 137.

To return to the Family Page from the Notes dialog box, from the **View** menu, select **Family Page**.

SCRAPBOOKS: THE BASICS

In Scrapbooks, you can store virtually any type of information about your family, including Kodak Photo CD Pictures; OLE objects such as sound files, video files, text files, and picture files; and non-OLE picture files such as bitmaps and TIFF files. Each individual and each marriage in your Family File has a Scrapbook, so you'll have wonderfully complete collections of family information to pass on from generation to generation.

Scrapbook pages allow you to use your creativity. For example, you could use scanned pictures, scanned school papers, and video files to create childhood pages in each of your children's Scrapbooks. Scanned photos of a couple's wedding and anniversary parties combined with special songs would make a beautiful record of a marriage. With all of the different types of pictures and objects that you can include in Scrapbooks, you have numerous possibilities!

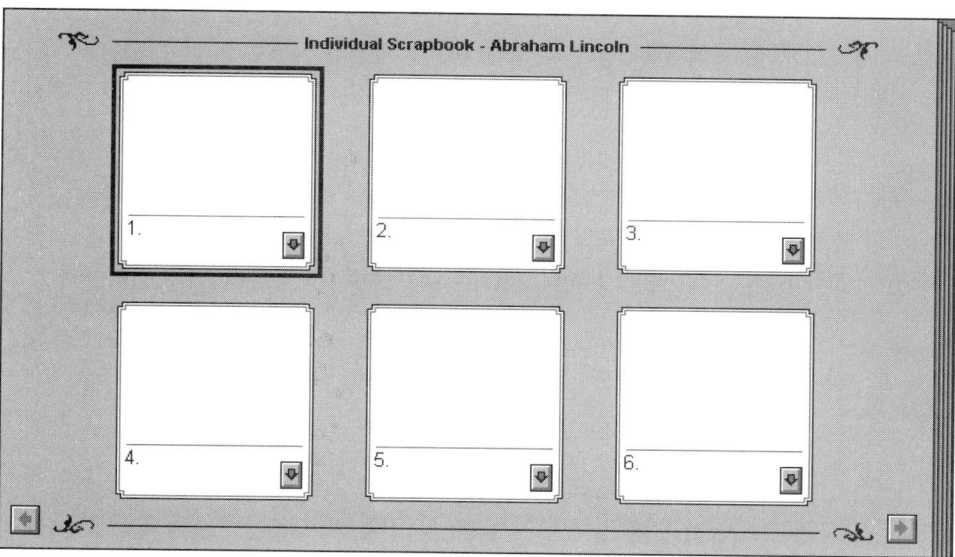

Figure 5-9. An empty Scrapbook page

Opening a Scrapbook for an Individual or Marriage

You can open Scrapbooks from any view. However, we'll first explain how to open Scrapbooks from the Family Page.

To display an individual's or a marriage's Scrapbook:

1. Go to the Family Page containing the individual or the marriage whose Scrapbook you want to see.

    The Index of Individuals and Find Individual are two quick ways to locate an individual's Family Page. The Index of Individuals is described on page 117. Find Individual is described on page 122.

2. On the Family Page, place the cursor either on the name of the individual or on the marriage whose Scrapbook you want to see.

3. From the **View** menu, select **Scrapbook**.

    Family Tree Maker displays the individual's or marriage's Scrapbook. If this is the first time you have opened this Scrapbook, you will be on the first page. If you have opened this Scrapbook before, you will be on the same page as when you last closed the Scrapbook.

If you want to open a Scrapbook from a view other than the Family Page, simply do step 3 while you are in that view. Family Tree Maker will display the Individual Scrapbook for the **primary individual**.

The primary individual is the main individual in the view. For example, in a Descendant tree, the primary individual is the individual at the top of the tree. Some views, such as the Report view or the Labels/Cards view, don't have a "main" individual. In these views, the primary individual is the primary individual from the previous view.

Note: If the Scrapbook that Family Tree Maker displays is not for the individual that you want, you can navigate to their Scrapbook easily. From the **View** menu, select **Index of Individuals**, select the individual whose Scrapbook you want to see, and then click **OK**.

What Goes into a Scrapbook?

You can store virtually any type of family information in a Scrapbook, including your family photographs and any other paper memorabilia that's been **scanned**; **pictures**, and other items that can be pasted to and from the Clipboard; sound clips, video clips, and other **OLE objects**; **Kodak Photo CD pictures**; and **text**. Once one of these items is stored in a Scrapbook, we refer to it as a **Picture/Object**. If you're uncertain about what these different terms refer to, keep reading; each one is described below.

Note: If you are planning to include large images and video clips in your Scrapbooks, keep the capabilities of your computer in mind. If you only have the minimum system requirements, your machine will run slowly when you work with large images and video clips. In fact, if your machine does not have enough RAM, you may not be able to load particularly large files. In addition, you will need quite a bit of free space on your hard drive to store large images and video clips. See "Picture Size and Your Computer," page 413, for more information.

Kodak Photo CD Pictures

A Kodak Photo CD is a CD-ROM disc containing pictures that came from your undeveloped film, negatives, or old photos. Placing your pictures on a Kodak Photo CD is easy to do and a great way to prepare family photos for use with Family Tree Maker. For more information about creating Kodak Photo CDs, see Appendix C.

To use Kodak Photo CDs, the only special equipment you need is a CD-ROM player on your computer that can read a Kodak Photo CD (many of the early CD-ROM players cannot). If you have one of these CD-ROM players, Family Tree Maker can read and import your Photo CD Pictures.

Pictures

"Pictures," sometimes called "graphics," are electronic images. There are many ways to get pictures:

- Take your undeveloped film, old photos, or negatives to a Kodak processor and have the images placed on a Kodak Photo CD.

- Create, scan, or purchase pictures that you can store on your hard disk in a graphics file. You can create your own pictures using a graphics software program. Scanning is described in the next section. Pictures are available for purchase in many software packages; check your local software dealer.

- Cut or copy an image from another software program, another Scrapbook in Family Tree Maker, or another view in Family Tree Maker and store it temporarily on the Clipboard as a bitmap or metafile.

- Cut or copy an image from any OLE server application and store it temporarily on the Windows Clipboard.

Pictures can be stored in many different file formats. Some common formats are bitmap (.BMP) and Tagged Image File Format (.TIF). When you have pictures in these or one of several other file formats, you can place them into your Family Tree Maker Scrapbooks. Placing pictures into Family Tree Maker is described in "Scrapbooks: Inserting Items" on page 153.

Scanning

"Scanning" is making an electronic reproduction of a paper item, such as a photograph, newspaper clipping, birth certificate, or diploma. In effect, scanning is a way of making your own pictures, just like those described in "Pictures," on page 149. Scanning is a great way to preserve family memorabilia, because scanned images won't fade or become brittle like paper and photographs tend to do after many years. And, once you have a scanned image of an item, you can store it safely on your computer.

To scan an item, you must have a scanner and scanner software. Family Tree Maker does not scan items for you, nor can it act as scanning software. There are many different types of scanners made by many different companies. Most scanners come with their own software. If you are interested in scanning your paper memorabilia, the best thing to do is to talk with your local computer dealer. They should be able to help you choose the scanner that is right for you. Of course, you'll also want to read the manuals for the scanner so that you can correctly create electronic images to place in your Scrapbooks.

Object Linking and Embedding (OLE)

Object Linking and Embedding (OLE) is a technology that lets you create items in one software program and place them in another software program. For example, you can use video capture software to transfer clips of your home videos onto your computer. Then, with the help of Object Linking and Embedding you can transfer video clips from your video capture software into Family Tree Maker Scrapbooks.

OLE objects are items, such as the video clips described on page 150, that can be transferred from one software program to another. The types of objects you might want to use in Scrapbooks include sound clips; video clips; still images or pictures; and text objects from a word processor, spreadsheet, or database.

An **OLE server** is a software program, such as the video capture software described on page 150, that creates OLE objects. Any Windows 3.1 (or higher) compatible program *can* be an OLE server. Not all are, so it is important to read the box carefully before making a purchase. Most software manufacturers will advertise OLE server capability if they have it, or you can call the manufacturer to ask before purchasing.

An **OLE client** is a software program, such as Family Tree Maker, into which OLE objects can be placed. Think of it in terms of a restaurant: the server creates the food and serves it to the client, and the client eats (or stores) it. For a more thorough description of Object Linking and Embedding, see the index of your Microsoft Windows 3.1 (or later) User's Guide.

Text

While the Notes dialog box is generally where you store text, there may also be cases when you want to store text in the Scrapbook. For example, if your child used a word processor to write a report for school or a letter to grandma, you might want to save the word processor file in the Scrapbook.

To store text (word processor files) in the Scrapbook, you cannot just use the Edit menu to copy and paste it into the Scrapbook. Instead, you need to treat the text as an OLE object. For more information about OLE objects, see "Object Linking and Embedding (OLE)" on page 150.

Setting Defaults for Picture Resolution and Compression

You can set a default degree of compression and resolution for any pictures that you bring into Scrapbooks. Even if you set a default, you can change the settings for individual pictures at any time.

To set default levels of compression and resolution for pictures:

1. From the **Prefs** menu, select **Pictures/Objects**.

    Family Tree Maker displays the Pictures/Objects dialog box.

2. You can now select the default compression and/or resolution. Each of your options is described below.

    Degree of Compression — Select the option button corresponding to the degree of compression that you want for your picture. Higher ratios give you a greater loss in picture quality, but the pictures will take up less space on your hard disk. (Family Tree Maker uses the industry standard JPEG compression method.) Lower ratios give you pictures with less loss in quality, but will take more disk space. The "1:1" setting will not reduce the quality of your picture at all, but will take up the most space on your hard disk. In general, the "recommended" setting is a good balance between quality loss and disk space.

    Photo CD — This option is only available for Kodak Photo CD Pictures. Select the option button corresponding to the resolution that you want for your picture. "Resolution" refers to the size of your picture. A higher resolution will create a larger picture, and a larger picture will be sharper and have more detail. If the default resolution that you choose here is not available for one of the images that you import, Family Tree Maker will import it at the next available lower resolution.

    Choosing resolutions higher (larger) than the recommended "256 x 384" will use up large amounts of your hard disk space. In addition, you may not be able to load a picture at a very high resolution if your computer does not have a sufficient amount of RAM (memory). See "Picture Size and Your Computer," page 413, for more information.

3. Click **OK** when you've made your selections.

    Family Tree Maker remembers and applies your selections until you change them again.

SCRAPBOOKS: INSERTING ITEMS

There are five different ways to insert items into a Scrapbook. The method that you use will depend on what it is that you want to insert. Use Figure 5-10 to help determine which method you should use in each case.

When you are ready to insert a new item, you can place it either between two Picture/Objects or to the immediate right of the last Picture/Object. To insert an item between two Picture/Objects, select the Picture/Object on the right and then use a command from the Picture/Object menu to insert the new item. When you insert an item after the last Picture/Object in the Scrapbook, you cannot leave empty spaces between the last Picture/Object and the new item. The new item must be inserted directly after the last Picture/Object.

When you have...	Use this menu choice...
A Kodak Photo CD Picture.	Picture/Object: Insert Photo CD Picture, described on page 154.
A graphic file, such as a scanned image or clip art, stored on your computer's hard disk. Compatible file formats include (*.BMP), (*.GIF), (*.PCX), (*.TIF), (*.JPG), and (*.JFF).	Picture/Object: Insert Picture from File, described on page 157.
An OLE object in a file. Also use this method when you want to create a new OLE object and then insert it into the Scrapbook.	Picture/Object: Insert Object, described on page 159.
Items that you have cut or copied to the Clipboard, such as an Ancestor tree, or even a Picture/Object that you are copying from one Scrapbook to another.	Edit: Paste, described on page 162.
OLE objects on the Clipboard, such as pictures, text, video, and sound.	Edit: Paste or Edit: Paste Special, described on page 162.

Figure 5-10. Commands for inserting items into Scrapbooks

Picture/Object: Insert Photo CD Picture

Using the Insert Photo CD Picture command on the Picture/Object menu, you can insert pictures from Kodak Photo CD-ROM discs. When you insert pictures, keep the capabilities of your computer in mind. If you insert large picture files, your machine may run slowly. In fact, if your machine does not have enough RAM, you may not be able to load particularly large files. In addition, you will need quite a bit of free space on your hard drive to store large images and video clips. See "Picture Size and Your Computer," page 413, for more information.

To insert a Kodak Photo CD picture into a Scrapbook:

1. In the Scrapbook, select the area into which you want to insert the picture.

    If you insert a picture when an empty Picture/Object area is selected, the picture goes into that Picture/Object area. If you insert a picture when an occupied Picture/Object area is selected, Family Tree Maker moves the existing Picture/Objects to the right and inserts a new Picture/Object area for the new picture.

2. From the **Picture/Object** menu, select **Insert Photo CD Picture**.

    Family Tree Maker displays the Insert from Photo CD dialog box. You have several options.

You can use your computer keyboard to move around and select pictures in this dialog box. Figure 5-11 on the next page shows which keys work as selection and navigation keys. Your other options are described below the figure.

Press this key...	To do this...
$\boxed{\uparrow}$	Move to the picture above the currently selected picture
$\boxed{\downarrow}$	Move to the picture below the currently selected picture
$\boxed{\leftarrow}$	Move to the picture to the left of the currently selected picture
$\boxed{\rightarrow}$	Move to the picture to the right of the currently selected picture
$\boxed{\leftrightarrows}$ (tab)	Move forward between the buttons in the dialog box
$\boxed{\text{⇧ Shift}} + \boxed{\leftrightarrows}$	Move backwards between the buttons in the dialog box
$\boxed{\text{home}}$	Move to the first picture on the current screen
$\boxed{\text{end}}$	Move to the last picture on the current screen
$\boxed{\text{Ctrl}} + \boxed{\text{home}}$	Move to the first picture on the CD
$\boxed{\text{Ctrl}} + \boxed{\text{end}}$	Move to the last picture on the CD
$\boxed{\text{PgUp}}$	Move to the picture one screen up
$\boxed{\text{PgDn}}$	Move to the picture one screen down

Figure 5-11. Moving the cursor in the Insert from Photo CD dialog box

Find — Use this button to go to a particular picture on the Photo CD. Simply type the number of the picture in the **Find photo number** field and then click **OK**. Family Tree Maker returns you to the Insert from Photo CD dialog box and selects the picture with that number.

View — Use this button to display the currently selected picture at full size in the View Picture dialog box. In the View Picture dialog box you can use the scroll bars and the **Zoom** buttons to get a better look at your picture. The choices that you make here do not change the picture; they are only for viewing purposes. Click **OK** in the View Picture dialog box to return to the Insert from Photo CD dialog box.

Resolution — Use this button to change the resolution and compression with which this picture will be stored in the Scrapbook. See "Controlling Picture Resolution and Compression" on page 178 for a complete description of the Compression/Resolution dialog box. In most cases, you do not need to change the compression and resolution. However, if you have a reason for altering the resolution, go ahead and do it now.

3. Click **OK** in the Insert from Photo CD dialog box when you are ready to insert a picture.

Family Tree Maker displays the Edit Picture dialog box where you can select editing options. The editing options fall into three categories: rotating, flipping, and cropping. Rotating allows you to re-orient pictures that are sideways or upside down, flipping is for adjusting pictures that are backwards, and cropping allows you to select the area of the picture that you want to place in the Scrapbook. See "Editing Picture/Objects" on page 172 for instructions on using this dialog box.

Note: If you want to edit a picture, this is the best time to do it. This is because Family Tree Maker compresses images for storage unless you select 1:1 compression. Once you have placed a picture in the Scrapbook, it must be decompressed and recompressed each time you edit it again. Decompressing and recompressing a picture multiple times reduces the quality of the picture. (Family Tree Maker uses the industry standard JPEG compression method.) Please note that printing and viewing your picture at different sizes do not involve compression and will not reduce the quality of your picture.

When you click **OK** to leave the Edit Picture dialog box, Family Tree Maker compresses and saves your picture in the Family File. The picture is now visible in the Scrapbook at a reduced size, called a **thumbnail**. The thumbnail's small size allows you to see several different images on the screen at once. The real, full-sized images will be used for printing and viewing.

Once you have inserted a picture into the Scrapbook, you should use the More About Picture/Object dialog box to create a caption and to tell Family Tree Maker in which documents you want the picture to print. See "Recording Important Picture/Object Information" on page 164.

Picture/Object: Insert Picture from File

Using the Insert Picture from File command on the Picture/Object menu you can insert pictures from files into a Scrapbook. The Scrapbook accepts the following file formats:

- Windows Bitmap (*.BMP)

- CompuServe Bitmap (*.GIF)

- ZSoft Image (*.PCX)

- Tagged Image Format (*.TIF)

- JPEG Interchange Format (*.JPG, *.JFF)

When you insert pictures, keep the capabilities of your computer in mind. If you insert large picture files, your machine may run slowly. In fact, if your machine does not have enough RAM, you may not be able to load particularly large files. In addition, you will need quite a bit of free space on your hard drive to store large images. See "Picture Size and Your Computer," on page 413, for more information.

To insert a picture into a Scrapbook with the Insert Picture from File command:

1. In the Scrapbook, select the area into which you want to insert the picture.

   If you insert a picture when an empty Picture/Object area is selected, the picture goes into that Picture/Object area. If you insert a picture when an occupied Picture/Object area is selected, Family Tree Maker moves the existing Picture/Objects to the right and inserts a new Picture/Object area for the new picture.

2. From the **Picture/Object** menu, select **Insert Picture from File**.

   Family Tree Maker displays the Insert Picture dialog box.

3. In the **Drives** and **Directories** fields, select the drive and directory where the picture file you want to insert is located. If you are unsure where your file is, click **Find file** and follow the instructions in "Finding Files" on page 392.

4. Click the **List Files of Type** drop-down list and select the format of the file that you want to open.

5.   Select the name of your file in the **File Name** field.

     After selecting a file name, you have several options:

     Preview Picture — Select this check box to view the picture at reduced size in the "Preview" field.

     View — Use this button to display the picture at full size in the View Picture dialog box.

     Compression — Use this button to change the compression with which this picture will be stored. See "Controlling Picture Resolution and Compression" on page 178 for a description of this dialog box. In most cases, you do not need to change the compression.

6.   Click **OK** in the Insert Picture dialog box.

Family Tree Maker displays the Edit Picture dialog box where you can select editing options. The editing options fall into three categories: rotating, flipping, and cropping. Rotating allows you to re-orient pictures that are sideways or upside down, flipping is for adjusting pictures that are backwards, and cropping allows you to select the area of the picture that you want to place in the Scrapbook. See "Editing Picture/Objects" on page 172 for instructions on using this dialog box.

Note: If you want to edit a picture, this is the best time to do it. This is because Family Tree Maker compresses images for storage unless you select 1:1 compression. Once you have placed a picture in the Scrapbook, it must be decompressed and recompressed each time you edit it again. Decompressing and recompressing a picture multiple times reduces the quality of the picture. (Family Tree Maker uses the industry standard JPEG compression method.) Please note that printing and viewing your picture at different sizes do not involve compression and will not reduce the quality of your picture.

When you click **OK** to leave the Edit Picture dialog box, Family Tree Maker compresses and saves your picture in the Family File. The picture is now visible in the Scrapbook at a reduced size, called a thumbnail. The thumbnail's small size allows you to see several different images on the screen at once. The real, full-sized images will be used for printing and viewing.

Once you have inserted a picture into the Scrapbook, you should use the More About Picture/Object dialog box to create a caption and to tell Family Tree Maker in which documents you want the picture to print. See "Recording Important Picture/Object Information" on page 164.

Picture/Object: Insert Object

With the Insert Object command, you can insert existing OLE objects into the Scrapbook. In addition, you can create new OLE objects and then insert them into the Scrapbook. OLE objects include pictures, text, spreadsheets, sound clips, and video clips. When you insert pictures, video, or sound files, keep the capabilities of your computer in mind. If you insert large files, your machine may run slowly. In fact, if your machine does not have enough RAM, you may not be able to load particularly large files. In addition, you will need quite a bit of free space on your hard drive to store large images and video clips. See "Picture Size and Your Computer," page 413, for more information.

Inserting Existing OLE Objects into the Scrapbook

To insert an *existing* OLE object with the Insert Object command:

1. In the Scrapbook, select the area into which you want to insert the object.

   If you insert an OLE object when an empty Picture/Object area is selected, the OLE object goes into that Picture/Object area. If you insert an OLE object when an occupied Picture/Object area is selected, Family Tree Maker moves the existing Picture/Object to the right and inserts a new Picture/Object area for the new OLE object.

2. From the **Picture/Object** menu, select **Insert Object**.

   Family Tree Maker displays the Insert Object dialog box.

3. Select the **Create from File** option button.

4. In the **File** field, type the path and name of the file containing the OLE object that you want to insert into the Scrapbook.

   For example, if you had a file called "sound.wav" in the "windows" directory on your C:\ drive, you would type `C:\windows\sound.wav`

   If you do not remember the exact name and location of your file, click **Browse** to display the Browse dialog box. In the Browse dialog box, use the **Drives** and **Directories** fields to locate your file. Click **OK** to return to the Insert Object dialog box once you have the correct file path and name.

   If you want to view an icon in the Scrapbook instead of the OLE object itself, select the **Display As Icon** check box. You may want to do this if you are pasting in a text file or some other object that isn't attractive when it's shrunk down to fit into the Picture/Object area.

When you select this option, you can change the appearance of the icon by clicking **Change Icon**. In the Change Icon dialog box, you can either type the file name for the new icon in the **From File** field, or search for an icon file by clicking **Browse**. Click **OK** to return to the Insert Object dialog box once you have the correct file path and name.

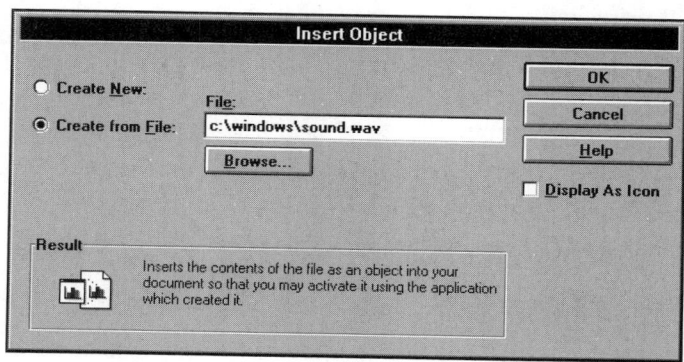

Figure 5-12. The Insert Object dialog box — inserting from a file

5. When the correct file name is in the **File** field, click **OK**.

    Family Tree Maker places the OLE object in the Scrapbook.

Once you have inserted an OLE object into the Scrapbook, you should use the More About Picture/Object dialog box to create a caption and to tell Family Tree Maker in which documents you want the item to print. See "Recording Important Picture/Object Information" on page 164. You can also edit an OLE object once it's in the Scrapbook. See "Editing OLE Objects" on page 176.

Creating and Inserting New OLE Objects into the Scrapbook

To create a *new* OLE object to insert into a Scrapbook:

1. In the Scrapbook, select the area into which you want to insert the object.

    If you insert an OLE object when an empty Picture/Object area is selected, the OLE object goes into that Picture/Object area. If you insert an OLE object when an occupied Picture/Object area is selected, Family Tree Maker moves the existing Picture/Objects to the right and inserts a new Picture/Object area for the new OLE object.

2. From the **Picture/Object** menu, select **Insert Object**.

    Family Tree Maker displays the Insert Object dialog box.

3. Select the **Create New** option button.

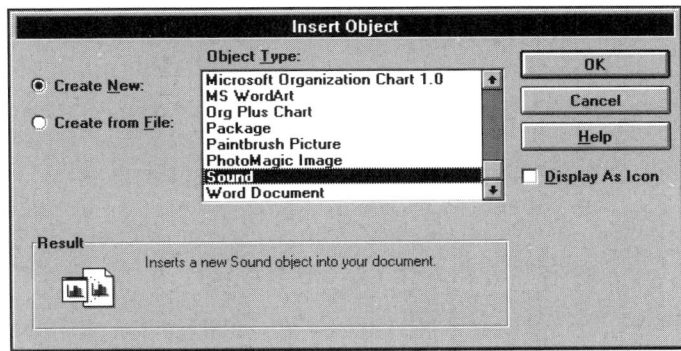

Figure 5-13. The Insert Object dialog box — creating a new file

4. In the **Object Type** scrolling list, click the name of the OLE object that you want to insert into the Scrapbook.

    Microsoft Windows opens the software program in which you can create the OLE object.

5. In the other software program, create the OLE object.

    If you need instructions for using that program, please refer to its manual.

6. When you are finished creating the new OLE object, from the **File** menu of that software program, select **Exit and Return to Family Tree Maker**.

    Microsoft Windows closes the software program and returns you to Family Tree Maker. (Windows may also ask you if you want to update or save your information; answer **Yes** or **OK**.) Family Tree Maker places the OLE object in the Scrapbook.

Once you have inserted an OLE object into the Scrapbook, you should use the More About Picture/Object dialog box to create a caption and to tell Family Tree Maker in which documents you want the item to print. See "Recording Important Picture/Object Information" on page 164. You can also edit an OLE object once it's in the Scrapbook. See "Editing OLE Objects" on page 176.

Edit: Paste and Edit: Paste Special

With the Paste command you can insert items that you have cut or copied to the Clipboard, such as items from other software programs, Picture/Objects from other Scrapbooks, and OLE objects like pictures, sound clips, video clips, and word processor documents. You can also insert OLE Objects with the Paste Special command. When you insert OLE objects with, the Paste Special command, you have slightly more control over the process.

When you insert pictures, video, and sound, keep the capabilities of your computer in mind. If you insert large files, your machine may run slowly. In fact, if your machine does not have enough RAM, you may not be able to load particularly large files. In addition, you will need quite a bit of free space on your hard drive to store large files. See "Picture Size and Your Computer," page 413, for more information.

To paste an item from the Clipboard into a Scrapbook:

1. Make sure that the item you want to paste is on the Clipboard.

   In general, to copy an item to the Clipboard, you first select that item. Then from the **Edit** menu, select **Copy**. If the item is in a software program other than Family Tree Maker, the process may be slightly different. Please refer to that software program's manual for instructions.

2. In the Scrapbook, select the area into which you want to paste the item.

   If you paste an item from the Clipboard when an empty Picture/Object area is selected, the item will be pasted into that Picture/Object area. If you paste an item from the Clipboard when an occupied Picture/Object area is selected, Family Tree Maker moves the existing Picture/Objects to the right and inserts a new Picture/Object area for the new item.

3. From Family Tree Maker's **Edit** menu, select either **Paste** or **Paste Special**.

   If you are using the Paste command, skip the remaining two steps and read the paragraphs after step 5. If you are using the Paste Special command, continue with step 4.

4. Family Tree Maker displays the Paste Special dialog box. In the **As** list, click the data type corresponding to the OLE object that you want to paste into the Scrapbook.

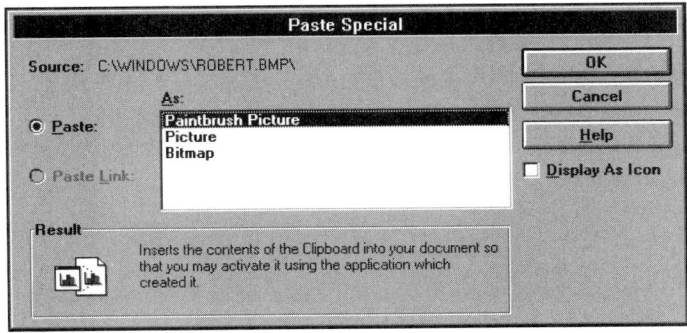

Figure 5-14. The Paste Special dialog box

If you want to view an icon in the Scrapbook instead of the OLE object itself, select the **Display As Icon** check box. You may want to do this if you are pasting in a text file or some other object that isn't attractive when it's shrunk down to fit into the Picture/Object area.

When you select this option, you can also change the appearance of the icon by clicking **Change Icon**. In the Change Icon dialog box, you can either type the file name for the new icon in the **File name** field, or search for an icon file by clicking **Browse**. Click **OK** to return to the Paste Special dialog box once you have the correct file path and name.

5. Click **OK**.

Family Tree Maker places the OLE object in the Scrapbook.

Once you have pasted an item into the Scrapbook, you should use the More About Picture/Object dialog box to create a caption and to tell Family Tree Maker in which documents you want the item to print. See "Recording Important Picture/Object Information" on page 164.

You can also edit and change the compression of an item once it's in the Scrapbook. See "Editing Picture/Objects" on page 172 and "Controlling Picture Resolution and Compression" on page 178. To edit an OLE object, see "Editing OLE Objects" on page 176.

SCRAPBOOKS: WORKING WITH PICTURE/OBJECTS

Once you have Picture/Objects in your Scrapbooks, there are many things that you can to do with them. For example, you can view pictures at full size or play videos and sounds. You can even play a whole Scrapbook at once in a "slide show." You can also edit Picture/Objects, as well as store information about them in the More About Picture/Object dialog box. All of these functions are described in the following sections.

If you want to print your Picture/Objects in trees, see Chapter 8, "Creating and Printing Trees." If you want to print your Picture/Objects in another document, see Chapter 9. Also see "Recording Important Picture/Object Information," below, for more about printing Picture/Objects in trees and other documents.

Recording Important Picture/Object Information

Each Picture/Object has its own More About Picture/Object dialog box. This dialog box is for recording captions and other important information about your Picture/Objects, such as what they are and when they were created. Another very important function of this dialog box is that you use it to select the types of documents in which you want your Picture/Objects to print. The More About Picture/Object dialog box is also for indicating whether or not you want each Picture/Object to be included when the Scrapbook is played.

To record captions and other information about your Picture/Objects:

1. Select the Picture/Object whose More About dialog box you want to open.

2. From the **Picture/Object** menu, select **More About**. You can also press Ctrl + **M** or click the downward-pointing arrow next to the Picture/Object.

   Family Tree Maker displays the More About Picture/Object dialog box. A reduced-size image of your Picture/Object should be in the upper right-hand corner of the Jialog box. Make sure that it's the Picture/Object that you want to record information about. You now have several options, each of which is described below.

   Caption — Type a caption for your Picture/Object in this field.

   Category — Type a category of your own creation in this field. Categories are useful when it's time to print or search for a Picture/Object. For example, if you wanted to look at all of the Picture/Objects related to childhood birthdays and you had given all of the childhood birthday

Picture/Objects the category "Childhood Birthday," you'd be able to locate all of these birthday pictures easily.

Put some thought into the creation of your categories — you will find that it pays off when you print documents in which you want to include Picture/Objects. Think about the types of documents you will want to print in the future. Will you want family trees containing a portrait of each individual as an adult? How about creating special anniversary address labels that contains each couple's wedding picture? Thinking about the types of documents that you want to print should help you create your categories.

Depending on the number of Picture/Objects that you place in Scrapbooks, you may want your categories to be fairly specific. For example, if you have several different portraits for each individual, you wouldn't want to put them all in the category "Portrait." Instead, it would be a good idea to create categories such as "Portrait - Childhood," "Portrait - Teen", and so on.

In general, you will want to base your categories on the event that the Picture/Object portrays. For example, "Wedding - Reception" and "Wedding - Ceremony" for wedding pictures. "Graduation," "Bar Mitzvah," "Thanksgiving," and "Vacation," are other examples. To get an idea of how categories work, you may want to see the section "Picture/Objects on Labels and Cards" on page 300.

Date of origin — Type the date on which the original item was created. For pictures, you would want to type the date when the photograph was taken.

Type — Click this drop-down list and select the type that applies to the currently selected Picture/Object. If the currently selected Picture/Object is a Kodak Photo CD picture or a picture inserted from a file, Family Tree Maker has already selected the type for you.

Description — Type a description of the Picture/Object in this field. You can include more detailed information than in the caption.

Include in show — Select this check box if you want Family Tree Maker to include this Picture/Object when you play the Scrapbook. For more information about playing Scrapbooks, see "Playing a Scrapbook," page 170.

Include in printed Scrapbook — Select this check box if you want Family Tree Maker to print this Picture/Object when you print the Scrapbook. Items that you might not want to print include sound clips, because they will only print as icons.

Preferred Picture/Object #1 - #3 for trees — To make it easier to select Picture/Objects to print in trees, Family Tree Maker allows you to select the three Picture/Objects that you are most likely to print for an individual. You can designate your three choices using the "Preferred Picture/Object for trees" check boxes.

For example, if you picked each individual's birthday photo as the "Preferred Picture/Object #1 for trees" and told Family Tree Maker to include "Preferred Picture/Object #1 for trees" when you printed a tree, the tree would contain each individual's birthday photo.

Please note that for each individual's Scrapbook, you can only designate one Picture/Object as the "Preferred Picture/Object #1 for trees." The same holds for "Preferred Picture/Object #2 for trees" and so on. This means that if you already have selected one picture as the "Preferred Picture/Object #1 for trees" and then select it for a second picture, the first picture is no longer the "Preferred Picture/Object #1 for trees."

Although Family Tree Maker only allows you to designate three "preferred" Picture/Objects for trees, you can include any other Picture/Object in a tree. You will simply use Categories, described above, when it is time to print.

Preferred Picture/Object for Labels/Cards — To make it easier to select Picture/Objects to print on labels or cards, Family Tree Maker allows you to select the Picture/Object that you are most likely to print for an individual. You can designate your choice using the "Preferred Picture/Object for Labels/Cards" check box.

All of the same rules apply to "Preferred Picture/Object for Labels/Cards" as for "Preferred Picture/Object for trees," described above.

Preferred Picture/Object for Fam Grp Sheets — To make it easier to select Picture/Objects to print on Family Group Sheets, Family Tree Maker allows you to select the Picture/Object that you are most likely to print for an individual. You can designate your choice using the "Preferred Picture/Object for Fam Grp Sheets" check box.

All of the same rules apply to "Preferred Picture/Object for Fam Grp Sheets" as for "Preferred Picture/Object for trees," described above.

CD#, Photo#, Resolution — When the currently selected Picture/Object is a Kodak Photo CD picture, Family Tree Maker displays this information.

Finding Picture/Objects in a Scrapbook

Using the Find Picture/Object command, you can locate a Picture/Object in the Scrapbook that is currently open. If you want to search all of the Scrapbooks in your Family File at the same time, you must use the Find Individual command. See "Locating Individuals in Your Family File" on page 122.

To find a Picture/Object in a Scrapbook:

1. Make sure you're in the Scrapbook that you want to search.

2. From the **Edit** menu, select **Find**.

   Family Tree Maker displays the Find Picture/Object dialog box.

3. Click the **Search** drop-down list and select the name of the field that you want to search.

4. In the **for** field, type the information that you want to find.

   If the field that you are searching only has certain legal values (such as "yes" or "no"), Family Tree Maker will display a drop-down list in the "for" field. In this case, just click the item that you want to search for.

5. Click **Find next** to start the search.

   Family Tree Maker goes to and selects the first Picture/Object that matches your request. If no matches are found, Family Tree Maker tells you so.

   If you like, you can edit this Picture/Object and then continue your search by clicking **Find next**.

6. Click **Find next** to continue your search.

   Continue clicking **Find next** until you're done searching or until Family Tree Maker runs out of matches. To go back to previous matches, you can click **Find previous**.

7. To quit the search, click **Cancel**.

   If you didn't find the Picture/Object you were looking for, try again with a less restrictive request. For example, search for a portion of a caption rather than a complete caption.

Moving Around in a Scrapbook

One way to move around in a Scrapbook is with your mouse. Just move the mouse pointer to the Picture/Object you want to select and then click the primary mouse button.

To turn Scrapbook pages with the mouse, click the page-turning buttons in the lower right- and left-hand corners of your screen. When you're on the first page of a Scrapbook, the backward page-turn button will not work. When you're on the last page of a Scrapbook, the forward page-turn button will not work.

You can also use your computer keyboard to move around in a Scrapbook. Figure 5-15 on the next page shows which keys work as navigation keys.

Viewing Pictures at Full Size

Although pictures appear in Scrapbooks at a reduced size, called a **thumbnail**, you can view them at full size. (This only applies to non-OLE pictures.)

To view a non-OLE picture at full size:

1. In the Scrapbook, select the Picture/Object that you want to view.

2. From the **Picture/Object** menu, select **View Picture**. You can also double-click the Picture in the Scrapbook.

    Family Tree Maker displays the View Picture dialog box. Use the **Zoom** buttons to view your picture at larger or smaller sizes. When your whole picture is not visible in the dialog box, Family Tree Maker places scroll bars on the bottom and right sides of the picture. You can use these scroll bars to view different sections of your picture.

3. Click **OK** to close the View Picture dialog box.

    Family Tree Maker returns you to the Scrapbook view.

Press this key...	To do this...
[↑]	Move to the Picture/Object above the currently selected Picture/Object
[↓]	Move to the Picture/Object below the currently selected Picture/Object
[←]	Move to the Picture/Object to the left of the currently selected Picture/Object. Family Tree Maker turns the page if the next Picture/Object is on the next page.
[→]	Move to the Picture/Object to the right of the currently selected Picture/Object. Family Tree Maker turns the page if the next Picture/Object is on the next page.
[⇥] (tab)	Move to the next Picture/Object. Family Tree Maker turns the page if the next Picture/Object is on the next page.
[⇧ Shift] + [⇥]	Move to the previous Picture/Object. Family Tree Maker turns the page if the next Picture/Object is on the next page.
[home]	Move to the first Picture/Object on the current page
[end]	Move to the last Picture/Object on the current page
[Ctrl] + [home]	Move to the first Picture/Object on the first page of the Scrapbook
[Ctrl] + [end]	Move to the last Picture/Object on the last page of the Scrapbook
[PgUp]	Move to the previous page in the Scrapbook
[PgDn]	Move to the next page in the Scrapbook
[Ctrl] + [M]	Display the More About Picture/Object dialog box for the currently selected Picture/Object

Figure 5-15. Keys for moving and selecting Picture/Objects in a Scrapbook

Playing OLE Objects

Once you have placed OLE objects in a Scrapbook, you can "play" them. For example, you can listen to sound files and watch video files.

To play an OLE object:

1. Double-click the Picture/Object that you want to play.

    What happens after you double-click depends on the OLE object's server. In most cases, video and sound files will play. Picture files will most likely appear at full size and spreadsheets will open.

2. If the OLE server opened, you can return to Family Tree Maker by closing the server. From the **File** menu of the server, select **Exit and Return to Family Tree Maker**.

    Note: If the program does not have a menu choice such as "Exit and Return" or "Update," refer to that program's manual for instructions.

Playing a Scrapbook

Once you have Picture/Objects in a Scrapbook, you can easily create a "slide show" to display each of the Picture/Objects in sequence. All you need to do is indicate which Picture/Objects you want to include in the show and for how long you want each Picture/Object to appear on the screen.

To play the Picture/Objects in a Scrapbook sequentially:

1. Open the Scrapbook for which you want to create a show. Do **not** go into Scrapbook Print Preview.

2. Open the More About Picture/Object dialog box for each of the Picture/Objects that you want to include in the show. You can do this by clicking the downward-pointing arrow next to each Picture/Object. Make sure that the **Include in show** check box is selected.

    You may also want to ensure that the **Include in show** check box is *not* selected for those Picture/Objects that you do not want in the show.

3. Make sure that the Picture/Objects are in the order in which you want them to appear in the show. If not, you can move them. See "Moving or Copying Picture/Objects Between Scrapbooks" on page 180 or "Sorting a Scrapbook" on the next page.

4. From the **Picture/Object** menu, select **Play Scrapbook**.

   Family Tree Maker displays the Play Scrapbook dialog box.

5. Enter a number in the **Time between Picture/Objects** field.

   You can enter from 1 to 999. The number that you enter is the number of seconds for which Family Tree Maker will display each picture on the screen during the show.

6. Click **OK**.

   Family Tree Maker begins the show. Each Picture/Object is centered on the screen for the number of seconds that you selected. Picture/Objects that can be "played," such as sounds and videos, are played. If you click on the screen while a picture is displayed, Family Tree Maker will skip the time delay and move on to the next Picture/Object.

Sorting a Scrapbook

You may want the Picture/Objects in your Scrapbooks in a particular order. You can choose the order quickly and easily with Family Tree Maker's sorting feature. When you choose a sorting order, it only affects the Scrapbook that is currently open.

To sort a Scrapbook:

1. From the **Format** menu, select **Sort Scrapbook**.

   Family Tree Maker displays the Sort Scrapbook dialog box.

2. Click the option button for the type of sorting you prefer.

   You can sort on captions, categories, or dates. For captions or categories, Family Tree Maker sorts alphabetically, beginning with the first word.

3. Click **OK** when you've made your selection.

   Family Tree Maker sorts the current Scrapbook and returns you to the Scrapbook view.

Editing Picture/Objects

You can edit a picture both as you insert it into a Scrapbook and after inserting it into the Scrapbook. If you want to edit an OLE object, see "Editing OLE Objects," on page 176.

Editing a Picture as You Place it in a Scrapbook

When you place a picture in a Scrapbook, Family Tree Maker automatically displays the Edit Picture dialog box. If you would like to edit your picture, this is the best time to do it. Instructions for rotating, flipping, and cropping are below.

When you click **OK** to leave the Edit Picture dialog box, Family Tree Maker compresses and saves your picture in the Family File. The picture is placed in the Scrapbook at a reduced size, called a **thumbnail**. The thumbnail's small size allows you to see several different images on the screen at once. The real, full-sized images will be used for printing and viewing.

Once you have inserted a picture into the Scrapbook, you should use the More About Picture/Object dialog box to create a caption and to tell Family Tree Maker in which documents you want the picture to print. See "Recording Important Picture/Object Information" on page 164.

Editing a Picture after Placing it in a Scrapbook

Editing a picture after placing it in the Scrapbook involves decompressing and recompressing it. Unless you selected 1:1 compression when you initially imported the picture, repeated decompression and recompression reduce the quality of the picture. (Family Tree Maker uses the industry standard JPEG compression method.) For this reason, Family Tree Maker asks you to retrieve the original picture before you edit it. See "Preparing to Edit a Picture," on the next page. Please note that printing and viewing your pictures at different sizes do not involve compression and will not reduce the quality of your picture.

Preparing to Edit a Picture

If you are currently in the process of placing a picture in the Scrapbook and the Edit Picture dialog box is already open, you can skip these instructions. Only use these instructions when you are editing a picture that was previously inserted into the Scrapbook.

To open a picture for editing:

1. In the Scrapbook, select the picture that you want to edit.

2. From the **Picture/Object** menu, select **Edit**.

3. Family Tree Maker asks if you want to open and edit the original file. In general, editing the original file will give you the best quality picture. If you click **Yes**, go to step 4. If you click **No**, Family Tree Maker displays your picture for editing. Skip the remaining steps and begin editing now.

    Note: If the picture is either black and white, a Kodak Photo CD picture, stored with 1:1 compression, or was pasted into Family Tree Maker, you will not need to get the original file. Skip the remaining steps and begin editing now.

4. Family Tree Maker displays the Insert Picture dialog box. Select the name of your file.

5. Click **OK**.

    Family Tree Maker displays your picture in the Edit Picture dialog box. To rotate, flip, or crop the picture, continue reading on the next page.

Rotating a Picture

Sometimes when you scan a picture, newspaper clipping, or other paper memorabilia, the image turns out sideways or upside down.

To rotate a picture:

1. If the picture is not open, follow the instructions in "Preparing to Edit a Picture," on page 174.

2. Click one of the three following buttons:

    Rotate L — Use this button to rotate the picture ninety degrees to the left (counter-clockwise).

    Rotate R — Use this button to rotate the picture ninety degrees to the right (clockwise).

    180 — Use this button to rotate the picture 180 degrees.

3. If you are finished editing the picture, click **OK** to have Family Tree Maker place the newly-rotated picture into the Scrapbook.

    If you have previously placed this picture in other Scrapbooks, Family Tree Maker will ask if you want to change all copies of the picture. Click **No** if you only want to change the copy in the currently open Scrapbook.

Flipping Pictures

To flip a picture:

1. If the picture is not open, follow the instructions in "Preparing to Edit a Picture," on page 174.

2. You can flip the picture using two different buttons:

    Mirror — Use this button to flip the picture so that it is right to left instead of left to right.

    Flip — If the items in your picture are upside down instead of right side up, use this button to flip the picture.

3. If you are finished editing the picture, click **OK** to have Family Tree Maker place the newly-flipped picture into the Scrapbook.

   If you have previously placed this picture in other Scrapbooks, Family Tree Maker will ask if you want to change all copies of the picture. Click **No** if you only want to change the copy in the currently open Scrapbook.

Cropping Pictures

Cropping pictures allows you to perfect them for your Scrapbook. For example, you can remove empty background space so that the picture focuses on the people. Or, you can use a family photograph to make individual portraits of each family member.

To crop a picture:

1. If the picture is not open, follow the instructions in "Preparing to Edit a Picture," on page 174.

2. Move the cursor onto the image.

   The cursor becomes a cross-hair (large plus sign).

3. Position the cross-hair over the exact spot where you want the top left corner of the cropped picture to be.

   If you want to select a very small portion of the picture, click **Zoom In** to enlarge the picture on the screen. This will allow you to select the cropping area more accurately. If you want to select a large portion of the picture when your picture does not fit inside the Edit Picture dialog box, you can click **Zoom Out**.

4. Press and hold the mouse button while you drag diagonally to the exact spot where you want the lower right corner of the cropped picture to be, then release the mouse button.

   The area inside the box is what will remain after the picture is cropped. If you do not like the position of the box, simply repeat steps 2 and 3 to create a new box.

5. When you have a box around the area that you want to keep, click **Crop**.

    Family Tree Maker deletes the part of the picture that you chose to crop off, showing you what the cropped picture will look like. If you want to remove even more of the original picture, repeat steps 2, 3, and 4. If you feel that you have cropped too much of the picture, click **Cancel** to start again.

6. If you are finished editing the picture, click **OK**.

    Family Tree Maker permanently crops the picture and places the newly-cropped version in the Scrapbook.

    If you have previously placed this picture in other Scrapbooks, Family Tree Maker will ask if you want to change all copies of the picture. Click **No** if you only want to change the copy in the currently open Scrapbook.

Editing OLE Objects

Family Tree Maker does not control the editing of OLE objects. Instead, you edit the objects in the software program that originally created the object.

To edit an OLE object:

1. Select the Picture/Object, and then from the **Picture/Object** menu, select **Edit**.

    Microsoft Windows opens the software program in which the Object was originally created. If Family Tree Maker cannot find the correct software program, check to see that you have not deleted the software program or moved it to a new location.

2. Edit the Object as needed.

    Please refer to the manual for that software program for instructions.

3. From the **File** menu of that software program, select **Exit and Return to Family Tree Maker**.

    Note: If the program does not have a menu choice such as "Exit and Return" or "Update," refer to that program's manual for instructions.

    Microsoft Windows closes the program and returns you to Family Tree Maker. (Windows may also ask if you want to update or save your information; answer **Yes** or **OK**, unless you don't want to save your changes.) Family Tree Maker places the OLE object in the Scrapbook.

Controlling Picture/Object Brightness and Contrast

The Brightness and Contrast controls allow you to change the shading in the non-OLE pictures that you have placed in your Scrapbooks. If the color in an individual picture isn't quite right, you can change that picture's contrast. If all of your pictures tend to print too darkly, you can change the brightness for all of the pictures at once.

Changing the Contrast for a Single Picture/Object

To change the contrast setting for a single Picture/Object:

1. Select the Picture/Object whose contrast you want to change.

2. From the **Picture/Object** menu, select **Contrast**.

    Family Tree Maker displays the Contrast dialog box.

3. Click and drag the **Contrast** scroll box to change the contrast.

4. Click **OK**.

    Family Tree Maker returns you to the Scrapbook.

Changing the Brightness for All Picture/Objects in a View

When you change the brightness setting for all Picture/Objects at once, you are changing it for a specific view, not for all views. For example, if you are printing an Ancestor tree and you change the brightness setting while you're in the Ancestor Tree view, every Ancestor tree that you print afterwards will have the same brightness setting. However, Descendant trees would not have this brightness setting. If you wanted your Descendant trees to have the same brightness setting as your Ancestor trees, you would need to switch to the Descendant Tree view and change the brightness setting there, too.

To change the brightness setting for all Picture/Objects in a view:

1. Make sure you are in a view that can print Picture/Objects, such as the Scrapbook view or the Ancestor Tree view.

2. From the **File** menu select **Print Setup**.

    Family Tree Maker displays the Print Setup dialog box.

3. Click **Brightness**.

    Family Tree Maker displays the Brightness dialog box.

4. Click and drag the **Contrast** scroll box to change the contrast.

5. Click **OK**.

   Family Tree Maker returns you to the Print Setup dialog box.

6. Click **OK** to close the Print Setup dialog box.

Controlling Picture Resolution and Compression

Selecting the degree of compression for your color and grayscale pictures lets you control the tradeoff between the quality of your pictures and the amount of disk space they take up. Black and white pictures are always compressed because compression does not change their quality. You cannot change the compression of black and white pictures. You can also control the resolution of Kodak Photo CD pictures.

You can change the compression of a picture from several places:

- from the Insert Picture dialog box when you are placing a picture into a Scrapbook from a file.

- from the Insert from Photo CD dialog box when you are placing a new Photo CD Picture in the Scrapbook.

- from the Change Compression/Resolution dialog box whenever you are in the Scrapbook.

In addition, if you want to set a default compression or resolution for all pictures that you place in the Scrapbook in the future, see the topic "Selecting Defaults for Picture Resolution and Compression" on page 152.

To change compression or resolution:

1. Select the picture whose compression or resolution you want to change.

2. Open the Compression/Resolution dialog box. How you open this dialog box depends on your current location:

   If you are in the Import Picture dialog box, click **Compression**.

   If you are in the Import from Photo CD dialog box, click **Resolution**.

   If you are in a Scrapbook, from the **Picture/Object** menu, select **Compression/Resolution**. If Family Tree Maker displays a message telling you to get the original picture, click **OK**. Then, in the Insert Picture dialog box, click either **Compression** or **Resolution**.

3. You can now change the compression and/or resolution. Each of your options is described below.

    Degree of Compression — Select the option button corresponding to the degree of compression that you want for your picture. Higher ratios give you a greater loss in picture quality, but the pictures will take up less space on your hard disk. (Family Tree Maker uses the industry standard JPEG compression method.) Lower ratios give you pictures with less loss in quality, but will take up the most disk space. The "1:1" setting will not reduce the quality of your picture at all, but will take up the most space on your hard disk.

    In general, the "Recommended" setting is a good balance between quality loss and disk space. However, if you're importing a file that contains a lot of text, such as a scanned article or birth certificate, you may want to use a compression that's lower than the recommended level. It will make the text easier to read.

    Picture resolution — This option is only available for Kodak Photo CD pictures. Select the option button corresponding to the resolution that you want for your picture. "Resolution" refers to the size of your picture. A higher resolution will create a larger picture, and a larger picture will be sharper and more detailed. If a particular resolution is not available for the image you are currently working with, the option button will be grayed out.

    Choosing resolutions higher (larger) than the recommended "256 x 384" will use up large amounts of your hard disk space. In addition, you may not be able to load a picture at a very high resolution if your computer does not have a sufficient amount of RAM (memory). You only need to use high resolutions when you want to print large, very high-quality images on a high-quality printer or when you plan to crop a small part of the picture. See "Picture Size and Your Computer," page 413, for more information.

    Disk Space Needed — This shows the approximate amount of disk space needed to store the picture that you are currently working with. Each time you change one of the options in this dialog box, the numbers in the "Disk Space Needed" field will change. Note that this is an approximation; the actual size may vary slightly when the picture is actually compressed.

4. Click **OK** when you've made your selections.

    Family Tree Maker changes the compression and/or resolution of the picture and places it in the Scrapbook.

Moving or Copying Picture/Objects Between Scrapbooks

You can move or copy Picture/Objects within a Scrapbook and also from one Scrapbook to another, as long as the two Scrapbooks are in the same Family File. When you edit a Picture/Object that is in more than one Scrapbook, you can choose whether or not your edits affect all of the copies of the Picture/Object or just the copy in the Scrapbook that is currently open.

To move or copy a Picture/Object, start with the Scrapbook containing the Picture/Object you want to move or copy:

1. Select the Picture/Object that you want to move or copy.

2. From the **Edit** menu, select **Cut** to remove the Picture/Object from this location. Select **Copy** to copy the Picture/Object to another Scrapbook.

    Because the Picture/Object is now on the Clipboard, you can use the Paste command to insert the Picture/Object into any location in a Scrapbook.

    If you want to place the Picture/Object in a new location in the **same** Scrapbook, select the new location and then from the **Edit** menu, select **Paste**. You can skip the rest of these steps.

    If you want to place the Picture/Object in a **different** Scrapbook, continue with step 3.

3. Go to the Family Page containing the individual or the marriage whose Scrapbook you want to paste the Picture/Object into.

    Use the Index of Individuals or Find Individual to locate the individual's Family Page. The Index of Individuals is described on page 117. Find Individual is described on page 122.

4. On the Family Page, place the cursor either on the name of the individual or on the marriage whose Scrapbook you want to open.

5. From the **View** menu, select **Scrapbook**.

    Family Tree Maker displays the individual's or marriage's Scrapbook.

7. Select the area where you want to paste the Picture/Object.

8. From the **Edit** menu, select **Paste**.

    Family Tree Maker pastes the Picture/Object from the Clipboard into the Scrapbook and repositions any existing Picture/Objects if necessary.

Since the Clipboard is not erased until you use the Copy or Cut command again, you can paste the same Picture/Object or caption as many times as you like.

Removing Picture/Objects from a Scrapbook

You cannot delete a Picture/Object by selecting it and attempting to insert a new Picture/Object in its place. This will only move the Picture/Object that you wanted to delete to the right and create a space for the new Picture/Object.

To remove Picture/Objects from the Scrapbook:

1. Select the Picture/Object that you want to remove.

2. Press delete or ←BkSp to permanently remove the Picture/Object from the Scrapbook. Or, from the **Edit** menu, select **Cut** to cut the Picture/Object to the Clipboard.

    Family Tree Maker displays a confirmation dialog box. If you really want to delete the Picture/Object, click **Yes**. Otherwise, click **No**.

    Family Tree Maker removes the Picture/Object from the Scrapbook, as well as any More About information associated with it. The Picture/Objects remaining in the Scrapbook move to the left to fill up the empty space.

If you accidentally delete the wrong Picture/Object, from the **Edit** menu, select **Undo** immediately.

Chapter 6

FIXING RELATIONSHIP MISTAKES

Posing as a Greek goddess in 1906 is Grace Irene Porter, age sixteen.
Grace was an artist, whose career included painting gowns for the couturière
Madame Jeanette in the 1920's. Grace is the great grandaunt of
Kimberly Mullin, one of Banner Blue's technical writers.

FIXING RELATIONSHIP MISTAKES

From time to time you may find that you've accidentally married someone to the wrong individual or given someone the wrong parents. You may even discover that an individual doesn't belong in your Family File at all. The commands described in this section allow you to modify any relationships that you've created by mistake.

REMOVING AN INDIVIDUAL FROM YOUR FAMILY FILE

If you find that you've added an individual to your Family File by mistake, you can use the **Delete Individual** command to remove him or her. You can only delete one individual at a time using this command.

Note: If you've made a mistake entering a single piece of information, such as an incorrect date or location, you don't need to use Delete Individual; just type over the incorrect information. Do *not* type over an individual's *name* unless you are just changing the spelling. If you need to *move* an individual to a different Family Page, use the Attach and Detach commands described later in this chapter.

To delete an individual:

1. Go to the Family Page of the individual that you want to delete and place the cursor on the individual's name.

2. From the **People** menu, select **Delete Individual**.

    Family Tree Maker asks you to confirm the deletion.

Note: It's important to remember that the Delete Individual command severs all ties that the deleted individual created between any other individuals in your tree. This means that when you've deleted an individual, you may have to reconnect other individuals in your tree. For example, if you delete a single parent, you've disconnected all of that parent's children from the rest of their relatives. Since children are related to other family members only through the parental connection, you must re-attach children to a parent to re-establish their family ties. See "Linking Children to Their Parents" on page 188 for instructions.

The following four commands allow you to change relationships in your Family File without removing anyone permanently.

DETACHING A CHILD FROM THE WRONG PARENTS

If a child in your Family File appears with the wrong parents, you can use the **Detach Child** command to separate the child from those parents. If the individual you are detaching has children, those children will remain with the individual after he or she is detached. Only the relationship between the individual that you detach and his or her parents will be severed.

To detach a child from his or her parents:

1. Go to the Family Page containing the set of parents and the child that you want to detach from each other.

    Note: You must be on the Family Page where the individual is in the "Children" list. If you're on a page where the individual appears as a husband or wife, click the tab for the individual's parents. This tab is on the right side of your screen.

2. Place the cursor on the child you want to detach.

3. From the **People** menu, select **Fix Relationship Mistakes**.

4. From the **Fix Relationship Mistakes** submenu, select **Detach Child**.

    Family Tree Maker asks you to confirm the detachment.

    If the child has siblings, Family Tree Maker asks if the siblings should be detached as well. If you select "Yes," Family Tree Maker will detach all siblings from the parents at once and they will remain together as siblings. If you select "No," Family Tree Maker will only detach the selected individual.

To reattach this individual elsewhere in the tree, see "Linking Children to Their Parents," on page 188.

DETACHING INCORRECT SPOUSES FROM EACH OTHER

If Family Tree Maker shows two individuals as married when they actually never had this type of relationship, use the **Detach Spouse** command to separate them from each other. If these spouses have children listed on their Family Page, the children will remain with the spouse who is not being detached. Use the **Detach Child** command (described on page 186) if you also need to detach the children from the remaining spouse.

You do not need to use this command if a couple divorces. Instead, you can indicate a divorce in the More About Marriage dialog box for that couple. See "Entering Brief Marriage Facts" on page 145. In addition, if an individual remarries, you can create a new Family Page containing the new couple. See "Creating Additional Spouses" on page 110.

To detach someone from his or her spouse:

1. Go to the Family Page containing the individual you want to detach.

   Note: You must be on the Family Page where the individual appears as a husband or wife, not as a child. If you're on a page where the individual is in the "Children" list, click the tab with the individual's name on it. This tab is on the right side of your screen.

2. Place the cursor on the spouse you want to detach.

3. From the **People** menu, select **Fix Relationship Mistakes**.

4. From the **Fix Relationship Mistakes** submenu, select **Detach Spouse**.

   Family Tree Maker asks you to confirm the detachment.

If the individual you are detaching has children, the children will remain with the spouse who was not detached.

To reattach this individual elsewhere in the tree, see "Linking Individuals by Marriage" on page 189.

LINKING CHILDREN TO THEIR PARENTS

If an individual and his or her parents are in your Family File, but the individual does not appear on the parents' Family Page, use the **Attach Child** command. You only need to use this command when both the child and parents are already in your Family File. If one of them is not in the Family File, just type his or her name on the appropriate Family Page (see "Entering Family Information" on page 77 for more information).

To attach a child to his or her parents:

1. Go to the Family Page where you want the individual to appear as a child (the page that shows the child's parents as spouses).

2. From the **People** menu, select **Fix Relationship Mistakes**.

3. From the **Fix Relationship Mistakes** submenu, select **Attach Child**.

    Family Tree Maker displays a list of everyone in your Family File.

4. Click the name of the individual that you want to attach as a child.

    If you click the name of an "illegal" individual, Family Tree Maker displays an error message and asks you to select another individual. An "illegal" individual is someone that, for logical reasons, could not possibly be the child of the individual. For example, you could not attach an individual's mother as the individual's child.

5. Click **OK**.

6. If the child has siblings, Family Tree Maker asks whether you want to associate those siblings with the new set of parents. Click either **Yes** or **No**.

    If you choose "Yes," Family Tree Maker attaches any siblings that have the same preferred parents (see page 116).

7. If the child already has another set of parents, Family Tree Maker displays the Set Relationship dialog box. Click the drop-down list next to each parent's name and select the word that describes the relationship between the parent and the child.

    Family Tree Maker gives the siblings that you are also attaching the same relationship to the new parent(s), unless the siblings would then have too many natural parents. In this case Family Tree Maker gives them a step-relationship. If the children actually have different relationships, you can go to each child's Lineage dialog box (see page 134) and choose the correct relationship.

8. Click **OK** after making your selections.

   Family Tree Maker displays the Family Page.

LINKING INDIVIDUALS BY MARRIAGE

If two individuals are in your Family File, but aren't listed on a Family Page as husband and wife, use **Attach Spouse** to join them. You only need to use this command if both spouses are already in your Family File, but are not married to each other. If only one of the individuals is already in your Family File, just enter the other spouse's name on that individual's Family Page (see "Entering Family Information" on page 77 for more information).

Note: Before you can attach a spouse, you must have an opening for him or her on the Family Page. If two spouses are already on the Family Page, you will need to create a spot for the new one that you're attaching. See "Creating Additional Spouses" on page 110.

To attach two individuals as spouses:

1. Go to the Family Page where one of the individuals appears in the "Husband" or "Wife" field.

   Note: You must be on the Family Page where the individual to whom you want to attach a spouse appears as a husband or wife, not as a child. If you're on a page where the individual is shown in the "Children" list, click the tab for that individual's Family Page. The tab is on the right side of your screen.

   In order to ensure that the children from this marriage will appear on the same Family Page as their parents, make sure that you are on the Family Page where the children and one of the parents appear. That way, Family Tree Maker knows to keep the children with the marriage you are creating.

2. From the **People** menu, select **Fix Relationship Mistakes**.

3. From the **Fix Relationship Mistakes** submenu, select **Attach spouse**.

   Family Tree Maker displays a list of everyone in your Family File.

4. Click the name of the individual that you want to attach as a spouse.

   If you click the name of an "illegal" individual, Family Tree Maker displays an error message and asks you to select another individual. An "illegal" individual is someone that, for logical reasons, could not possibly be the spouse of the individual. For example, you can't attach someone as a spouse if doing so would make them their own parent.

5. Click **OK**.

   Family Tree Maker asks you to confirm your selection.

Chapter 7

SEARCHING ARCHIVES AT HOME

*With visions of sugarplums dancing in their heads...Cathi (Skyles) Fineran, age 4,
and her brother Bill Skyles, age 3, sit on Santa's lap in 1963. Cathi is currently
a Project Manager at Banner Blue Software.*

SEARCHING ARCHIVES AT HOME

Family Tree Maker's specialties have always been organizing family information and creating family trees. Now, however, Family Tree Maker can also help you with your family research!

How Can Family Tree Maker Help with Family Research?

If you have a CD-ROM drive, you can use the FamilyFinder view to read **Family Archives** and the **FamilyFinder Index**. Family Archives are CDs containing information from a variety of records, such as census records, marriage records, Social Security death benefits records, and linked pedigrees. You can think of a Family Archive as a book with pages that you can turn to find family information. The FamilyFinder Index is the index to all of the Family Archives. It helps you find the right page in the Family Archive books.

If you own the Deluxe Edition of Family Tree Maker, you already have the FamilyFinder Index — it came on the same CD as your Family Tree Maker program. You can purchase Family Archives and the FamilyFinder Index from Brøderbund, and you can also find them in selected libraries.

How Do the Family Archives and FamilyFinder Index Work?

The FamilyFinder view is equipped with a special tool called the **Search Expert**. The Search Expert can help you locate the names of your ancestors in the FamilyFinder Index and Family Archives. When the Search Expert finds a matching name in the FamilyFinder Index, it tells you which Family Archive contains more information about the name. Reading the information in that Family Archive will help you determine if you've actually found your ancestor, or just someone with a similar name. When you do find one of your ancestors, you can add information from the Family Archive directly to your Family File.

Often, the information in the Family Archive is so complete that you won't need to go to the actual record (marriage, census, etc.) that the information in the Family Archive came from. However, if you do want to see the actual record, the Family Archive can help you find it. For example, if you are looking for a census record, the Family Archive will tell you on which microfilm roll the record is located. Then, you can go directly to a library or National Archives branch and ask for the correct roll.

What Can I Do with Information from Family Archives?

The information in Family Archives can help you find small facts that are missing from your family tree, or even add entire branches to it. In most cases, you can copy information from the Family Archive directly into your Family File. There are four different types of Family Archives:

- **Data** Family Archives consist of information from marriage records, death records, and much more. You can copy this information directly into your Family File.

- **World Family Tree** Archives are a special set of Family Archives. They contain family trees that were submitted to the World Family Tree Project by Family Tree Maker customers just like yourself (see page 362). When you find a link between your Family File and one of these family trees, you can append the family tree to your Family File. World Family Tree Archives work slightly differently than the other Family Archives, so you'll see separate sets of instructions for them throughout this chapter.

- **Image** Family Archives contain scanned images of records, such as military records. You can read these images to get family information, and copy the images to the Clipboard or into Family Tree Maker Scrapbooks.

- **Text** Family Archives contain paragraphs of information from books, such as genealogies. You can scroll through the pages in this Family Archive to look for more family information.

Why Use Family Archives and the FamilyFinder Index?

As many family historians can tell you, genealogy is a time-consuming pursuit. You can spend quite a bit of time making trips to the library, hunting down the right indexes, and searching through indexes before you even find out if a record containing the right information exists. The FamilyFinder Index and Family Archives let you bypass the library trips and searching. Instead, you use your computer to find the records, to learn what information those records contain, and to find out where the actual record is. In addition, you can copy information from Family Archives directly to your Family File. This not only saves you data-entry time, but eliminates the chance of making transcription errors.

OPENING FAMILY ARCHIVES AND THE FAMILYFINDER INDEX

To open the FamilyFinder Index or a Family Archive:

1. Insert the CD in your computer's CD-ROM drive.

2. From the **View** menu, select **FamilyFinder**.

   Family Tree Maker displays the Introduction page of the FamilyFinder Index or Family Archive. If this is the first time that you've opened a particular Family Archive, you will see a license agreement. Please read it carefully.

Moving Around in Family Archives and the FamilyFinder Index

Both the Family Archives and the FamilyFinder Index have labeled tabs along the right side of the screen. You can click these tabs to turn to the Introduction, Contents, Index, and Information pages. You always know what page you are on, because each page has an identifying title up at the top, such as "FamilyFinder Index — Master Table of Contents."

Where to Go from Here

Once you have opened the FamilyFinder Index or a Family Archive, you can search it for information, print and copy information, add information directly to your Family File, and more, depending on which Family Archive you're in.

If you would first like a brief introduction to each type of page in the FamilyFinder Index and Family Archives, continue reading the next few sections. They describe how to use the Introduction, Contents, Index, and Information pages.

If you would like to jump right in and begin searching with the Search Expert, go right ahead! Instructions for searching in the FamilyFinder Index begin on page 203, instructions for searching in Family Archives begin on page 208, and instructions for searching in World Family Tree Archives begin on page 214.

ALL ABOUT INTRODUCTION PAGES

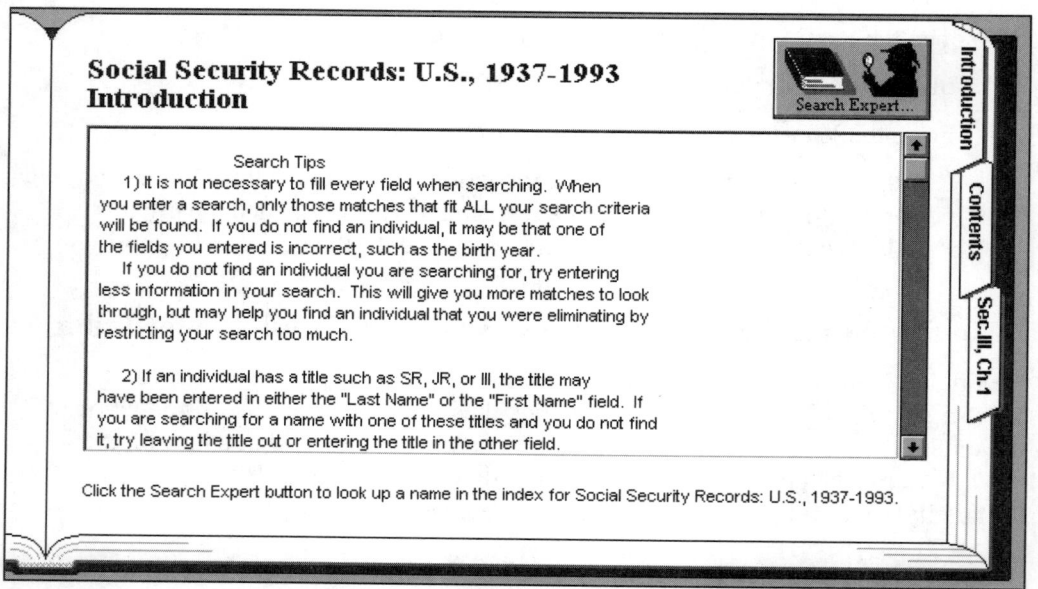

Figure 7-1. A sample Introduction page

Introduction pages give you general information about the contents of Family Archives and the FamilyFinder Index. They also provide you with important information about searching in different types of records. Understanding this information can help you research your family more effectively.

ALL ABOUT CONTENTS PAGES

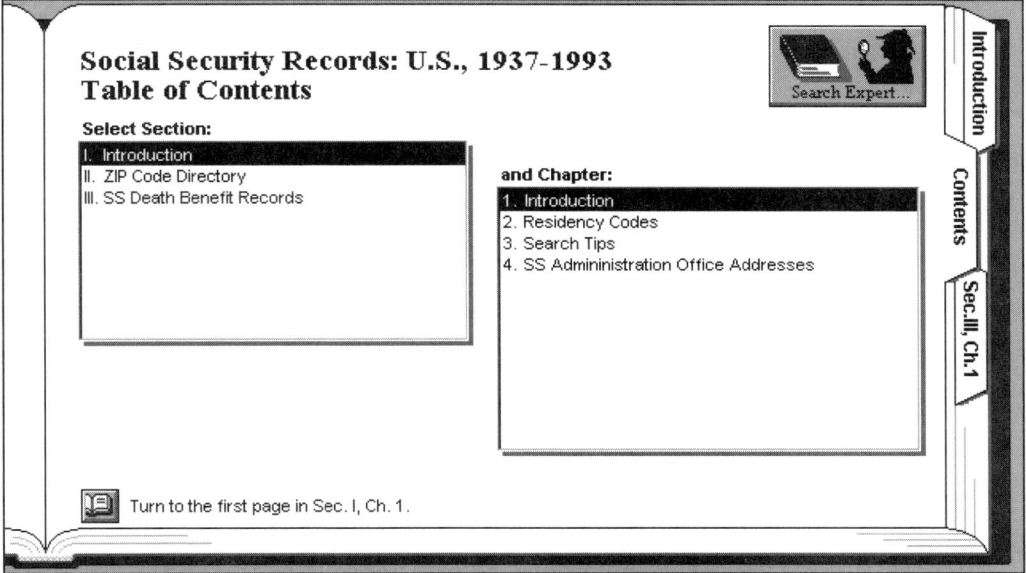

Figure 7-2. A sample Contents page

The Contents pages of most Family Archives are similar to the contents pages of a book: they tell you how the information is divided into sections and chapters. For example, in some Family Archives, each section contains information from a state, and each chapter contains information from a county in that state. The FamilyFinder Index Contents page lists all of the Family Archives.

You can use the Contents page to go to information that interests you:

- In the FamilyFinder index, for details about the information in the currently selected Family Archive click **Find out**. To view the information in a Family Archive that you own, select the Family Archive's title and click **Open**. The titles of the Family Archives that you own will have CD icons to the left of them.

- In Family Archives, select the section and chapter that you want to see and click **Turn to**.

ALL ABOUT INDEX PAGES

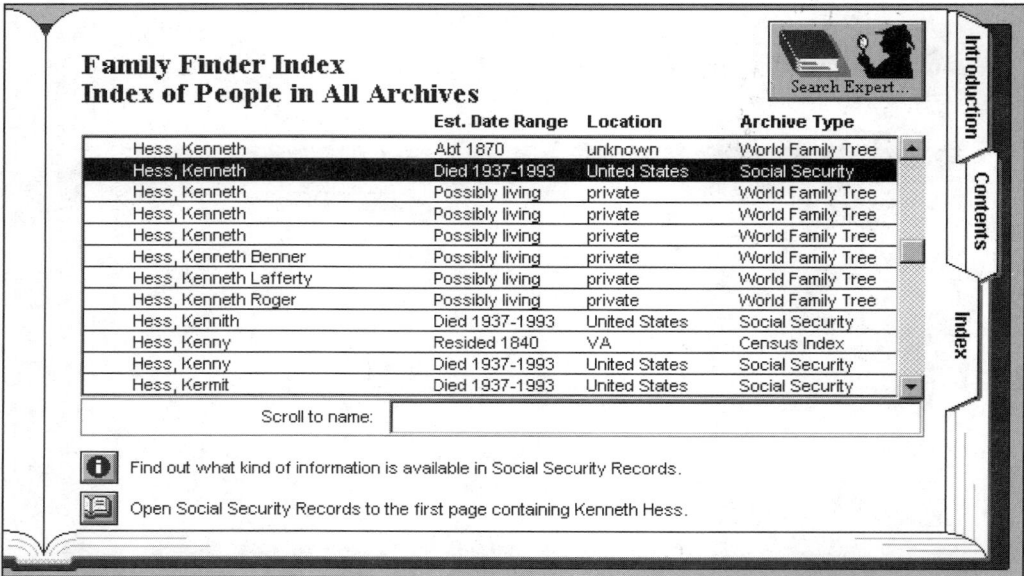

Figure 7-3. A sample Index page

Index pages provide you with more detailed information than Contents pages: they list the names of the individuals in the Family Archives. The Index page in the FamilyFinder Index lists all names from all Family Archives (approximately 115 million). The Index page of a Family Archive shows the name of every individual in that particular Family Archive.

You can use the Index page to go to information that interests you:

- When you're in the FamilyFinder Index, for details about the information in the currently selected Family Archive click **Find out**. To view the information in a Family Archive that you own, select the Family Archive's title and click **Open**. The titles of the Family Archives that you own will have CD icons to the left of them.

- In Family Archives, select a name and click **Turn to**. When you are in a World Family Tree Archive, you will see a number listed to the right of each name. This is the number of the pedigree in which you can find that name.

Also listed are the individual's birth date and the state, country, or geographic area of their birth, death, or marriage, if available.

To casually browse through an index, you can use the scroll bar, the arrow keys on your keyboard, or the "Scroll to name" field (see "Scrolling Through an Index," below.) When you want to do a complete search for a name, be sure to use the Search Expert. See "Locating Names with the Search Expert" on page 202.

Scrolling Through an Index

The "Scroll to name" field is for jumping from one section of the index to another when you are browsing through the names. Do not use it to do a thorough search for a name. Instead, when you want to do a thorough search, use the Search Expert. See "Locating Names with the Search Expert" on page 202.

To scroll to a name in an index:

1. Click in the **Scroll to name** field.

2. Start typing the last name of the individual that you want to scroll to.

   With each character you type, you will get closer to the name you are looking for. You can type part or all of the name, as long as it is in the following format: Last name, First name Middle name.

ALL ABOUT FAMILY ARCHIVE INFORMATION PAGES

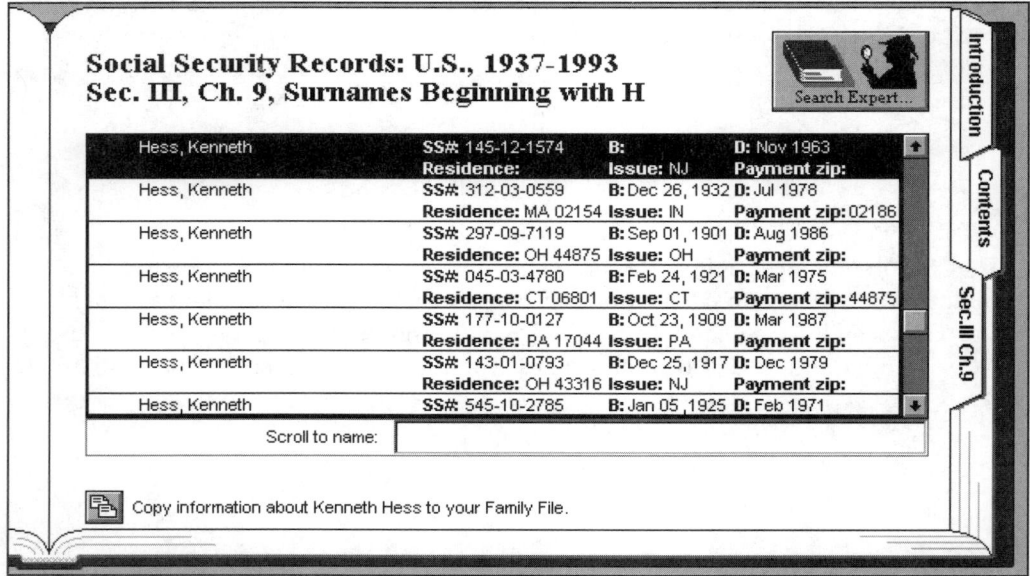

Figure 7-4. A sample Information page

The Information pages are the most interesting part of the Family Archives because they contain actual genealogical information. In addition, they can tell you where to go to find the record that the information in the Family Archive was taken from. Information pages come in four different varieties:

- First, there are **record** Information pages. They contain records about individuals or marriages. You can copy the information in these records directly to your Family File. When a field contains too much information to fit in the allotted space, Family Tree Maker places an ellipsis button (**...**) to the right of it. Click the button to see the rest of the information.

- Second, there are **text** Information pages. They contain free-form text that you can select and copy to the Notes pages in your Family File.

- Third, there are **image** Information pages. These are images of records and book pages, as though someone took pictures of them. You can print the images, or copy them to the Clipboard or to Scrapbooks in your Family File.

- Finally, there are **World Family Tree** Information pages. These contain family trees that were submitted to the World Family Tree Project by Family Tree Maker customers just like yourself (see page 362). You can view and print them on Family Pages or in trees, reports, Family Group Sheets, and more. When you find a connection to your family, you can append these family trees directly to your Family File.

Scrolling Through the Information Pages

When you want to browse through the information in a Family Archive, you can use the scroll bars, the "Scroll to name" field, or the "Go To Page" command. Instructions for the "Scroll to name" field and the "Go To Page" command are below. Please note that the "Scroll to name" field is only available when the information in the Family Archive is organized alphabetically. The "Go To Page" command is only available for Text and Image Family Archives. When you want to do a thorough search for a name, see "Locating Names with the Search Expert" on the next page.

To scroll with the "Scroll to name" field:

1. Click in the **Scroll to name** field.

2. Start typing the last name of the individual that you want to find.

   With each character you type, you will get closer to the name you are looking for. You can type part or all of the name, as long as it is in the following format: Last name, First name Middle name.

To use the "Go To Page" command:

1. From the **Edit** menu, select **Go To Page**.

   Family Tree Maker displays the Go To dialog box.

2. Type in the page you want to see.

3. Click **OK**.

   Family Tree Maker displays the page you requested.

LOCATING NAMES WITH THE SEARCH EXPERT

When you want to find a name in the FamilyFinder Index or in a Family Archive, it's best to let the Search Expert do the work. Not only can the Search Expert locate matches more quickly, but in some cases it can use information from your Family File to find more and better matches. For more control over what the Search Expert looks for, see "Preferences for Searching," below.

When you are ready to search, there are three sets of instructions: one for searching in the FamilyFinder Index (see page 203), one for searching in Family Archives (see page 208), and one for searching in World Family Tree Archives (see page 214).

Preferences for Searching

You can choose whether or not the Search Expert uses **Soundex codes** to find possible matches. Soundex coding is a system that gives a unique code to all names that sound the same, even when they are spelled differently, such as "Smith" and "Smithe." Using Soundex codes can help you find records that you may otherwise not know to look for. Please note that Soundex searching may not be available in all Family Archives.

To choose preferences for searching:

1. From the **Prefs** menu, select **FamilyFinder**.

   Family Tree Maker displays the FamilyFinder dialog box.

2. If you want the Search Expert to use Soundex codes while searching, select the **Similar last names using Soundex** check box. Otherwise, deselect it.

3. Click **OK**.

   Family Tree Maker returns you to the FamilyFinder view.

Searching in the FamilyFinder Index

You can begin a search from any page in the FamilyFinder Index:

1. Click **Search Expert**.

   Family Tree Maker displays the Search Expert dialog box.

2. To find matches for someone who is in your Family File, click **Search for Someone from your Family File**. When you select this option, Family Tree Maker will use the information in your Family File, such as birth dates, death dates, married names, maiden names, and nicknames to help find matches for the individual that you choose in step 3. To find matches for any other name, click **Search for Someone NOT from your Family File**.

3. Now you must tell Family Tree Maker what to search for.

   If you chose "Search for Someone from your Family File," Family Tree Maker displays a list of the individuals from your Family File. Select a name from the list.

   If you chose "Search for Someone NOT from your Family File," Family Tree Maker displays a dialog box containing a "Name" field. Type a name in any of the formats shown in Figure 7-5 on page 204.

4. Click **Start search**.

   If there are no matches, FamilyFinder displays a message telling you this. You may want to read "What if I Can't Find My Ancestor's Name?" on page 218. Otherwise, Family Tree Maker places a magnifying glass to the left of the matches. The best match will also be highlighted.

What can you do with these matches? Your options are listed below.

- Click **Next** to move forward and click **Previous** to move backwards through the matches. **First** will take you to the very first match, and **Final** will take you to the last match.

- Select and deselect index entries so you can print a list of them or copy a list to the Clipboard. These lists can be handy when you order or use Family Archives. See "Selecting and Deselecting Index Entries for Printing and Copying" on page 205.

- Find out what type of information is available in a Family Archive that contains a match. See "Getting More Information About a Match" on page 206.

- If you own a Family Archive containing a match, you can open it and view the information associated with the match. See "Opening Family Archives from Within the FamilyFinder Index" on page 207.

- If you do not own a Family Archive containing a particular match, you can get purchasing information by highlighting the match and clicking **How to order**.

You can also use the scroll bars and the "Scroll to name" field to move through the FamilyFinder Index and look at names other than the matches, if you like. The current matches will remain marked until you begin another search, leave the FamilyFinder view, or choose the **Clear Search** command from the **Edit** menu.

If you type this...	You find this...
Last	Entries only containing the surname
First Last *or* Last, First	Entries containing the first name and surname
, First	Entries only containing the first name
, First Middle	Entries only containing the first name and middle name
Last, First Middle *or* First Middle Last	Entries containing the first name, middle name, and surname

Figure 7-5. Name formats for the Name field

Selecting and Deselecting Index Entries for Printing and Copying

When you see index entries that interest you, you can place check marks next to them to select them for printing or copying. The table below describes how to select index entries.

To do this...	Do this...
Select a single entry	Highlight the entry and press the spacebar, or from the **Edit** menu, choose **Select Entry**
Deselect a single entry	Highlight the entry and press the spacebar, or from the **Edit** menu, choose **Deselect Entry**
Select all matching entries	From the **Edit** menu, choose **Select All Matching Entries**
Deselect all matching entries	From the **Edit** menu, choose **Deselect All Matching Entries**

Figure 7-6. Selecting and deselecting index entries

Once you have made your selections, you can either print the entries in a list or copy the list to the Clipboard. The list that you create will include the individual's name, as well as the information listed to the right of the name, such as the Family Archive number and date range. Instructions for printing and copying begin on the next page.

Printing Selected Entries

To print selected entries:

1. Turn on your printer.

2. From the **File** menu, select **Print Selected Entries**.

   Family Tree Maker first reminds you how to change the text formatting; click **OK** to clear the message. (For instructions on changing the text formatting, see "Formatting Text" on page 308.) Family Tree Maker then displays the Print dialog box where you can select printing options. See "Printing Your Document" on page 319 if you need instructions.

3. Click **OK** when you've selected your printing options.

   Family Tree Maker prints the list.

Copying Selected Entries to the Clipboard

To copy selected entries to the Clipboard:

1. From the **Edit** menu, choose **Copy Selected Entries**.

   Family Tree Maker places a list of the names on the Clipboard.

2. You can now use the Paste command to insert the contents of the Clipboard wherever you like. In most cases, you probably want to open a Windows word processor or spreadsheet and paste them in there.

   If you need help with another Windows program, please refer to that program's manual.

Getting More Information About a Match

To find out what information a Family Archive contains about a match, highlight the match and click **Find out**. Family Tree Maker displays the More About dialog box. It summarizes what type of information is available in the Family Archive. For more details about the Family Archive, click **Archive info**. For purchasing information, click **To order**.

Opening Family Archives from Within the FamilyFinder Index

When you are searching in the FamilyFinder Index and you open a Family Archive containing matches, Family Tree Maker automatically places a magnifying glass next to each match. This way, you don't have to re-specify the search that you began in the FamilyFinder Index.

To open a Family Archive from within the FamilyFinder Index:

1. Highlight a matching name and click **Open**.

2. Insert the correct Family Archive into your CD-ROM drive when Family Tree Maker asks you to do so.

3. Family Tree Maker opens the Family Archive and displays the Information page containing the first match.

What can you do with these matches? Your options are listed below.

- Click **Next** to move forward and click **Previous** to move backwards through the matches. **First** will take you to the very first match, and **Final** will take you to the last match.

- Copy matching information directly to a Family File, either merging it with an existing individual's information or creating a new individual. See "Copying Information from Family Archives to Your Family File" on page 210.

- From image Information pages, copy images to the Clipboard or select them for printing. See "Copying Images" on page 212 or "Printing Images" on page 213.

Searching in Family Archives

To search in a Data or Image Family Archive, begin with step 1 below. If you want to search in a World Family Tree Archive, it's better to use the instructions in "Searching in World Family Tree Archives" on page 214.

You can begin a search from any page in a Family Archive:

1. Click **Search Expert**.

   Family Tree Maker displays the Search Expert dialog box.

2. If you want to find matches for someone who is in your Family File, click **Search for Someone from your Family File**. When you select this option, Family Tree Maker will use the information in your Family File, such as birth dates, death dates, married names, maiden names, and nicknames to help find matches for the individual that you choose in step 3. If you want to find matches for a name that is *not* in your Family File, click **Search for Someone NOT from your Family File**.

   If you decide that instead of searching only this Family Archive, you want to search all Family Archives simultaneously, click **Search all archives**. Family Tree Maker will ask you to insert the FamilyFinder Index and will then display the FamilyFinder Index Search Expert. Continue with step 2 on page 203.

3. Now you must tell Family Tree Maker what to search for. There are two options, as described below.

   If you chose "Search for Someone from your Family File," Family Tree Maker displays a list of the individuals from your Family File. Select a name from the list.

   If you chose "Search for Someone NOT from your Family File," Family Tree Maker displays a dialog box containing a "Name" field. Type a name in any of the formats shown in Figure 7-5 on page 204.

4. Click **Start search**.

   If there are no matches, FamilyFinder displays a message telling you this. You may want to read "What if I Can't Find My Ancestor's Name?" on page 218. Otherwise, Family Tree Maker displays the first Information page containing a match. If the Family Archive contains images, there will be a magnifying glass next to the page number below the image.

If the information in the Family Archive is in records, there will be a magnifying glass to the left of each match. When a field in a record contains too much information to fit in the allotted space, Family Tree Maker places an ellipsis button (...) to the right of it. Click the button to see the remaining information.

What can you do with these matches? Your options are listed below.

- Click **Next** to move forward and click **Previous** to move backwards through the matches. **First** will take you to the very first match, and **Final** will take you to the last match.

- From record Information pages, copy matching information directly to a Family File, either merging it with an existing individual's information or creating a new individual. See "Copying Information from Family Archives to Your Family File" on page 210.

- On image Information pages, view the image at different sizes. See "Changing the Size of an Image" on page 212.

- From image Information pages, copy images to the Clipboard or select them for printing. See "Copying Images" on page 212 or "Printing Images" on page 213.

You can also use the scroll bars and the "Scroll to name" field to move through the Family Archive and look at names other than the matches, if you like. The current matches will remain marked until you begin another search, leave the FamilyFinder view, or choose the **Clear Search** command from the **Edit** menu.

Copying Information from Family Archives to Your Family File

Copying information directly from a Family Archive into a Family File is much faster than copying it by hand. In addition, you avoid the possibility of making transcription errors. The instructions for copying information differ, depending on what it is that you are copying:

- If you are copying individual records or marriage records, use the instructions in "Copying Individual and Marriage Records," below.

- If you are copying images, see "Copying Images" on page 212.

Copying Individual and Marriage Records

Before you begin with the steps below, be sure that you have the correct Family File open.

To copy information to a Family File:

1. Select the record that you want to copy by clicking it.

    Family Tree Maker highlights the record.

2. Click **Copy information**.

    Family Tree Maker displays the Copy Information to Family File dialog box.

3. If you want to merge the information with an existing individual's or marriage's information, click **Copy to Someone (a Marriage) in your Family File**. Family Tree Maker displays the Index of Individuals, continue with "Merging Information," below. If you want to create a new individual or marriage, click **Copy to Someone (a Marriage) NOT in your Family File** and continue with "Adding New Information," on the next page.

Merging Information

4. Highlight the individual or marriage you want to merge the information into and then click **OK**.

    Family Tree Maker displays the Fields to Include dialog box. To use this dialog box, you can generally follow the instructions in steps 1 through 6 under "Mapping Information Between the Source and Destination Files" on page 381. The main difference is that the list on the left is labeled **Fields to import** and the list on the right is labeled **Fields in Family Tree Maker**.

5. Click **OK** in the Fields to Include dialog box after making your selections.

   Family Tree Maker adds the information to appropriate fields in your Family File. Some of the fields that Family Tree Maker fills with information may have sources (see page 101). When this is the case, Family Tree Maker adds a description of the Family Archive on which you found the information to the corresponding Source field.

6. If some of the fields already contain information, Family Tree Maker lets you choose which information to keep in your Family File. Click **OK** after making your selections.

   Family Tree Maker returns you to the Family Archive's Information page.

Adding New Information

4. Family Tree Maker tells you that it is adding a new individual or marriage to your Family File. If this is what you want to do, click **Copy information**.

   Family Tree Maker displays the Choose Sex dialog box.

5. Select the option button corresponding to the sex of the individual listed in the dialog box and then click **OK**.

   Family Tree Maker displays the Fields to Include dialog box. To use this dialog box, you can generally follow the instructions in steps 1 through 6 under "Mapping Information Between the Source and Destination Files" on page 381. The main difference is that the list of the left is labeled **Fields to import** and the list on the right is labeled **Fields in Family Tree Maker**.

6. Click **OK** in the Items to Include dialog box after making your selections.

   Family Tree Maker adds the individual or marriage to your Family File and returns you to the Family Archive's Information page. The individual(s) you created will not be linked to anyone else in your Family File. You will need to use one of the Attach commands to create links with other individuals. See "Linking Children to Their Parents" on page 188 or "Linking Individuals by Marriage" on page 189.

   Some of the fields that Family Tree Maker fills with information may have sources (see page 101). When this is the case, Family Tree Maker adds a description of the Family Archive on which you found the information to the corresponding Source field.

Changing the Size of an Image

There are two ways to change the size of an image:

- You can make the text in the image larger or smaller by clicking **Zoom In** or **Zoom Out**. Please note, however, that these buttons only affect the size of the image on the screen and will not change the size of the printed image.

- You can increase the size of the viewing area and see more of the image at once by clicking **View**. Family Tree Maker will display the image in the View dialog box. You can move from image to image by clicking the **PrevPg** and **NextPg** buttons, and you can use **Zoom In** and **Zoom Out** to change the size of the text in the image. However, most menu commands and toolbar buttons are unavailable while you are in the View dialog box. To close the View dialog box and return to the Image page, click **Cancel**.

Copying Images

To copy an image to the Clipboard or Scrapbook:

1. Display the image that you want to copy.

2. Click either **Copy this image to your Family File** or **Copy this image to the Clipboard**.

   If you are copying the image to the Clipboard, you can now paste the image wherever you want; skip the remaining steps. If you are copying the image to a Scrapbook, Family Tree Maker displays the Copy Image to Family File dialog box; continue with step 3.

3. Select the individual whose Scrapbook you want to add the image to.

4. Click **Add image to Scrapbook page**.

   Family Tree Maker adds the image to the individual's Scrapbook. In addition, Family Tree Maker adds a sentence of source information to the "Description" field in the image's More About dialog box (see "Recording Important Picture/Object Information" on page 164). This sentence gives information about the Family Archive from which you copied the text.

Printing Images

To print an image:

1. Display the image that you want to print.

2. From the **Edit** menu, choose **Select Image for Printing**.

   Family Tree Maker places a printer icon in the upper-left corner of the dialog box.

Figure 7-7. A printer icon

3. Repeat step 2 for any additional images that you want to print.

4. When you have selected all of the images you want to print, from the **File** menu, choose **Print Selected Images**.

   Family Tree Maker asks you to confirm that you want to print all of the images you have selected.

5. Click **Yes** to print them.

   Each image is printed on a separate page. At the bottom of each page, Family Tree Maker prints source information about the Family Archive from which you copied the image.

Searching in World Family Tree Archives

You can begin a search from either the Index or Introduction page of a World Family Tree Archive:

1. Click **Search Expert**.

   Family Tree Maker displays the Search Expert dialog box.

2. If you want to find matches for someone who is in your Family File, click **Search for Someone from your Family File**. When you select this option, Family Tree Maker will use the information in your Family File, such as birth dates, death dates, married names, maiden names, and nicknames to help find matches for the individual that you choose. If you want to find matches for a name that is *not* in your Family File, click **Search for Someone NOT from your Family File**.

   If you decide that instead of searching only this Family Archive, you want to search all Family Archives simultaneously, click **Search all archives**. Family Tree Maker will ask you to insert the FamilyFinder Index and will then display the FamilyFinder Index Search Expert. Continue with step 2 on page 203.

3. Now you must tell Family Tree Maker what to search for. There are two options, as described below.

   If you chose "Search for Someone from your Family File," Family Tree Maker displays a list of the individuals from your Family File. Select a name from the list.

   If you chose "Search for Someone NOT from your Family File," Family Tree Maker displays a dialog box containing a "Name" field. Type a name in any of the formats shown in Figure 7-5 on page 204.

4. Click **Start search**.

   If there are no matches, FamilyFinder displays a message telling you this. You may want to read "What if I Can't Find My Ancestor's Name?" on page 218. Otherwise, Family Tree Maker places a magnifying glass to the left of the matches. The best match will also be highlighted.

What can you do with these matches? Your options are listed below.

- Click **Next** to move forward and click **Previous** to move backwards through the matches. **First** will take you to the very first match, and **Final** will take you to the last match.

- Select and deselect matching index entries so that you can print a list of them or copy a list to the Clipboard. See "Selecting and Deselecting Matches" on page 205.

- Find out what type of information the World Family Tree pedigree contains about a matching name. See "Getting More Info About a Name from the World Family Tree" on page 215.

- Go to the family tree containing the information associated with a match. Once the pedigree is open you can look through it and print it. You can also add the information to your Family File if you believe that it is part of your family. See "Turning to a World Family Tree Pedigree" on page 216 and "Merging a World Family Tree Pedigree with a Family File" on page 217.

You can also use the scroll bars and the "Scroll to name" field to move through the Index page of the World Family Archive and look at names other than the matches, if you like. The current matches will remain marked until you begin another search, leave the FamilyFinder view, or choose the **Clear Search** command from the **Edit** menu.

Getting More Info About a Name from the World Family Tree

To find out what type of information the World Family Tree contains about a name, highlight the name on the Index page and click **Find out**. Family Tree Maker displays the More About dialog box. It summarizes what type of information is available in the World Family Tree pedigree.

Turning to a World Family Tree Pedigree

To view a pedigree that's in a World Family Tree Archive, click **Turn to** from the Index page. Family Tree Maker goes into a special **World Family Tree mode** that allows you to look at the pedigree just as if you were looking at your own Family File — on Family Pages, in trees, and in reports.

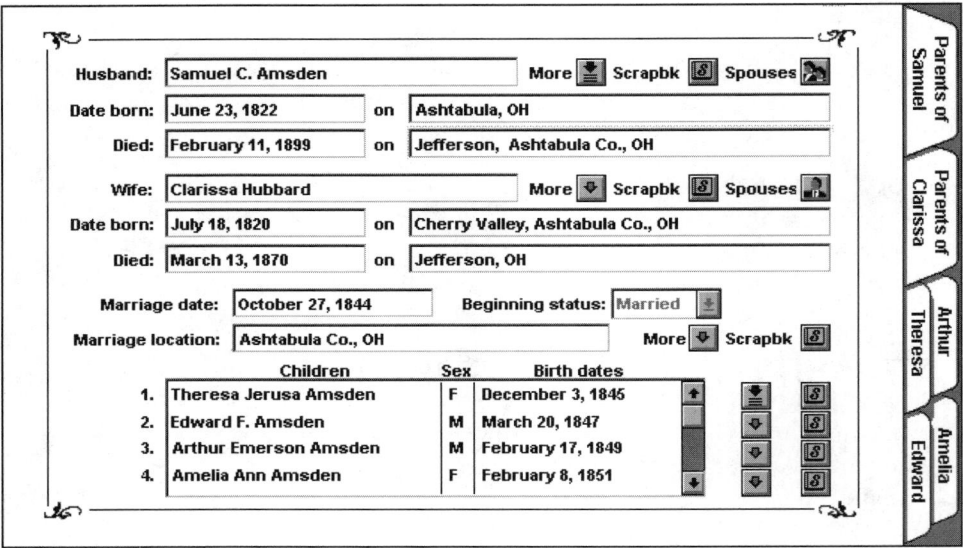

Figure 7-8. Family Tree Maker in World Family Tree mode

When you open a pedigree, Family Tree Maker displays a Family Page from the pedigree. As shown in Figure 7-8 above, the Family Page in World Family Tree mode looks very similar to a regular Family Page. The main difference is that it has a different background color than the regular Family Pages. In addition, the title bar at the very top of your screen will say, for example, "WFT Pedigree #323" instead of listing the name of your Family File.

To look at the information in a World Family Tree Pedigree, you can click the tabs along the right side of the screen to move between Family Pages. In addition, to look at reports and different types of trees, click the toolbar buttons or use the commands on the **View** menu, just as you would with your own

Family File. Once you're in a tree, for example, you can control the formatting options, such as which individuals and information appear in the tree.

If you find it easier to look at information on paper, you can print trees, reports, and other documents, just as with your own Family File. Simply go to the view that you want to print and use the commands on the **Contents** and **Format** menus to set up the document as you want it. Then, use the **Print** command on the **File** menu to print it. If you need information about any of the formatting options, see page 239 for help with trees or page 278 for help with reports.

Please note that you cannot edit the information in a World Family Tree pedigree. While you are in World Family Tree mode, the editing commands on the pull-down menus have been removed, and you can't change the information in fields. If you find a link to your family and you merge the pedigree with your Family File, you can edit the information after it is in your Family File.

Merging a World Family Tree Pedigree with a Family File

If you decide that a World Family Tree pedigree has a link to your family, you can merge the pedigree with your Family File. If you have more than one Family File, be sure to open the correct one before you start merging. When you are ready to merge a World Family Tree pedigree into a Family File, from the **People** menu, select **Merge Pedigree**.

Family Tree Maker displays the Individuals to Include dialog box. In this dialog box you can select individuals from the source file (the World Family Tree pedigree) to merge into the destination file (your Family File). Continue with "Selecting Individuals to Include" on page 380.

Exiting World Family Tree Mode

If you click the **FamilyFinder** toolbar button or choose **FamilyFinder** from the view menu, Family Tree Maker asks if you would like to merge the World Family Tree pedigree with your own Family File. If you do, click **Yes** and continue with the paragraph directly above this one. If not, Family Tree Maker closes the World Family Tree Pedigree and returns you to the Index page in the Family Archive.

WHAT IF I CAN'T FIND MY ANCESTOR'S NAME?

It is possible that the name you are looking for will not be found in the FamilyFinder Index. If this occurs, don't despair! There are two things you should realize before giving up:

First, it may be that the individual whose record you want to locate really is listed in the FamilyFinder Index, but their name has been disguised by errors or a name change. Because the FamilyFinder Index is composed from many different sources, including hand-written census records more than a century old, there are spelling errors, misinterpretations of names, transpositions of first and last names, first initials being used instead of first names, abbreviations being used instead of full or middle names (like Edw. Wm. instead of Edward William), and other errors. Even name changes may play a part in "hiding" a name you are looking for. For example, if you are looking for the name of a female in the Social Security Death Benefits Records Index, most likely you should be looking under her married name rather than her maiden name. For these reasons, as you look through the FamilyFinder Index, don't rule out entries that are similar, but not exact matches of the names that you are looking for.

There are two places you can go for advice and more examples of what types of errors you should be aware of. First, click the **Introduction** tab on the Family Archive in which you could not find your ancestor's name. You may find helpful information there. Second, if you have the Deluxe Edition of Family Tree Maker, see the important topic "Issues with using the FamilyFinder Index (and Family Archives)" in the Genealogy "How-To" Guide.

To read this topic:

1. From the **Help** menu, select **Genealogy "How-To" Guide**.

2. On the first screen of the Genealogy "How-To" Guide, select **FamilyFinder Index**.

    Family Tree Maker displays the topic "All About the FamilyFinder Index."

3. From that topic, select **Issues with using the FamilyFinder Index (and Family Archives)**.

Second, even if you can't locate your ancestor's name in the FamilyFinder Index, it is still possible that a record with your ancestor's name exists. It just happens that the record was not in an index that is available electronically, and therefore couldn't be included in the FamilyFinder Index.

Purchasing Family Archives

Family Archives were created by the Automated Archives division of Brøderbund. For more information about or to purchase Family Archives, call Brøderbund's Customer Support at (415) 382-4770. The fax number is (415) 382-4419. Lines are open Monday through Thursday, 6 AM to 4:45 PM and Friday, 6 AM to 3:45 PM, Pacific time. You can also write to the address below (include your address and phone number so that we can contact you).

Brøderbund Customer Support
PO Box 6125
Novato, CA 94948-6125

If you need technical support when using a Family Archive, call Brøderbund's Banner Blue Division at (510) 794-6850 and choose technical support. You can speak directly to a technical support representative Monday through Friday, 8:00 AM to 5:00 PM, Pacific time.

In addition, Banner Blue's Technical Support Department now has an **interactive automated help system**, which consists of pre-recorded voice instructions and the ability to fax back written instructions. It is available 24 hours a day, seven days a week by calling (510) 794-6850.

Purchasing Family Archives for use in your home will allow you to locate ancestors without even leaving your computer. In addition, you avoid the time limits that libraries often must impose on computer use. Contact Brøderbund's Customer Support for purchasing information, and see how easy it can be!

You can also find the Family Archives at selected libraries. Check with your local libraries for more information about their CD-ROM index collection.

THE "HOW-TO" GUIDE

The CD-ROM version of Family Tree Maker For Windows also contains a Genealogy "How-To" Guide to help you trace your family tree. This step-by-step guide tells you what questions to ask, where to go, and how to find important facts about your ancestors from sources both in the United States and abroad.

To open the Genealogy "How-To" Guide, from the **Help** menu, select **Genealogy "How-To" Guide**. Family Tree Maker will display the Contents screen. To see instructions for using the Genealogy "How-To" Guide, select the first topic, "All about using the Genealogy 'How-To' Guide."

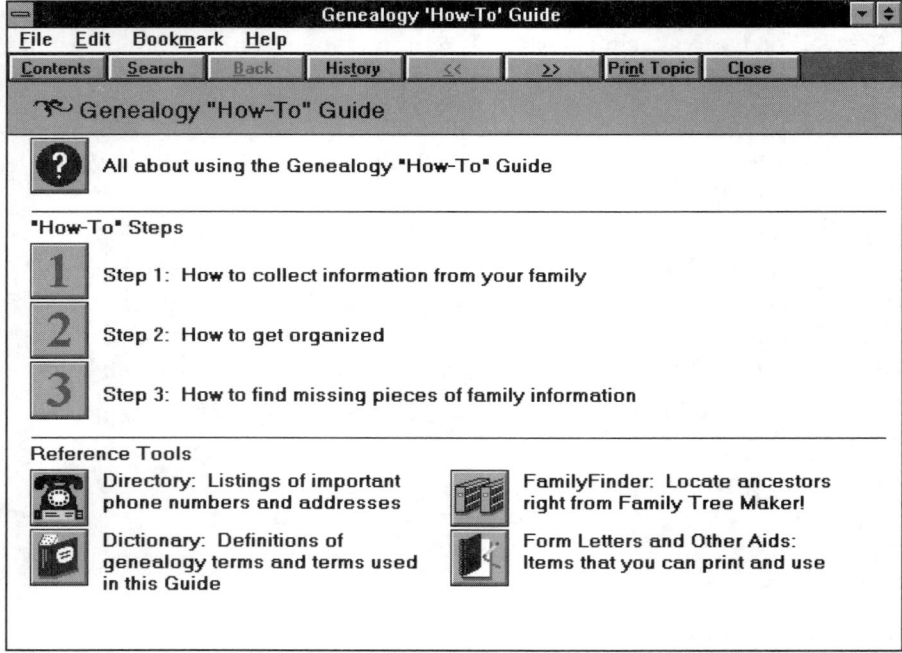

Figure 7-9. With the Genealogy "How-To" Guide, learning how to use census records is easy!

A small portion of the information covered in the "How-To" Guide is in Appendix A, beginning on page 397. However, you will find that the "How-To" Guide covers many more topics in greater detail.

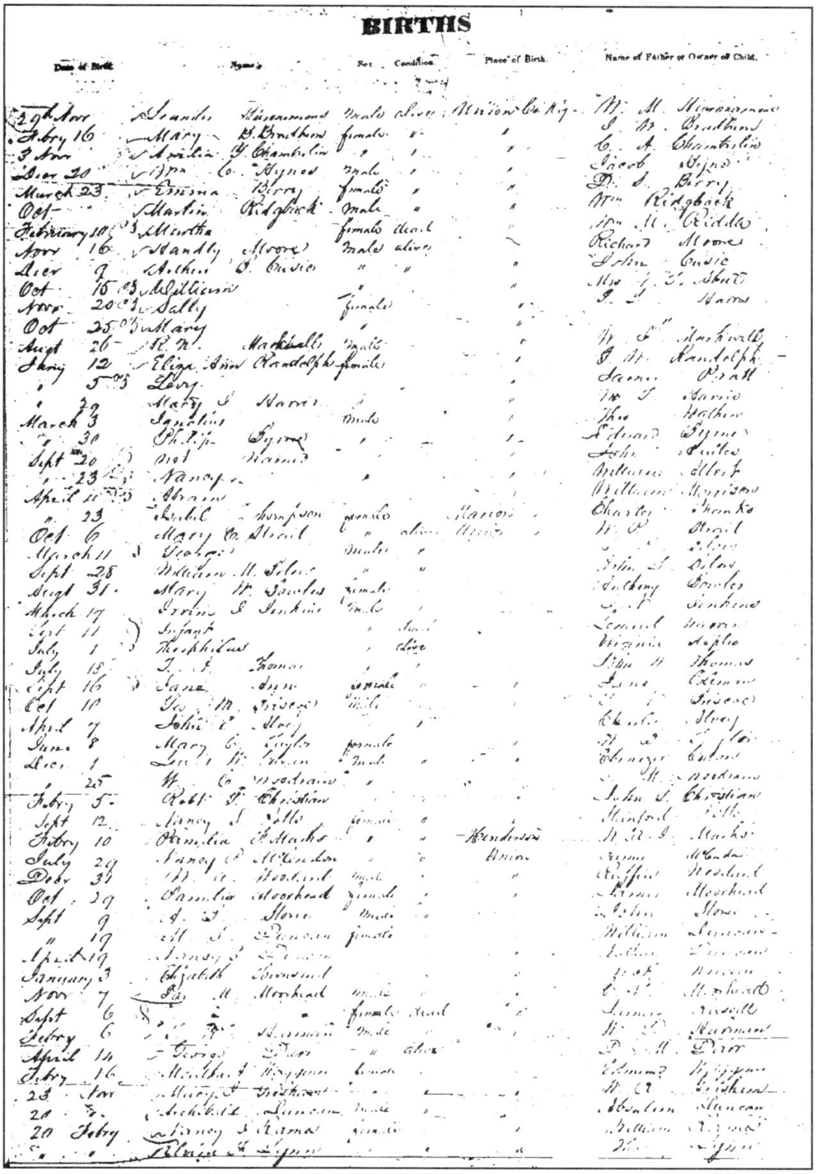

Figure 7-10. The Genealogy "How-To" Guide includes tips on reading old handwriting. This would be useful if you had to obtain information from a document such as this birth registry.

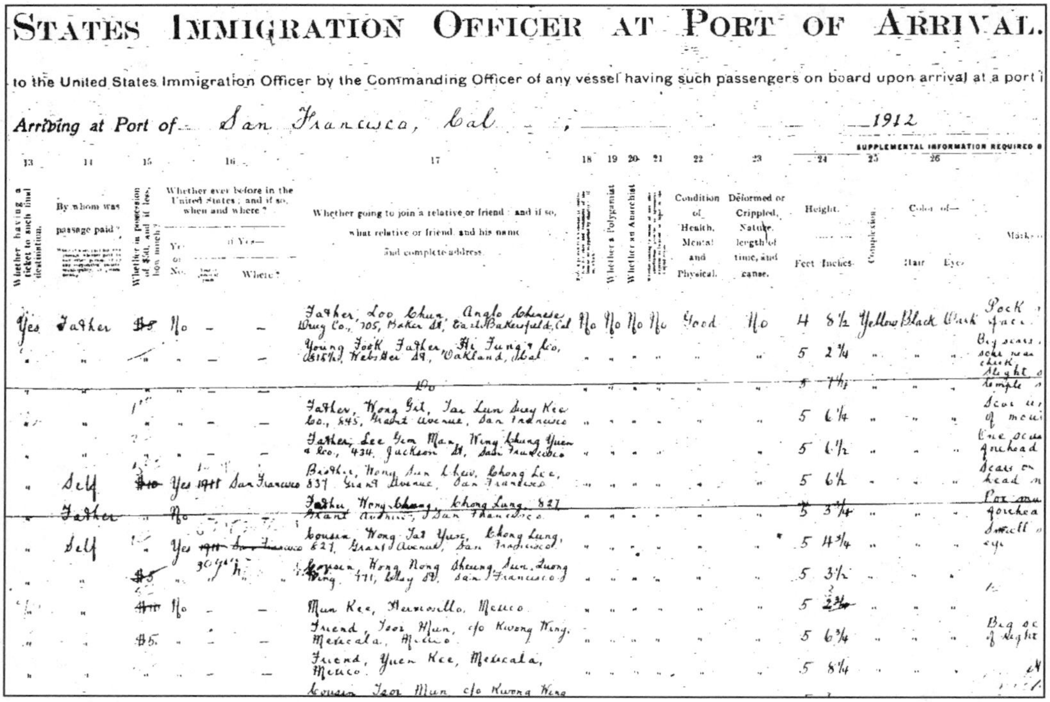

STATES IMMIGRATION OFFICER AT PORT OF ARRIVAL.

to the United States Immigration Officer by the Commanding Officer of any vessel having such passengers on board upon arrival at a port i

Arriving at Port of San Francisco, Cal. 1912

SUPPLEMENTAL INFORMATION REQUIRED B

13 Whether having a ticket to such final destination.	14 By whom was passage paid?	15 Whether in possession of $50, and if less, how much?	16 Whether ever before in the United States; and if so, when and where?	17 Whether going to join a relative or friend; and if so, what relative or friend, and his name and complete address.	18	19 Whether a Polygamist.	20 Whether an Anarchist.	21	22 Condition of Health, Mental and Physical.	23 Deformed or Crippled. Nature, length of time, and cause.	24 Height. Feet Inches	25 Complexion.	26 Color of— Hair Eyes	Marks
Yes	Father	$5	No	Father, Loo Chun, Anglo Chinese Drug Co., 705, Baker St., East Bakersfield, Cal.	No	No	No	No	Good	No	4 8½	Yellow	Black Dark	Pock face
"	"	"	"	Young Look, Father, Hi Fung & Co., 815½, Webster St., Oakland, Cal.	"	"	"	"	"	"	5 2¾	"	" "	Big scars cheek
"	"	"	"		"	"	"	"	"	"	5 7½	"	" "	Slight temple
"	"	"	"	Father, Wong Gil, Tai Lun Suey Kee Co., 845, Grant Avenue, San Francisco	"	"	"	"	"	"	5 6¼	"	" "	Scar of mou
"	"	"	"	Father, Lee Yem Man, Wing Chung Yuen & Co., 434, Jackson St., San Francisco	"	"	"	"	"	"	5 6½	"	" "	One scar forehead
"	Self	$10	Yes 1911 San Francisco	Brother, Wong Sun Chew, Chong Lee, 837, Grant Avenue, San Francisco	"	"	"	"	"	"	5 6½	"	" "	Scar on head
"	Father	"	No	Father, Wong Chong, Chong Lung, 827 Grant Avenue, San Francisco	"	"	"	"	"	"	5 3¼	"	" "	Pox mar forehead
"	Self	"	Yes 1911 San Francisco	Cousin, Wong Sai Yuen, Chong Lung, 827, Grant Avenue, San Francisco	"	"	"	"	"	"	5 4¾	"	" "	Small eye
"	"	$5	"	Cousin, Hong Nong Sheung, Sun Luong Wing, 111, Alley St., San Francisco	"	"	"	"	"	"	5 3½	"	" "	
"	"	$10	No	Mun Kee, Hermosillo, Mexico	"	"	"	"	"	"	5 [illegible]	"	" "	
"	"	$5	"	Friend, Yee Hun, c/o Kwong Wing, Mexicala, Mexico	"	"	"	"	"	"	5 6¾	"	" "	Big sc of right
"	"	"	"	Friend, Yuen Kee, Mexicala, Mexico	"	"	"	"	"	"	5 8¼	"	" "	
				Cousin Yeo Mun c/o Kwong Wing										

Figure 7-11. Using passenger arrival records to find genealogical information can be tricky, but our Genealogy "How-To" Guide helps demystify the process.

The "How-To" Guide has several different sections. It contains everything from information about basic research techniques to a directory of hundreds of addresses and phone numbers that will be useful in your genealogical research. And, unlike genealogy books, this guide is interactive. You can go straight to the information regarding your heritage and bypass any information that isn't useful to you. It even contains census abstracts and form letters that you can print.

Using Family Archives Responsibly

Software programs, just like books and movies, are protected by U.S. copyright laws and international treaties. By explaining what copyright laws say and how they affect Family Archive users, we hope to shed more light on what is acceptable use of Family Archives.

Acceptable Use

For your own research, you may use any and all data from the Family Archives you buy. If you have an opportunity to collaborate with others on family research, that's great! Copyright laws permit sharing of *small quantities* of data with family members and friends, and if applicable, with clients of your professional genealogical services.

For Family Archive users, "small quantities" can mean the following:

- Information about one nuclear family.

- The names of all individuals with the same first or last name, living in an *exact* county in an *exact* decade.

- Complete information about one individual on the Family Archive.

Note that the examples listed above are all very *specific* pieces of information. The key thing to remember is that it's OK to use your Family Archive to help someone else quickly fill in a small blank in their family research. But if they want to rely on your Family Archive for anything more than a name here or a date there, they should buy their own copy to use.

When you're not sure if something is OK, consider these rules of the "Fair Use" doctrine of U.S. copyright law.

- **Purpose and Character of the Use** — If it is for non-profit or educational purposes, it may be fair; if it is for commercial gain it may be unfair.

- **Amount and Substantiality of the Portion Used** — Must not be too large compared to the copyrighted work as a whole.

- **Effect of the Use on the Copyrighted Work** — Must not harm the potential market for, or value of, the work.

If a publisher such as a software company perceives that his copyright has been abused, he can bring legal action against the person or company suspected. Courts then use these Fair Use rules to determine whether the copyright actually has been violated.

Why are Family Archives Copyrighted?

Another rule of Fair Use defines what can be copyrighted:

- **Nature of Copyrighted Work** — The work must be original to deserve copyright protection.

We start with information dispersed in public and private records. Then, our professional staff adds value to that data by *selecting* which records and data fields to compile, *filling in* missing or incomplete areas, *interpreting* ambiguous information, *arranging* their compilation in a unique format, and *adding retrieval software* to make the data easy to search. These five points produce a work of original authorship that merits a copyright.

Abuse of Copyright

Businesses like ours will only be able to keep publishing genealogical CD-ROMs as long as it makes sense economically, so we must insist that users be conscientious in observing copyright law.

These four uses are considered copyright violations:

- Systematically making a Family Archive available to more than one person at a time.

- Systematically making large parts of a Family Archive's contents available to others.

- Uploading all or part of a Family Archive's contents onto an electronic bulletin board.

- Circulating a printout taken straight off the Family Archive.

Examples of "large parts" that are too much to share are (1) the whole Family Archive, or (2) the results of more than two blanket searches (all or most records that match a search for name, date of birth, or other generic characteristic). If someone else wants to use your Family Archive for such a broad search, they are clearly expecting to find a lot of useful information on the Family Archive. That makes them a potential Family Archive customer, so allowing such free access to your Family Archive is a violation of Fair Use.

We trust you to use your best judgment when deciding what is and isn't acceptable use of a Family Archive. However, you should remember that when Family Archive owners ignore their responsibility, we can't renew the resources needed to keep bringing valuable data and software to genealogists.

Frequently Asked Questions

Can I charge people a fee to let them use my Family Archive?

No. It is not Fair Use to "rent" your Family Archives. Such use, especially if you publicize an offer, is a violation of Fair Use because it harms our potential market. You may, however, charge people a fee for your research services if you look up information for them on your Family Archive. That's because you add your own value to the information. Still, the information you deliver to your clients should not be copied electronically off the Family Archive (as a screen download or printout), because that requires no expertise, takes only mechanical effort, and does not add any value to the copyrighted work. Instead, you would want to deliver the information in the form of a pedigree tree, for example. Asking someone to pay for a screen download is so similar to renting your Family Archive that it's not considered Fair Use.

What if my neighbor wants to look up her grandfather on my Family Archive?

That's fine. Your neighbor has a specific person in mind, and she'll only be using a tiny portion of the data from your Family Archive. If she later buys a different Family Archive of her own, hopefully she'll return the favor and let you do a search or two!

Can I use a Family Archive to answer a search request on an electronic bulletin board?

No. Posting the results of a broad search onto an electronic bulletin board is always a violation of copyright, because the information is projected to a large number of people. On the other hand, if you and another *specific person* want to use e-mail to communicate with each other, it's fine to share small quantities of *specific data* from your Family Archive. As long as your messages aren't being broadcast to an entire bulletin board community, e-mail can be a real time-saver for checking and finding family history facts quickly.

Chapter 8

CREATING AND PRINTING TREES

Hugo Paz, one of Family Tree Maker's programmers, is pictured here with his family. Hugo, his wife Elizabeth, and his daughter Elizabeth Christine posed for this picture at Disneyland in 1992.

CREATING AND PRINTING TREES

Printing beautiful family trees is one of the most rewarding features of using Family Tree Maker. When you print a family tree, you have an easy way to see a portion of the information that you've entered into Family Tree Maker.

Printing family trees is easy. You create a tree by choosing to view your family information as a tree, just as you can choose to view your information on a Family Page or in the Index of Individuals.

TYPES OF TREES

There are three tree views: the **Ancestor Tree** view, the **Descendant Tree** view, and the **Outline Descendant Tree** view. The Ancestor Tree view can create Fit to Page Ancestor trees and Custom Ancestor trees. The Descendant Tree view and Outline Descendant Tree views can create both Descendant trees and Direct Descendant trees. Each tree type is described on the next few pages, or you can refer to the quick reference tables on pages 231 and 236.

Fit to Page Ancestor Trees

A **Fit to Page Ancestor tree** is a one-page Ancestor tree. Ancestor trees include an individual and that individual's parents, grandparents, great-grandparents, and so on. It does not show that individual's aunts, uncles, nieces, nephews, or cousins. A sample Ancestor tree is shown in Figure 8-1 on page 230.

Print a Fit to Page Ancestor tree when you want a single-page Ancestor tree. However, remember that because Fit to Page Ancestor trees are limited to one page, you have less control over your tree's appearance. For example, the number of generations you can include in a single tree is limited. In addition, Family Tree Maker controls things like the tree's layout, font size, and the amount of information that prints in the boxes.

Custom Ancestor Trees

A **Custom Ancestor tree** is an Ancestor tree that can have any number of pages. In addition, you have complete control over its appearance, from the information that it contains to the color and size of the text.

Choose to print a Custom Ancestor tree when you want a tree that's bigger than a single page or when you want to customize trees for yourself or to give as gifts. Each tree can be a little bit different — there are hundreds of combinations.

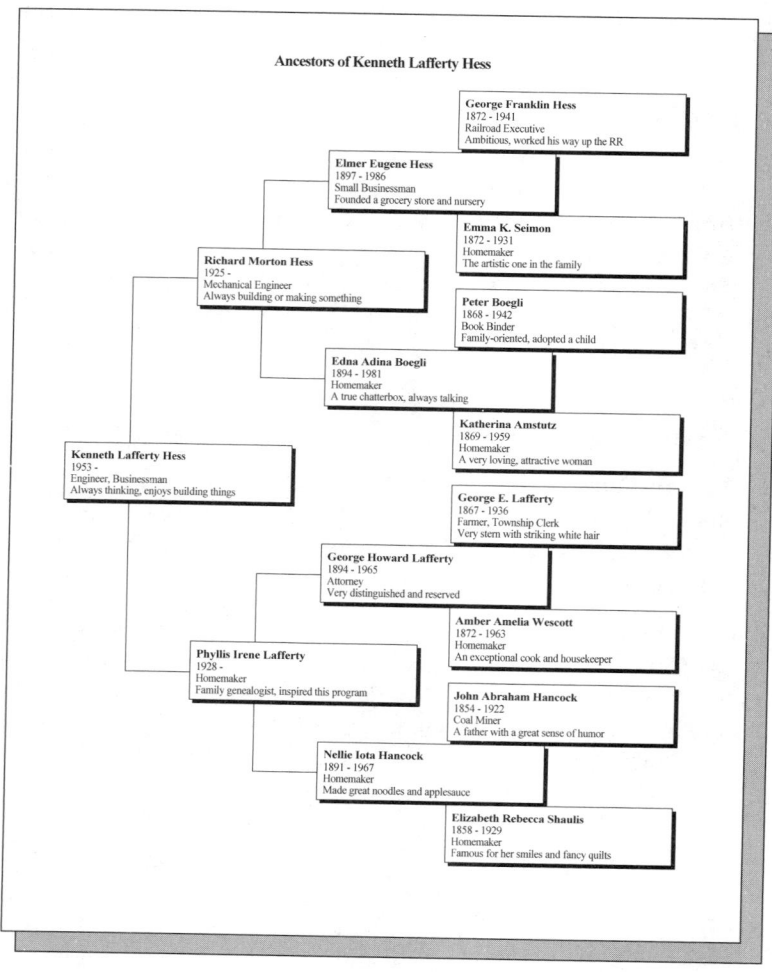

Figure 8-1. An Ancestor tree

This tree type...	Has these features...
Fit to Page Ancestor trees	• One page *only* • Limited number of generations • Limited number of fields in each box • Can print Ahnentafel numbers • Limited text size and box size, no word wrapping • No control over tree layout and box width • No control over the way the boxes are connected • Choose box, line, and border styles • Add a title and footnote • Print column labels and empty branches
Custom Ancestor trees	• Any number of pages; up to 800,000" x 800,000" • Up to 99 generations • Up to 50 fields in each box • Can print Ahnentafel numbers • Choose box, line, and border styles • Add a title and footnote • Print column labels and empty branches • Options for text size and box size • Options for tree layout and box width • Options for the way the boxes are connected

Figure 8-2. Characteristics of Ancestor Trees

Descendant Trees

A **Descendant tree** shows an individual and that individual's children, grandchildren, great-grandchildren, and so on. Because Descendant trees include so many individuals, they can grow to several pages very quickly.

With Descendant trees you can have up to 99 generations and all types of information in your boxes. Many other formatting options are available so that you can create a tree to suit your tastes. A sample Descendant tree is shown in Figure 8-3.

Direct Descendant Trees

A **Direct Descendant tree** is similar to a Descendant tree, but it is much smaller. It starts with a relative in the distant past and shows the line of descent to a relative in a later generation. Siblings can be included, but siblings' spouses, cousins, and others who aren't direct descendants cannot.

With Direct Descendant trees you can have up to 99 generations and all types of information in your boxes. Many other formatting options are available so that you can create a tree to suit your tastes.

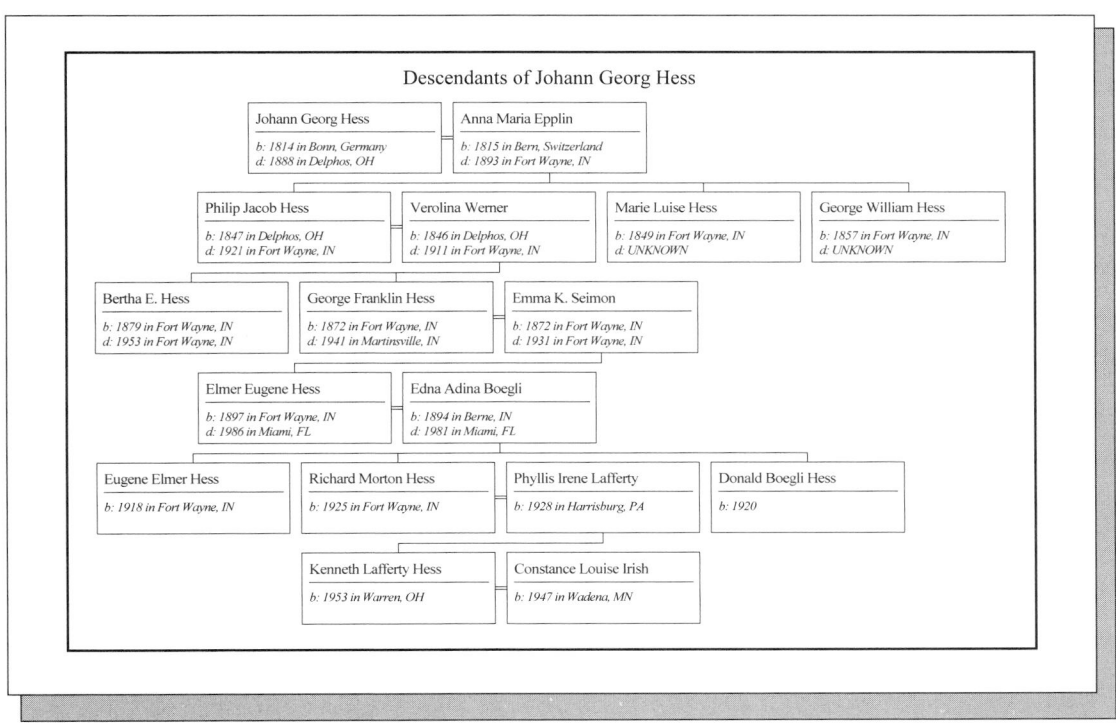

Figure 8-3. A Descendant tree

Outline Descendant Trees

An **Outline Descendant tree** contains the same type of information as a Descendant tree: an individual and that individual's children, grandchildren, great-grandchildren, and so on. However, instead of showing each individual in a box, the individuals are in outline form. Each individual's information is on a separate line, and each generation is indented slightly more than the one before it. Each descendant's spouse is directly beneath him or her and is marked with a plus sign (+). These trees can fit many generations on a single page.

Outline Descendant trees can have up to 250 generations. In addition, you can choose what information prints, font sizes and styles, and much more. A sample Outline Descendant tree is shown in Figure 8-4.

Outline Direct Descendant Trees

An **Outline Direct Descendant tree** is similar to an Outline Descendant tree, but it is much smaller. It starts with a relative in the distant past and shows the line of descent to a relative in a later generation. Siblings can be shown, but siblings' spouses, cousins, and others who aren't direct descendants cannot. However, instead of showing each individual in a box, the individuals are in outline form. Each individual's information is on a separate line, and each generation is indented slightly more than the one before it. Each descendant's spouse is directly beneath him or her and is marked with a plus sign (+). These trees can fit many generations on a single page.

Outline Direct Descendant trees can have up to 250 generations. In addition, you can choose what information prints, font sizes and styles, and much more.

Descendants of Thomas Sprunger

```
1  Thomas Sprunger  1645 - UNKNOWN
..  +Regina Buergi  1649 - UNKNOWN
.........  2 Hans Sprunger  1668 -
...................  3 Deiter Sprunger
.......................  +Elizabeth Neuenschwander
...............................  4 Christian Amstutz  1772 -
.....................................  +Katherina Nussbaum  1773 -
.............................................  5 Johannes Ulrich Amstutz  1817 - 1869
.............................................  +Elisabeth Sprunger  1832 - 1902
....................................................  6 Katherina Amstutz  1869 - 1959
....................................................  +Peter Boegli  1868 - 1942
....................................................  6 Lena Amstutz  1860 -
....................................................  6 Marianna Amstutz  1861 -
....................................................  6 Jakob U. Amstutz  1862 -
....................................................  6 John J. Amstutz  1864 -
....................................................  6 Japhet Amstutz  1865 -
....................................................  6 Elisabeth U. Amstutz  1867 -
....................................................  6 Twin Amstutz  1867 -
....................................................  6 Jakob Sprunger  1830 -
....................................................  6 Katharina Sprunger  1833 -
....................................................  6 David Sprunger  1836 -
....................................................  6 Marianna Sprunger  1838 -
.............................................  5 Elisabeth Amstutz  1797 -
.............................................  5 Johannes Amstutz  1800 -
.............................................  5 Christian Amstutz  1802 -
.............................................  5 Regina Amstutz  1803 -
.............................................  5 Anna Amstutz  1804 -
.............................................  5 Durs Dorsey Amstutz  1805 -
.............................................  5 Michael Amstutz  1807 -
.............................................  5 Jakob Amstutz  1808 -
.............................................  5 Kathrine Amstutz  1810 -
.............................................  5 Magdalena Amstutz  1815 -
...............................  4 Johann Amstutz  1771 -
...............................  4 Michael Amstutz  1779 -
.........  2 Hans Sprunger  1668 -
.........  2 Hans Peter Sprunger  1669 -
.........  2 Barbara Sprunger  1671 -
.........  2 Catharina Sprunger  1673 -
.........  2 Sebastian Sprunger  1675/76 -
.........  2 Salomon Sprunger  1676/77 -
.........  2 Salmon Sprunger  1679/80 -
```

Figure 8-4. An Outline Descendant tree

This tree type...	Has these features...
Descendant trees and Direct Descendant trees	• Any number of pages; up to 800,000" x 800,000" • Up to 99 generations • Up to 50 fields in each box • Options for box, line, and border styles • Add a title and footnote • Print row labels • Options for text size, box size, and box width • Options for tree layout, but not box connections
Outline Descendant trees and Outline Direct Descendant trees	• A tree in outline form • Any number of pages • Up to 250 generations • Up to 50 fields per individual • Options for border styles • Add a title, footnote, and page numbers • Options for text size • Print generation numbers for each individual

Figure 8-5. Characteristics of Descendant and Outline Descendant trees

CREATING ANCESTOR TREES

To create an Ancestor tree:

1. In any view, highlight the name of the individual who you want to be the **primary individual**. For example, you could highlight the individual's name on a Family Page or in the Index of Individuals.

   The "primary individual" in an Ancestor tree is the leftmost individual in the tree. This individual's ancestors are shown in the rest of the tree.

2. From the **View** menu, select **Ancestor Tree**.

3. From the **Format** menu, select **Tree Format**.

   Family Tree Maker displays the Tree Format dialog box.

4. Select either the **Fit to Page** or **Custom** option button and click **OK**.

   We'll describe the other options in this dialog box later.

   Note: If you choose Fit to Page Ancestor tree when you have a Custom Ancestor tree on the screen, Family Tree Maker modifies your tree so that it can fit on a single page. Typically, Family Tree Maker will decrease the number of generations and the size of the text in the boxes. There may be other changes too.

   Likewise, if you make a change to a Fit to Page Ancestor tree that makes it too large to fit on a single page, Family Tree Maker asks if you want to reverse the changes, reduce the amount of information in each box, or let the tree grow larger than one page.

5. You can either print your tree right away (see "Printing Your Tree" on page 263), or customize it and then print (see "Customizing Trees," on page 239).

CREATING ALL TYPES OF DESCENDANT TREES

To create a Descendant, Direct Descendant, Outline Descendant, or Outline Direct Descendant tree:

1. In any view, highlight the name of the individual who you want to be the **primary individual**. For example, you could highlight the individual's name on a Family Page or in the Index of Individuals.

   The "primary individual" in Descendant, Direct Descendant, Outline Descendant, and Outline Direct Descendant trees is the individual at the top of the tree.

2. From the **View** menu, select either **Descendant Tree** or **Outline Descendant Tree**.

3. From the **Contents** menu, select **Individuals to Include**.

   Family Tree Maker displays the Individuals to Include dialog box.

   All descendants — If you want to create a regular Descendant or Outline Descendant tree, select this option button and click **OK**. Skip to step 7.

   Direct Descendants only from ... to — If you want to create a Direct Descendant tree or Outline Direct Descendant tree, select this option button.

   Include siblings of direct descendants — Select this check box if you would like to include each individual's brothers and sisters in the Direct Descendant tree or Outline Direct Descendant tree.

4. Click **Change secondary individual**.

   Family Tree Maker displays the Change secondary individual dialog box (see Figure 8-6 on the next page).

5. Select the name of the secondary individual (the individual that you want at the bottom of your tree) and click **OK**.

   If you have trouble locating the correct individual, you can type their name in the **Name** field or click **Find**. For instructions, see "Doing a Quick Search" on page 118 or "Using Find Name" on page 119.

6. Click **OK** to close the Individuals to Include dialog box.

7. You can either print your tree right away (see "Printing Your Tree" on page 263), or customize it and then print (see "Customizing Trees," on page 239).

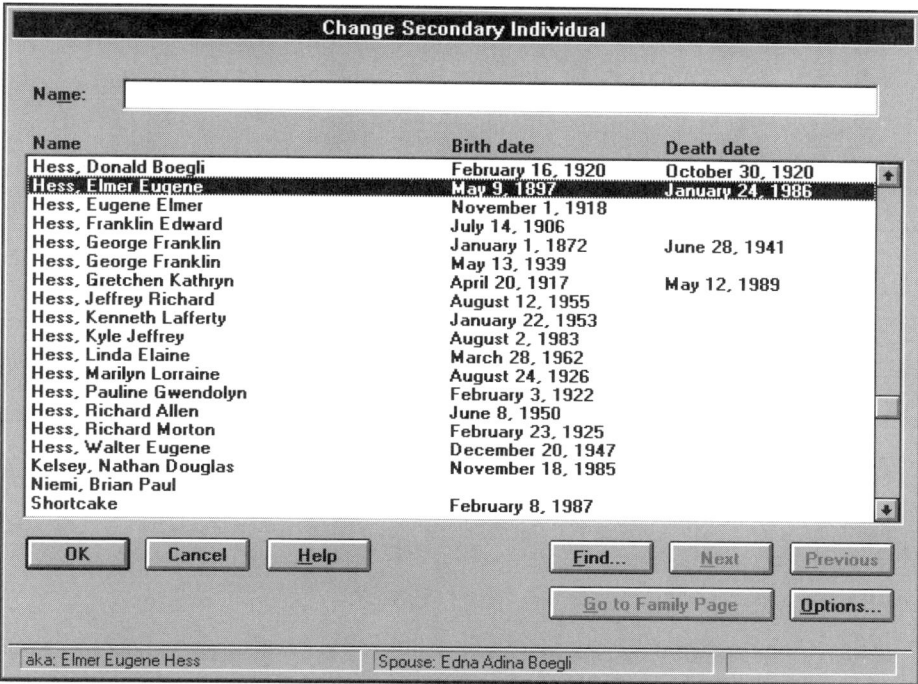

Figure 8-6. The Change secondary individual dialog box

CUSTOMIZING TREES

Once you've created your basic tree, you can customize it by adding color and borders, changing fonts and font styles, including different types of information, and much more. A complete list is below. You can go through these sections in any order you want, so experiment with the options until you find a tree that suits your tastes. Then, when you're happy with your tree, see "Printing Your Tree" on page 263.

Your tree customization options include the following (some are not available for Fit to Page Ancestor trees):

- Selecting the number of generations to include in the tree, page 242

- Selecting information to include in the tree, page 243

- Formatting the information in the tree, page 247

- Formatting text, including color, font, size, and style, page 253

- Selecting colors and box, border, and line styles and for the tree, page 254

- Adding a title and footnote to the tree, page 254

- Selecting the layout for box-style trees, page 255

- Selecting the layout for outline-style trees, page 256

- Selecting the width for boxes and Picture/Objects in the tree, page 258

- Other printing options, page 259

Other helpful options include the following: viewing your tree at different sizes on the screen (see "Zooming," below), showing and hiding the lines that indicate where the page breaks are (see "Showing Page Lines" on the next page), and navigating through your Family File by clicking names in your trees (see "Using Your Mouse in Trees" on the next page).

Zooming

With the Zoom command, you can make your tree appear larger on screen so it's easier to read the text. You can also shrink it down so you can see the entire tree at once. Please note that the Zoom command does not control how large your tree is when you print.

To use the Zoom command:

1. From the **View** menu, select **Zoom**.

   Family Tree Maker displays the Zoom dialog box.

2. Select the option button for the size that you prefer.

   "Size to Window" fits your entire tree on the screen. "Actual Size" makes the tree the approximate size that it is when it prints. "200%" is the largest size at which you can view your tree.

3. Click **OK** when you've made your selection.

   When your whole tree is not visible on the screen, Family Tree Maker places scroll bars on the bottom and right sides of the tree. You can use these scroll bars to view different sections of the tree.

Showing Page Lines

You can control whether or not dotted lines indicating page margins appear on the screen. From the **View** menu, select **Show Page Lines**. If this option has a check next to it, the page lines will be visible. Otherwise, they won't be. Page lines never appear on your printed documents.

Using Your Mouse in Trees

You can click in trees to do two different things. First, you can navigate through Family Tree Maker, moving to different views and making different individuals the primary individual. Second, you can activate Picture/Objects, either viewing pictures at full size or "playing" OLE objects. For more information about including Picture/Objects in your trees see "Selecting Information to Include in Your Tree" on page 243.

Whether you navigate through Family Tree Maker or activate your Picture/Objects depends on what you click and whether you double-click or single-click. The table below describes each of the functions.

Do this...	To do this...
Click once anywhere in a box, or click an individual's name in outline-style trees.	Select the individual. You can then use the menus or the toolbar to change to any view. The selected individual becomes the primary individual.
Double-click any text in a box, or double-click an individual's name in outline-style trees.	Go to the individual's Family Page.
Double-click a Picture/Object in a box (not available for outline-style trees).	If the Picture/Object is an OLE object, Family Tree Maker opens the OLE server and "plays" the object. For example, it plays sound and video files. If the Picture/Object isn't an OLE object, Family Tree Maker displays it in the View Picture dialog box.

Figure 8-7. Using your mouse in trees

Choosing the Number of Generations

The number of generations that a tree can have depends on the tree type. Descendant trees and Custom Ancestor trees can have up to 99 generations. Fit to Page Ancestor trees can have up to 6 generations, and Outline Descendant trees can have up to 250 generations. This option is not available for Direct Descendant and Outline Direct Descendant trees, because for those tree types you show how two individuals are connected, rather than showing a specific number of generations.

Remember, the more generations you add, the bigger your tree will be. For example, a 10-generation Ancestor tree can have 512 boxes in its rightmost column because each of us has 512 seventh great-grandparents (assuming no one married a cousin).

To choose the number of generations to include in your tree:

1.   From the **Contents** menu, select **# of Generations to Show**.

     Family Tree Maker displays the # of Generations to Show dialog box.

2.   Select the number of generations that you want to include in your tree.

3.   Click **OK** when you've made your selection.

     Family Tree Maker returns you to the tree view.

When you look at a Fit to Page Ancestor tree, you may notice that Family Tree Maker needed to abbreviate some of the names, locations, and biographical information to make the tree fit on a single page. This can happen especially with trees that include five or more generations. If your Fit to Page Ancestor tree grows too large to fit on a single page, Family Tree Maker will warn you of this.

Selecting Information to Include in Your Tree

With Family Tree Maker, you can choose what information to include in your trees. Each item that you choose will appear in your tree's boxes, or in the case of outline-style trees, on a line.

From the **Contents** menu, select **Items to Include**. Family Tree Maker displays the Items to Include dialog box (see Figure 8-8). It contains two lists: the list on the right shows which items will be included in your tree, and the list on the left shows which items you can add to your trees. You can add and delete items to and from the list on the right as often as you like. Remember, however, the more items you choose to include in your tree, the fewer individuals will fit on a page.

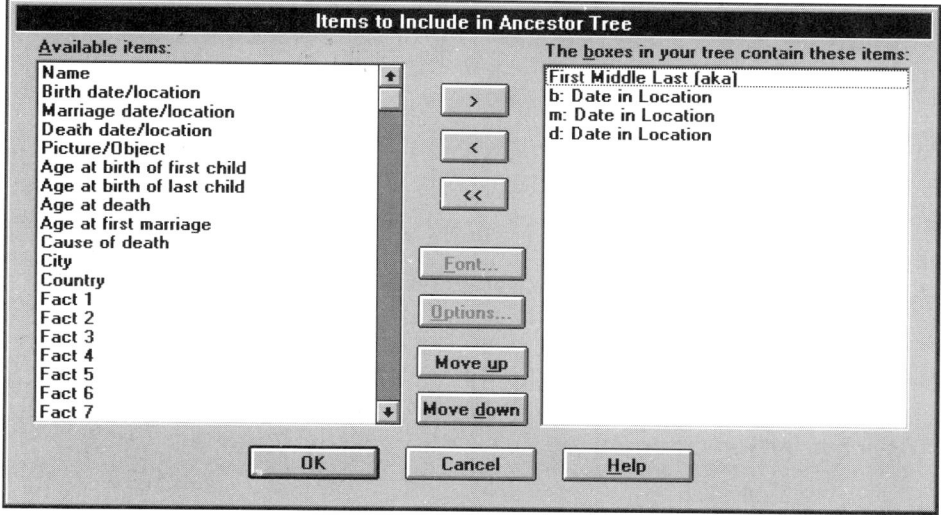

Figure 8-8. Items to Include dialog box

Among the items that you can choose to include are names, dates, facts, addresses, relationship information, and reference numbers. If you have placed Picture/Objects in Scrapbooks, you can include them in your tree's boxes — for individuals and/or for marriages. To include a Picture/Object for each individual or for each marriage, select either **Picture/Object** or **Marriage Picture/Object** from the list on the left. Family Tree Maker displays the Options: Picture/Object dialog box. In this dialog box you can select which Picture/Object will be included in each individual's box. When you include Picture/Objects, it's a good idea not to include too much other information. Otherwise, you won't be able to fit as many generations on a single page.

If an individual does not have a Picture/Object, Family Tree Maker will insert a substitute graphic where the Picture/Object normally would be. For more information about substitute graphics, see "Missing Picture/Objects" on page 250.

You can also insert lines and blank rows in a tree's boxes by selecting **Line in box** or **Blank row** from the list on the left. In fact, if you do not have Picture/Objects in each individual's Scrapbook and you want to manually attach photos to your trees after you've printed them, you can add several blank rows to leave space for the photos. The number of blank rows that you will need to add depends on the size of your photos.

Using the **Custom field** item, you can add up to 80 characters of text to each individual's information in the tree. Remember, what you type in this field will appear as part of *every* individual's information.

You can also include the sources of your family information. See "Formatting the Information in Your Tree," on page 247.

To add items to or remove items from your tree:

1. Click an item in the list on the left if you want to add that item. If you want to remove an item, click that item in the list on the right.

    Family Tree Maker highlights the item.

2. Click either the **Include** button (the arrow pointing to the right) or the **Remove** button (the arrow pointing to the left). See Figure 8-9.

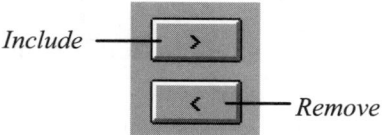

Figure 8-9. The Include and Remove buttons

If you chose to add the item, it is added to the list on the right. If you chose to remove the item, it is removed from the list on the right. You can include up to fifty items per individual, although you will probably want to include far fewer.

Instead of selecting an item and then clicking "Include" or "Remove," you can just double-click the item's name. Double-clicking items in the list on the left automatically adds them. Double-clicking items in the list on the right automatically removes them. In addition, if you want to delete all items from the list on the right, click the **Remove all** button (the double arrow pointing to the left).

Some items, such as names and dates, require you to make formatting choices. Family Tree Maker automatically displays a dialog box that asks you to make a formatting choice when it is necessary. You can also format an item by selecting it in the list on the right and then clicking **Options**. For more information about making formatting choices for the items in your trees, see "Formatting the Information in Your Tree" on page 247.

You can also choose sizes and styles for the text in your trees by clicking **Font**. See "Formatting Text" on page 253.

3. Once the list on the right contains all of the items that you want, you can change the order in which they appear. Simply click an item and then click either **Move up** or **Move down** to move that item up or down one space. The item at the top of the list will appear at the top of the box, or as the first item on the line in outline-style trees.

4. Click **OK** when you've made your selections.

    Family Tree Maker returns you to the tree view.

Notes About Ancestor Trees

-   With Ancestor trees, you can optionally choose to print the primary individual and the primary individual's spouse in the same box. To do this, select **Spouse (primary individual only)** as an item to print. All of the other individuals' spouses already appear in the tree.

-   Both Reference numbers and Standard numbers can appear either in front of an individual's name or on separate lines in Ancestor trees (see page 247). Reference numbers are numbers that you can create for your own filing system. You can enter these numbers in the Lineage dialog box (see page 134). Standard numbers (Ahnentafel numbers) are automatically generated by a formula. The formula states that an individual's father is twice that individual's number, and an individual's mother is twice that individual's number plus 1. If your Ahnentafel number is 1, your father's number is 2, and your mother's is 3. When you choose to include Standard numbers in your tree, you can specify the starting number for the primary individual; Family Tree Maker calculates the rest of the numbers for you.

- If you include any marriage information in Ancestor trees, such as "Marriage date/location" or "Marriage Picture/Object," it will only appear in the husband's box.

Notes About Descendant Trees

- Reference numbers are numbers that you can create for your own filing system. They can appear either in front of an individual's name or on their own separate line in Descendant trees. You can enter these numbers in the Lineage dialog box (see page 134). Standard numbers (Ahnentafel numbers) cannot appear in Descendant trees.

- If you include any marriage information in Descendant trees, such as "Marriage date/location" or "Marriage Picture/Object," it will only appear in the box of the bloodline descendant's spouse.

Notes About Outline Descendant Trees

- When an individual has had more than one spouse, Family Tree Maker lists them in the order in which the marriages took place. If Family Tree Maker is not displaying spouses in the correct order, check the marriage dates on the applicable Family Pages. When you do not have an exact marriage date, use approximate dates so that the spouses will print in the correct order. For help with estimated dates, see Figure 3-5 on page 87.

Formatting the Information in Your Tree

Many of the items that you choose in the Items to Include dialog box (see page 243) have formatting options, such as whether or not to use labels or include source information. You can format these items when you first select them (see directly below) and also after they've already been selected (see page 252).

Formatting Items As You Select Them

When you're selecting items to include in your trees, Family Tree Maker displays an Options dialog box for those items that have formatting options. Simply make your formatting selections and then click **OK** to continue. The Options dialog boxes are described on the next few pages.

Using different formatting options can be a good way to control the size of trees. For example, some date formats allow you to print the date and location on the same line (making the box shorter but wider) and others allow you to print them on separate lines (making the box taller but narrower).

Names

When you choose to include names in your tree, Family Tree Maker displays the Options: Name dialog box. Click the **Format** drop-down list to select a format for the names in your tree. For example, you could choose to omit middle names or split names onto two lines. A line split is indicated by "\\".

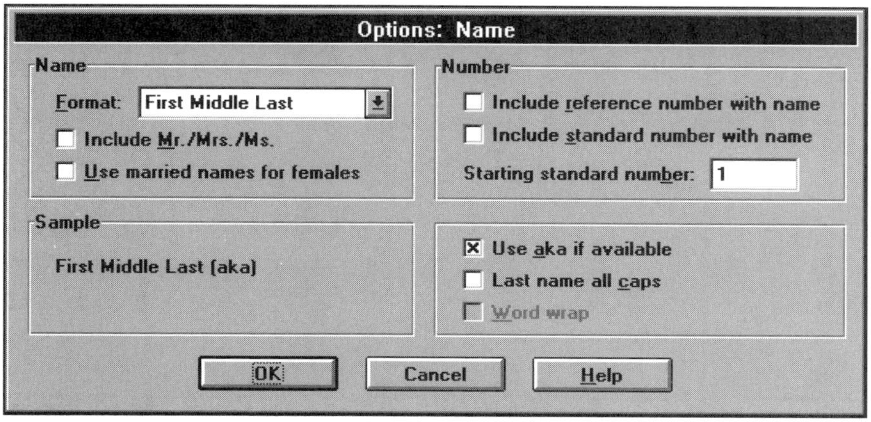

Figure 8-10. The Options: Name dialog box

There are other options in this dialog box, although not all of them are available for all types of trees. If you would like titles to appear in your tree, select the **Include Mr./Mrs./Ms.** check box. To use married names instead of maiden names for women, select the **Use married names for females** check box.

If you use reference numbers in your Family File (see page 134), you can include them in front of people's names by selecting the **Include reference number with name** check box. You can also have Family Tree Maker calculate Standard (Ahnentafel) numbers for you in Ancestor trees. Simply select the **Include standard numbers with name** check box and type the number for the primary individual in the **Starting standard number** field. If you prefer to include nicknames instead of given names, select the **Use aka if available** check box.

Facts

Family Tree Maker displays the Options: Fact dialog box when you choose to include facts from the More About Facts dialog box. In the **Include** and **Labels** group boxes, choose options for formatting dates and labels. If you want to include source information for facts in your tree, select the **Include source information** check box. If you are including a fact field that contains more than a few words, select the **Word wrap** check box.

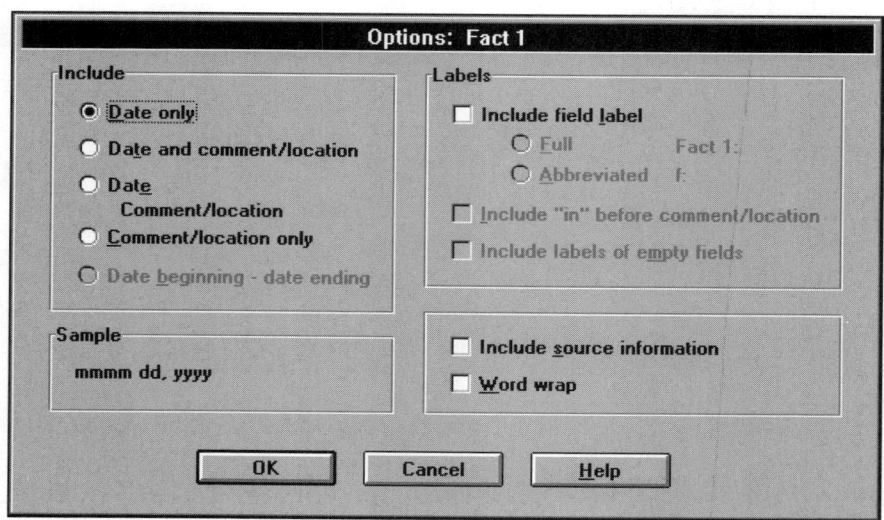

Figure 8-11. The Options: Fact dialog box

Picture/Objects

You can include Picture/Objects in your Ancestor trees and Descendant trees, but not in Outline Descendant trees. If you choose Picture/Objects in the Items to Include dialog box, Family Tree Maker displays the Options: Picture/Object dialog box. This is where you choose which of each individual's Picture/Objects will appear in the tree. Select one of the **Preferred Picture/Object** option buttons to include Picture/Objects that you chose as "Preferred Picture/Object for trees" in the More About Picture/Object dialog boxes. For more information about the More About Picture/Object dialog box, see page 164.

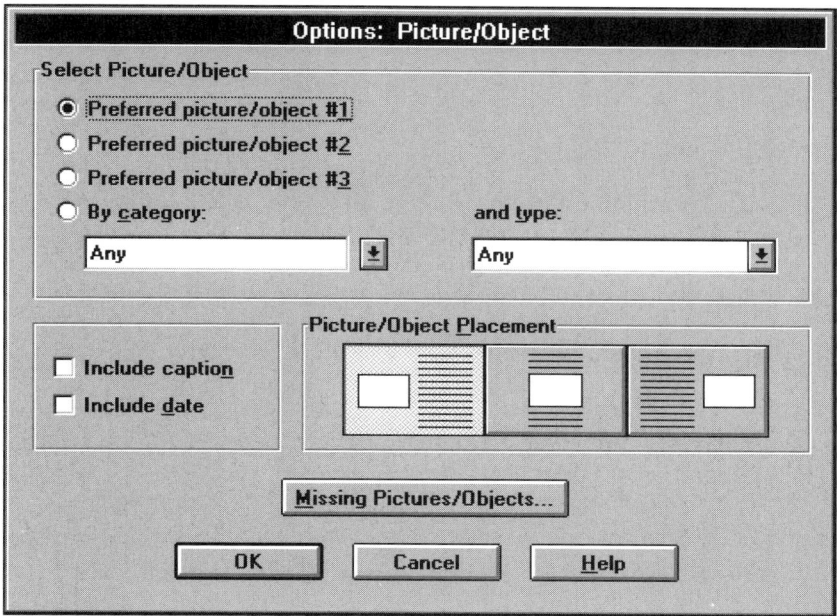

Figure 8-12. The Options: Picture/Object dialog box

Instead of using the "Preferred" Picture/Objects, you can choose to include Picture/Objects of a particular **category** and **type**. You use the More About Picture/Object dialog box (see page 164) to assign categories and types to Picture/Objects. Categories are classifications that you create. For example, you could create a "Birthday" category in which to place birthday pictures. Or, you could create a "Child Portrait" category in which to place portraits that were taken when the individuals were young. Types are chosen from a drop-down list in the More About Picture/Object dialog box. They describe what Picture/Objects are, such as "Pictures" or "Sound Clips."

The **By Category** and **and Type** fields work together to find the Picture/Objects that you want to include in your tree. For example, if you choose the category "Birthdays" and the type "Picture," Family Tree Maker searches for Picture/Objects that fulfill **both** requirements. However, both of the fields have an "Any" option, which, in effect, allows you to search only one of the two fields. If the category that you assigned to a Picture/Object does not appear in the "By Category" drop-down list, just type it into the field. When there is more than one Picture/Object of the category and type that you select, Family Tree Maker uses the first one that it finds.

If you wish to include the Picture/Object's caption or date, select the **Include caption** or **Include date** check box. You can also limit the size of the Picture/Objects that you include in your trees. See "Limiting the Width of Boxes and Picture/Objects," on page 258.

To choose how the text and Picture/Objects are arranged in your tree's boxes, select the **Picture/Object Placement** button picturing the placement that you prefer. The Picture/Object can be to the right or left of the text, or both the text and the Picture/Object can be centered in the box.

Missing Picture/Objects

You may not have a Picture/Object for all of the individuals that you are including in the tree. When this is the case, Family Tree Maker substitutes a graphic (or a blank space) where the Picture/Object normally would be. The default is a blank space. To choose the substitute graphic, click **Missing Picture/Objects** in the Options: Picture/Object dialog box. Family Tree Maker displays the Missing Picture/Objects dialog box. You can either:

- Click the button for the graphic that you prefer or choose the blank space and then click **OK** to return to the Options: Picture/Object dialog box, or

- Choose to use your own picture file as a substitute graphic. The graphic can be in any of the following file formats: Windows Bitmap (*.BMP), CompuServe Bitmap (*.GIF), ZSoft Image (*.PCX), Tagged Image Format (*.TIF), or JPEG Interchange Format (*.JPG, *.JFF). To choose your own picture, click **Choose Picture**. Family Tree Maker displays the Import Picture from File dialog box. If you need instructions, see "Picture/Object: Insert Picture from File" on page 157. When you have selected a picture to insert, click **OK** twice to return to the Options: Picture/Object dialog box.

Standard Numbers

If you choose to include Standard numbers, Family Tree Maker displays the Options: Standard number (Ahnentafel) dialog box. Type the starting number for the primary individual; Family Tree Maker calculates the rest of the numbers for you. Since Ahnentafel numbering is calculated based on an individual's position in an Ancestor tree, this option only applies to Ancestor trees.

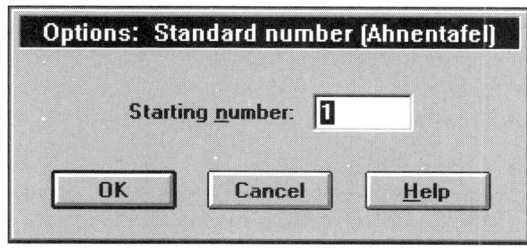

Figure 8-13. The Options: Standard Number dialog box

Other

Some fields, such as "Phone" just have a simple set of options, such as whether or not to include field labels or use the word wrapping function. Word wrapping allows the text to wrap onto multiple lines if it is too long to fit on one line.

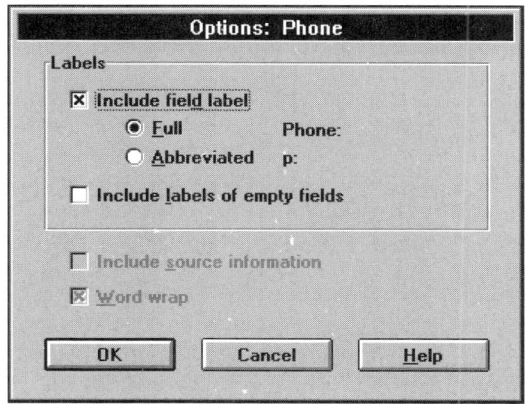

Figure 8-14. The Options: Phone dialog box

Formatting Items After They've Been Selected

To change the formatting of an item that's already in the list on the right side of the Items to Include dialog box:

1. Select the item in the list on the right by clicking it.

    Family Tree Maker highlights the item.

2. Click **Options**.

    Family Tree Maker displays an Options dialog box. Each of the Options dialog boxes are described above in "Formatting Items as You Select Them."

    Note: If you select an item in the scrolling list on the right and "Options" stays grayed out, that item does not have any formatting options.

    Statistics, such as age at death, or number of children, do not have formatting options. They always print with their field labels (for example, "Age at death: 40"). If "est" prints, as in "Age at death: 40 est," it means that a date was uncertain. If a "?" prints, it means that there is no information in a date field. (Entering an uncertain date is always better than entering nothing.)

3. Make your selections and then click **OK**.

    When you have finished formatting and selecting items to include in your tree, click **OK** in the Items to Include dialog box. Family Tree Maker returns you to the tree view.

From the Items to Include dialog box, you can also change the text font, style, or size for any of the items you choose to print:

1. Select the item in the list on the right by clicking it.

    Family Tree Maker highlights the item you selected.

2. Click **Font**.

    Family Tree Maker displays the Text Font, Style & Size dialog box, described in the next section.

Formatting Text

Each text item that appears in your tree, including the title and footnote, can be formatted differently. For example, you might want to bold the names in your tree, or even make them bigger than the other information in each box.

To format the text items in your tree:

1. From the **Format** menu, select **Text Font, Style, & Size**.

   Family Tree Maker displays the Text Font, Style, & Size dialog box. You can also format text from the Items to Include dialog box (described on page 243). In that case, click the item in the list on the right that you want to format, then click **Font**.

2. In the **Items to format** list on the left, select an item that you want to format, such as **Name**.

   When an item is selected, you can choose formatting options for it. Each of the formatting options is described below. The "Sample" field shows how your formatted text will appear.

   Font — Click this field to display a list of fonts and then click the name of the font you want.

   Size — Click this field to display a list of text sizes and then click the size you want.

   Note: The Size option is not available for Fit to Page Ancestor trees. Family Tree Maker automatically sizes text in these trees.

   Style — Click this field to display a list of text styles, such as "Bold" or "Italics," and then click the style you want.

   Color — Click this field to display a list of colors and then click the color you want. If you do not have a color printer, the colors will print in shades of gray.

   Alignment — Click this field to display a list of text alignments, such as "Centered," and then click the alignment you want.

   Note: The Alignment option is not available for Outline Descendant and Outline Direct Descendant trees.

   Underline — Select this check box to underline the item.

3. Click **OK** when you've made your selections.

   Family Tree Maker returns you to the tree view.

Choosing Styles for Boxes, Lines, & Tree Borders

You can make each tree unique by selecting different styles of boxes and tree borders. In addition, you can choose colors for boxes, borders, shadows, and the tree background. If you have a color printer, your trees will print in color. If your printer is black and white, the trees will print in shades of gray.

To select formatting options for boxes, borders, and lines:

1. From the **Format** menu, select **Box, Line, & Border Styles**.

   Family Tree Maker displays the Box, Line, & Border Styles dialog box. If you are formatting an Outline Descendant or Outline Direct Descendant tree, this dialog box is labeled "Line & Border Styles."

2. Make your selections by clicking the buttons with the pictures of the borders, lines, and boxes that you like. Each tree can only have one box style and one border style. Of course, Outline Descendant and Outline Direct Descendant trees don't have box style options.

3. You can also choose colors for each of these elements. Click the color field for each element of the tree and then select a color from the list that Family Tree Maker displays.

4. Click **OK** when you've made your selections.

   Family Tree Maker returns you to the tree view.

Adding a Title and Footnote

Adding a title and footnote to your tree gives it a personal touch. However, if you're trying to save space, you might want to skip these options.

To add a title or footnote to your tree:

1. From the **Contents** menu, select **Title & Footnote**.

   Family Tree Maker displays the Title & Footnote dialog box. Each of your options is described below.

   Title — Titles print at the top center of your tree. Select the **Automatic title** option button if you want Family Tree Maker to create a title for you, such as "Ancestors of Jane Smith." If you want to create your own title, select the **Custom title** option button and type your title in the field provided. With Outline Descendant trees, you can select the **Print title on every page** check box to include the title at the top of each page.

Page Number — Select the **Include page number** check box to include page numbers at the bottom of each page of your tree. Click the up and down arrows on the **Starting number** field to change the starting page number.

Note: This option is only available for Outline Descendant and Outline Direct Descendant trees.

Footnote — Type your footnote in the field provided. It can be up to four lines long and will print in the lower left corner of your tree. You can place a box around it by selecting the **Draw box around footnote** check box.

2. Click **OK** when you've made your selections.

Family Tree Maker returns you to the tree view.

Selecting the Layout for Box-Style Trees

Selecting a more compact layout can help you save space in your tree. If you want to change the layout for an outline-style tree, see "Selecting the Layout for Outline-Style Trees" on page 256.

To choose a layout for box-style trees:

1. From the **Format** menu, select **Tree Format**.

Family Tree Maker displays the Tree Format dialog box. Each of your options is described below.

Type — This option is only available for Ancestor trees. Select the **Fit to page** option button if you only want one-page trees. Select **Custom** if you want to allow your trees to grow larger than one page.

Note: If you choose Fit to Page Ancestor tree when you have a Custom Ancestor tree on the screen, Family Tree Maker modifies your tree so that it can fit on a single page. Typically, Family Tree Maker will decrease the number of generations and the size of the text in the boxes. There may be other changes too.

Likewise, if you make a change to a Fit to Page Ancestor tree that makes it too large to fit on a single page, Family Tree Maker asks if you want to reverse the changes, reduce the amount of information in each box, or let the tree grow larger than one page.

Layout and **Connections** — Click the buttons showing the Layout and Connections that you prefer. Tighter Layout and Connections allow you to fit more information on each page. Please note that Connections options are not available for Descendant trees.

Center tree on page(s) — Select this check box if you would like your tree to be centered between the left, right, top, and bottom margins.

Make all boxes same size — De-select this check box if you want to allow the tree's boxes to vary in size, which saves space.

2. Click **OK** when you've made your selections.

Family Tree Maker returns you to the tree view.

Selecting the Layout for Outline-Style Trees

Outline-style trees have special layout options because they don't use boxes to display each individual's information.

To select the layout for outline-style trees:

1. From the **Format** menu, select **Tree Format**.

Family Tree Maker displays the Tree Format dialog box. Each of your options is described below.

Indentation — In outline-style trees, each generation is indented slightly more than the generation above it. Some people find it easier to distinguish between generations when there are leader dots (........) extending from the left margin of the page to each individual's name. If you want leader dots in your tree, enter a period (.) in the **Indent with which character** field. If you want to indent with a character other than leader dots, enter that character into the field. Leave it blank if you don't want anything at all.

To increase or decrease the size of each generation's indentation, click the up arrow or down arrow in the **Indent each generation by** field. A larger number will create a wider tree, and a smaller number will create a narrower tree. When you change the size of the indentation, you are changing it for all generations in the tree.

Generation Numbers — Generation numbers can help you see who belongs to which generation and are especially helpful when your tree is very long. To include generation numbers, select the **Place a generation number before each descendant's name** check box.

Normally, "1" is the first generation number in a tree. However, you can enter any number, up to 9999, in the **Starting generation number** field. If you were creating a series of several trees, you might want to enter a different number.

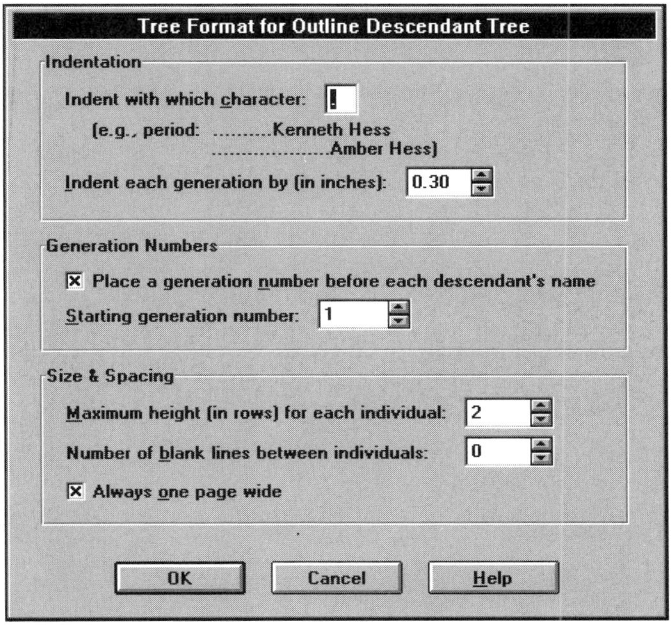

Tree Format for Outline Descendant Tree

Indentation

Indent with which character: [!]

(e.g., period: ....Kenneth Hess
.....................Amber Hess)

Indent each generation by (in inches): [0.30]

Generation Numbers

[X] Place a generation number before each descendant's name

Starting generation number: [1]

Size & Spacing

Maximum height (in rows) for each individual: [2]

Number of blank lines between individuals: [0]

[X] Always one page wide

[OK]   [Cancel]   [Help]

Figure 8-15. The Tree Format dialog box

Size & Spacing — If you choose to include a lot of information for each individual in your tree, it may not always fit on a single line. To allow an individual's information to wrap over more than one line, enter a number greater than one in the **Maximum height (in rows) for each individual** field. To limit each individual to one line only, enter "1" in the field.

Blank lines between each individual's information can make outline-style trees easier to read, but they will also decrease the amount of information that you can fit on a single page. To include blank lines between each individual in your tree, enter a number greater than zero in the **Number of blank lines between individuals** field.

Selecting the **Always one page wide** check box means that Family Tree Maker will not let the tree grow wider than one page. If any individual's information is too wide to fit on one page, Family Tree Maker will try reducing the size of the text in the tree to make the information fit. You can avoid this by increasing the number in the **Maximum height (in rows) for each individual** field. This allows information to wrap onto multiple lines.

2. Click **OK** when you've made your selections.

   Family Tree Maker returns you to the tree view.

Limiting the Width of Boxes and Picture/Objects

Setting a maximum box width and a maximum Picture/Object width can help you fit more information on a single page. This option is not available for Fit to Page Ancestor trees, because Family Tree Maker automatically controls this setting for you. Likewise, this option is not available for Outline Descendant and Outline Direct Descendant trees, because they do not have boxes.

To set a maximum width for your tree's boxes and Picture/Objects:

1. From the **Format** menu, select **Maximum Width for Each Box & Picture/Object**.

   Family Tree Maker displays the Maximum Width for Each Box & Picture/Object dialog box.

2. Enter a number in the **Maximum box width** field. To get a smaller tree, enter a smaller number. You can enter any width between .1 and 99.99 inches.

3. Enter a number in the **Maximum Picture/Object width** field. To allow the Picture/Objects to fit inside their boxes, this number must be slightly smaller than the number in the "Maximum box width" field. If it is too large, Family Tree Maker displays an error message.

4. Click **OK** when you've made your selections.

   Family Tree Maker returns you to the tree view.

   Note: If necessary, Family Tree Maker abbreviates your information to make it fit in the box size you specify. For example, if you select a very long name format, but a small maximum box width, Family Tree Maker may have to change the name format to a smaller one.

Other Printing Options

Each type of tree has its own set of special printing options. To display these special printing options, from the **Contents** menu, select **Options**. Read the appropriate section below for descriptions of the options.

Ancestor Tree Options

All of these options are available for both Fit to Page Ancestor trees and Custom Ancestor trees.

Label columns as "Parents," "Grandparents," etc. — Column labels identify each generation of your tree as the parents, grandparents, great-grandparents, etc., of the primary individual. These labels appear at the top of each column and make it easy to understand the tree at a glance.

Include duplicate ancestors each time they appear — If you have an instance of intermarriage in your family (for example, a cousin marrying back into the family), you will have some duplicate individuals in your tree. Select this check box if you want these individuals to print in your tree more than once.

Include siblings of primary individual — Usually an ancestor tree doesn't include the siblings of the primary individual. Instead, it only shows the ancestors of the primary individual. However, you can select this option if you wish to include them. Even when you select this option, the siblings will be left out of Fit to Page Ancestor trees if there is not enough space for them.

Include empty branches — Printing empty branches is useful when you want to collect more information about your family. You can fill out the boxes by hand and later transfer the information into your computer.

Descendant and Direct Descendant Tree Options

Label rows as "Children," "Grandchildren," etc. — Row labels identify each generation of your tree as the children, grandchildren, great-grandchildren, etc., of the primary individual. These labels appear at the left margin of the page.

Include duplicate descendants each time they appear — If you have an instance of intermarriage in your family (for example, a cousin marrying back into the family), you will have some duplicate individuals in your tree. Select this check box if you want these individuals to print in your tree more than once.

Outline Descendant and Outline Direct Descendant Tree Options

Print spouses — Select this check box to include descendants' spouses in your Outline Descendant tree. Each descendant's spouse will be directly beneath him or her and will be marked with a plus sign (+).

Include duplicate descendants each time they appear — If you have an instance of intermarriage in your family (for example, a cousin marrying back into the family), you will have some duplicate individuals in your tree. Select this check box if you want these individuals to print in your tree more than once.

CONTROLLING THE SIZE OF YOUR TREE

You can print a tree that contains as much information as you want, as long as it doesn't exceed 800,000" x 800,000" inches! Family Tree Maker prints the tree on as many pages as it takes to show the information and then you can then piece the pages together to create one large, beautiful tree.

If you want to reduce the size of your tree, experiment with the options in the following two tables. If you want just single-page trees, see "Creating a Set of Trees" on page 264. If you want to print large trees on one sheet of paper, see "How Can I Print Extra-large Trees on One Piece of Paper?" on page 265.

If Your Tree is Too Tall...

- If you print dates, choose a format that includes the date and location on the same line or only prints the date. (See "Selecting Information to Include in Your Tree" on page 243.)

- Include fewer generations in a single tree. Print multiple trees instead. (See "Choosing the Number of Generations" on page 242.)

- Print fewer items for each individual. (See "Selecting Information to Include in Your Tree" on page 243.)

- Omit borders, titles, and footnotes. (See "Choosing Styles for Boxes, Lines, and Tree Borders" on page 254 and "Adding a Title and Footnote" on page 254.)

- Don't use column labels. (See "Other Printing Options" on page 259.)

- Omit empty branches and the siblings of the primary individual. (See "Other Printing Options" on page 259.)

- Select a smaller font size, a smaller font, and the style "Regular." (See "Formatting Text" on page 253.)

- Try switching page orientation to "Portrait." (See "Print Setup" on page 266.)

- For Outline Descendant trees, reduce the number of rows per individual. (See "Selecting the Layout for Outline-Style Trees" on page 256.)

Figure 8-16. Making tall trees shorter

If Your Tree is Too Wide...

- If you print dates, choose a format that separates the date and location onto two lines or only prints the date. (See "Selecting Information to Include in Your Tree" on page 243.)

- Choose a name format that omits middle names. (See "Selecting Information to Include in Your Tree" on page 243.)

- Include fewer generations in a single tree. Print multiple trees instead. (See "Choosing the Number of Generations" on page 242.)

- If you print "Fact" fields, shorten the information entered in them (see "Entering Brief Biographical Facts" on page 130.)

- Omit borders, titles, and footnotes. (See "Choosing Styles for Boxes, Lines, and Tree Borders" on page 254 and "Adding a Title and Footnote" on page 254.)

- Don't use row labels. (See "Other Printing Options" on page 259.)

- Omit empty branches and the siblings of the primary individual. (See "Other Printing Options" on page 259.)

- Select a smaller font size, a smaller font, and the style "Regular." (See "Formatting Text" on page 253.)

- Reduce the width of the boxes with the Maximum Box and Picture/Object Width option. (See "Limiting the Width of Boxes and Picture/Objects" on page 258.)

- Try switching the page orientation to "Landscape." (See "Print Setup" on page 266.)

- For Outline Descendant trees, select the "Always One Page Wide" option. (See "Selecting the Layout for Outline-Style Trees" on page 256.)

Figure 8-17. Making wide trees narrower

PRINTING YOUR TREE

Once you have created your tree using the options on pages 229-262, you're ready to print it.

To print a tree:

1. Make sure you're in a tree view — there should be a tree on your screen.

2. Turn on your printer.

3. From the **File** menu, select **Print**.

   Family Tree Maker displays the Print dialog box where you can select printing options. Each of these options is described below.

   Note: You can also control items such as paper orientation, paper size, margins, and which printer prints your tree. If you want to change any of these items, see "Print Setup" on page 266.

   Print range — Use this option to select the pages to print. If you want to print all of the pages, select the **All** option button. If you want to print a range of pages, type the page number of the first page that you want to print in the **From** field and type the page number of the last page you want to print in the **To** field. If you want to print only one page, type the number of that page in both the **From** and **To** fields.

   Print quality — Use this option to select the quality of your printed materials. The higher the print quality you choose, the darker and sharper your printed materials will be. However, items printed in high print quality also take longer to print. If your printer does not support different print qualities, this option will not be available to you.

   Copies — In this field, type the number of copies that you want to print.

   Print to file — If you want to be able to print your tree to a file and send it to your printer at a later time, select this check box. This option is especially useful if you want to print your tree on a printer or plotter owned by someone who doesn't have Family Tree Maker. When you print, Family Tree Maker will ask for an "Output File Name." For general instructions for printing to a file, see page 264.

   Note: If you intend to print the file on a printer other than your own, you will need to change the settings in "Print Setup" to match the printer you will be using. See "Print Setup" on page 266.

Collate copies — Select this check box if you are printing multiple copies of a multiple-page tree and want to print complete trees instead of several copies of the first page, then several copies of the second page, and so on.

Print empty — Select this check box if you want to print an empty tree. Empty trees are useful when you're doing research away from your computer. You can write in the empty boxes, and then enter the information into your computer later.

Note: This option is not available for Outline Descendant trees.

Print color — If you have a color printer, select this check box to print in color. De-select it if you just want to print in black and white. If you don't have a color printer, select this check box to print in black, white, and shades of gray.

4. Click **OK** when you've made your selections.

   Family Tree Maker prints your tree.

CREATING A SET OF TREES

Rather than printing a tree on multiple pages and then piecing the pages together to form a single, large tree, consider printing a set of smaller trees. Print one tree that shows you through your grandparents (in the case of an Ancestor tree) or grandchildren (in the case of a Descendant tree). Then print additional trees for each grandparent (or grandchild) spanning a few more generations. You will end up with a set of trees showing exactly the same information as you would have had with a single, large tree.

To print a set of small trees:

1. Choose a small number of generations. For Ancestor trees, you'll usually want to print about three generations. For Descendant trees, you'll probably be able to fit two. Experiment to find out how much you can fit on a page.

2. Repeat step 1 as often as you like, with a grandparent or grandchild on one tree becoming the primary individual on a subsequent tree.

You will end up with a set of trees instead of one big tree.

How Can I Print Extra-Large Trees on One Large Piece of Paper?

If you can get access to a large plotter, you can print your tree on a poster-size piece of paper. To find a plotter, check with engineering and architectural service bureaus in your area. When you find a service bureau that can plot your tree, follow the instructions below:

1. Find out what type of plotter they use and then install that plotter's printer driver in Windows on your computer. For information about installing printer drivers, see your Microsoft Windows User's Guide.

2. Change the settings in Family Tree Maker's Print Setup dialog box so that they match the plotter on which you will print your tree. See "Print Setup" on page 266.

3. Create your tree.

4. Put a floppy disk in your disk drive.

5. From the **File** menu, select **Print**.

   Family Tree Maker displays the Print dialog box.

6. Select the **Print to file** check box. Also make sure to select **Print color** if you want the tree printed in color and have selected appropriate colors in the process of creating your tree.

7. Click **OK**.

   Family Tree Maker displays the Print to File dialog box.

8. In the **Output file name** field, type the letter of the drive where your floppy disk is located and a name for the tree.

   For example, if your floppy disk was in drive a:\ and you were creating a tree for the Hess family, you might type something like **A:\hesstree.prn** Remember, the file name must be no longer than eight characters with a three letter extension.

9. Click **OK**.

   Family Tree Maker prints your tree to your diskette.

You can now take the floppy disk to the service bureau and they can print your tree. The service bureau does not need a copy of Family Tree Maker to print your tree. They will simply copy the file directly to the plotter. For example, if the plotter was connected to LPT 1 and your floppy disk was in drive a:\ of their computer, they would type **copy/b A:\hesstree.prn LPT1**

PRINT SETUP

With the Print Setup dialog box, you can control the following items: paper orientation, paper size, paper source, margins, whether or not your pages overlap, which printer prints your documents, and other printer-specific options. Changing these settings can affect the number of pages needed to print a multiple page tree. Normally, you won't have to change any of these settings because Family Tree Maker uses the same print setup as your other Windows programs.

When you change print setup, you are changing it for a specific view, not for all views. For example, if you are printing an Ancestor tree and you change the print setup while you're in the Ancestor Tree view, every Ancestor tree that you print afterwards will have the same setup. However, Descendant trees would not have this setup. If you wanted your Descendant trees to have the same setup as your Ancestor trees, you would need to switch to the Descendant Tree view and change the print setup.

To change the print setup:

1. From the **File** menu, select **Print Setup**. Or, if you're in the Print dialog box, click **Setup**.

    Family Tree Maker displays the Print Setup dialog box.

    Default/Specific Printer — Use this field to select a printer. The default printer is the printer that you normally use with your other Windows programs. Select the **Default printer** option button to use this printer. If you wish to use a different printer, select the **Specific printer** option button and select a printer from the list that Family Tree Maker displays.

    Note: If the printer you wish to use is not shown in the "Specific Printer" drop-down list, then you need to install that printer's driver. Consult your Microsoft Windows User's Guide for information about installing printer drivers.

    Portrait/Landscape — If you want your document to print with the short edge of the paper at the bottom (as a letter normally prints) select the **Portrait** option button. If you want your document to print with the long edge of the paper at the bottom (sideways), select the **Landscape** option button. Ancestor trees usually take fewer pages in portrait orientation and Descendant trees usually take fewer pages in landscape orientation. This option is not available to printers using 14" x 11" paper.

Size/Source — Click the arrow next to the **Size** field to choose a paper size, and **Source** to choose your paper source.

Margins — Use the **Top**, **Bottom**, **Left**, and **Right** fields to change the margins on your pages.

Print continuous forms — If your printer uses continuous forms, you can select this check box to tell Family Tree Maker to print across the perforations in your paper. This does not apply to laser printers that automatically feed in single sheets of paper.

Overlap pages — If you want information on the edge of one page to be repeated on the edge of the next page so that it's easier to tape pages together, select this check box.

Brightness — Use this button to display the Brightness dialog box. In the Brightness dialog box you can control the color level for all of the Picture/Objects that are printed in the current view. When you have selected a brightness setting, click **OK** in the Brightness dialog box to return to the Print Setup dialog box.

Options — Use this button to display the Options dialog box. The options available to you depend on your printer. Make your selections from this dialog box, and then click **OK** to return to the Print Setup dialog box.

2. Click **OK** when you've made your selections.

   Family Tree Maker returns you to the current view.

Chapter 9

PRINTING DETAILED INFORMATION

*Pictured here are Ted Terashi Nomura and his bride Junko Nakazato. The couple
moved to the United States shortly after their wedding in Tokyo, Japan on May 12, 1960.
Their daughter, Tina Nomura is Banner Blue's Operations Supervisor.*

PRINTING DETAILED INFORMATION

With Family Tree Maker, you can create and print many other documents besides family trees. In this chapter, we tell you how to print labels and cards, Family Group Sheets, reports, and Scrapbooks. To print trees, see Chapter 8 "Creating and Printing Trees." For calendars, Family Pages, More About dialog boxes, and batch printing, see Chapter 10 "Other Printing."

Printing documents such as reports and Scrapbooks can be a lot of fun, so don't be afraid to experiment! Remember, if you get lost, you can always press [F1] to get on-screen help.

THE BASICS OF PRINTING

There are three main steps to printing each of these documents. First, you select the view for the document that you want to print. Second, you customize the document so that it looks the way you want. Third, you print your finished document. It's really quite simple, and we'll guide you along the way.

In the first part of this chapter, we give a short description of each of the documents that you can print. Along with the descriptions are instructions for displaying the basic version of each document. It's this basic document that you can customize and then print.

In the second part of this chapter, we give instructions for using each of the customization commands. You can use these commands in any combination to personalize your family documents. Please note that not all commands can be used with all documents. To help clarify when you can use a command, the description of each document includes a listing of the customization commands that you can use with that document.

Be creative when you customize! By trying different options, you'll find the styles that suit you best.

ALL ABOUT LABELS AND CARDS

Labels and cards have all kinds of valuable uses. For example, you can print address labels when it's time to send out invitations or holiday greetings. If you need to do a family mailing, you can print addresses directly onto postcards. Making "Hello, my name is..." stickers for large family reunions can help everyone get acquainted, and printing rolling index cards or address book pages allows you to keep family phone numbers close at hand. For a list of the different sizes and types of labels and cards that Family Tree Maker can print, look in the Print Setup dialog box from the Labels/Cards view (see page 282).

Family Tree Maker allows you to select a group of individuals to print your labels or cards for so that you don't always have to print them for everyone. In addition, each time you print, Family Tree Maker lets you choose whether to print one label or card per household or per individual. For example, if you print address labels for holiday cards, you probably only want one for each household. If you print name tags, you would want one for each individual.

Because Family Tree Maker recognizes the relationships between the individuals in your family tree, it prints labels and cards intelligently. For example, if you choose to print one address label per household, Family Tree Maker realizes that not everyone fits into the precise mold of a nuclear family. This means that it would print address labels that said "The John and Jane Doe Family" for any nuclear families, "John and Jane Doe" for any couples without children, and "Jane Doe" or "John Doe" for any single adults. No one would be excluded just because they aren't part of a household that has two parents and children.

Creating Labels and Cards

You create labels and cards by choosing the Labels/Cards view, just as you can choose the Family Page view or the Ancestor Tree view. When you choose the Labels/Cards view, Family Tree Maker displays a page of basic labels or cards for you. You can then make some customization selections, or just print the labels or cards as they are.

To create labels or cards:

1. From the **View** menu, select **Labels/Cards**.

    Family Tree Maker displays a sheet of labels or cards. Their size and shape depend which labels or cards are currently selected in the Print Setup dialog box. We will show you how to change the label or card size in "Label/Card Size and Print Setup," on page 282.

2. You can either print your labels or cards right away (see "Printing Your Document" on page 319), or customize them and then print (see "Customizing Labels and Cards," below).

Customizing Labels and Cards

For labels and cards, your customization options include the following:

- Selecting the label size, page 282

- Selecting individuals to print labels or cards for, page 283

- Selecting information to include on your labels or cards, page 293

- Formatting the information on your labels or cards, page 297

- Formatting text, including color, font, size, and style, page 308

- Selecting borders and colors for the labels or cards, page 313

- Selecting a size for Picture/Objects on the labels or cards, page 314

- Other printing options, such as whether to print for households or individuals, page 316

- Selecting the order in which the labels or cards print, page 318

Other helpful options include the following: viewing labels and cards at different sizes on the screen (see page 280), showing and hiding the lines that indicate where the page breaks are (see page 281), and navigating through your Family File by clicking names on labels and cards (see page 281).

ALL ABOUT FAMILY GROUP SHEETS

A Family Group Sheet is a detailed report about a single nuclear family (two parents and their children) including names, birth dates, death dates, marriage dates, and more. You can also include Picture/Objects for each individual, as well as a Picture/Object for the marriage.

Creating a Family Group Sheet

You create a Family Group Sheet by choosing the Family Group Sheet view, just as you can choose the Family Page view or the Ancestor Tree view. When you choose the Family Group Sheet view, Family Tree Maker creates a basic Family

Group Sheet for you. You can then make some customization selections, or just print the Family Group Sheet as it is.

To create a Family Group Sheet:

1. Go to the Family Page containing the individual whose Family Group Sheet you want to see.

   Use the Index of Individuals or Find Individual to locate that individual's Family Page. The Index of Individuals is described on page 117. Find Individual is described on page 122.

   Make sure you go to the Family Page of the husband and wife for whom you want to print a Family Group Sheet. If either of them was married more than once and the Family Page shows a spouse other than the one that you want, you can navigate to the correct spouse by clicking **Spouses**.

2. From the **View** menu, select **Family Group Sheet**.

   Family Tree Maker displays the Family Group Sheet.

3. You can either print your Family Group Sheet right away (see "Printing Your Document" on page 319), or customize it and then print (see "Customizing a Family Group Sheet," below).

Customizing a Family Group Sheet

For Family Group Sheets, your customization options include the following:

- Selecting information to include on your Family Group Sheet, page 293
- Formatting the information to include on your Family Group Sheet, page 297
- Formatting text, including color, font, size, and style, page 308
- Adding a title and footnote, page 310
- Choosing whether each individual's information is printed on a separate sheet, page 316

Other helpful options include the following: viewing Family Group Sheets at different sizes on the screen (see page 280), and showing and hiding the lines that indicate where the page breaks are (see page 281).

ALL ABOUT REPORTS

Family Tree Maker creates two different types of columnar reports: **Predefined reports** and **Custom reports**. With Predefined reports, Family Tree Maker chooses the contents, although you can still choose formatting options, such as fonts, borders, and titles. In some cases you can also choose who appears in a Predefined report. There are seven different types of Predefined reports to choose from: Kinship: Canon & Civil, Kinship: Relationship Only, Data Errors, Medical Information, Address, Birthdays of Living Individuals, and Parentage. When you are in LDS mode, there are two additional Predefined reports: PAF: Incomplete Individual Ordinances and PAF: Incomplete Marriage Sealings. Predefined reports are easy to use because Family Tree Maker does most of the work for you.

There are two kinds of Custom reports: Individual and Marriage. The only difference is that the Marriage report lists each individual's spouse. Otherwise, with Custom reports, you choose the contents as well as the formatting. Custom reports can contain up to 100 columns of almost any type of information. You also can choose whom to include. For example, you can print a report that contains only the people born before a certain date or in a certain place. Custom reports can be useful or just fun. Be creative — you can probably think of all kinds of facts that you want to know about your family.

Creating a Report

You create a report by choosing the Report view, just as you can choose the Family Page view or the Ancestor Tree view. When you choose the Report view, Family Tree Maker displays the last report that you created.

First you will choose what type of report you want to create. Then, you can make some formatting selections and print the report:

1. If you are planning to create a Kinship report, select the primary individual by highlighting his or her name on a Family Page or in another document.

    The primary individual in a Kinship report is the individual to whom everyone else in the report is related.

2. From the **View** menu, select **Report**.

    Family Tree Maker displays the last report you created.

3. From the **Format** menu, select **Report Format**.

    Family Tree Maker displays the Report Format dialog box.

4. In the **Select a format for your report** list, click the report format that you want to create. Each format is described below.

    Individual Custom — With Individual Custom reports, you choose the contents, as well as the formatting. You also can choose to include all of the individuals in your Family File or just a smaller group. Select this type of report when none of the other reports contain the information that you want.

    Marriage Custom — The only difference between the Individual Custom report and the Marriage Custom report is that the Marriage report lists each individual's spouse.

    Kinship: Canon & Civil — Kinship reports list the names, relationships, and relationship degrees of the primary individual's blood relatives, spouses of blood relatives, and blood relatives of the primary individual's spouse(s). Adopted children, foster children, and children of unknown status will appear in Kinship reports unless you choose to exclude them. See "Entering Nicknames, Titles, and Parental Relationship Information" on page 134 for information about excluding individuals.

    The "degree" of a relationship is a legal term. It refers to the number of "steps" between two individuals who are blood relatives. The degree in civil law represents the total number of steps through the bloodline that separate two individuals. For example, there are two steps from you to your grandparent and then two steps back down to your first cousin, so the degree is four.

    The degree in Canon law measures the maximum number of steps from the nearest common ancestor. Your grandparent is the nearest common ancestor between you and your first cousin, so in this case the degree would be two. Canon law is used in most of the United States.

    If two individuals are related in more than one way, Family Tree Maker displays each of the relationships in the Kinship report. For example, if two cousins marry, each of the relationships between them would be included.

    Kinship: Relationship Only — This type of Kinship report lists each individual's name, birth date, and relationship with the primary individual.

Data Errors — This report helps you locate and fix possible errors in your Family File. A complete listing of the types of errors that it finds begins on page 371. Select this type of report when you want to clean up your file. If you're planning to submit your file to the World Family Tree Project (see page 362), you may want to do this beforehand.

Medical Information — This report lists each individual's name, birth date, and any medical information from their Medical dialog box. See page 133 for information about the Medical dialog box.

Address — This report lists each individual's name, address, and phone number, if available. The addresses and phone numbers are taken from the individual's Address dialog box. See page 132 for information about the Address dialog box.

Birthdays of Living Individuals — This report lists each living individual's name, birth date, and age at next birthday. Family Tree Maker uses your computer's internal clock to calculate how old each individual is. Be sure that the clock is set correctly before you generate this type of report. See your Windows User's Guide for instructions on setting the clock.

Parentage — This report lists each individual's name, his or her parents' names, and the nature of the relationship between the individual and each parent. For example, it could show someone as a "Stepmother."

If the currently open Family File is in LDS mode (see page 78), you have the following additional options:

PAF: Incomplete Individual Ordinances — This report lists each individual in the Family File that is missing at least one of the following dates: birth or christening, death, baptism, endowment, and seal to parents.

PAF: Incomplete Marriage Sealings — This report lists each individual in the Family File that is missing at least one of the following dates: marriage or sealing.

5. Click **OK** after making your selection.

6. You can either print your report right away (see "Printing Your Document" on page 319), or customize it and then print (see "Customizing a Report," on the next page).

Customizing a Report

For reports, your customization options include the items in the list below. Please note that not all options are available for every type of report.

- Selecting individuals to include in the report, page 283
  Not available for Kinship, Parentage, and PAF reports

- Selecting the number of generations to include in the report, page 292
  Only available for Kinship reports

- Selecting information to include in the report, page 293
  Only available for Custom reports and Data Errors reports

- Formatting the information included in the report, page 297
  Available for all report types

- Formatting text, including color, font, size, and style, page 308
  Available for all report types

- Adding a title and footnote, page 310
  Available for all report types

- Selecting borders and colors for the report, page 313
  Available for all report types

- Selecting the width for the columns in the report, page 315
  Available for all report types

- Selecting the order in which the individuals appear in the report, page 318
  Available for all report types

Other helpful options include the following: viewing reports at different sizes on the screen (see page 280), showing and hiding the lines that indicate where the page breaks are (see page 281), and navigating through your Family File by clicking names in reports (see page 281).

ALL ABOUT PRINTED SCRAPBOOK PAGES

Printed Scrapbook pages are great documents to add to family books or other collections of printed family information. You can print Scrapbook pages with as many or as few Picture/Objects per page as you like. To personalize them, you can add a title and decorative borders, too.

Displaying Scrapbook Pages

You create Scrapbook pages by choosing the Scrapbook view, just as you can choose the Family Page view or the Ancestor Tree view. When you choose the Scrapbook view, Family Tree Maker displays a Scrapbook page. You can make some customization selections, or just print the Scrapbook pages as they are.

To display a Scrapbook page:

1. Go to the Family Page containing the individual or the marriage whose Scrapbook you want to print.

    The Index of Individuals and Find Individual are two quick ways to locate an individual's Family Page. The Index of Individuals is described on page 117. Find Individual is described on page 122.

2. On the Family Page, place the cursor either on the name of the individual or on the marriage whose Scrapbook you want to print.

3. From the **View** menu, select **Scrapbook**.

    Family Tree Maker displays the Scrapbook.

4. You can either print your Scrapbook pages right away (see "Printing Your Document" on page 319), or customize them and then print (see "Customizing Scrapbook Pages," below).

Customizing Scrapbook Pages

For Scrapbooks, your customization options include the following:

*   Selecting information to include in your Scrapbooks, page 293

*   Formatting text, including color, font, size, and style, page 308

*   Adding a title and page numbers, page 310

*   Selecting how many Picture/Objects to print per Scrapbook page, page 312

*   Selecting borders and colors for the Scrapbook, page 313

*   Setting other print options, such as which Picture/Objects to print, page 316

*   Selecting the order in which Picture/Objects appear, page 318

Formatting and printing for Scrapbooks works differently than for other documents in Family Tree Maker. With Scrapbooks, you can *only* make formatting changes when you switch to Print Preview. To go into Print Preview, from the **File** menu, select **Print Preview**.

In Print Preview, you can use the **Zoom** buttons to get a better view of the Scrapbook pages, the **Setup** button to change the Print Setup, the **Print** button to print the pages, and the **Scrapbk** button to return to the Scrapbook view. In addition, you can use the commands on the **Contents** and **Format** menus to change your formatting selections. Finally, the **Show Page Lines** command on the **View** menu lets you show and hide lines that indicate where one page ends and another page begins.

CUSTOMIZING YOUR DOCUMENTS

Instructions for using each of the customization commands are in the next several sections. Please note that some of the customization commands work slightly differently for each document. For this reason, some sections contain notes to help you use the command correctly. Be sure to read the notes about the document that you are currently working with.

Zooming

With the Zoom command, you can make your document appear larger on screen so it's easier to read the text. You can also shrink it down so you can see the whole thing at once. Please note that the Zoom command does not control how large your document is when you print.

To use the Zoom command:

1. From the **View** menu, select **Zoom**.

    Family Tree Maker displays the Zoom dialog box.

2. Select the option button for the size that you prefer.

    "Size to Window" fits your entire document on the screen. "Actual Size" makes the document the approximate size that it is when it prints. "200%" is the largest size.

3. Click **OK** when you've made your selection.

    When your whole document is not visible on the screen, Family Tree Maker places scroll bars on the bottom and right sides of it. You can use these scroll bars to view different sections of it.

Showing Page Lines

You can control whether or not dotted lines indicating page margins appear on the screen. From the **View** menu, select **Show Page Lines**. If this option has a check next to it, the page lines will be visible. Otherwise, they won't be. These lines never appear on your printed documents.

Using Your Mouse in Reports and Labels and Cards

You can navigate through Family Tree Maker simply by clicking names in reports or on labels and cards and then clicking the toolbar or using the menus. You can also activate the Picture/Objects on labels and cards, either viewing pictures at full size or "playing" OLE objects. For information about including Picture/Objects on labels and cards, see "Selecting Information to Include in Your Document" on page 293.

Whether you navigate through Family Tree Maker or activate your Picture/Objects depends on what you click and whether you double-click or single-click. The table below describes each of the functions.

Do this...	To do this...
Click once anywhere on a label or card, or click an individual's name in a report.	Select the individual. You can then use the menus or the toolbar to change to any view. The selected individual becomes the primary individual.
Double-click any text on a label or card, or double-click an individual's name in a report.	Go to the individual's Family Page.
Double-click a Picture/Object on a label or card (not available for reports).	If the Picture/Object is an OLE object, Family Tree Maker opens the OLE server and "plays" the object. For example, it plays sound and video files.
	If the Picture/Object is a not an OLE object, Family Tree Maker displays it in the View Picture dialog box.

Figure 9-1. Using your mouse in reports and labels and cards

Label/Card Size and Print Setup

Labels and cards have their own special Print Setup dialog box. Print setup for all other documents is on page 266.

To change the print setup for labels and cards:

1. Make sure you're in the Labels/Cards view. There should be a set of labels or cards on the screen.

2. From the **File** menu, select **Print Setup**.

    Family Tree Maker displays the Print Setup dialog box. Each of your options is described below.

    Default/Specific Printer — Use this field to select a printer. Select the **Default printer** option button to use the printer that you normally use with your other Windows programs. If you wish to use a different printer, click the **Specific printer** drop-down list and select a printer from the list that Family Tree Maker displays.

    Note: If the printer you wish to use is not shown, then you need to install that printer's driver. Consult your Microsoft Windows User's Guide for information about installing printer drivers.

    Portrait/Landscape — If you want your sheet of labels or cards to print with the short edge of the sheet at the bottom select the **Portrait** option button. If you want the sheet to print with the long edge of the sheet at the bottom (sideways), select the **Landscape** option button.

    Source — To choose a paper source, click the **Source** drop-down list and then make a selection from the list that Family Tree Maker displays.

    Avery® products — Use this list to select the type and size of the label or card on which to print. Family Tree Maker supports dozens of different card and label sizes, including address labels, name badges, rotary cards, video cassette labels, index cards, address book pages, and more. The card and label types are based on the Avery line of office products, although you can use any brand. You can even print on plain 8 1/2" x 11" paper if you just want to print block-style reports.

    Family Tree Maker indicates the product number, style, and size of each label or card so that you can get a general idea of the label's or card's appearance. If you want to see exactly what a label looks like, select the label type in the **Avery products** list and click **OK**. Family Tree Maker will draw the label or card on your screen. If you do not like the style of the label or card, simply re-open the Print Setup dialog box to select a new style.

Brightness — Use this button to display the Brightness dialog box. The Brightness level that you select through this dialog box will only apply to Picture/Objects that are printed on labels and cards. When you have selected a brightness setting, click **OK** in the Brightness dialog box to return to the Print Setup dialog box.

Options — Use this button to display the Options dialog box. The options available to you depend on your printer. Make your selections from this dialog box, and then click **OK** to return to the Print Setup dialog box.

3. Click **OK** when you've made your selections.

    Family Tree Maker returns you to the Labels/Cards view.

Selecting Individuals to Include in Your Document

When you create Custom reports and labels and cards, you can use the Individuals to Include dialog box to select a group of individuals to print. Instructions for using this feature begin in the paragraph below. However, this feature works slightly differently for different documents, so be sure also to read the special note for the document that you are creating:

- Labels and cards, page 290

- Reports, page 290

1. From the **Contents** menu, select **Individuals to Include**.

    Family Tree Maker displays the Include dialog box.

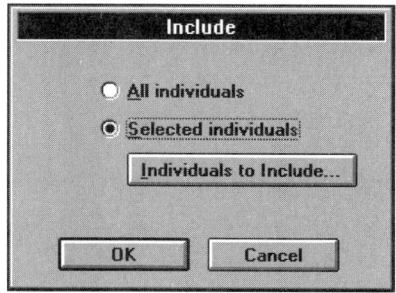

Figure 9-2. The Include dialog box

2. If you want everyone in your Family File to print, choose **All individuals** and click **OK**. You can then skip the remaining steps. Otherwise, choose **Selected individuals** and then click **Individuals to Include**.

When you click "Individuals to Include," Family Tree Maker displays the Individuals to Include dialog box. This is the dialog box that you will use to create a group of individuals to print. The list on the right shows the group of individuals who will be printed. The list on the left shows which individuals you can add to the group. The individuals in the list on the left are in alphabetical order by last name. Nicknames (aka's) are on different lines than the given names. See Figure 9-3, below.

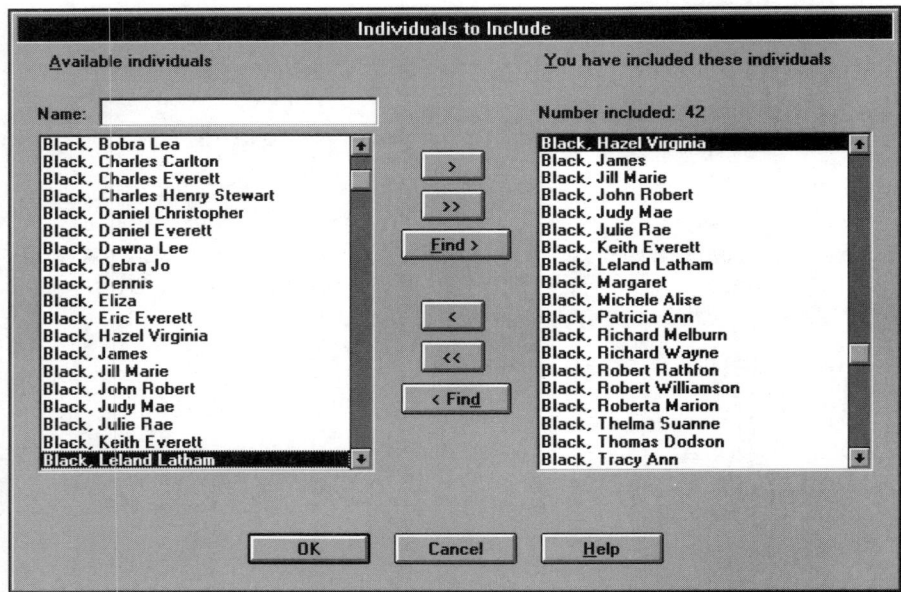

Figure 9-3. The Individuals to Include dialog box

3. Now you must create the group of individuals to print. You can do this by selecting individuals and adding them to or removing them from the list on the right. The table below shows the three methods that you can use. You can use any combination of these methods to create your group.

To do this...	Use this button...	See page...
Include or remove individuals one-by-one.	"Include" or "Remove" (the single arrows)	286
Include all of the individuals currently in your Family File or remove all of the individuals currently in the group.	"Include All" or "Remove All" (the double arrows)	287
Choose categories of individuals to include or remove all at once.	"Find and Include" or "Find and Remove"	288

Figure 9-4. Methods for creating groups

In general, you do not need to worry about the order in which you add individuals because Family Tree Maker can sort them for you later. The sorting orders include "Last name (A first)," "Last name (Z first)," "Birth date (oldest first)," and "Birth date (youngest first)." If you want individuals in an order other than those offered in the Sort dialog box, add them to the list in that order. Then, in the Sort dialog box, select the **Don't sort individuals** option button.

Note: There is *one* Individuals to Include dialog box for all views in Family Tree Maker. The group of individuals that you create in one view, such as Labels/Cards, is available to you in the other views that allow you to choose groups: Report, Calendar, and batch print. Even if you exit Family Tree Maker, the group that you create in the Individuals to Include dialog box will remain the same until you change it again. Of course, if you make changes to the group in one view, such as the Report view, the group will change in all other views as well.

4. When you're done creating the group, click **OK** in the Individuals to Include dialog box.

Family Tree Maker will return you to the document view.

Using the "Include" and "Remove" Buttons

With the "Include" and "Remove" buttons you can add and remove individuals to and from the group one at a time.

To create a group using the "Include" and "Remove" buttons:

1. Click an individual's name in the list on the left to add that individual to the group. If you want to remove an individual from the group, click his or her name in the list on the right.

2. Click either the **Include** button (the arrow pointing to the right) or the **Remove** button (the arrow pointing to the left). See Figure 9-5.

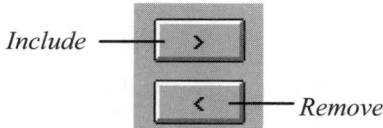

Figure 9-5. The Include and Remove buttons

If you chose to add the individual, his or her name is added to the list on the right and the "Number included" increases by one. If you chose to remove the individual, his or her name is removed from the list on the right, and the "Number included" decreases by one.

Instead of selecting an individual and then clicking "Include" or "Remove," you can just double-click the individual's name. Double-clicking names in the list on the left automatically adds them to the group. Double-clicking names in the list on the right automatically removes them from the group.

Using the "Include All" and "Remove All" Buttons

With the "Include All" button, one click adds all of the individuals currently in your Family File to the group. With the "Remove All" button, one click removes all of the individuals from the group. See Figure 9-6.

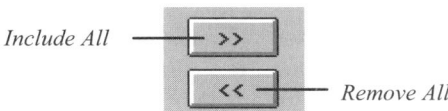

Include All

Remove All

Figure 9-6. The Include All and Remove All buttons

The best time to use the "Include All" button is when you want to create a group that includes almost all of the individuals that are currently in your Family File. For example, if there are only a few people that you don't want to include in the group, click the **Include All** button (the double arrows pointing to the right) to move all of the individuals to the list on the right. Then use the **Remove** button (the arrow pointing to the left) to remove the few individuals that you don't want in the group. This is much faster than including all of the individuals one by one. The "Remove" button is described in "Using the 'Include' and 'Remove' Buttons" on page 286.

If you want to include all of the individuals in your Family File, don't use the "Include All" button. Instead, from the **Contents** menu, select **Individuals to Include**. Then, in the Include dialog box, select **All Individuals**. This way, individuals that you add to your Family File later will be included automatically. If you use the "Include All" button to include everyone, individuals that are added to your Family File later will *not* be added to the group automatically.

The best time to use the "Remove All" button is when you already have several individuals in the group and you want to start over. Click the **Remove All** button (the double arrows pointing to the left) to remove all of the individuals from the group. Then use any method to begin adding individuals to the group again.

Using the "Find and Include" and "Find and Remove" Buttons

With the "Find and Include" and "Find and Remove" buttons, Family Tree Maker will search your Family File for individuals, such as those who were born before a certain date or those who are ancestors of a particular individual, and add them to or remove them from the group.

To create a group using the "Find and Include" and "Find and Remove" buttons:

1. Decide which individuals you want to add to or remove from the group. For example, do you want to add your ancestors? Do you want to add the individuals who were merged or appended? Do you want to remove all of the individuals who were born before a particular date?

    If you want to add or remove a group of individuals that are relatives of a particular individual, make sure to highlight the name of that individual in the list on the left before moving on to step 2. For example, if you wanted to add all of your ancestors, you would highlight your name.

2. Click either the **Find and Include** ("Find" with the arrow pointing to the right) or **Find and Remove** button ("Find" with the arrow pointing to the left). See Figure 9-7.

    Family Tree Maker displays either the Add Individuals or Remove Individuals dialog box. In this dialog box you specify which individuals you want Family Tree Maker to find and add to or remove from the group.

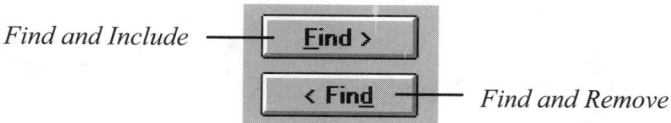

Find and Include ———— [**Find** >]
[< **Find**] ———— *Find and Remove*

Figure 9-7. The Find and Include and Find and Remove buttons

3. Click in the **Search** field.

    If you want to find the individuals who are all relatives of a particular individual, choose **Relatives** from the drop-down list. Family Tree Maker automatically fills the "of" field with the name of the individual that was highlighted in step 1. Using the **Limit relationships to** fields, select the individuals that you want to find. For example, to find all of the individual's ancestors, you would enter a large number in **Generations of Ancestors** and zeros in the other two fields. When you've made your selections, click **OK** and skip to step 5.

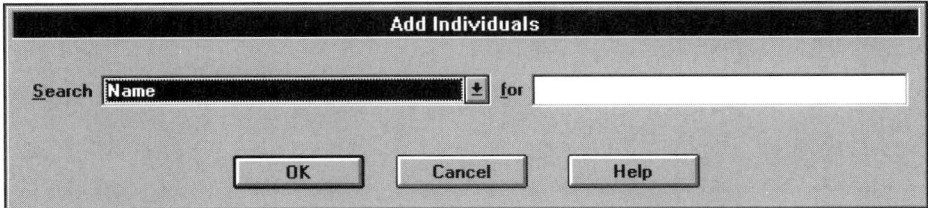

Figure 9-8. The Add Individuals dialog box

If you want to find individuals who have something in common, such as a birthplace, use the drop-down list to choose the name of the field that contains that information. For example, if you wanted to find all individuals who were born in a particular place, you would select "Birth location." When you've selected a field, continue with step 4.

4. In the **for** field, type the information that you want to search for. If the field that you are searching only has certain legal values (such as "male," "female," and "unknown"), Family Tree Maker will display a drop-down list in the "for" field. In this case, just click the item that you want to search for.

   For example, if you chose "Birth location" in step 3, and you wanted Family Tree Maker to find everyone that was born in Cleveland, Ohio, then you would type **Cleveland, Ohio** in the "for" field. If you are searching a date field, see Figure 4-12 on page 125 for searching tips.

5. Click **OK**.

   Family Tree Maker searches your Family File for individuals who match your request. If no matches are found, Family Tree Maker tells you so. If you chose to add the individuals, their names are added to the list on the right and the "Number included" increases. If you chose to remove the individuals, their names are removed from the list on the right, and the "Number included" decreases.

Special Note for Labels and Cards

When you print labels and cards, you can choose to print one label or card for each household or for each individual. For example, if you are printing address labels for holiday cards, you probably only want to print one label per household. If you are printing name tags, however, you would probably want to print one for each individual.

As you create your list of individuals to print, make sure to include *all* of the individuals whose names you want to appear on a label or card. If you are printing labels or cards for individuals and you leave a name off of the list, a label or card won't print for that individual. If you are printing labels or cards for households, and you accidentally leave out a member of a household, the information on the label or card may not print as you want it to.

Once you have created your list of individuals to print, you will be able to tell Family Tree Maker whether you want to print your labels or cards separately for each individual, or whether you want to print one label or card for each household. To make this choice, you will use the Options dialog box on the Contents menu. This dialog box is described on page 316.

You will also be able to select name formats for your labels or cards. The name formatting choices let you control how formal or informal your labels or cards are. For example, you can choose to use titles such as "Mr." and "Mrs." or you can just choose to use first names. You also can control how the names in a household print. For example, you may choose a name format such as "Mr. & Mrs. Doe and Family." On the other hand you may prefer to list out all of the names of the individuals in the household. There are several options; the choice that you make will probably depend on your reason for printing labels or cards. To make this choice, you will use the Options: Name dialog box, described on page 298.

Special Note for Reports

Please note that the Individuals to Include option is not available for Marriage, Parentage, and PAF reports.

Finding Individuals in Reports

This feature is available in all reports that include names and are sorted in alphabetical order by last name, except the Parentage report, the Marriage report, and the PAF: Incomplete Marriage Sealings report.

You can find an individual in a report just by typing their name:

1. Click in the **Type name** field at the top of the screen.

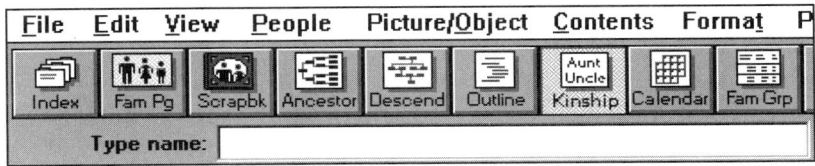

Figure 9-9. The Type name field

2. Start typing the last name of the individual that you want to find.

    With each character you type, you will get closer to the name you are looking for. You can type part or all of the name, as long as it is in the same format as the report (Last name, First name Middle name).

Choosing the Number of Generations for Kinship Reports

Family Tree Maker lets you choose how many generations of ancestors and descendants to include in Kinship reports. In addition, you can limit the degrees of cousinship that a Kinship report contains (5th cousins, 6th cousins, 7th cousins, and so on).

To choose the number of generations for a Kinship report:

1. From the **Contents** menu, select **# of Generations to Show**.

   Family Tree Maker displays the # of Generations to Show dialog box. Each of your options is described below.

   Limit size of Kinship report to show — Select this check box if you would like to limit the number of individuals in your Kinship report. Leave this check box unchecked if you want to include all possible relatives in your Kinship report. When this check box is unchecked, the next three options in the dialog box are not available.

   Generations of Ancestors *and* **Generations of Descendants** — Click the up or down arrows in these fields to choose how many generations of the primary individual's ancestors and descendants to include. You can choose any number from 1 to 99.

   Degrees of Cousins — Click the up or down arrows in this field to choose how many cousins to include. For example, if you don't want to include individuals more distantly related than 5th cousins, select "5" in this field. You can choose any number from 1 to 99.

   Report only closest relationship for each individual — The individuals in your Family File can be related in more than one way, especially when intermarriage exists. If you select this check box, Family Tree Maker will include only one relationship between the primary individual and each of the other individuals in the Kinship report.

   Display only natural parental relationships — Select this check box to include only natural parents in the Kinship report.

2. Click **OK** when you've made your selections.

   Family Tree Maker returns you to the Kinship report.

Selecting Information to Include in Your Document

When you create labels and cards, Family Group Sheets, reports, and Scrapbooks, you can use the Items to Include dialog box to choose what information to include in them. Instructions for using this feature begin in the paragraph below. This feature works slightly differently for different documents, so be sure also to read the special note for the document that you are creating:

- Labels and cards, page 295

- Family Group Sheets, page 296

- Reports, page 296

- Scrapbooks, page 296

From the **Contents** menu, select **Items to Include**. (For Scrapbooks, you must first be in Print Preview.) Family Tree Maker displays the Items to Include dialog box (see Figure 9-10). It contains two lists: the list on the right shows which items will be included in the document. The scrolling list on the left shows which items you can add to the document. Each document has a default group of items that are already included. However, you can add and delete items to and from the list on the right as often as you like. When you're done selecting information, click **OK**. Family Tree Maker will return you to the document view.

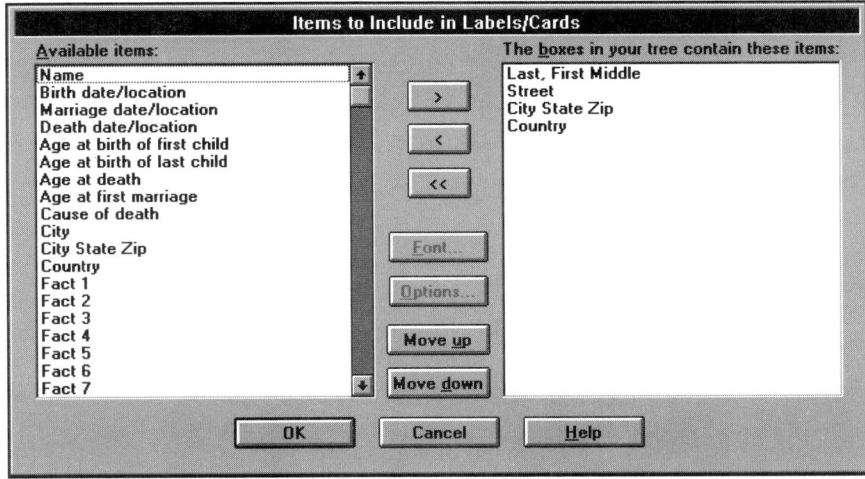

Figure 9-10. Items to Include dialog box

Adding and Removing Items to and from Documents

To add items to or remove items from a document:

1. Click the name of an item in the list on the left to add it. To remove an item from the list, click the name of the item in the list on the right.

2. Click either the **Include** button (the arrow pointing to the right) or the **Remove** button (the arrow pointing to the left). See Figure 9-11.

   If you chose to add the item, it is added to the list on the right. If you chose to remove the item, it is removed from the list on the right.

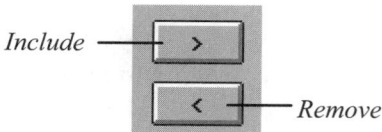

Include

Remove

Figure 9-11. The Include and Remove buttons

Instead of selecting an item and then clicking "Include" or "Remove," you can just double-click the item. Double-clicking items in the list on the left automatically adds them. Double-clicking items in the list on the right automatically removes them. In addition, if you want to delete all items from the list on the right, just click the **Remove all** button (the double arrow pointing to the left).

Some items, such as names and dates, require you to make formatting choices. Family Tree Maker automatically displays a dialog box that asks you to make a formatting choice when it is necessary. You can also format an item by selecting it in the list on the right and clicking **Options**. See "Formatting the Information in Your Document" on page 297.

3. Once the list on the right contains all of the items that you want, you can change the order in which they appear. Simply click an item in the list on the right and then click either **Move up** or **Move down** to move that item up or down one space.

   You can also choose sizes and styles for the text in your documents by clicking **Font**. See "Formatting Text" on page 308 for more information.

Special Note for Labels and Cards

When you're printing labels or cards that include addresses, you should know that Family Tree Maker takes addresses from the Address dialog box, described on page 132. You do not have to type an address into every individual's Address dialog box, because individuals can inherit addresses from their spouses or parents. If an individual does not have an address in his or her Address dialog box, Family Tree Maker first checks to see if the individual's spouse has an address. If the individual's spouse does not have an address, Family Tree Maker uses the address of the individual's parents. If the parents do not have an address either, then the individual has no address. You can tell when an address has been inherited because the label will have a dotted line around it on your screen. (The dotted line will not print on the label or card.)

You can include up to fifty items per label or card, although you will probably want to include far fewer unless you are printing a block-style report on regular paper. There are a few items of special interest for labels and cards:

- If you have placed Picture/Objects in each individual's Scrapbook, you can include Picture/Objects on your labels or cards. Simply select **Picture/Object** from the list on the left. Family Tree Maker will display the Options: Picture/Object dialog box. In this dialog box you can select which Picture/Object will be included on each individual's label or card and where it is placed in relation to the text. If an individual does not have a Picture/Object, Family Tree Maker will insert a small substitute graphic in the box instead. For more information about substitute graphics, see "Missing Picture/Objects" on page 302.

- Using the **Custom field** item, you can add up to 80 characters of text to your labels or cards. What you type in this field will appear on every label or card that you print. The **Custom field** field is most useful for adding phrases such as "Hello, my name is..." or "Holiday Greetings for" at the top of name tags or address labels.

- Also useful for labels and cards is the item **City State Zip**. This item allows you to print addresses in the correct format. If you tried to create a label using the three separate items **City**, **State**, and **Zip**, they would print on three separate lines instead of on one long line.

Special Note for Family Group Sheets

One page of your Family Group Sheet can contain the basic information; this page is called the Standard Page. You can also choose to include information from the More About dialog boxes, which will appear on additional pages.

If you have placed Picture/Objects in Scrapbooks, you can include them on the Standard Page — one for each individual and one for the marriage. Simply select **Standard Page with Picture/Objects** from the list on the left. If the marriage or an individual does not have a Picture/Object, Family Tree Maker will insert a substitute graphic instead. For more information about substitute graphics, see "Missing Picture/Objects" on page 302. Please note that this is not available if you selected the LDS option in the Labels dialog box (see page 78).

Special Note for Reports

In the Report view, the Items to Include command is only available for Custom reports and Data Errors reports. In Custom reports, the items that you choose appear in columns, from left to right. For example, you would choose **Name** first if you wanted each individual's name to be in the leftmost column. You would choose **Death date** last if you wanted this information to appear in the rightmost column. You can include up to one hundred items per report, limited by paper size, however.

In Data Errors reports, you are choosing which types of errors you want Family Tree Maker to locate and include in the report. In this case, the "Options" button is not available.

Special Note for Scrapbooks

Among the items you can include on a printed Scrapbook are the caption, the description, and the date. However, the more information you include, the smaller the Picture/Objects will be. In addition, if you choose to include more items than can fit on each Scrapbook page, Family Tree Maker simply will not print those items that do not fit, starting with the last item you choose.

The items that you choose to include will be printed in "blocks." For example, if you chose to include "Picture/Object" and then "Picture/Object Caption," each Picture/Object would print with its caption directly beneath it.

Formatting the Information in Your Document

Many items that you can include in Family Group Sheets, reports, and labels and cards have formatting options. Instructions for this feature begin in the paragraph below. This feature works slightly differently for different documents, so be sure to read the special note for the document that you are creating:

- Labels and cards, page 298
- Family Group Sheets, page 305
- Reports, page 307

Formatting Items As You Select Them

When you're selecting items to include in your documents, Family Tree Maker displays an Options dialog box for those items that have formatting options. Simply make your selections and then click **OK** to continue. The list above shows on which page the Options dialog boxes for each document are described.

Formatting Items After They've Been Selected

To change the formatting of an item that's already in the list on the right:

1. Click the item in the list on the right.

   Family Tree Maker highlights the item.

2. Click **Options**.

   Family Tree Maker displays an Options dialog box. Each of the Options dialog boxes is described below in the sections about each document.

   Note: If you select an item in the list on the right and **Options** stays grayed out, that item does not have any formatting options.

   Statistics, such as age at death, or number of children, do not have formatting options. They always print with their field labels (for example, "Age at death: 40"). If a "?" prints, it means that there is no information in a date field. If "est" prints, as in "Age at death: 40 est," it means that a date was uncertain. (Entering an uncertain date is always better than entering nothing.)

3. Make your selections and then click **OK**.

   Family Tree Maker closes the Options dialog box.

From the Items to Include dialog box, you can also change the text font, size, or style for any or all of the items you choose to print:

1. Select the item in the list on the right by clicking it.

   Family Tree Maker highlights the item you selected.

2. Click **Font**.

   Family Tree Maker displays the Text Font, Style & Size dialog box. This dialog box is described in "Formatting Text" on page 308. Please note that the "Font" button is not available for reports. To change text formatting in reports, see "Formatting Text" on page 308.

Special Note for Labels and Cards

With labels and cards, you have special formatting options for names, facts, Picture/Objects, and a few other items. Formatting options for names are described directly below. Formation options for Picture/Objects are described on page 300, facts are on page 303, and other items are on page 304.

Names on Labels and Cards

When you choose to include names on labels or cards, Family Tree Maker displays the Options: Name dialog box. See Figure 9-12. In this dialog box, you can choose the format in which all names will print in this set of labels or cards.

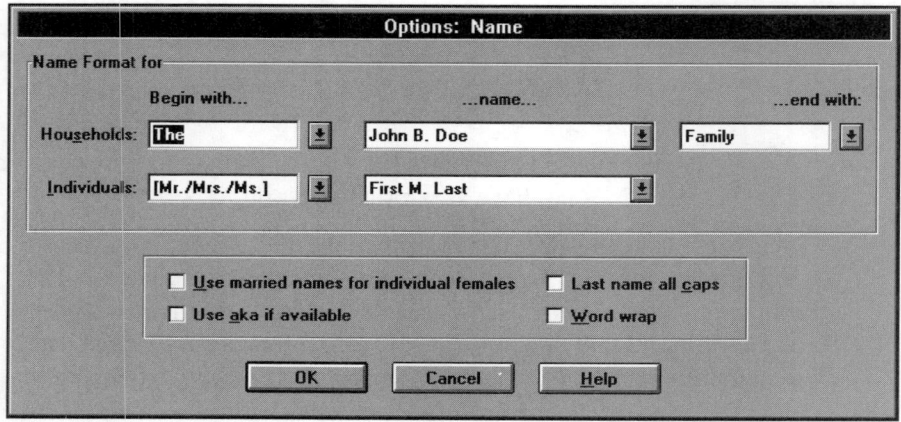

Figure 9-12. The Options: Name dialog box for labels and cards

Note: There may be a few individuals in your Family File who use different titles. For example, some individuals may use the title "Dr." or "Reverend." You can create special titles for those individuals in their Lineage dialog boxes. See "Entering Nicknames, Titles, and Parental Relationship Information" on page 134. However, the majority of the individuals in your Family File will get their titles from the Options: Name dialog box.

There are two different name formats that you can set in this dialog box: one when the individuals are printed on a label or card as part of a household, and one when the individuals are printed as individuals. Each of these name formats has multiple parts that work together to create the whole printed name.

Before you begin making your selections, here are a few examples:

To get	Begin with	name	end with
The John B. Doe Family	The	John B. Doe	Family
John & Jane Doe and Children	(Blank)	John & Jane Doe	and Son/Daughter/ Children
Mr. and Mrs. Doe	Mr. and Mrs.	Doe	N/A
Ms. Jane S. Doe	Mr./Mrs./Ms.	First M. Last name	N/A

Figure 9-13. Name format samples

To set the name format:

1. Click in the **Households/Begin with** drop-down list. You can either type in your own word(s), leave the field blank, or select an item from the drop-down list.

   The drop-down list generally uses the titles "Mr." and "Mrs." However, if you prefer different titles, you can change them in the Titles dialog box, described on page 86.

2. Click in the **Households/name** field and select an appropriate name format

3. Click in the **Households/end with** field. You can either select an item from the drop-down list or type in your own word(s).

    This field is only available for Households.

4. Repeat steps 1 and 2 for the **Individuals** fields.

5. If you would like Family Tree Maker to print nicknames when they are available, select the **Use aka if available** check box. If you would like all last names printed in capitals, select the **Last name all caps** check box. To allow long name formats to wrap onto two lines, select the **Word wrap** check box. Finally, select the **Use married names for individual females** check box if you want to use married names for women when you are printing labels and cards for individuals instead of households.

6. Click **OK** when you've made your selections.

    Family Tree Maker returns you to the Items to Include dialog box.

Picture/Objects on Labels and Cards

If you choose to include Picture/Objects on your labels or cards, Family Tree Maker displays the Options: Picture/Object dialog box. This is where you choose which of each individual's Picture/Objects will appear on the label or card. Select the **Preferred Picture/Object #1** option button to include the Picture/Object that you chose as the "Preferred Picture/Object for Labels/Cards" in the More About Picture/Object dialog box. For more information about the More About Picture/Object dialog box, see page 164.

Instead of using the "Preferred Picture/Objects," you can choose to include a Picture/Object of a particular **category** and **type**. Categories are classifications that you create. For example, you could create a "Birthday" category in which to place birthday pictures. Or, you could create a "Child Portrait" category in which to place portraits that were taken when the individuals were young.

Types are chosen from a drop-down list in the More About Picture/Object dialog box. They describe what Picture/Objects are, such as "Pictures" or "Sound Clips." Categories and types are assigned to each Picture/Object in the More About Picture/Object dialog box.

The **By Category** and **and Type** fields work together to find the Picture/Objects that you want to place on your labels or cards. For example, if you choose the category "Birthdays" and the type "Picture," Family Tree Maker searches for Picture/Objects that fulfill *both* requirements. However, both of the fields have an "Any" option, which, in effect, allows you to search only one of the two fields. If the category that you assigned to a Picture/Object does not appear in the "By Category" drop-down list, just type it into the field. When there is more than one Picture/Object of the category and type that you select, Family Tree Maker uses the first one.

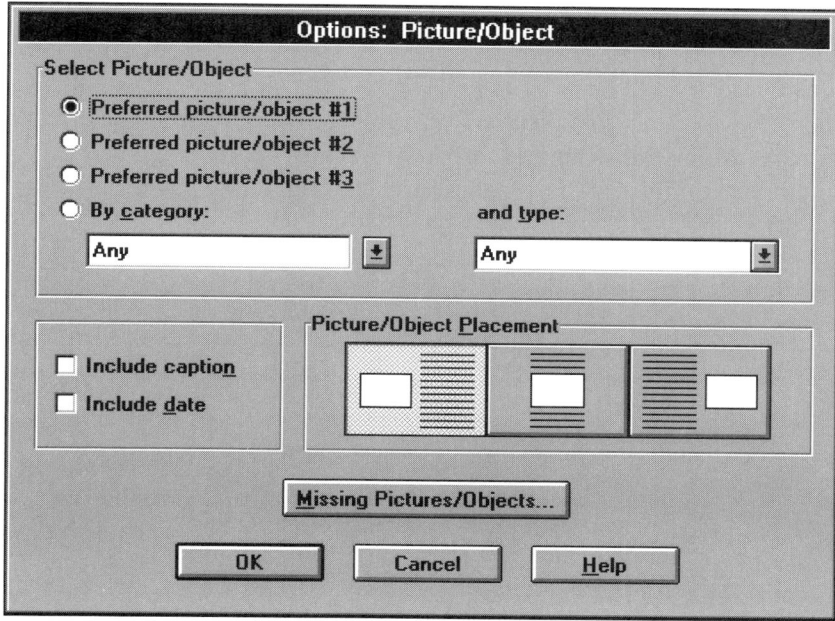

Figure 9-14. The Options: Picture/Object dialog box

If you wish to add the Picture/Object's caption or date, select the **Include caption** or **Include date** check box. You can also limit the size of the Picture/Objects that you include in your trees. See "Limiting the Width of Picture/Objects," on page 314.

To choose how the text and Picture/Objects are arranged in your tree's boxes, select the **Picture/Object Placement** button picturing the placement that you prefer. The Picture/Object can be to the right or left of the text, or both the text and the Picture/Object can be centered in the box.

Missing Picture/Objects

You may not have a Picture/Object for all of the individuals that you are printing. When this is the case, Family Tree Maker substitutes a graphic or leaves a blank space where the Picture/Object normally would be. The default is a blank space. To choose a substitute, click **Missing Picture/Objects**. Family Tree Maker displays the Missing Picture/Objects dialog box. You can either:

- Click the button for the graphic that you prefer or choose the blank space and then click **OK** to return to the Options: Picture/Object dialog box, or

- Choose to use your own picture file as a substitute graphic. The graphic can be in any of the following file formats: Windows Bitmap (*.BMP), CompuServe Bitmap (*.GIF), ZSoft Image (*.PCX), Tagged Image Format (*.TIF), or JPEG Interchange Format (*.JPG, *.JFF). To choose your own picture, click **Choose Picture**. Family Tree Maker displays the Import Picture from File dialog box. If you need instructions, see "Picture/Object: Insert Picture from File" on page 157. When you have selected a picture to insert, click **OK** twice to return to the Options: Picture/Object dialog box.

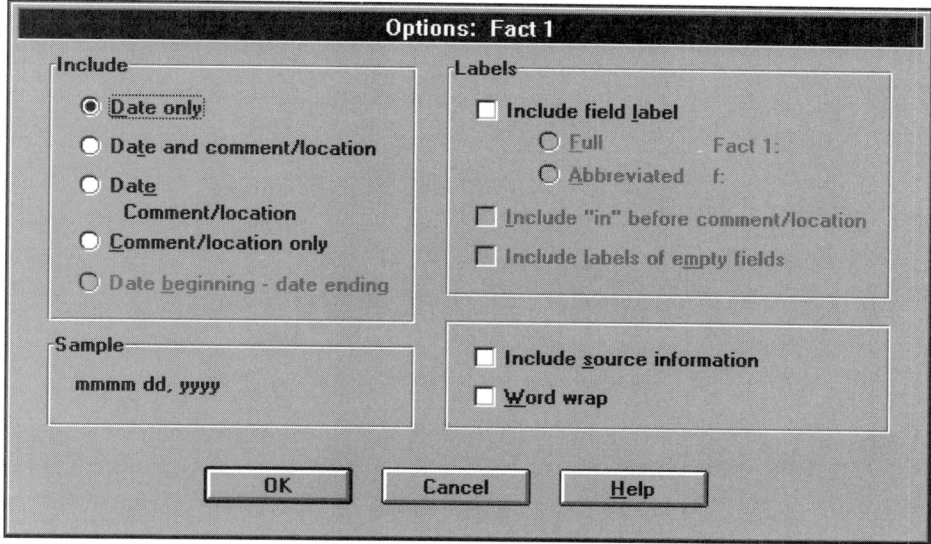

Figure 9-15. The Options: Fact dialog box

If you choose to include facts on your labels or cards, Family Tree Maker displays the Options: Fact dialog box. This dialog box gives you several options for formatting your fact fields, including whether you want field labels to print and how you want them to print. If you want to include source information for facts in your tree, select the **Include source information** check box.

Other Items on Labels and Cards

Some fields, such as phone number, also have options such as including field labels or using word wrap. See Figure 9-16, below. You can even include source information for some fields, although this option is not available for the phone number field. Click the check boxes which correspond to the options you wish to use.

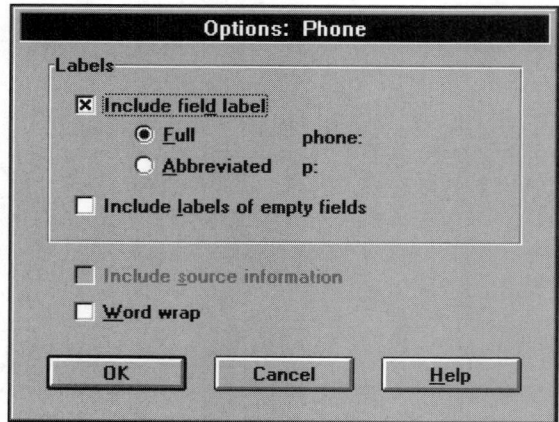

Figure 9-16. The Options: Phone dialog box

Special Note for Family Group Sheets

In Family Group Sheets, you can format the Standard Page, the Standard Page with Picture/Objects, and the More About dialog boxes. Formation options for the Standard Page and the Standard Page with Picture/Objects are on this page. Formatting options for More About dialog boxes are on page 307.

Standard Page in Family Group Sheets

When you choose to include the Standard Page in your Family Group Sheet, Family Tree Maker displays the Options: Standard Page dialog box. You can use this dialog box to choose whether all spouses or only the preferred spouse prints. In addition, there is an **Include labels of empty fields** check box. Select this check box if you want to print labels for fields that don't contain information. If you want to have empty rows print so you can fill in information about more children, select the **Include blank rows for additional children** check box. This option is useful when you are researching.

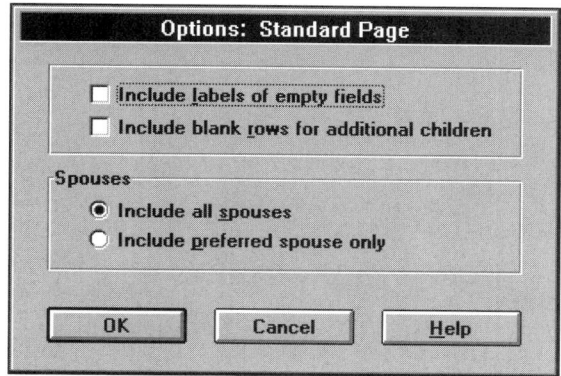

Figure 9-17. The Options: Standard Page dialog box

Standard Page with Picture/Objects in Family Group Sheets

If you choose to include the Standard Page with Picture/Objects in your Family Group Sheet, Family Tree Maker displays the Options: Standard Page with Picture/Objects dialog box. Select the **Preferred Picture/Object** option button to include the Picture/Object that you chose as the "Preferred Picture/Object for Fam Grp Sheets" in the More About Picture/Object dialog box. The Picture/Object that you chose in the Marriage Scrapbook will appear at the top of the Family Group Sheet and the Picture/Object that you chose in the Individual

Scrapbooks will appear next to each individual. For more information about the More About Picture/Object dialog box, see page 164.

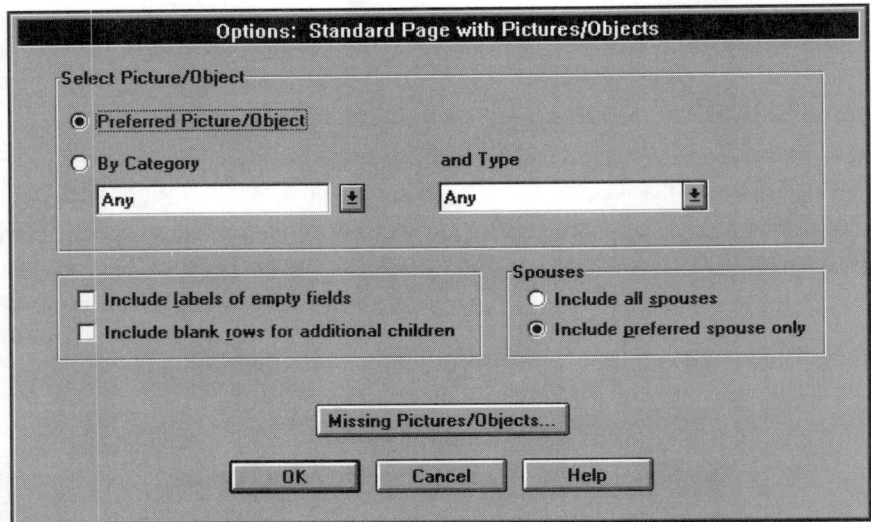

Figure 9-18. The Options: Standard Page with Picture/Objects dialog box

Instead of using the "Preferred Picture/Objects," you can choose to include a Picture/Object of a particular **category** and **type**. Categories are classifications that you create. For example, you could create a "Birthday" category in which to place birthday pictures. Or, you could create a "Child Portrait" category in which to place portraits that were taken when the individuals were young.

Types are chosen from a drop-down list in the More About Picture/Object dialog box. They describe what Picture/Objects are, such as "Pictures" or "Sound Clips." Categories and types are assigned to each Picture/Object in the More About Picture/Object dialog box.

The **By Category** and **and Type** fields work together to find the Picture/Objects that you want to place on your Family Group Sheet. For example, if you choose the category "Birthdays" and the type "Picture," Family Tree Maker searches for Picture/Objects that fulfill *both* requirements. However, both of the fields have an "Any" option, which, in effect, allows you to search only one of the two fields. If the category that you assigned to a Picture/Object does not appear in the "By Category" drop-down list, just type it into the field. When there is more than one Picture/Object of the category and type that you select, Family Tree Maker uses the first one.

If an individual does not have a Picture/Object, Family Tree Maker will insert a graphic where the Picture/Object normally would be. For more information about substitute graphics, see "Missing Picture/Objects" on page 302.

More About Dialog Boxes in Family Group Sheets

If you selected any of the listed More About dialog boxes (Facts, Address, Medical, Marriage Facts), Family Tree Maker will display an Options dialog box. In this dialog box you can choose to include sources for your information, if they are available. In addition, to print labels for fields which contain no information, you can select the **Include labels of empty fields** check box.

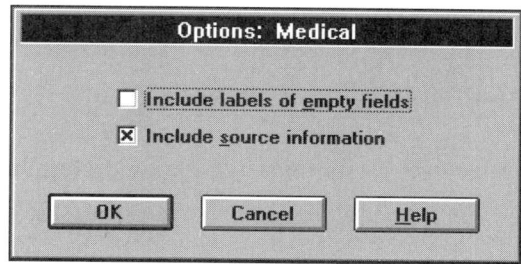

Figure 9-19. An Options dialog box for the More about dialog boxes

Special Note for Reports

In reports, you can only format names. For all other items, Family Tree Maker automatically chooses the format that is best for the report. Formatting options for names are described directly below.

Names in Reports

When you choose to include names, aka's (nicknames), or spouses in your report, Family Tree Maker displays the Options: Name dialog box. In this dialog box, you can choose the format in which the names will print in your report. Click the **Format** drop-down list to select a format for the names in your tree. For example, you could choose to use initials instead of full names or split names onto two lines. A line split is indicated by "\\". If you would like titles to appear in your tree, select the **Include Mr./Mrs./Ms.** check box. To use women's married names instead of their maiden names, select the **Use married names for females** check box. When you've made your formatting selections, click **OK**.

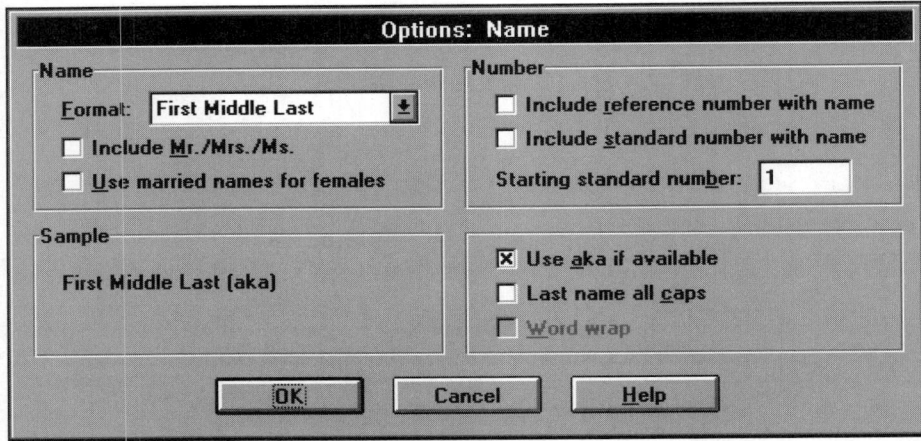

Figure 9-20. The Options: Name dialog box

Formatting Text

When you choose a font size, keep the size of your document in mind. If you choose a font that's too large, not all of the information will fit attractively. In the case of Scrapbooks and labels and cards, any information that does not fit simply will not print.

To format text that appears in your documents:

1. From the **Format** menu, select **Text Font, Style, & Size**.

   Family Tree Maker displays the Text Font, Style, & Size dialog box.

   With Scrapbooks, you must first switch to Print Preview before you can make formatting changes. To switch to Print Preview when you are in the Scrapbook view, from the **File** menu, select **Print Preview**.

   With Family Group Sheets, labels and cards, and Scrapbooks, you can also format text from the Items to Include dialog box. In the list on the right, click the item that you want to format, then click **Font**.

2. In the **Items to format** list, select an item that you want to format.

    When an item is selected, you can choose formatting options for it. Each of the formatting options is described below. The "Sample" field shows what your choices will look like.

    Font — Click this field to display a list of fonts and then click the name of the font you want.

    Size — Click this field to display a list of text sizes and then click the text size you want.

    Note: If you have selected the LDS option in the Labels dialog box (see page 78), the Size option is not available for the Standard Pages in Family Group Sheets.

    Style — Click this field to display a list of text styles, such as "Bold" or "Italics," and then click the style you want.

    Color — Click this field to display a list of colors and then click the color you want.

    Alignment — Click this field to display a list of text alignments, such as "Centered," and then click the alignment you want.

    Note: The Alignment option is not available for Family Group Sheets and Reports.

    Underline — Select this check box to underline the item.

    Note: The Underline option is not available for reports.

3. Click **OK** when you've made your selections.

    Family Tree Maker returns you to the document view.

Adding a Title and Footnote

When you create Family Group Sheets, reports, and Scrapbooks, you can use the Title & Footnote dialog box to add a title and footnote or page numbers. Instructions for using this feature begin in the paragraph below. This feature works slightly differently for different documents, so be sure also to read the special note for the document that you are creating:

- Family Group Sheets, page 310
- Scrapbooks, page 311
- Reports, page 311

To add a title and footnote or page numbers to your document:

1. From the **Contents** menu, select **Title & Footnote**.

    For Scrapbooks, you must first be in Print Preview. To switch to Print Preview when you are in the Scrapbook view, from the **File** menu, select **Print Preview**.

    Family Tree Maker displays the Title & Footnote dialog box.

2. Make your selections in the dialog box.

    The options for each different document are described below.

3. Click **OK** when you've made your selections.

    Family Tree Maker returns you to the document view.

Special Note for Family Group Sheets

Title — Select the **Automatic title** option button if you want Family Tree Maker to create a title for you. To create your own title, select the **Custom title** option button and type your title in the field provided. Titles print at the top left of the page.

Page Number — Select the **Include page number** check box if you want Family Tree Maker to print page numbers at the bottom of each page. You can also enter a starting page number in the **Starting number** field.

Preparer Information — Enter your personal information and the current date in these fields so that people who look at the Family Group Sheet will know who prepared it. This information prints as a footnote.

Special Note for Scrapbooks

Title — Select the **Automatic title** option button if you want Family Tree Maker to create a title for you. If you want to create your own title, select the **Custom title** option button and type your title in the field provided. If you would like the title to print on every page, select the **Print title on every page** check box.

Page number — Select the **Include page number** check box to include page numbers on your Scrapbook pages. Click the up and down arrows on the **Starting number** field to change the page number of the first page.

Special Note for Reports

Title — Select the **Automatic title** option button if you want Family Tree Maker to create a title for you. If you want to create your own title, select the **Custom title** option button and type your title in the field provided. If you would like the title to print on every page, select the **Print title on every page** check box.

Page Number — Select the **Include page number** check box to include page numbers at the bottom of each page of your report. Click the up and down arrows in the **Starting number** field to change the page number of the first page.

Footnote — Use this field to include a footnote on your report. The footnote will appear in the lower left corner of the last page.

Draw box around footnote — Select this check box to draw a box around your footnote.

Choosing the Layout for Scrapbooks

The **layout** refers to the placement of each Picture/Object on a Scrapbook page.

To choose the Scrapbook page layout:

1. Make sure you're in Scrapbook Print Preview.

    To switch to Print Preview when you are in the Scrapbook view, from the **File** menu, select **Print Preview**.

2. From the **Format** menu, select **Scrapbook Format**.

    Family Tree Maker displays the Format for Printed Scrapbook dialog box.

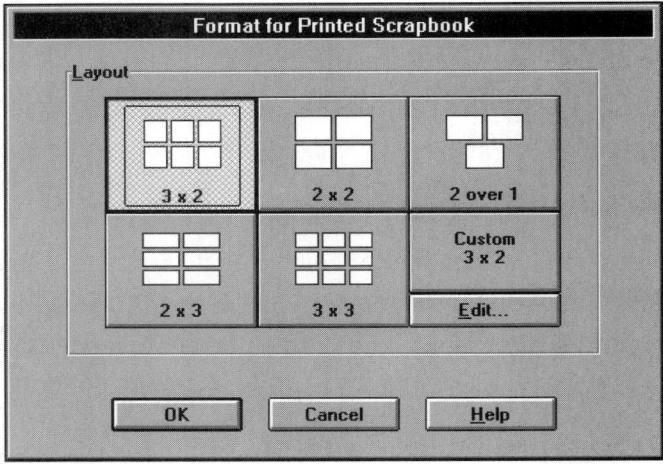

Figure 9-21. The Format for Printed Scrapbook dialog box

3. Click the button showing the Picture/Object layout you want.

    To create your own special Scrapbook page layout, click **Edit**. In the Custom Layout dialog box that Family Tree Maker displays, enter the number of Picture/Objects you want across and down each page. You can choose from 1 to 50. Remember, however, the more Picture/Objects on each page, the smaller they will be. Click **OK** to return to the Format for Printed Scrapbook dialog box.

4. Click **OK** when you've made your selection.

    Family Tree Maker returns you to Scrapbook Print Preview.

Choosing Borders and Line Styles

Family Tree Maker has several different border styles, box styles, and line styles for labels and cards, reports, and Scrapbooks. In addition, you can select colors for different elements in your documents, such as the background and borders. Instructions for using this feature begin below. This feature works slightly differently for different documents, so be sure also to read the special note for the document that you are creating:

- Labels and cards, page 313
- Scrapbooks, page 314
- Reports, page 314

To select these formatting options:

1. From the **Format** menu, select **Box, Line, & Border Styles**.

   For Scrapbooks, you must first be in Print Preview. To switch to Print Preview when you are in the Scrapbook view, from the **File** menu, select **Print Preview**.

   Family Tree Maker displays the Box, Line, & Border Styles dialog box.

2. Make your selections by clicking the buttons with the styles that you like.

   You may only choose one style for each element. For example you can only choose one border style per document.

3. You can also select colors for various parts of your document, depending on which document it is. Click the color field for each element of the document and then select a color from the list that Family Tree Maker displays. The colors will only print if you have a color printer, otherwise they will print in shades of gray.

4. Click **OK** when you've made your selections.

   Family Tree Maker returns you to the document view.

Special Note for Labels and Cards

With labels and cards, you can select box and line styles. The box is drawn around the edge of the label or card. Choosing not to have a box will give you the most space for text on your label or card. The line color that you select will be the color with which the box is drawn. The fill color will be inside the box.

Special Note for Scrapbooks

With Scrapbooks, you can select a border style, a box style, and a line style. The border is drawn around the edge of each page and the boxes are drawn around each Picture/Object.

The border color that you select will be the color with which the border is drawn and the background color will cover the entire background of each Scrapbook page. The line color that you select will be the color with which the boxes are drawn around each Picture/Object, and the fill color will be inside each box.

Special Note for Reports

With reports, you can select border styles. The border is drawn along the top and bottom edges of the report.

The border color that you select will be the color with which the border is drawn. The background color will cover the entire background of the report.

Limiting the Width of Picture/Objects

When you choose to include Picture/Objects on your labels or cards, setting a maximum width can help you fit more information on each one.

To set a maximum width for Picture/Objects on labels and cards:

1. From the **Format** menu, select **Maximum Width for Each Picture/Object**.

2. Enter a number in the **Maximum Picture/Object width** field. To get a smaller Picture/Object, enter a smaller number. You can enter any width between 0.1 inch and 99.99 inches. Your Picture/Objects will fit into a square with sides of that length.

3. Click **OK** when you've made your selection.

   Family Tree Maker returns you to the Labels/Cards view.

   Note: If necessary, Family Tree Maker will abbreviate your information to make it fit in the label or card size you specify. For example, if you select a very long name format, but a small label or card, Family Tree Maker may have to change the name format to a smaller one.

Choosing Column Widths and Spacing in Reports

Normally, Family Tree Maker chooses appropriate widths for each column in a report and spaces the columns .25" apart. However, if you prefer, you can choose your own column widths and spacing.

To select column widths and spacing in reports:

1. From the **Format** menu, select **Maximum Width**.

    Family Tree Maker displays the Maximum Width for Each Column dialog box. On the left side of the dialog box there are numbers that correspond to the columns in your report; "1" is the leftmost column. On the right side of the dialog box is a list titled "Column item." This list tells you what information each column contains.

    If a column that you want to edit is not visible, use the scroll bar on the left side of the dialog box to scroll through the list. When you are ready, you can begin to edit the columns. Each of your options is described below.

    Set widths automatically — Select this option button if you prefer to have Family Tree Maker choose the widths and spacing for each column. In this case, none of the other options in the dialog box are available.

    Choose widths manually — Select this option button if you prefer to manually set the widths and spacing for each column.

    Width — Click either the up or down arrow to change how much space a column occupies. If you choose a width that is too narrow for the text in the column, Family Tree Maker will try abbreviating the text. If the abbreviated text does not fit, it will be truncated.

    Spacing — Click either the up or down arrow to change the distance between a column and the column to the right of it.

    Total report width — This field shows how wide your entire report will be with the currently selected column widths and spacing. To change these numbers, you must change the numbers in the "Width" and "Spacing" fields.

2. Click **OK** after you've made your changes.

    Family Tree Maker returns you to the Report view.

Choosing the Family Group Sheet Format

When you print your Family Group Sheets, you can choose whether or not each individual's information begins on a new page.

To select a Family Group Sheet printing format:

1. From the **Format** menu, select **Format**.

   Family Tree Maker displays the Format dialog box.

2. If you want each individual's information to begin on a new page, select the **Begin each person on a new page** check box. Otherwise, make sure that the check box is not selected.

3. Click **OK** when you've made your choice.

   Family Tree Maker returns you to the Family Group Sheet view.

Setting Other Printing Options

Both Scrapbooks and labels and cards have other important printing options. To display the dialog box where you choose special printing options, from the **Contents** menu, select **Options**. (For Scrapbooks, you must first be in Print Preview. To switch to Print Preview when you are in the Scrapbook view, from the **File** menu, select **Print Preview**.) These options are described below.

- Labels and cards, page 316
- Scrapbooks, page 317

Special Note for Labels and Cards

Use Name Format for — When you print labels or cards, you must decide if you want to print one label or card for each household or for each individual. For example, if you are printing address labels for holiday cards, you probably only want to print one label per household. If you are printing name tags, however, you would want to print one for each individual.

If you select **Individual**, Family Tree Maker will use the "Individuals" name format you selected in the Options: Name dialog box (page 298) and will print a label or card for each individual in your list of Individuals to Include (page 283). If you select **Household**, Family Tree Maker will use the "Household" name format you selected in the Options: Name dialog box (page 298) and will print a label or card for each group of individuals who share the same address. Family

Tree Maker is smart enough to adjust the name format for all different types of households:

- A family group, such as parents and children, that shares the same address will print on one label with the "Household" name format you have selected. For example "Mr. and Mrs. Doe and Family."

- A couple that shares the same address will print on one label with a variation of the "Household" name format. For example "Mr. and Mrs. Doe."

- A single individual with a unique address will print alone on a label with another variation of the "Household" name format. For example, "Ms. Doe."

That way, all of your labels or cards have the same basic style, but are suitable to the type of household. The exact name format printed on your labels or cards will depend on your selections in the Options: Name dialog box (see page 298).

Print blank rows when fields are empty — When the **Print blank rows when fields are empty** check box is selected, Family Tree Maker will insert a blank row in the label or card when it comes across an empty field.

Special Note for Scrapbooks

When you print Scrapbook pages, there may be some Picture/Objects that you do not want to include. For example, sound clips would only be represented as icons. To exclude a Picture/Object from Scrapbook pages, open the Picture/Object's More About dialog box (see page 164) and deselect the **Include in Printed Scrapbooks** check box. In the Options for Printed Scrapbook dialog box, you can further control which Picture/Objects print on the Scrapbook pages.

If you wish to print all Picture/Objects that are marked for printing, select the **All** option button. Alternatively, you can choose to include Picture/Objects of a particular **category** and **type**. Categories are classifications that you create. For example, you could create a "Birthday" category in which to place birthday pictures. Or, you could create a "Child Portrait" category in which to place portraits that were taken when the individuals were young.

Types are chosen from a drop-down list in the More About Picture/Object dialog box. They describe what Picture/Objects are, such as "Pictures" or "Sound Clips." Categories and types are assigned to each Picture/Object in the More About Picture/Object dialog box.

The **By Category** and **and Type** fields work together to find the Picture/Objects that you want to place in your Scrapbook. For example, if you choose the category "Birthdays" and the type "Picture," Family Tree Maker searches for

Picture/Objects that fulfill **both** requirements. However, both of the fields have an "Any" option, which, in effect, allows you to search only one of the two fields. If the category that you assigned to a Picture/Object does not appear in the "By Category" drop-down list, just type it into the field.

Choosing the Sorting Order

When you print labels and cards and reports, you can select the order in which the names print. You can also select the order in which Picture/Objects are arranged in Scrapbooks. Instructions for using this feature begin below. This feature works slightly differently for different documents, so be sure also to read the special note for the document that you are creating:

- Labels and cards, page 318

- Reports, page 318

- Scrapbooks, page 318

Selecting a Sorting Order

To select a sorting order:

1. From the **Format** menu, select **Sort**.

   Family Tree Maker displays the Sort dialog box.

2. Click the option button for the type of sorting you prefer.

3. Click **OK** when you've made your selection.

   Family Tree Maker returns you to the document view.

Special Note for Reports and Labels and Cards

If you want the individuals to print in the order in which you added them to the group in the Individuals to Include dialog box (see page 283), select **Don't Sort Individuals**. This is especially useful for printing individuals in an Ancestor or Descendant order.

Special Note for Scrapbooks

Please note that when you choose a sorting order in Scrapbooks, it only affects the Scrapbook that is currently open.

Printing Your Document

Once you have created your document, you are ready to print.

To print a document:

1. Make sure you're in the view for the document that you want to print.

   If you're printing a Scrapbook, you can print from both the Scrapbook view and Scrapbook Print Preview.

2. Turn on your printer.

3. From the **File** menu, select **Print**.

   Family Tree Maker displays the Print dialog box where you can select printing options. Each of these options is described below.

   Note: You can also control items such as paper orientation, margin size, and which printer prints your document. If you want to change any of these items, see "Print Setup," on page 266. To control these options for labels and cards, see "Label/Card Size and Print Setup" on page 282.

   Print range — Use this option to select the pages to print. If you want to print all of the pages, select the **All** option button. If you want to print a range of pages, type the page number of the first page that you want to print in the **From** field and the page number of the last page you want to print in the **To** field. If you want to print only one page, type the same number in both the **From** and **To** fields.

   Print quality — Use this option to select the quality of your printed materials. The higher the print quality you choose, the darker and sharper your printed materials will be. However, items printed in high print quality also take longer to print. If your printer does not support different print qualities, this option will not be available to you.

   Copies — In this field, type the number of copies that you want to print.

   Collate copies — Select this check box if you are printing multiple copies of your document and want to print complete sets instead of several copies of the first page, then several copies of the second page, and so on.

Print to file — If you want to print to a file and send it to your printer at a later time, select this check box. This option is especially useful if you want to print on a printer or plotter owned by someone who doesn't have Family Tree Maker. When you print, Family Tree Maker will ask for an "Output File Name." For general instructions for printing to a file, see page 265.

Note: If you intend to print the file on a printer other than your own, you will need to change the settings in "Print Setup" to match the printer you will be using. See "Print Setup" on page 266.

Print empty — If you want to print an empty document, select this check box. Empty documents can be useful when you're doing research away from your computer. You can write the information in and then enter it into your computer later.

Print color — If you have a color printer, select this check box to print in color. If you have a black and white printer, select this check box to print in grayscale. De-select this check box if you just want to print in black and white. If you have a black and white printer, color Picture/Objects will always print in grayscale.

Note: Please note that this option is only available for Family Group Sheets.

4. Click **OK** when you've made your selections.

   Family Tree Maker prints your document.

Chapter 10

OTHER PRINTING

Courtney Kermeen, Family Tree Maker's Product Manager, is pictured here playing with a family friend's sunglasses and drum in 1974. The picture was later sent to her grandfather, who played drums in a Dixieland band.

OTHER PRINTING

Family Tree Maker can print many other documents besides family trees: calendars, labels, cards, Scrapbook pages, Family Group Sheets, and reports. You can also print the information contained on your Family Pages and More About dialog boxes. This chapter tells you how to print calendars and the information contained in Family Pages and More About dialog boxes. For labels and cards, Scrapbook pages, Family Group Sheets, and reports, see Chapter 9. Information about printing trees is in Chapter 8.

Printing documents such as calendars can be a lot of fun, so don't be afraid to experiment! Remember, if you get lost, you can always press [FI] to get on–screen help.

CALENDARS

You can print a calendar to help you keep track of family members' birthdays and anniversaries year 'round. If you like, your calendar can also include people's ages and the number of years that they've been married.

Creating a Calendar

To create a calendar, from the **View** menu, select **Calendar**. Family Tree Maker displays a calendar containing your family's birthdays and anniversaries. If more events occur on a single day than will fit in the space for that day, Family Tree Maker prints a second page of that month to hold the overflow.

You can move around in your calendar using the scroll bars and arrow keys. In addition, clicking the double up and down arrows on the scroll bar will take you to the previous or next month if you've chosen to create a yearlong calendar. To make your calendar bigger and easier to read on screen, from the **View** menu, select **Zoom**, and then choose a size from the dialog box. The larger the percentage, the bigger your calendar will be on screen.

Note: The Zoom command does not control how large your calendar will be when you print.

You can also control whether or not dotted lines appear on the screen to show you where your margins are set. From the **View** menu, select **Show Page Lines**. If this option has a check next to it, then page lines will be visible. Otherwise, they won't be. These lines will not appear on your printed calendar.

If you notice that anyone is missing from your calendar, go to that individual's Lineage dialog box (see page 134) and check to see that the **Exclude from calendars** check box is not selected. Also make sure that you haven't excluded that individual from the group of individuals to include in the calendar. See "Selecting Individuals to Include in Your Calendar" below.

You can either print your calendar right away (see "Printing a Calendar" on page 333), or customize it and then print (see "Customizing a Calendar" below).

CUSTOMIZING A CALENDAR

For calendars, your customization options include the following: which information to include, which individuals to include, how the text is formatted, the style of the borders, the colors in the calendar, and whether or not the calendar has a footnote. Each of these options are described in the next few sections.

Selecting Individuals to Include in Your Calendar

When you create calendars, you can use the Individuals to Include dialog box to select a group of individuals to print:

1. From the **Contents** menu, select **Individuals to Include**.

   Family Tree Maker displays the Include dialog box.

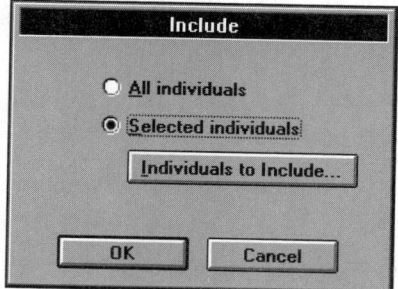

Figure 10-1. The Include dialog box

2. If you want everyone in your Family File to print, choose **All individuals** and click **OK**. You can then skip the remaining steps. Otherwise, choose **Selected individuals** and then click **Individuals to Include**.

When you click "Individuals to Include," Family Tree Maker displays the Individuals to Include dialog box. This is the dialog box that you will use to create a group of individuals to print. The list on the right shows the group of individuals who will be printed. The list on the left shows which individuals you can add to the group. The individuals in the list on the left are in alphabetical order by last name. Nicknames (aka's) are on different lines than the given names. See Figure 10-2, below.

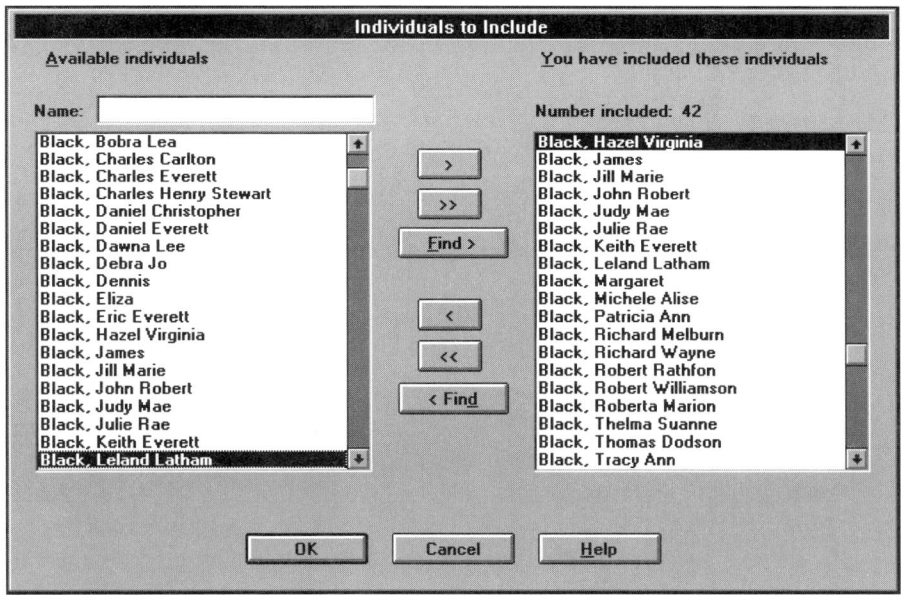

Figure 10-2. The Individuals to Include dialog box

3. Now you must create the group of individuals to print. You can do this by selecting individuals and adding them to or removing them from the list on the right. The table below shows the three methods that you can use. You can use any combination of these methods to create your group.

To do this...	Use this button...	See page...
Include or remove individuals one-by-one.	"Include" or "Remove" (the single arrows)	327
Include all of the individuals currently in your Family File or remove all of the individuals currently in the group.	"Include All" or "Remove All" (the double arrows)	328
Choose categories of individuals to include or remove all at once.	"Find and Include" or "Find and Remove"	329

Figure 10-3. Methods for creating groups

Note: There is *one* Individuals to Include dialog box for all views in Family Tree Maker. The group of individuals that you create in one view, such as Labels/Cards, is available to you in the other views that allow you to choose groups: Report, Calendar, and batch print. Even if you exit Family Tree Maker, the group that you create in the Individuals to Include dialog box will remain the same until you change it again. Of course, if you make changes to the group in one view, such as the Report view, the group will change in all other views as well.

4. When you're done creating the group, click **OK** in the Individuals to Include dialog box.

Family Tree Maker will return you to the Calendar view.

Using the "Include" and "Remove" Buttons

With the "Include" and "Remove" buttons you can add and remove individuals to and from the group one at a time.

To create a group using the "Include" and "Remove" buttons:

1. Click an individual's name in the list on the left to add that individual to the group. If you want to remove an individual from the group, click his or her name in the list on the right.

2. Click either the **Include** button (the arrow pointing to the right) or the **Remove** button (the arrow pointing to the left). See Figure 10-4.

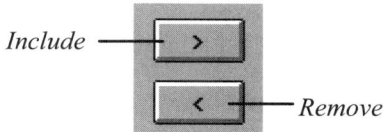

Figure 10-4. The Include and Remove buttons

If you chose to add the individual, his or her name is added to the list on the right and the "Number included" increases by one. If you chose to remove the individual, his or her name is removed from the list on the right, and the "Number included" decreases by one.

Instead of selecting an individual and then clicking "Include" or "Remove," you can just double-click the individual's name. Double-clicking names in the list on the left automatically adds them to the group. Double-clicking names in the list on the right automatically removes them from the group.

Using the "Include All" and "Remove All" Buttons

With the "Include All" button, one click adds all of the individuals currently in your Family File to the group. With the "Remove All" button, one click removes all of the individuals from the group. See Figure 10-5.

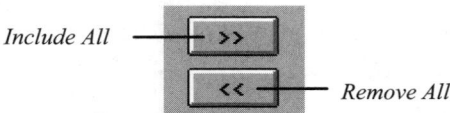

Figure 10-5. The Include All and Remove All buttons

The best time to use the "Include All" button is when you want to create a group that includes almost all of the individuals who are currently in your Family File. For example, if there are only a few people that you don't want to include in the group, click the **Include All** button (the double arrows pointing to the right) to move all of the individuals to the list on the right. Then use the **Remove** button (the arrow pointing to the left) to remove the few individuals that you don't want in the group. This is much faster than including all of the individuals one by one. The "Remove" button is described in "Using the 'Include' and 'Remove' Buttons" on page 327.

If you want to include all of the individuals in your Family File, don't use the "Include All" button. Instead, from the **Contents** menu, select **Individuals to Include**. Then, in the Include dialog box, select **All Individuals**. This way, individuals that you add to your Family File later will be included automatically. If you use the "Include All" button to include everyone, individuals that are added to your Family File later will *not* be added to the group automatically.

The best time to use the "Remove All" button is when you already have several individuals in the group and you want to start over. Click the **Remove All** button (the double arrows pointing to the left) to remove all of the individuals from the group. Then use any method to begin adding individuals to the group again.

Using the "Find and Include" and "Find and Remove" Buttons

With the "Find and Include" and "Find and Remove" buttons, Family Tree Maker will search your Family File for individuals, such as those who were born before a certain date or those who are ancestors of a particular individual, and add them to or remove them from the group.

To create a group using the "Find and Include" and "Find and Remove" buttons:

1. Decide which individuals you want to add to or remove from the group. For example, do you want to add your ancestors? Do you want to add the individuals who were merged or appended? Do you want to remove all of the individuals who were born before a particular date?

    If you want to add or remove a group of individuals that are relatives of a particular individual, make sure to highlight the name of that individual in the list on the left before moving on to step 2. For example, if you wanted to add all of your ancestors, you would highlight your name.

2. Click either the **Find and Include** ("Find" with the arrow pointing to the right) or **Find and Remove** button ("Find" with the arrow pointing to the left). See Figure 10-6.

    Family Tree Maker displays either the Add Individuals or Remove Individuals dialog box. In this dialog box you specify which individuals you want Family Tree Maker to find and add to or remove from the group.

Find and Include ——— **Find >**

< Find ——— *Find and Remove*

Figure 10-6. The Find and Include and Find and Remove buttons

3. Click in the **Search** field.

    If you want to find the individuals who are all relatives of a particular individual, choose **Relatives** from the drop-down list. Family Tree Maker automatically fills the "of" field with the name of the individual that was highlighted in step 1. Using the **Limit relationships to** fields, select the individuals that you want to find. For example, to find all of the individual's ancestors, you would enter a large number in **Generations of Ancestors** and zeros in the other two fields. When you've made your selections, click **OK** and skip to step 5.

If you want to find individuals who have something in common, such as a birthplace, use the drop-down list to choose the name of the field that contains that information. For example, if you wanted to find all individuals who were born in a particular place, you would select "Birth location." When you've selected a field, continue with step 4.

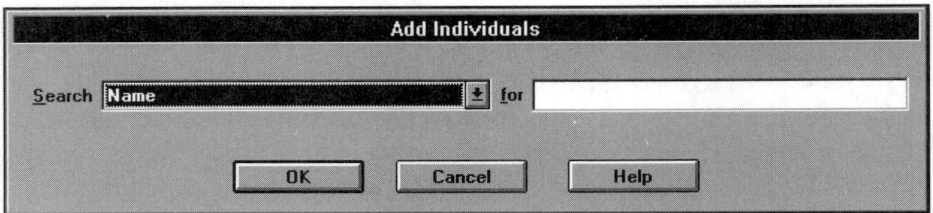

Figure 10-7. The Add Individuals dialog box

4. In the **for** field, type the information that you want to search for. If the field that you are searching only has certain legal values (such as "male," "female," and "unknown"), Family Tree Maker will display a drop-down list in the "for" field. In this case, just click the item that you want to search for.

   For example, if you chose "Birth location" in step 3, and you wanted Family Tree Maker to find everyone that was born in Cleveland, Ohio, then you would type **Cleveland, Ohio** in the "for" field. If you are searching a date field, see Figure 4-12 on page 125 for searching tips.

5. Click **OK**.

   Family Tree Maker searches your Family File for individuals who match your request. If no matches are found, Family Tree Maker tells you so. If you chose to add the individuals, their names are added to the list on the right and the "Number included" increases. If you chose to remove the individuals, their names are removed from the list on the right, and the "Number included" decreases.

Selecting Information to Include in Your Calendar

To choose information to include in your calendar:

1. From the **Contents** menu, select **Items to Include**.

   Family Tree Maker displays the Items to Include dialog box.

2. Make your selections. Each option is described below.

   Year — Use the up or down arrow in this field to select a year.

   Month — Click this drop-down list and select **All** if you want to print a full year. Otherwise, select the month that you want to print.

   Name format — Click this drop-down list and select the format in which you want each individual's name to appear.

   Use married names for female family members — Select this check box if you want to print women's married names instead of their maiden names.

   Use aka if available — Select this check box if you want nicknames to appear in the calendar when they are available.

   Last name all caps — Select this check box if you want to print all last names in capital letters.

   Print only if still alive — Select this check box to exclude information about individuals for whom you have entered death dates or who are more than 120 years old.

   Birthdays, Anniversaries, Both — Select an option button according to the type of information you want in your calendar.

   Include age for birthdays & years for anniversaries — Select this check box to have Family Tree Maker calculate individuals' ages on their birthdays and the number of years they have been married on their anniversaries. This number will appear next to their names. If a "?" prints, it means that there is no information in the associated date field. If the word "est" prints, as in "Bonnie Anderson - 85 est," it means that you entered an uncertain date.

   Events that fall on February 29th will appear on February 28th if the calendar is not for a leap year.

3. Click **OK** when you've made your selections.

   Family Tree Maker returns you to the Calendar view.

Formatting Text

You can choose different formatting for each item in your calendar, such as day names, month names, and the information that prints in each day.

To format the text in a calendar:

1. From the **Format** menu, select **Text Font, Style & Size**.

   Family Tree Maker displays the Text Font, Style & Size dialog box.

2. In the **Items to format** list, select an item that you want to format.

   When an item is selected, you can choose formatting options for it. Each of the formatting options is described below. The "Sample" field shows what your choices will look like.

   Font — Click this field to display a list of fonts and then click the name of the font you want.

   Size — Click this field to display a list of text sizes and then click the text size you want.

   Style — Click this field to display a list of text styles, such as "Bold" or "Italics," and then click the style you want.

   Color — Click this field to display a list of colors and then click the color you want.

3. Click **OK** when you're done making changes.

   Family Tree Maker returns you to the Calendar view.

Adding a Subtitle and Footnote

Family Tree Maker automatically includes the month in place of a title, but you can add a subtitle and footnote. The subtitle will appear beneath the name of the month and the footnote will appear in the lower-right corner of the page.

To add a subtitle or footnote to a calendar:

1. From the **Contents** menu, select **Title & Footnote**.

   Family Tree Maker displays the Title & Footnote dialog box. Each of your options is described below.

   Subtitle — If you wish to have a subtitle below the name of the month, type one in this field.

Footnote — Use this field to include a footnote in your calendar.

Draw box around footnote — Select this check box to draw a box around your footnote.

2. Click **OK** when you're done creating your title and footnote.

   Family Tree Maker returns you to the Calendar view.

Borders, Background Colors, and Fill Colors

You can add interest to your calendar by choosing borders and colors. A border is a design that Family Tree Maker draws around each month in your calendar. The fill color is the color that appears inside the box for each day and the background color is the color that surrounds each month. If you have a color printer, your calendar will print in color. If your printer is black and white, the calendar will print in shades of gray.

To change border, background, or fill colors on your calendar:

1. From the **Format** menu, select **Box, Line, & Border Styles**.

   Family Tree Maker displays the Box, Line, & Border Styles dialog box.

2. Make your selections by clicking the buttons with the pictures of the borders and boxes that you like. Each calendar can only have one box style and one border style.

3. You can also choose colors for each of these elements. Click the color drop-down list for each element of the calendar and then select a color from the list that Family Tree Maker displays.

4. Click **OK** when you've made your selections.

   Family Tree Maker returns you to the Calendar view.

Printing a Calendar

When you have finished creating your calendar, you're ready to print.

To print your calendar:

1. Make sure you're in the Calendar view.

2. Turn on your printer.

3. From the **File** menu, select **Print Calendar**.

Family Tree Maker displays the Print Calendar dialog box. Each of your options is described below.

Note: You can also control items such as paper orientation, paper size, margins, and which printer prints your calendar. If you want to change any of these items, see "Print Setup" on page 266.

Print range — Use this option to select the pages to print. If you want to print all of the pages, select the **All** option button. If you want to print a range of pages, type the page number of the first page that you want to print in the **From** field and type the page number of the last page you want to print in the **To** field. If you want to print only one page, type the number of that page in both the **From** and **To** fields.

Print quality — Use this option to select the quality of your printed materials. The higher the print quality you choose, the darker and sharper your printed materials will be. However, items printed in high print quality also take longer to print. If your printer does not support different print qualities, this option will not be available to you.

Copies — In this field, type the number of copies that you want to print.

Collate copies — Select this check box if you are printing multiple copies of a calendar and want to print complete sets. De-select this check box if you want multiple copies of the first page, of the second page, and so on.

Print to file — If you want to be able to print your calendar to a file and send it to your printer at a later time, select this check box. This option is especially useful if you want to print your calendar on a printer or plotter owned by someone who doesn't have Family Tree Maker. When you print, Family Tree Maker will ask for an "Output File Name." For general instructions for printing to a file, see page 265.

Print empty — Select this check box to print an empty calendar.

Print color — If you have a color printer, select this check box to print in color. If you have a black and white printer, select this check box to print in grayscale. De-select this check box if you want to print in black and white.

4. Click **OK** when you've made your selections.

Family Tree Maker prints your calendar.

FAMILY PAGES AND MORE ABOUT DIALOG BOXES

The Family Page and More About dialog boxes contain all of the biographical data about an individual and his or her family. Family Tree Maker lets you print this information in a few concise reports. You can also print out blank forms to take with you when you do your research.

Printing Family Page Information

To print the information contained in a Family Page:

1. Go to the Family Page containing the information you want to print.

2. Turn on your printer.

3. From the **File** menu, select **Print**.

    Family Tree Maker displays a message telling you where you can change the fonts for this document. Then, Family Tree Maker displays the Print dialog box. Each of your options is described below.

    Print range — If a couple has several children, their Family Page information can be more than one page long. If you want to print all of the pages, select the **All** option button. If you want to print a range of pages, type the page number of the first page that you want to print in the **From** field and type the page number of the last page you want to print in the **To** field. If you want to print only one page, type the number of that page in both the **From** and **To** fields.

    Print quality — Use this option to select the quality of your printed materials. The higher the print quality you choose, the darker and sharper your printed materials will be. However, items printed in high print quality also take longer to print. If your printer does not support different print qualities, this option will not be available to you.

    Copies — In this field, type the number of copies that you want to print.

    Collate copies — Select this check box if you are printing multiple copies of the Family Page information and want to print complete sets. De-select this check box if you want multiple copies of the first page, of the second page, and so on.

Print to file — If you want to be able to print your Family Page to a file and send it to your printer at a later time, select this check box. This option is especially useful if you want to print your Family Page on a printer owned by someone who doesn't have Family Tree Maker. When you print, Family Tree Maker will ask for an "Output File Name." For general instructions for printing to a file, see page 265.

Print empty — Select this check box to print an empty Family Page. Empty Family Pages can be useful when you're doing research away from your computer. You can write the information on the Family Page, and then enter it into your computer later.

Print color — If you have a color printer, select this check box to print in color. If you have a black and white printer, select this check box to print in grayscale. De-select this check box if you want to print in black and white.

4. Click **OK** when you've made your selections.

   Family Tree Maker prints your Family Page information.

Printing More About Information

To print the information contained in your More About dialog boxes:

1. Go to the Family Page containing the individual or marriage whose More About dialog boxes you want to see.

2. Place your cursor on the individual or marriage.

3. From the **View** menu, select **More About**. From the submenu, select the name of the dialog box that you want to see.

   If you go to an individual's Notes dialog box, you will only be able to print that individual's Notes. If you go to any of the individual's other More About dialog boxes, you can print the information contained in all of the individual's More About dialog boxes, except Notes.

4. Turn on your printer.

5. From the **File** menu, select **Print**.

   Family Tree Maker displays a message telling you where you can change the fonts for this document. Then, Family Tree Maker displays the Print dialog box. Each of your options is described on the next page.

Print range — Use this option to select the pages to print. If you want to print all of the pages, select the **All** option button. If you want to print a range of pages, type the page number of the first page that you want to print in the **From** field and type the page number of the last page you want to print in the **To** field. If you want to print only one page, type the number of that page in both the **From** and **To** fields.

Print quality — Use this option to select the quality of your printed materials. The higher the print quality you choose, the darker and sharper your printed materials will be. However, items printed in high print quality also take longer to print. If your printer does not support different print qualities, this option will not be available to you.

Copies — In this field, type the number of copies that you want to print.

Collate copies — Select this check box if you are printing multiple copies of the More About dialog boxes and want to print complete sets. De-select this check box if you want multiple copies of the first page, multiple copies of the second page, and so on.

Print to file — If you want to be able to print your More About dialog boxes to a file and send it to your printer at a later time, select this check box. This option is especially useful if you want to print your More About dialog boxes on a printer owned by someone who doesn't have Family Tree Maker. When you print, Family Tree Maker will ask for an "Output File Name." For general instructions for printing to a file, see page 265.

Note: If you intend to print the file on a printer other than your own, you will need to change the settings in "Print Setup" to match the printer you will be using. See "Print Setup" on page 266.

Print empty — Select this check box to print empty More About dialog boxes (except the Notes dialog box).

Print color — If you have a color printer, select this check box to print in color. If you have a black and white printer, select this check box to print in grayscale. De-select this check box if you want to print in black and white.

6.   Click **OK** when you've made your selections.

Family Tree Maker prints your More About information.

BATCH PRINTING

When you want to print a lot of information, use the Batch Print command. It is available for Family Group Sheets, Notes dialog boxes, and Scrapbooks. The Batch Print command lets you specify what document you want to print, what information it contains, and also provides page-numbering functions.

Here are the basic steps to start a batch print (details follow):

1. Choose what type of document you want to print.

2. Choose which individuals' information you want to print.

3. Specify the print settings.

4. Tell Family Tree Maker to print the documents.

Selecting and Setting Up the Document Type

With batch printing, you first need to decide what document you want to print.

To select and set up a document for batch printing:

1. Go to the document that you want to print.

   To print Family Group Sheets, from the **View** menu, select **Family Group Sheet**.

   To print Notes for individuals or marriages, place the cursor either on the name of the individual or on the marriage. Then from the **View** menu, select **More About**. From the submenu, select **Notes**.

   To print Scrapbooks for individuals or marriages, place the cursor either on the name of the individual or on the marriage. Then from the **View** menu, select **Scrapbook**.

2. Use the commands on the **Contents** and **Format** menus to set up the document for printing.

   For example, use the **Items to Include** command to choose which items you want to include in all of the documents. You also might want to format the text in the documents using the **Text Font, Style, & Size** command.

3. At this time, you may also want to check your print setup, which controls items such as paper orientation, paper size, and margins. If you want to change any of these items, see the section titled "Print Setup" on page 266.

   Continue with "Selecting a Print Order and Individuals to Print."

Selecting a Print Order and Individuals to Print

After you've chosen the type of document you want to print, you're ready to select a printing order and choose individuals to print.

From the **File** menu, select **Batch Print**. Family Tree Maker displays the Individuals to Include dialog box. In this dialog box you can create a group of individuals to include in the batch print. However, you first need to select a printing order.

Selecting a Print Order

To select a printing order:

1. Click **Sort order**.

   Family Tree Maker displays the Sort Batch Print dialog box.

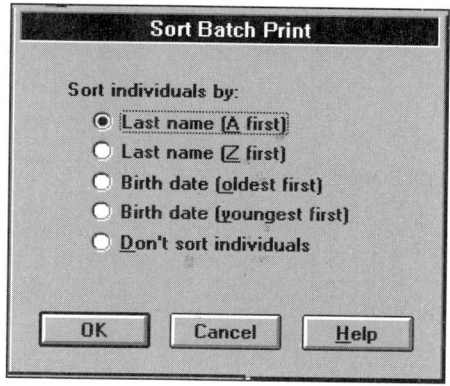

Figure 10-8. The Sort dialog box

2. Click the option button for the type of sorting you prefer.

   If you want individuals to print in the order in which you will choose them in the Individuals to Include dialog box, select **Don't sort individuals**.

3. Click **OK** when you've made your selection.

   Family Tree Maker returns you to the Individuals to Include dialog box. Now you can choose the individuals to print.

Selecting Individuals to Print

The Individuals to Include dialog box contains two lists. The list on the right shows the group of individuals who will be printed. The list on the left shows which individuals you can add to the group. The individuals in the list on the left are in alphabetical order by last name. Nicknames (aka's) are on different lines than the given names. See Figure 10-9, below.

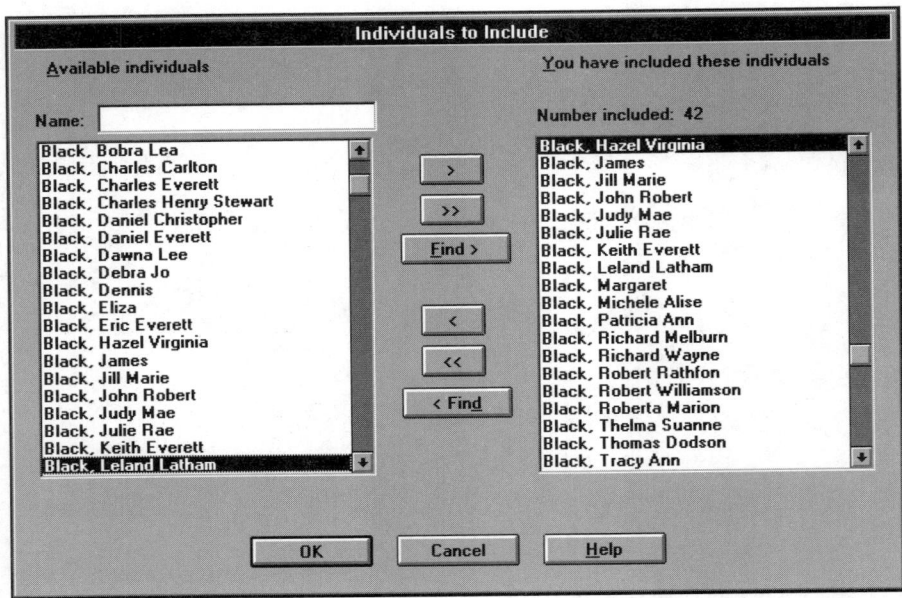

Figure 10-9. The Individuals to Include dialog box

To create the group of individuals:

1. Select individuals and add them to or remove them from the list on the right. The table below shows the three methods that you can use. You can use any combination of these methods to create your group.

To do this...	Use this button...	See page...
Include or remove individuals one-by-one.	"Include" or "Remove" (the single arrows)	342
Include all of the individuals currently in your Family File or remove all of the individuals currently in the group.	"Include All" or "Remove All" (the double arrows)	343
Choose categories of individuals to include or remove all at once.	"Find and Include" or "Find and Remove"	344

Figure 10-10. Methods for creating groups

Note: There is *one* Individuals to Include dialog box for all views in Family Tree Maker. The group of individuals that you create in one view, such as Labels/Cards, is available to you in the other views that allow you to choose groups: Report, Calendar, and batch print. Even if you exit Family Tree Maker, the group that you create in the Individuals to Include dialog box will remain the same until you change it again. Of course, if you make changes to the group in one view, such as the Report view, the group will change in all other views as well.

2. When you're done creating the group, click **OK** in the Individuals to Include dialog box.

   Family Tree Maker will display the Batch Print dialog box.

Using the "Include" and "Remove" Buttons

With the "Include" and "Remove" buttons you can add and remove individuals to and from the group one at a time.

To create a group using the "Include" and "Remove" buttons:

1. Click an individual's name in the list on the left to add that individual to the group. If you want to remove an individual from the group, click his or her name in the list on the right.

2. Click either the **Include** button (the arrow pointing to the right) or the **Remove** button (the arrow pointing to the left). See Figure 10-11.

    If you chose to add the individual, his or her name is added to the list on the right and the "Number included" increases by one. If you chose to remove the individual, his or her name is removed from the list on the right, and the "Number included" decreases by one.

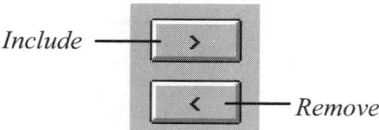

Figure 10-11. The Include and Remove buttons

Instead of selecting an individual and then clicking "Include" or "Remove," you can just double-click the individual's name. Double-clicking names in the list on the left automatically adds them to the group. Double-clicking names in the list on the right automatically removes them from the group.

Using the "Include All" and "Remove All" Buttons

With the "Include All" button, one click adds all of the individuals currently in your Family File to the group. With the "Remove All" button, one click removes all of the individuals from the group. See Figure 10-12.

Include All 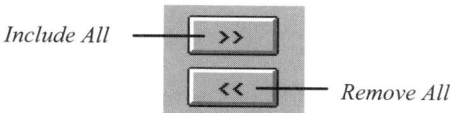 Remove All

Figure 10-12. The Include All and Remove All buttons

The best time to use the "Include All" button is when you want to create a group that includes almost all of the individuals that are currently in your Family File. For example, if there are only a few people that you don't want to include in the group, click the **Include All** button (the double arrows pointing to the right) to move all of the individuals to the list on the right. Then use the **Remove** button (the arrow pointing to the left) to remove the few individuals that you don't want in the group. This is much faster than including all of the individuals one by one. The "Remove" button is described in "Using the 'Include' and 'Remove' Buttons" on page 342.

The best time to use the "Remove All" button is when you already have several individuals in the group and you want to start over. Click the **Remove All** button (the double arrows pointing to the left) to remove all of the individuals from the group. Then use any method to begin adding individuals to the group again.

Using the "Find and Include" and "Find and Remove" Buttons

With the "Find and Include" and "Find and Remove" buttons, Family Tree Maker will search your Family File for individuals, such as those who were born before a certain date or those who are ancestors of a particular individual, and add them to or remove them from the group.

To create a group using the "Find and Include" and "Find and Remove" buttons:

1. Decide which individuals you want to add to or remove from the group. For example, do you want to add your ancestors? Do you want to add the individuals who were merged or appended? Do you want to remove all of the individuals who were born before a particular date?

   If you want to add or remove a group of individuals that are relatives of a particular individual, make sure to highlight the name of that individual in the list on the left before moving on to step 2. For example, if you wanted to add all of your ancestors, you would highlight your name.

2. Click either the **Find and Include** ("Find" with the arrow pointing to the right) or **Find and Remove** button ("Find" with the arrow pointing to the left). See Figure 10-13.

   Family Tree Maker displays either the Add Individuals or Remove Individuals dialog box. In this dialog box you specify which individuals you want Family Tree Maker to find and add to or remove from the group.

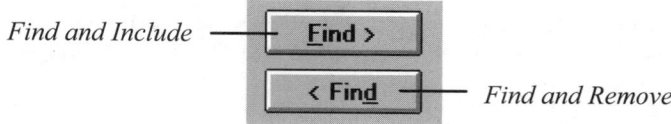

Find and Include —— **Find >**

< Find —— *Find and Remove*

Figure 10-13. The Find and Include and Find and Remove buttons

3. Click in the **Search** field.

   If you want to find the individuals who are all relatives of a particular individual, choose **Relatives** from the drop-down list. Family Tree Maker automatically fills the "of" field with the name of the individual that was highlighted in step 1. Using the **Limit relationships to** fields, select the individuals that you want to find. For example, to find all of the individual's ancestors, you would enter a large number in **Generations of Ancestors** and zeros in the other two fields. When you've made your selections, click **OK** and skip to step 5.

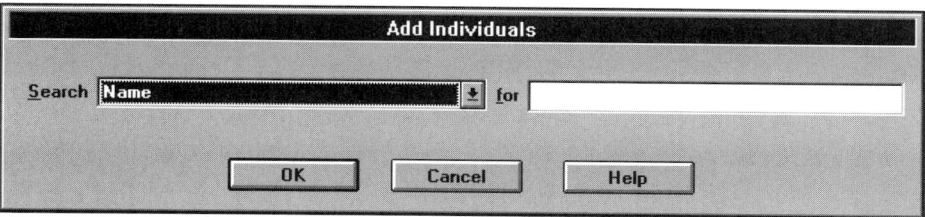

Figure 10-14. The Add Individuals dialog box

If you want to find individuals who have something in common, such as a birthplace, use the drop-down list to choose the name of the field that contains that information. For example, if you wanted to find all individuals who were born in a particular place, you would select "Birth location." When you've selected a field, continue with step 4.

4. In the **for** field, type the information that you want to search for. If the field that you are searching only has certain legal values (such as "male," "female," and "unknown"), Family Tree Maker will display a drop-down list in the "for" field. In this case, just click the item that you want to search for.

   For example, if you chose "Birth location" in step 3, and you wanted Family Tree Maker to find everyone that was born in Cleveland, Ohio, then you would type **Cleveland, Ohio** in the "for" field. If you are searching a date field, see Figure 4-12 on page 125 for searching tips.

5. Click **OK**.

   Family Tree Maker searches your Family File for individuals who match your request. If no matches are found, Family Tree Maker tells you so. If you chose to add the individuals, their names are added to the list on the right and the "Number included" increases. If you chose to remove the individuals, their names are removed from the list on the right, and the "Number included" decreases.

Selecting Print Settings

After you click **OK** in the Individuals to Include dialog box, Family Tree Maker displays the Batch Print dialog box. This is where you can select options for page numbering and print quality.

1. Make your selections in the Batch Print dialog box. Each of the options is described below.

    Print quality — Use this option to select the quality of your printed materials. The higher the print quality you choose, the darker and sharper your printed materials will be. However, items printed in high print quality also take longer to print. If your printer does not support different print qualities, this option will not be available to you.

    Page numbering — Select the option button for the page numbering scheme that you want for your batch print. If you choose to have page numbers, enter a starting number in the **Starting number** field. Please note that when you print Notes, the **Don't number pages** option button is not available. In addition, when you print Notes, you cannot select a starting number; all Notes start on page 1.

    Print color — If you have a color printer, select this check box to print in color. If you have a black and white printer, select this check box to print in grayscale. De-select this check box if you just want to print in black and white. If you have a black and white printer, color Picture/Objects will always print in grayscale.

2. Click **OK** when you've made your selections.

    Family Tree Maker begins the batch print.

Special Uses for Batch Printing

Batch printing comes in handy when you are doing family research. For example, you can batch print a set of Family Group Sheets to send to relatives so that they can verify the information. After printing the Family Group Sheets, you can easily switch to the Labels/Cards view and print mailing labels for the same group of people! This is because Family Tree Maker saves the group that you select in the Individuals to Include dialog box until you change it again.

Batch printing is also especially useful when you want to make family books. You can choose who to print the documents for and how to number the pages. You can also select the order in which the documents print — alphabetically, chronologically, or virtually any order you want! Many people like to print their documents in Ancestor or Descendant order, so we're including general instructions here:

To batch print in Ancestor or Descendant order:

1. When you first open the Individuals to Include dialog box, click the **Remove all** button (double arrows pointing to the left.)

2. Click **Sort order**.

   Family Tree Maker displays the Sort Batch Print dialog box.

3. Select the **Don't sort individuals** option button and then click **OK**.

   Family Tree Maker returns you to the Individuals to Include dialog box.

4. Select the individual whose ancestors or descendants you want to add and then click **Find and Include**.

   Family Tree Maker displays the Add Individuals dialog box.

5. In the **Search** field, select either **Ancestors** or **Descendants**.

6. Click **OK**.

   Family Tree Maker returns you to the Individuals to Include dialog box.

7. Click **OK**.

   Family Tree Maker displays the Batch Print dialog box.

8. Make your selections in the Batch Print dialog box.

9. Click **OK**.

   Family Tree Maker begins printing.

CREATING FAMILY BOOKS

Like most programs designed for Microsoft Windows, Family Tree Maker allows you to copy items from Family Tree Maker to the Windows Clipboard. You can then paste them into other Windows applications. This opens up many creative possibilities. For example, a family tree from Family Tree Maker could be pasted right into a book of family stories being written in a Windows word processor. Or, using a Windows desktop publishing program, you could create pages for a unique family album. Family trees and text from Family Tree Maker could also be combined with items such as scanned photographs and clip art.

Copying Items to Other Applications

You can place a copy of most Family Tree Maker items, such as trees, Family Group Sheets, and calendars, into other Windows applications. When you copy Outline Descendant trees and reports, Family Tree Maker copies a text file to the Clipboard. When you copy graphical items, such as box-style trees, Family Group Sheets, and calendars, Family Tree Maker places a **metafile** image on the Clipboard. A metafile is a graphics file format that many Windows word processors and graphics programs can read. Check the manual of your other software programs to see if they can read metafiles.

To copy and paste an item from Family Tree Maker into another Windows application:

1. Display the image that you want to copy.

2. From the **Edit** menu, select **Copy**.

   Family Tree Maker places a metafile image on the Clipboard.

3. Go to your other program and make any preparations that it requires.

4. From the **Edit** menu of that program, select **Paste**.

   An image will appear in that program.

   Note: You can also use these instructions to paste items into Family Tree Maker's Scrapbooks. If you decide to paste these types of items into a Scrapbook, we suggest that you only paste smaller items, such as trees with only a few boxes. When the items are too big, they do not fit attractively into the Scrapbook.

Chapter 11

MANAGING YOUR FILES

This is the 1978-1979 sixth grade class at Rockrimmon Elementary School in Colorado Springs, Colorado. Do you recognize anyone? The employees at Banner Blue Software sure do. One of Family Tree Maker's programmers, Kimberly (Williams) Paternoster, is pictured at the lower right corner.

MANAGING YOUR FILES

This chapter describes things that you can do with Family Files, such as opening them, checking them for errors, and exporting them to use with other programs.

CREATING NEW FAMILY FILES

To create a new Family File:

1. From the **File** menu, select **New Family File**.

    Family Tree Maker displays the New Family File dialog box.

2. Type a name for your file in the **File name** field.

    The name of your file must be eight letters or less and must have the extension .FTW. For example, you could type **myfamily.ftw** or **smith.ftw**

3. Click **OK**.

    Family Tree Maker creates your new Family File and then displays an empty Family Page.

OPENING EXISTING FILES

Using these instructions, you can open both Family Tree Maker for Windows and Family Tree Maker for DOS files. Instructions for opening PAF files are on page 352. Instructions for opening GEDCOM files begin on page 353.

To open a file in Family Tree Maker for Windows:

1. From the **File** menu, select **Open Family File**.

    Family Tree Maker displays the Open Family File dialog box.

2. In the **Drives** and **Directories** fields, select the drive and directory where the file you want to open is located. If you are unsure where your file is, click **Find file** and follow the instructions in "Finding Files" on page 392.

    Note: You cannot open a Family Tree Maker file (*.FTW) which is stored on a floppy diskette (or other removable media). You must transfer it to your hard drive before opening it. However, you can open Family Tree Maker Backup files (*.FBK and *.FBC) from floppy diskettes.

3. If your file is not a Family Tree Maker for Windows file, click the **File format** drop-down list and select the format of the file that you want to open.

   For example, if you want to open a Family Tree Maker for DOS file, select **Family Tree Maker for DOS (*.FTM)**.

4. Click the name of your file in the **File name** field and then click **OK**.

   If you are opening a Family Tree Maker for Windows file, your file is ready, so skip the remaining steps.

5. If your file is not a Family Tree Maker for Windows file, Family Tree Maker displays the New Family File dialog box. You must give your file a new name so that Family Tree Maker can make a copy of your original file and then convert the copy to a Family Tree Maker for Windows file.

   In the New Family File dialog box, you can either click **OK** to accept the name that Family Tree Maker suggests, or type a new name and then click **OK**. The name must be eight letters or less and must have the extension .FTW.

6. Click **OK** when you've given your file a new name.

   Family Tree Maker reloads your file as a Family Tree Maker for Windows file and then displays a Family Page containing one or more individuals from your file. You're ready to start working with your new Family File.

OPENING PAF FILES

If you simply want to open the PAF file in Family Tree Maker, use the instructions below. If you would like to add the information in the PAF file to the Family File that is currently open, see "Combining Files" on page 379.

To open a PAF file in Family Tree Maker for Windows (it must be from PAF version 2.1 or later):

1. From the **File** menu, select **Open Family File**.

   Family Tree Maker displays the Open Family File dialog box.

2. In the **Drives** and **Directories** fields, select the drive and directory where the file you want to open is located. If you are unsure where your file is, click **Find file** and follow the instructions in "Finding Files" on page 392.

3. Click the **File format** drop-down list and then select **Personal Ancestral File (INDIV2.DAT)**.

4. Click the name of the PAF file (INDIV2.DAT) in the **File name** field and then click **OK** to display the Open Personal Ancestral File dialog box.

5. In the Open Personal Ancestral File dialog box, you must give the PAF file a new name so that Family Tree Maker can make a copy of it and convert the copy to a Family Tree Maker for Windows file.

    Either click **OK** to accept the name that Family Tree Maker suggests or type a new name and then click **OK**. The name for your file must be eight letters or less and must have the extension .FTW.

    Family Tree Maker loads your PAF file as a Family Tree Maker for Windows file.

6. If Family Tree Maker encountered any difficulties while importing your file, it tells you that you can view a list of warnings and errors. After viewing the error list (if necessary) you can begin working with your Family File.

GEDCOM IMPORT AND EXPORT

GEDCOM is a standard file format for exchanging information between genealogy programs. The acronym GEDCOM stands for GEnealogical Data COMmunications. The Family History Department of the Church of Jesus Christ of Latter-day Saints (LDS Church) developed the GEDCOM standard.

You can use GEDCOM to transfer information into Family Tree Maker from another genealogy program that supports GEDCOM and vice versa. When you use GEDCOM, you avoid retyping.

Importing GEDCOM Files into Family Tree Maker

To open a GEDCOM file in Family Tree Maker for Windows:

1. From the **File** menu, select **Open Family File**.

    Family Tree Maker displays the Open Family File dialog box.

2. In the **Drives** and **Directories** fields, select the drive and directory where the file you want to open is located. If you are unsure where your file is, click **Find file** and follow the instructions in "Finding Files" on page 392.

3. Click the **File format** drop-down list and then select **GEDCOM (*.GED)**.

4. Click the name of the GEDCOM file in the **File name** field and then click **OK** to display the New Family File dialog box.

5. In the New Family File dialog box, you must give the GEDCOM file a new name so that Family Tree Maker can make a copy of it and convert the copy to a Family Tree Maker for Windows file.

   You can either click **OK** to accept the name that Family Tree Maker suggests or type a new name and then click **OK**. The name for your file must be eight letters or less and must have the extension .FTW.

   Family Tree Maker reloads your file as a Family Tree Maker for Windows file and then displays the Import from GEDCOM dialog box.

6. Some programs format information slightly differently than Family Tree Maker. Using the options listed below, you can reformat your information.

   Location — Some programs (like PAF) have longer location fields than Family Tree Maker does. For example, PAF can hold the location "Warren, Trumbull County, Ohio, United States of America." Select the **Keep first part if location fields are too long** option button to keep the first part of the location. The example above would become, "Warren, Trumbull County, Ohio." Select the **Keep last part if location fields are too long** option button to keep the last part of the location. The example above would become, "Ohio, United States of America."

   Delete underscore from names — Some programs (like PAF) add an underscore between compound names (for example, St._Germaine). Select this check box to replace the underscore with a space.

   Add spacing in location fields — Some programs also don't put spaces between the city, county, and state in location fields. Select this check box to add the normal space between these words, if necessary.

7. Now you must tell Family Tree Maker which information to import from your GEDCOM file. Family Tree Maker automatically imports an individual's name, sex, and the dates and locations of birth, death, and marriage. If you have sources for this information, they are also imported. If this is all of the information you want to import, click **OK** and skip the rest of these instructions. If you have additional information in your GEDCOM file and you want to import it, click **Fields to Import**. (This button may not be available if you do not have additional information to import.)

   Family Tree Maker displays the Fields to Import dialog box (see Figure 11-1 on the next page).

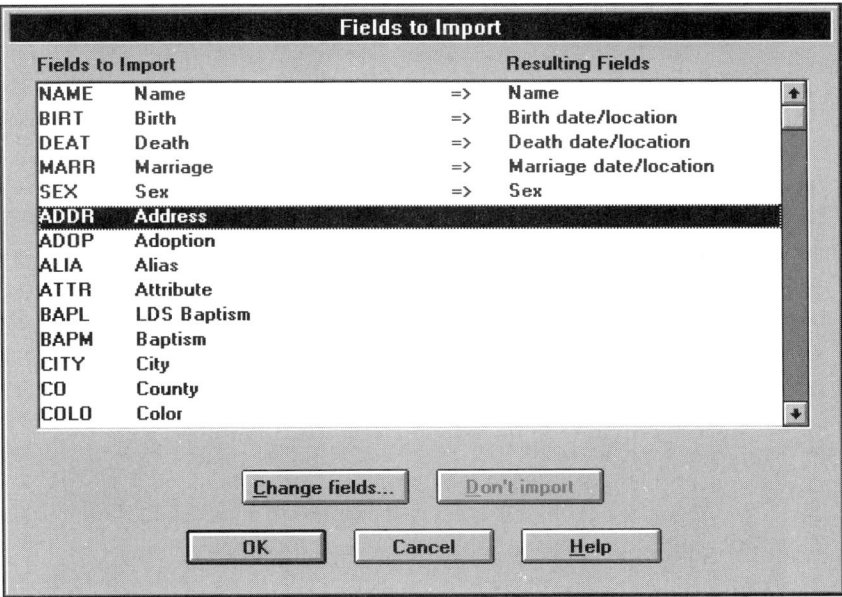

Fields to Import

Fields to Import			Resulting Fields
NAME	Name	=>	Name
BIRT	Birth	=>	Birth date/location
DEAT	Death	=>	Death date/location
MARR	Marriage	=>	Marriage date/location
SEX	Sex	=>	Sex
ADDR	Address		
ADOP	Adoption		
ALIA	Alias		
ATTR	Attribute		
BAPL	LDS Baptism		
BAPM	Baptism		
CITY	City		
CO	County		
COLO	Color		

Change fields...   Don't import

OK   Cancel   Help

Figure 11-1. The Fields to Import dialog box

There are two lists in this dialog box. The list on the left, **Fields to Import**, contains the GEDCOM tags from which the information is being imported. ("Tags" are labels for the different fields of information in the GEDCOM file. For example, the tag for occupation is "OCCU". For a list of tags, see pages 357 and 358.) The list on the right, **Resulting Fields**, shows which Family Tree Maker fields are being filled with information from the GEDCOM file.

8. To fill an additional Family Tree Maker field with GEDCOM information, click the name of that GEDCOM field in the "Fields to Import" list.

9. Click **Change fields**.

If there is more than one possible field into which that information can be imported, Family Tree Maker displays the Change Fields dialog box. In this case, continue with step 10 on the next page. If there is only one possible Family Tree Maker field into which that information can be imported, Family Tree Maker inserts the field name opposite the GEDCOM tag in the "Resulting Fields" list. In this case, skip to step 12.

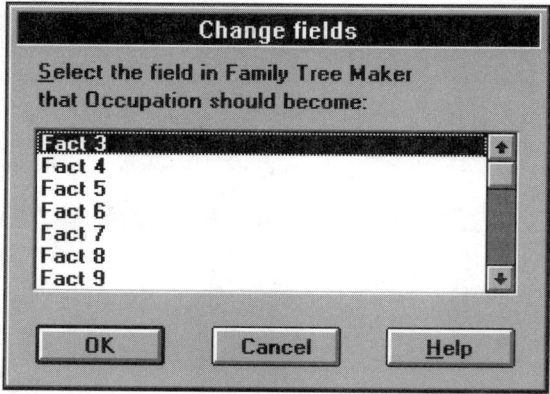

Figure 11-2. A Change Fields dialog box

10. In the Change Fields dialog box, click the name of the Family Tree Maker field that describes the information you selected in step 8.

11. Click **OK** to return to the Fields to Import dialog box.

If you later wish to change the mapping of a field, click the field name in the **Resulting Fields** list and then click **Change fields**. If this button stays grayed out, the mapping for that field is preset and cannot be changed.

12. Repeat steps 8 through 11 until all of the GEDCOM fields that you wish to map to Family Tree Maker fields are in the "Resulting Fields" list.

13. If you want to remove a field from the "Resulting Fields" list, click the field name and then click **Don't import**.

Family Tree Maker removes the field from the list.

14. Click **OK** when you've made your selections.

Family Tree Maker returns to the Import from GEDCOM dialog box.

15. Click **OK** again to create the Family File.

This tag	Stands for this	This tag	Stands for this
Addr	Address	Date	Date
Adop	Adoption	Dau	Daughter
Alia	Alias	Deat	Death
Afn	Ancestral file number	Dest	Destination
Anul	Annulment	Div	Divorce
Arvl	Arrival	Divf	Divorce filing
Asso	Associates	Dprt	Departure
Attr	Attribute	Dscr	Description
Bapl	Baptism LDS	Dwel	Dwelling
Bapm	Baptism	Educ	Education
Barm	Bar Mitzvah	Emig	Emigration
Basm	Bas Mitzvah	Endl	Endowment LDS
Birt	Birth	Enga	Engagement
Blsl	Blessing LDS	Even	Event
Buri	Burial	Fam	Family
Caus	Cause	Famc	Family child
Cast	Caste	Fams	Family spouse
Ceme	Cemetery	Fath	Father
Cens	Census	Fcom	First communion
Chan	Change	Fema	Female
Char	Character	File	File
Chil	Child	Fmt	Date format
Chr	Christening	Fost	Foster
Chra	Adult christening	Gedc	GEDCOM
City	City	Grad	Graduation
Co	County	Head	Header
Colo	Color	Hist ID	History ID #
Comm	Comment	Husb	Husband
Conc	Concatenate	Idno	Identification number
Conf	Confirmation	Ille	Illegitimate
Conl	Confirmation LDS	Immi	Immigration
Cont	Continuation	Indi	Individual
Corp	Corporation	Info	Information
Ctry	Country	Isa	Is a kind of
Cutoff Yr	Cutoff year	Labl	Label

Figure 11-3. Available tags

This tag	Stands for this		This tag	Stands for this
Lang	Language		Sibl	Sibling
Lds	LDS		Slgc	Sealing child
Lvg	Living		Slgp	Sealing parent
Male	Male		Son	Son
Marb	Marriage bann		Sour	Source
Marc	Marriage contract		Ssn	Social Security Number
Marl	Marriage License		Stae	State
Mars	Marriage settlement		Stake	Stake
Marr	Marriage		Stal	Stake LDS
Misc	Miscellaneous		Stil	Stillborn
Moth	Mother		Subm	Submitter
Name	Name		Surn	Surname
Namr	Name religious		Temp	Temple
Nati	Nationality		Text	Text
Natu	Naturalization		Titl	Title
Nchi	Number of children		Town	Town
Nmar	Number of marriages		Unit	Unit
Numb	Number		Vers	Version
Note	Note		Wife	Wife
Occu	Occupation		Will	Will
Ordl	Ordination LDS		Quay	Quality of date
Ordn	Ordination		Event1	_fa1
Phon	Phone number		Event2	_fa2
Plac	Place		Event3	_fa3
Post	Postal code		Event4	_fa4
Priv	Private		Event5	_fa5
Prob	Probate		Event6	_fa6
Race	Race		Event7	_fa7
Refn	Reference number		Event8	_fa8
Reli	Religion		Event9	_fa9
Rema	Remarks		Event10	_fa10
Resi	Residence		Event11	_fa11
Reti	Retirement		Event12	_fa2
Schema	Schema		Event13	_fa13
Sex	Sex			

Figure 11-4. Available tags, continued

Exporting GEDCOM Files from Family Tree Maker

To export your Family File to GEDCOM:

1. From the **File** menu, select **Copy/Export Family File**.

   Family Tree Maker displays the Copy/Export Family File dialog box.

2. Click the **File format** drop-down list and then select **GEDCOM (*.GED)**.

3. In the **File name** field, type a name for the GEDCOM file or keep the name that Family Tree Maker suggests. It must have the extension .GED.

4. In the **Drives** and **Directories** fields, select the drive and directory where you want to place your file.

5. Click **OK**.

   Family Tree Maker displays the Export to GEDCOM dialog box.

6. Make your selections. Each of the options is described below.

   File Type — The "Destination" field allows Family Tree Maker to check for requirements of the program that will read the GEDCOM file. Use the table below to make a selection. The **FTW** file type offers the most complete export; select it if you plan to later re-import the file into Family Tree Maker for Windows. If the program you are exporting to is not listed, choose **PAF**.

Select this...	To create this type of file...
ANSTFILE	Ancestral File of LDS church
NPS	Temple submission to LDS church
PAF	Personal Ancestral file, 2.1 or later
ROOTS	Roots II, Roots III, or Roots IV
FTM	Family Tree Maker for DOS
FTW	Family Tree Maker for Windows

Figure 11-5. Destination file types

When you make a selection in the "Destination" field, Family Tree Maker makes suggestions for the "GEDCOM" and "Character set" fields. However, if Family Tree Maker's suggestions are incorrect for your purposes, make your own selections. Whenever possible, choose **Version 5** in the "GEDCOM" field; it offers the best export.

Indent records — You can select this check box to make the file more readable in a word processor. However, some programs cannot read indented records, so it is best *not* to select this check box.

Abbreviate tags — Most programs use abbreviated tags instead of long tags, so it is best to select this check box. ("Tags" are labels for the different fields of information in the GEDCOM file. For example, the tag for occupation is "OCCU". For a list of tags, see pages 357 and 358.)

7. Now you must tell Family Tree Maker which information to export to your GEDCOM file. Family Tree Maker automatically exports most of the information, depending on your choices in step 6. If you have sources for this information, they are also exported. To see and/or change what is being exported, click **Fields to Export**. When you click "Fields to Export," Family Tree Maker displays the Fields to Export dialog box. Otherwise, click **OK** and skip the rest of these instructions.

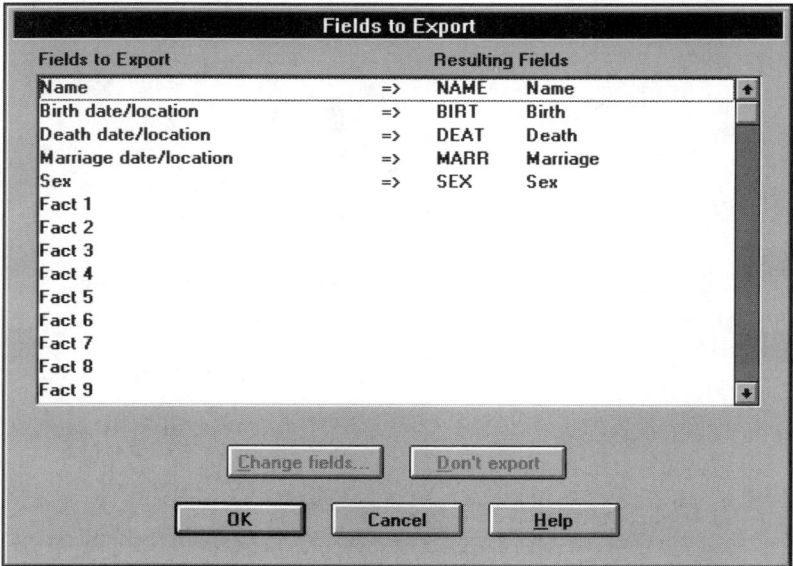

Figure 11-6. The Fields to Export dialog box

There are two lists in this dialog box. The list on the left, **Fields to Export**, contains all of the Family Tree Maker fields that you can export to the GEDCOM file. The list on the right, **Resulting Fields**, contains the GEDCOM tags to which the Family Tree Maker information is being exported. ("Tags" are labels for the different fields of information in the GEDCOM file. For example, the tag for occupation is "OCCU".)

Note: The "Resulting Fields" list defaults to contain all of the GEDCOM-supported fields, based on your choices in step 6. If you do not want to export all of this information, you can remove items from this list. See the next step for instructions.

8. If you want to remove a tag from the "Resulting Fields" list, click the tag name and then click **Don't export**.

9. To export a Family Tree Maker field that doesn't have a GEDCOM tag opposite it in the "Resulting Fields" list, click the name of the field.

10. Click **Change fields**.

If there is more than one possible GEDCOM tag to which that information can be exported, Family Tree Maker displays the Change Fields dialog box. In this case, continue with step 11 on the next page. If there is only one possible tag to which that information can be exported, Family Tree Maker automatically inserts the tag name in the list on the right, opposite the name of the Family Tree Maker field. In this case, skip to step 13.

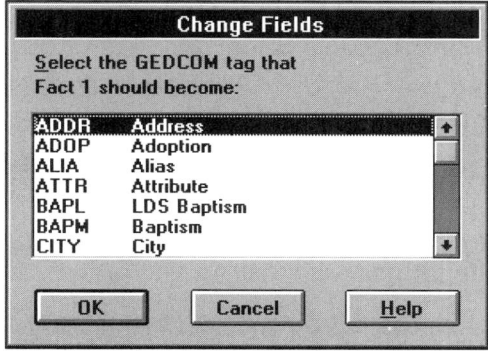

Figure 11-7. The Change Fields dialog box

11. In the Change Fields dialog box, click the name of the GEDCOM tag that describes the information you selected in step 9.

12. Click **OK** to return to the Fields to Export dialog box.

13. Repeat steps 8 through 12 until all Family Tree Maker fields that you wish to export have GEDCOM tags opposite them in the "Resulting Fields" list.

14. If you wish to change the mapping of a Family Tree Maker field, click it and then click **Change fields**. If this button stays grayed out, the mapping for that field is preset and cannot be changed.

15. Click **OK** when you've made your selections.

    Family Tree Maker returns to the Export to GEDCOM dialog box.

16. Click **OK** again.

    Family Tree Maker creates the GEDCOM file.

THE WORLD FAMILY TREE PROJECT

Banner Blue is inviting all Family Tree Maker customers to participate in a remarkable genealogical opportunity — the World Family Tree™ project. With over 500,000 copies sold, Family Tree Maker has been used by people just like you to collect information about hundreds of thousands of families. Now, in response to our customers' many requests, we've invested the equipment and know-how needed to compile all of those family trees into a massive database of family information.

With your participation, the World Family Tree could become the largest genealogical database in existence! As we collect family trees, we make them available on CD-ROM at affordable prices. We are also exploring other ways to give you access to the family trees, such as an on-line service.

Imagine uncovering generations of new information about your family without even leaving your computer — you'll be able to do that by finding just one shared ancestor among the millions of records available.

Details of Participation

As you consider adding your family information to the World Family Tree, there are some important issues to think about. The following sections might answer some of your questions.

Benefits of Sharing Your Family File

Submitting your file will be valuable to you and to other genealogists. By contributing to and accessing a shared collection of Family Tree Maker files, you can do the following:

- Extend your family tree when you locate the family trees of others who share your ancestry.

- Help others who may be searching for information that you have.

- Protect your family history data from loss or damage. Your family tree will be part of a readily-accessible database, to be archived at the Library of Congress in Washington, D.C.

- Preserve your family history data so that is can be accessed by your descendants. What a wonderful gift for future generations!

Protecting Your Privacy

In the interest of privacy, we suggest that you review the contents of your family tree before submitting it. If there is any information that you want to keep confidential, make a copy of your Family File, delete the information that you don't want to share with others, and then send the new, edited version of the file to the World Family Tree Project. When your tree becomes available on a World Family Tree CD, only the names, genders, and family links of living individuals will be published. We replace all other information about living individuals with "Private," "Any information hidden for privacy," or another similar message.

Ultimately, the more information we're able to include in the database, the better your chances are for linking family trees together, since you'll have more clues to connect individuals to your own family. You may end up with an expanded family reunion invitation list, not to mention a larger family tree!

When you send in your file, you will include your own name and address, and can also include your phone number if you wish. Although we will not publish this information with the CD, by submitting your Family File, you give Banner Blue the permission to provide your name and address to family history enthusiasts who are interested in contacting you. We urge you to let us know if your address changes so that we will always know how to get in touch with you.

Ensuring the Quality of the Database

We realize that much of the information in your family tree was probably collected by speaking with relatives. For this reason, we do not expect complete documentation of your family information. If you did get your information from sources outside of your family, however, we encourage you to record those sources in Family Tree Maker's Source fields (see "Recording Sources" on page 101). If you are not sure how to document your sources, check the genealogy books at your local library or ask a local genealogy society for more information.

We also understand that the potential for data errors exists, even in the most careful genealogist's family tree. Family Tree Maker can help you find possible errors (see "Checking Your File for Errors" on page 367), but it's still up to you to correct the mistakes. We want to remind participants to research carefully, and to try to avoid submitting confusing or misleading information.

By the same token, when you use the World Family Tree, you should recognize that it is meant to be a research tool, not a source of completely error-free data. The genealogical information in World Family Tree was submitted by genealogy enthusiasts like yourself, and has not been verified by Banner Blue. *Verify all information before adding it to your own collection of family information.*

Finally, we ask that you do not submit information that infringes on copyrights, invades the privacy of others, or is defamatory or profane in any way. Again, please review the contents of your file carefully before you submit it.

Your Participation is Important

Most genealogists feel that their work is never done, but we assure you that your family tree is valuable to other researchers, no matter how large or small, complete or incomplete. Whether you have just begun your family tree or you are looking to add more branches, submitting your family tree immediately is important to the creation of the World Family Tree.

We are sincerely excited about creating these opportunities for our customers. But don't forget, none of this can happen unless you submit your file. Continue reading on the next page for submission instructions. Become a part of the World Family Tree today!

How to Submit Your File

Before you begin, you should have an empty, formatted 3.5" or 5.25" diskette. You can use either size, depending on what is convenient for you. The diskette should be labeled with your name, address, and the present date; use a standard diskette label sticker if you have one.

To submit a copy of your Family File to the World Family Tree Project:

1. With the blank, formatted diskette in your diskette drive, start Family Tree Maker and open the Family File that you want to submit.

2. From the **File** menu, select **Submit to World Family Tree**.

   Family Tree Maker displays the Submit to World Family Tree dialog box.

3. Select the **Destination Drives** option button corresponding to the diskette drive that your blank diskette is in.

4. Type in the requested submitter information.

   Name, address — Banner Blue needs your name and address in case there is a problem with your Family File and we need to contact you. Family Tree Maker cannot finish the submission process until you have filled in your first name, last name, street address (or P.O. Box), city, state, and zip. If your address is in a country other than the United States, Family Tree Maker does not require the state and zip fields. However, please fill out the entire address needed for mail delivery.

   Phone (optional) — If you want Banner Blue and other World Family Tree users to be able to contact you by phone, include your phone number. Don't forget your area or country code!

   Date — Family Tree Maker uses the date from your computer's internal calendar. If the date is incorrect, please change it. It is vital to have the correct date on your Family File in case you later send us an updated version.

5. Click **OK**.

   Family Tree Maker displays the Submitter Agreement dialog box.

6. Read the information carefully and then click either **Yes** or **No**.

   By clicking "Yes," you indicate that you understand and accept your responsibilities as a submitter to the World Family Tree. In this case, Family Tree Maker copies your Family File to the diskette. If you click "No," Family Tree Maker cancels the submission process.

7. **Important:** When Family Tree Maker is finished copying your Family File onto the diskette, be sure to write your name and address on a label and place it on the diskette if you haven't already done so.

   Please don't skip this important step. If your diskette is damaged in transit, the Family File will be unreadable, and the label is the only way that we will know who sent the diskette.

8. Seal the diskette in a sturdy envelope and send it to:

   Banner Blue Software
   World Family Tree Project
   P.O. Box 760
   Fremont, CA 94537-0760

   Thank you for contributing to what will be a remarkable and unequaled source of linked genealogical data.

Your Rights as a Submitter to the World Family Tree

To ensure that you understand your rights as a submitter to the World Family Tree, please read the following information:

- By submitting your Family File to the World Family Tree Project, you give Brøderbund Software, Incorporated (Banner Blue's parent company) the permission to reproduce, compile, and distribute all information in your submitted Family File along with other submitted Family Files.

- The World Family Tree products are copyrighted; however, our copyright does not limit you from publishing your own family information as you see fit, nor from selling it or giving it to others.

- By submitting your Family File to the World Family Tree Project, you give Brøderbund Software, Inc. the permission to provide your name and mailing address to family history enthusiasts who are interested in contacting you.

- Do not submit information that infringes on the copyrights of others, invades the privacy of others, or is defamatory or profane in any way.

- Brøderbund Software, Inc. retains the right to edit your Family File before its final publication in the World Family Tree. However, Brøderbund recognizes the importance of maintaining the integrity of the data in your file and of not changing important family information.

- Submitting your Family File to the World Family Tree Project does not entitle you to any compensation, monetary or other.

- By submitting your Family File, you are indicating that you have read and accepted these rights and responsibilities.

- Family Tree Maker and the World Family Tree are trademarks of Brøderbund Software, Inc.

CHECKING YOUR FILE FOR ERRORS

Because collecting your family information involves tracking down so many dates, names, and other facts, there may be occasions when the information in your Family File is incorrect or incomplete. While Family Tree Maker cannot determine the accuracy of specific biographical information — such as the spelling of your relatives' names — it is able to identify facts that conflict with each other. We encourage you to use the error checking features so that your family information is as accurate as possible.

Family Tree Maker does some error checking automatically, while other types of error checking you initiate yourself. The three techniques are described below.

- **Data Entry Checking** With this method, Family Tree Maker screens information as you enter it, finding problems such as inconsistencies in birth and death dates. This method helps you catch errors immediately, while information about an individual is fresh in your mind. For more information, see "Data Entry Checking," on the next page.

- **The Find Error Command** This command lets you search your Family File for possible errors and fix them as they are found. This is an excellent method for finding errors, because it looks at all of the information in your Family File, not just the information that you are currently entering. In addition, you will locate all of the most common types of errors. For more information, see "The Find Error Command," on page 370.

- **Data Errors Report** With this method, you can print a report of the possible errors in your file and then later use that report to go through your Family File and correct the mistakes. This method is the most thorough, although not as easy to use because you must search your file manually to locate the errors that are listed in the report. For more information, see "Data Errors Reports," on page 371.

Data Entry Checking

Using the Data Entry Checking feature is easy. When it is on, Family Tree Maker automatically checks information as you enter it into the Family Page. When Family Tree Maker finds information that seems to be incorrect or conflicts with other information in your Family File, it prompts you to take a closer look at it and fix it, if necessary. For certain types of errors, such as random punctuation in a name, you can't turn the error checking off; Family Tree Maker always prompts you to fix these errors.

For instructions on turning the Data Entry Checking feature on and off, see "Data Entry Checking Preferences" on page 79. For a list of the errors that you can find with Data Entry Checking, see "Error Types" on page 371. For some samples of the dialog boxes that Family Tree Maker will display when it finds an error, see "Sample Error Checking Dialog Boxes," below.

Sample Error Checking Dialog Boxes

The error checking features in Family Tree Maker search for many different types of mistakes in names and dates. When Family Tree Maker locates a possible error, it displays a dialog box so that you can either fix the error or skip over it if it is not an error. There are five different types of dialog boxes, but they all work in fundamentally the same way. Two examples follow.

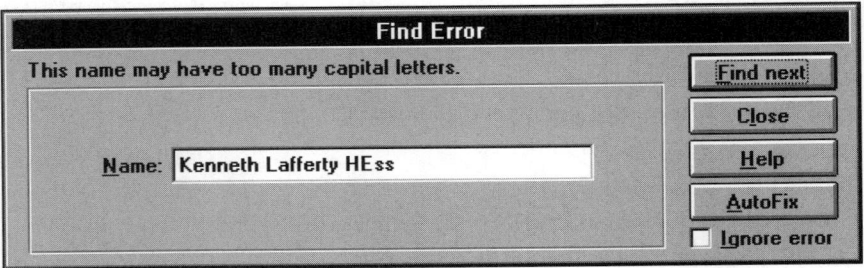

Figure 11-8. The Name Capitalization error dialog box

In the dialog box in Figure 11-8, Family Tree Maker believes that too many letters in the name are capitalized. To fix the error when you are using the Find Error command, you would re-type the name and then click **Find Next** to move on to the next error or **Close** to quit the search. To fix the error when you are using Data Entry Checking, all you need to do is re-type the name correctly and then click **OK**. ("OK" is not visible in Figure 11-8)

Alternatively, you could click **AutoFix**. In this case, Family Tree Maker would make its best attempt at fixing the error for you. When you click **AutoFix**, the button name changes to **Undo** so that you can reverse the change if Family Tree Maker fixed the error incorrectly.

If the name actually was capitalized correctly, you would select the **Ignore error** check box. This way, Family Tree Maker would not display this error for this individual again.

Let's look at another example. In the dialog box below, Family Tree Maker believes that you have entered an individual's nickname in the name field on the Family Page, instead of in the "aka" field in the Lineage dialog box.

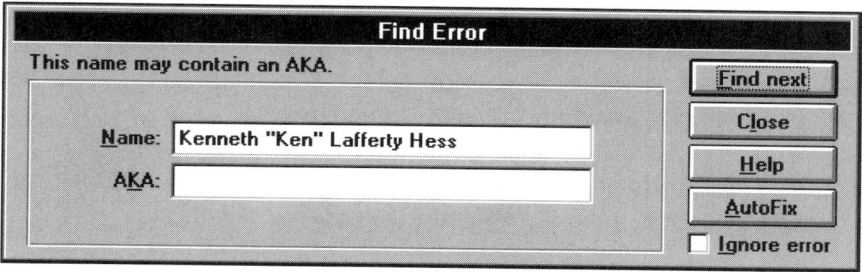

Figure 11-9. The AKA in name error dialog box

The **Name** field shows what is currently entered on the Family Page and the **aka** field shows what is in the More About Lineage dialog box. If you click **AutoFix**, Family Tree Maker will attempt to extract the nickname from the **Name** field and place it in the **aka** field. Otherwise, you can just type in the names correctly. Of course, if this wasn't an error, you would select the **Ignore error** check box.

The Find Error Command

Using the Find Error command is similar to spell-checking a word processing document: you go through the file from beginning to end and fix mistakes as you come across them. For a list of the errors that you can locate with the Find Error Command, see "Error Types" on page 371.

To check your Family File with the Find Error Command:

1. From the **Edit** menu, select **Find Error**.

   Family Tree Maker displays the Find Error dialog box. Each of your options is described below.

   Errors to find in search — Select the check boxes for the types of errors that you want Family Tree Maker to locate.

   Reset all ignored errors — If you previously chose to ignore some errors by selecting the "Ignore error" check box, described in step 3, click this button to include those errors in all future searches.

2. Click **OK** when you've made your selections.

   Family Tree Maker begins your error search.

3. When Family Tree Maker displays an error dialog box, you can either fix the error manually, fix it automatically by clicking **AutoFix**, or skip over it by selecting the **Ignore error** check box. When you select "Ignore error," Family Tree Maker flags that error so that it will not show up as an error in other places in your Family File and in subsequent searches.

   See "Sample Error Checking Dialog Boxes," on page 368, for specific examples.

4. Click **Find next** when you want to move on to the next error or click **Close** when you want to quit searching.

   You've reached the end of the search when Family Tree Maker returns you to a Family Page.

Data Errors Reports

A Data Errors report can show you all of the places in your Family File where there might be mistakes. It is very thorough in its checking, but in order to fix the mistakes, you have to go into your file and manually locate the errors listed in the report.

You create and print a Data Errors report in the Report view. For instructions, see "Creating a Report" on page 275. For a list of the errors that you can find with the Data Errors report, see "Error Types," below.

Error Types

This section lists the types of errors that Family Tree Maker can locate for you: name errors, date errors, and other types of errors. Each error message is listed in bold and is followed by a brief explanation and a suggestion for correcting it. Please note that Family Tree Maker does not search for some of these errors with all three types of error checking. This information is also included in the descriptions below the error messages.

Name Errors

"There may be too many APOSTROPHES in the name"
Available with all three types of error checking.
Family Tree Maker has found a name containing more than one apostrophe. Verify the spelling of the name and then delete any extra apostrophes.

"Possible misplaced DASH in the name"
Available with all three types of error checking.
Family Tree Maker has found a name with either two dashes in a row or a dash at the beginning or end of the name. Verify the spelling of the name and then delete any extra dashes.

"There may be a TITLE in the name field"
Available with all three types of error checking.
You may have typed an individual's title, such as "Dr." or "Reverend" in the name field on the Family Page instead of in the "Title" field in the Lineage dialog box (see page 134). Verify the spelling of the name, remove any titles, and type the titles in the "Title" field.

"The name may contain an illegal character"
Available with all three types of error checking.
Family Tree Maker has found a name containing one or more of the following characters: ~ ! @ # $ % ^ & * _ - + = \ | : ; " < > , / ( ) [ ] { } 1 2 3 4 5 6 7 8 9 0. Verify the spelling of the name and then delete any extra characters.

"Possibly used MARRIED instead of MAIDEN name"
Available with all three types of error checking.
Family Tree Maker has found a Family Page where the surname for both the husband and the wife is the same. Even though women usually assume their husbands' last names, most genealogists record women with their maiden (or family) surname instead of their married surname. Using this standard is helpful for tracking maternal lineage and for distinguishing between a man's sisters and spouses. Replace the married name with the maiden name.

"The name may have too many capital letters"
Available with all three types of error checking.
Family Tree Maker has found a word containing more than one capitalized letter. (Family Tree Maker understands surnames such as "Mac Donnell," "De Long," and "Von Trapp." Verify the spelling of the name and then switch any extra uppercase letters to lowercase letters.

"The name has mismatched BACKSLASHES"
Available with all three types of error checking.
Family Tree Maker has found a name containing either one backslash or more than two backslashes. In Family Tree Maker, you can place unusual last names between backslashes (Connie \Irish Hess\) so that Family Tree Maker recognizes them. You can also use two consecutive backslashes to indicate that someone does not have a last name (Running Bear \\). Verify the spelling of the name and then add or remove backslashes as needed.

"The name may have misplaced PERIODS"
Available with all three types of error checking.
Family Tree Maker has found a name with a period at the beginning, two periods in a row, or a period at the end. Verify the spelling of the name and then remove extra periods as needed.

"The name may contain an AKA"
Available with all three types of error checking.
You may have typed an individual's nickname in the name field on the Family Page instead of in the "aka" field in the Lineage dialog box (see page 134). Verify the spelling of the name, remove any nicknames, and type the nicknames in the "aka" field.

"LAST NAME possibly missing"

Available only with Data Errors reports.
Family Tree Maker has found a name field containing only one name part (word). Verify the name and type in any missing name parts. If you do not know what the missing name part is, type three question marks **???** in its place. For example, **John ???** If someone just does not have a last name, type two backslashes after their given name, such as **Hiawatha **.

Date Errors

"Born when parent <name> was under 13"

Available only with Data Errors reports.
According to the dates in your Family File, this individual was born before one (or both) of the parents reached age 13. Verify the birth dates, then make sure you have the correct relationship between the mother and child.

"<child's name> BIRTH DATE is after <mother's name> death date"

Available with all three types of error checking.
According to the dates in your Family File, this individual was born after the death date of his or her mother. Verify the birth and death dates, then make sure you have the correct relationship between the mother and child.

"<child's name> BIRTH DATE occurred too long after <father's name> death date"

Available with all three types of error checking.
According to the dates in your Family File, this individual was born more than 10 months after the death date of his or her father. Verify that the child is the natural child of the father and that their birth and death dates are correct.

"DEATH DATE is before birth date"

Available with all three types of error checking.
This individual's listed death date indicates that he died prior to his birth date. These two dates may simply have been entered in reverse order.

"EVENT DATE not before <name's> death date"

Available only with Data Errors reports.
An event that you have recorded for this individual is dated prior to his birth date or after his death date. Some events, such as burial, actually can happen outside of one's lifetime. However, if the event must have occurred during the individual's lifetime, verify the date of the event with another source.

"<Name's> MARRIAGE to <name> occurred before age 13"
Available only with Data Errors reports.
This individual was twelve years old or younger on the date of his or her marriage. Consult a municipal record for the marriage to ensure that you're using the most reliable source. Also double-check your original source for the marriage date and the birth dates of both spouses.

"EVENT DATE is empty"
Available only with Data Errors reports.
Family Tree Maker has found a date field that contains no text or numbers. Since events always correspond to a date, this indicates a gap in your research. For events where you do not know an exact date, you may want to use an estimated date (see page 87) or type **unknown** in the date field. Please note that this error message does not include the Fact fields in the Facts dialog box.

"DEATH DATE more than 120 years after birth"
Available with all three types of error checking.
Your Family File indicates that this individual had a life span of more than 120 years. Verify both the birth and death dates, making sure that the correct century is entered. If you do not have an exact death date for an individual, but do know that the individual is deceased, use an estimated death date (see page 87).

"<child's name> BIRTH DATE more than 20 years after <name> and <name> marriage date"
Available only with Data Errors reports.
Family Tree Maker has found an individual who was born more than 20 years after his or her parents were married. Verify both the birth and marriage dates, as well as the relationship between the parents and the child.

"<child's name> BIRTH DATE before <name> and <name> marriage date"
Available only with Data Errors reports.
Family Tree Maker has found an individual who was born before his or her parents were married. Verify both the birth and marriage dates, as well as the relationship between the parents and the child.

"Children of <name> and <name> are not listed in BIRTH ORDER"
Available only with Data Errors reports.
Family Tree Maker has found a Family Page on which the children are not listed in the order of their birth. Go to that Family Page and use the **Sort Children** command from the **People** menu to put them in the correct order (see page 99).

"Mother older than 50 at child's birth"
Available only with the Find Error Command.
Family Tree Maker has located a woman who was at least 50 years old on the birth date of one of her children. The listed child might instead be a grandchild or there could be a special circumstance such as adoption.

Other Errors

"Possible DUPLICATE individual"
Available only with the Data Entry Checking.
Family Tree Maker has found two people with identical names, sexes, and birth dates. Make sure that the individuals actually are distinct people. If you accidentally created more than one record for the same individual, you can eliminate the excess record by merging the information. See "Merging Duplicate Individuals" on page 387.

"NO PARENTS, NO CHILDREN, and NO SPOUSES"
Available with all three types of error checking.
Make sure you haven't omitted the individuals to whom this individual is related. If you don't yet know who they are, you'll at least know where to start your research! In some instances, you may have inadvertently unlinked an individual in order to fix a relationship mistake. For more information, see the Chapter 6, "Fixing Relationship Mistakes," on pages 185-190.

"<Fieldname> should have initial caps"
Available only with Data Errors reports.
Family Tree Maker has found a field where you have typed information in all capital letters or all lowercase letters. Check the capitalization.

BACKING UP YOUR FAMILY FILE

Family Tree Maker does not have a Save command, but a Backup command instead. This is because Family Tree Maker is a database program that saves your information regularly while you are using the program, as well as when you quit. Family Tree Maker saves your information both in your regular .FTW Family File and also in a special **backup** file that is in the same directory and has the same name as your Family File, but with the extension **.FBK**. The .FBK backup file is what Family Tree Maker would try to open if your original Family File was ever damaged.

Note: Since Family Tree Maker automatically saves the information that you enter, you cannot get rid of your latest changes by quitting the program without saving. To get rid of any changes, you must fix them manually. Or, following the directions below, make your own backup files regularly so you can revert to an old file.

You can also make your own compressed backup files to store on diskettes or in other directories. These backup copies that you create manually will have the extension **.FBC**. Making regular backup copies of your Family File can help ensure that you won't lose all of your genealogical information if something ever happens to the Family File that you work with regularly. If you are entering a lot of information, it's a good idea to backup as often as once every half hour — you never know when you will have a power failure! If you are planning to backup to a diskette drive, be sure to have blank, formatted diskettes handy.

If you want to make a copy of your Family File to share with someone, use the **Copy/Export Family File** command instead, described on page 389.

To manually backup your Family File:

1. From the **File** menu, select **Backup Family File**.

    Family Tree Maker displays the Backup Family File dialog box.

2. The "Currently selected backup destination" field lists where your backup copy would be if you clicked **OK** now. To change the location of your backup, select one of the option buttons in the **Backup Destination Choices** group box:

    Working directory will place your file in the directory where Family Tree Maker is installed. **Custom directory** lets you choose a different directory on your hard drive. The other option buttons let you place your file on a floppy diskette.

If you select **Custom directory**, click **Change filename or directory** to choose a new backup destination. In the Change filename or directory dialog box, use the **Drives** and **Directories** fields to select a location and then type a name in the **File name** field. The file name must be eight letters or less with the extension .FBC. If you want to find the location of a previous backup file, click **Find file** and then follow the instructions in "Finding Files" on page 392. Click **OK** when you've made your selections. Family Tree Maker returns you to the Backup Family File dialog box.

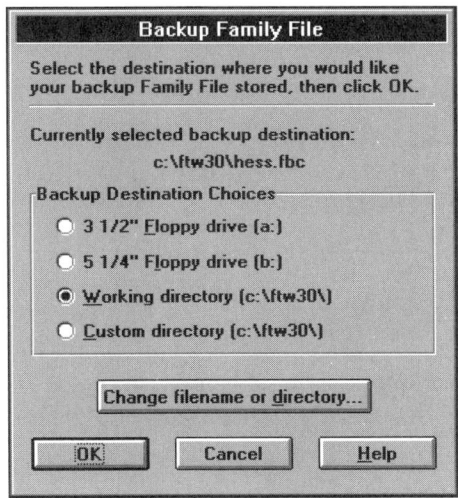

Figure 11-10. The Backup Family File dialog box

3. Click **OK** after making your selections.

    If the backup file that you want to create already exists, Family Tree Maker will warn you and may not let you create the file, depending on whether you have chosen to allow files to be overwritten. See "Selecting Startup Preferences" on page 26. Otherwise, Family Tree Maker copies your Family File to the file name and destination that you selected.

    If you are backing up a large file to a diskette drive, Family Tree Maker will ask you to insert new diskettes as needed. When the backup requires multiple diskettes, be sure to label them in the order in which they are used. At the end of the backup process, Family Tree Maker will ask you to reinsert the first diskette.

Opening Backup Files

If your original Family File is damaged or you want to revert to a previous copy, you will need to restore it from a backup, either .FBK or .FBC. (These two types of files are described on page 376.) This process will create a new file.

To open a backup file:

1. From the **File** menu, select **Open Family File**.

   Family Tree Maker displays the Open Family File dialog box.

2. In the **Drives** and **Directories** fields, select the drive and directory where your backup is located. If you are unsure where your file is, click **Find file** and follow the instructions in "Finding Files" on page 392.

3. Click the **File format** field and select either **Family Tree Backup (*.FBK)** or **Family Tree Maker Compressed Backup (*.FBC)**, depending on which type of backup you want to open.

4. Select the name of your file in the **File name** field and then click **OK**.

   If you are opening a Family Tree Maker Backup (*.FBK) file, Family Tree Maker displays the Open Backup Family File dialog box.

   If you are opening a Family Tree Maker Compressed Backup (*.FBC) file, Family Tree Maker displays Open Compressed Backup File dialog box.

5. You must give your file a new name so that Family Tree Maker can make a copy of your original file and then convert the copy to a Family Tree Maker for Windows file. Click **OK** to accept the name that Family Tree Maker suggests, or type a new name and then click **OK**.

   The name must be eight letters or less and must have the extension .FTW.

6. Click **OK** when you've given your file a new name.

   Family Tree Maker begins restoring your file. If you are restoring a file from diskettes, Family Tree Maker will prompt you to insert the diskettes as needed. When restoration is complete, Family Tree Maker displays a Family Page containing one or more individuals from your file.

COMBINING FILES

If you have several GEDCOM, PAF, Family Tree Maker for Windows, or Family Tree Maker for DOS files, you can join them together to create one large Family Tree Maker for Windows file. If your files contain overlapping information, Family Tree Maker helps you sort everything out by locating individuals who may be duplicates. Family Tree Maker automatically combines exact duplicates and then lets you compare possible duplicates so you can decide whether they should be combined.

Important: Be cautious when you join files. If you don't work carefully, you may accidentally combine two unique individuals. We suggest that you first make a backup copy of your file (see page 376) so you can return to a previous version in case your file doesn't turn out as you expected. Also, after you finish combining files, print some trees and reports so that it's easy to see whether or not you've made any mistakes

Opening the Files

The first step is to open the files that you want to combine:

1. Make sure that the correct Family Tree Maker **destination** file is open.

    The "destination" file is the file that you are adding information to; the "source" file is the file from which that information comes. The destination file will become larger, and the source file remains the same.

2. From the **File** menu, select **Open Family File**.

    Family Tree Maker displays the Open Family File dialog box.

3. In the **Drives** and **Directories** fields, select the drive and directory where the **source** file is located. If you are unsure where your file is, click **Find file** and follow the instructions in "Finding Files" on page 392.

4. Click the **File format** drop-down list and select the format of the file.

5. Click the name of your file in the **File name** list.

6. Select **Append file** and then click **OK**.

    Once you click "Append file," Family Tree Maker compares the field labels in the source and destination files. If all field labels are the same, Family Tree Maker displays the Individuals to Include dialog box; skip to "Selecting Individuals to Include" on page 382. Otherwise, continue with "Mapping Information Between the Source and Destination Files," on the next page.

Mapping Information Between the Source and Destination Files

If the two files contain different fields, you must use the Fields to Import dialog box to decide which fields in the destination file should be filled with which information from the source file.

The Fields to Include dialog box contains two lists. On the left, **Fields to Import** lists the fields in the source file. On the right, **Resulting Fields** lists the fields in the destination file that will be filled with information from the source file.

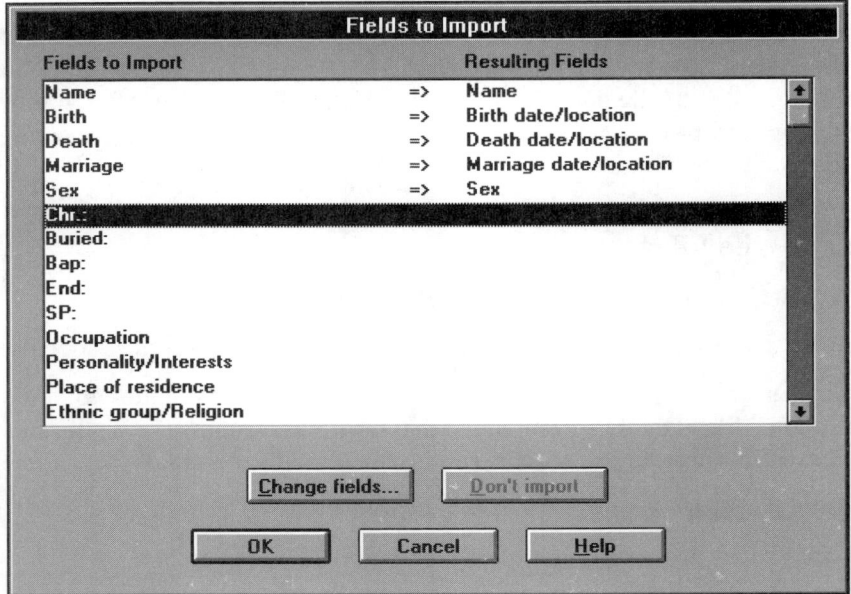

Figure 11-12. The Fields to Import dialog box

1. To map a field in your destination file to a field in your source file, click the field name in the **Fields to Import** list.

2. Click **Change fields**.

   If there is more than one possible match for the source field, Family Tree Maker displays the Change Fields dialog box. In this case, continue with step 3. If there is only one possible match for that source field, Family Tree Maker automatically inserts the destination field name in the "Resulting Fields" list. In this case, skip to step 5.

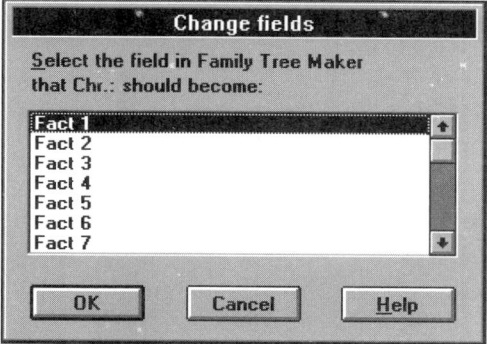

Figure 11-13. The Change Fields dialog box

3. In the Change Fields dialog box, click the name of the destination field that you want to fill with information from the source field you selected in step 1.

4. Click **OK** to return to the Fields to Include dialog box.

   If you later wish to change the mapping of a destination field, click the field name in the **Resulting Fields** list and then click **Change fields**. If this button stays grayed out, the mapping for that field is preset and cannot be changed.

5. Repeat steps 1 through 4 until all of the source fields that you wish to map have a destination field in the "Resulting Fields" list.

   All fields in the "Fields to Import" list that do not have a field opposite them in the "Resulting Fields" list will not be brought into the destination file.

6. If you want to remove a field from the "Resulting Fields" list, click the field name and then click **Don't import**.

   Family Tree Maker removes the field from the list.

7. Click **OK** when you've made your selections.

   Family Tree Maker displays the Individuals to Include dialog box. Continue with the next section.

Selecting Individuals to Include

When you click "OK" in the Fields to Import dialog box, Family Tree Maker displays the Individuals to Include dialog box. In this dialog box you can select individuals from the source file to merge into the destination file.

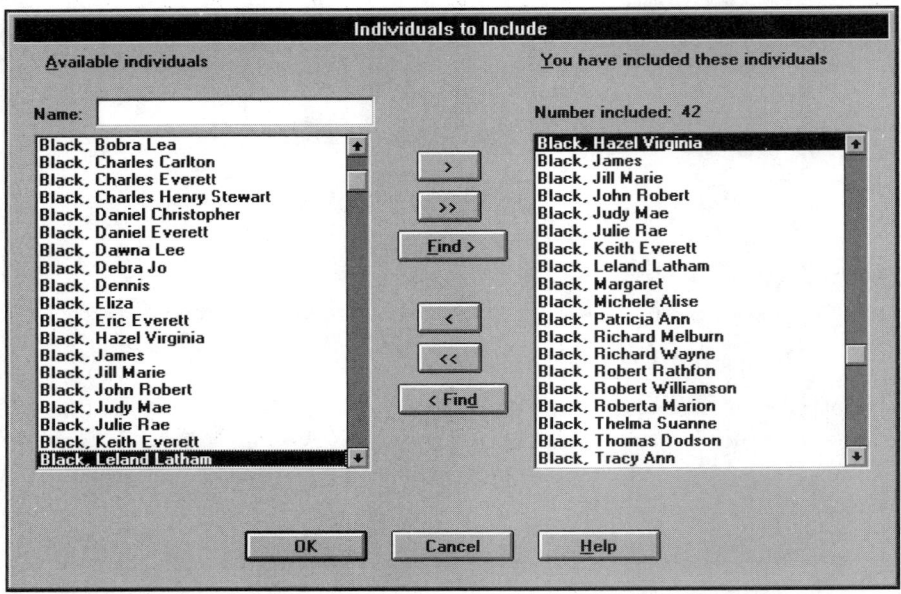

Figure 11-11. The Individuals to Include dialog box

1. Select a group of individuals to merge by adding them to or removing them from the list on the right.

    To add individuals one by one, select a name in the list on the left and click **Include** (the arrow pointing to the right). To add all of the individuals from the list on the left, click **Include all** (the double-arrows pointing to the right). To add special groups of individuals, click **Find and Include**. To remove individuals from the list on the right, you can use the bottom set of three buttons in the same way.

    For complete instructions on using each of these buttons, see "Using the 'Include' and 'Remove' Buttons" on page 327, "Using the 'Include All' and 'Remove All' Buttons" on page 328, and "Using the 'Find and Include' and 'Find and Remove' Buttons" on page 329.

To locate an individual in the list on the left quickly, click in the **Name** field at the top of the list and type the individual's name in the following format: Last name, First name Middle name. With each character you type, you will get closer to the name you are looking for.

2. Click **OK** once you've created a group of individuals to merge.

Family Tree Maker displays the Append File dialog box. Continue with "Appending and Merging Information," below.

Appending and Merging Information

The Append File dialog box gives you information about both the source file and the destination file. At this point, you have two choices. You can merge the information in the two files together, carefully eliminating possible duplicate information with Family Tree Maker's help. Alternatively, you can append all of the information from the source file to the destination file without checking for or eliminating any duplicates. You can then later go through your file and eliminate duplicate information using the instructions in "Merging Duplicate Individuals" on page 387. If you wish to completely quit this operation at this time, click **Cancel**. Otherwise, continue reading below.

You can do three different things from the Append File dialog box:

- Display a list that tells you whether each of the individuals in the source file is an exact match, possible match, or not a match for someone in the destination file. See "Displaying a Merge Report," on the next page. We strongly suggest that you read this report carefully before you begin any merging operations. This will help you avoid making mistakes.

- Begin merging information by viewing the exact matches and possible matches one at a time, deciding which information to keep and which information to discard. See "Merging Matches with Confirmation," on page 385.

- Add all of the information in the source file to the destination file, without merging anyone. See "Appending All Information," on page 387.

Displaying a Merge Report

A merge report is informational only; you cannot use it to change the contents of either file. However, you should read it carefully so that you know in advance how each individual will be treated if you proceed with a merge.

To see a merge report:

1. Click **Display Merge Report**.

   Family Tree Maker displays the Merge Report dialog box.

2. Carefully read the information displayed to the right of each name.

   The "Birth date" column helps you identify each individual in the list. The "Data differences" column tells you if an individual from the source file is a new individual, a possible match, or an exact match for someone already in the destination file.

   The words "New individual" indicate a new individual and the words "No differences" indicate an exact match. If someone is a possible match, the report lists which fields in the source and destination files contain differing information.

3. To see how the information in a field differs, highlight the field name and look at the **Individual #1** and **Individual #2** fields at the bottom of the dialog box.

   "Individual #1" comes from the individuals being merged. "Individual #2" comes from the existing individuals.

4. If you would like to print the report, turn on your printer and click **Print**. When Family Tree Maker displays the Print dialog box, you can click **OK** to print or click **Print Setup** to choose the printer, paper orientation, and size.

5. When you are finished reviewing the Merge Report, click **Done**.

   Family Tree Maker returns you to the Append File dialog box.

Merging Matches with Confirmation

To merge matching individuals one by one:

1. Click **Merge matching individuals**.

    If you have not already looked at the Merge Report, described on the previous page, Family Tree Maker will ask if you want to view it. Click **Yes** to see it, click **No** to move on.

    When you click "No," or if you have previously looked at the Merge Report, Family Tree Maker displays the Merge Individuals dialog box. In this dialog box, you can compare the information associated with the "possible match" individuals — individuals who appear to be the same person in both the source and destination files, but whose information differs slightly.

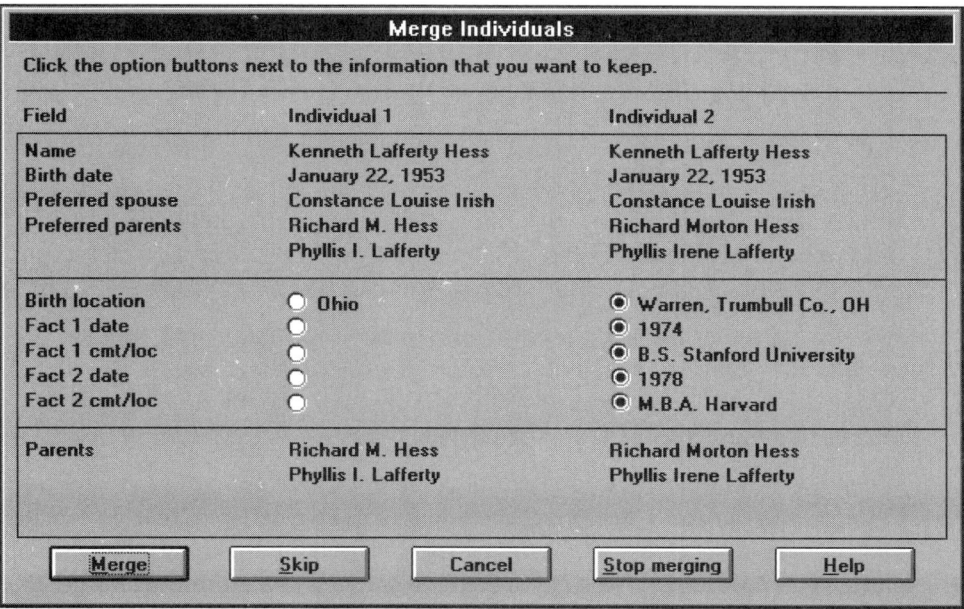

Figure 11-14. The Merge Individuals dialog box

2. Look through the information in the second and third columns. If you think that the information in these two columns belongs to the same individual, continue with step 3. If you think that it belongs to two separate individuals, click **Skip**.

When you click "Skip," Family Tree Maker does not merge the two individuals. Instead, both individuals will appear in your Family File. Repeat step 2 with the next set of information.

3. Carefully compare the information in the second and third columns line-by-line. On some lines there are option buttons next to the information. In this case, select the option buttons next to the information that you want to keep. The information that you do not select will be discarded.

The information on the lines without option buttons contains names of parents and names of spouses to help you identify the individual. This information will not be merged or discarded. It is there for informational purposes only.

4. After selecting the information that you want to keep, click **Merge**.

If there are two sets of Notes or two Scrapbooks for that individual, Family Tree Maker joins them together.

If there are more individuals to compare, Family Tree Maker displays the next set of information. In this case, return to step 2. If there are no more individuals to compare, Family Tree Maker displays a Family Page.

5. If at any time you wish to discontinue merging information and save the merges that you have already completed, click **Stop Merging**. If you do not wish to save any of your merges, click **Cancel** instead. Family Tree Maker returns to a Family Page.

6. When you are finished merging, print some trees and reports *before* you quit Family Tree Maker. Check over the documents to make sure that you didn't make any mistakes when merging the files. If you did make mistakes, you can reverse the merge by going to the **Edit** menu and selecting **Undo** *before* you quit Family Tree Maker. You cannot reverse a merge after quitting and restarting Family Tree Maker.

You can also use the Find command to see the results of your merge. From the **Edit** menu, select **Find individuals** to display the Find Individuals dialog box. Then, in the Find Individuals dialog box, select **Merged or appended individuals** in the **Search** field. For more complete instructions, see "Searching for Other Items" on page 123.

Appending All Information

To add all of the individuals from the source file to the destination file without merging any information:

1. Click **Append only (no merge)**.

   Family Tree Maker adds *all* individuals from the source file to the destination file.

2. Unless all of the individuals from the source file can be considered new individuals, you will need to use the **Merge Individuals** command later to remove the duplicate individuals from your Family File. See "Merging Duplicate Individuals" below for instructions.

MERGING DUPLICATE INDIVIDUALS

When you use the **Merge Individuals** command, Family Tree Maker searches through your Family File and locates **duplicate individuals**. Duplicate individuals are individuals who appear in your file twice. You can merge the two records for this individual together, choosing which information to keep if the records contain any differing information.

To use the Merge Individuals command:

1. From the **People** menu, select **Merge Individuals**.

   Family Tree Maker displays the Merge Individuals dialog box.

2. The Merge Individuals dialog box gives you information about the file you are working with. If you wish to quit the merge at this time, click **Cancel**. Otherwise, continue reading below.

You can do two different things from the Merge Individuals dialog box:

- Display a list that tells you whether each of the individuals in the source file is an exact match, possible match, or not a match for someone in the destination file. See "Displaying a Merge Report" on page 384. We strongly suggest that you read this report carefully before you begin any merging operations. This will help you avoid making mistakes.

- View the exact matches and possible matches one-by-one and decide which information to keep and which information to discard. See "Merging Duplicates with Confirmation," on the next page.

Merging Duplicates with Confirmation

To merge matching individuals one by one:

1. Click **Merge matching individuals**.

    If you have not already looked at the Merge Report, Family Tree Maker will ask if you want to view it. Click **Yes** to see it, click **No** to move on.

    When you click "No," or if you have previously looked at the Merge Report, Family Tree Maker displays the Merge Individuals dialog box. In this dialog box, Family Tree Maker lets you compare the information associated with the "possible match" individuals — individuals who may exist in two places, but whose information differs slightly.

2. Look through the information in the second and third columns. If you think that the information in these two columns belongs to the same individual, continue with step 5. If you think that it belongs to two separate individuals, click **Skip**.

    When you click "Skip," Family Tree Maker does not merge the two individuals. Instead, both individuals will appear in your Family File. Repeat step 2 with the next set of information.

3. Carefully compare the information in the second and third columns line-by-line. On some lines there are option buttons next to the information. In this case, select the option buttons next to the information that you want to keep. The information that you do not select will be discarded.

    The information on the lines without option buttons contains names of parents and names of spouses to help you identify the individual. This information will not be merged or discarded. It is there for informational purposes only.

4. After selecting the information that you want to keep, click **Merge**.

    If there are two sets of Notes or two Scrapbooks for that individual, Family Tree Maker joins them together. In addition, if two mothers or two fathers have a "Natural" relationship with the individual, one of the relationships is changed to "Unknown."

    If there are more individuals to compare, Family Tree Maker displays the next set. In this case, return to step 2. If there is no more information to compare, Family Tree Maker displays a Family Page.

5. If at any time you wish to discontinue merging information and save the merges that you have already completed, click **Stop Merging**. If you do not wish to save any of your merges, click **Cancel** instead.

   Family Tree Maker returns to a Family Page.

6. When you are finished merging, print some trees and reports *before* you quit Family Tree Maker. Check over the documents to make sure that you didn't make any mistakes when merging the individuals. If you did make mistakes, you can reverse the merge by going to the **Edit** menu and selecting **Undo** *before* you quit Family Tree Maker. You cannot reverse a merge after quitting and restarting Family Tree Maker.

COPYING AND EXPORTING FILES

To make a copy of your Family File or to export it to a different file format:

1. From the **File** menu, select **Copy/Export Family File**.

   Family Tree Maker displays the Copy/Export Family File dialog box.

2. Click the **File formats** drop-down list and select the format that you want for the copied file.

3. In the **File name** field, type a new file name.

4. In the **Drives** and **Directories** fields, select the drive letter and directory name to which you want your file copied.

5. Click **OK** when you've made your selections.

   Family Tree Maker copies or exports your file to the drive, directory, and file name that you chose.

EXPORTING AND DELETING GROUPS OF INDIVIDUALS

The **Copy/Export Individuals** command allows you to take a portion of the information contained in a Family File and save a copy of it in a new Family File. You might want to do this if you are sharing Family Files with another family member and you want to send him or her your newly-collected information. The **Delete Selected Individuals** command allows you to permanently remove multiple individuals from your Family File all at once.

You use both of these commands by first creating a document containing the group of individuals that you want to export or delete. This allows you to visually double-check that the correct individuals are in the group. Then, you use either the Copy/Export Individuals or Delete Selected Individuals command to export or delete the individuals. The process is described below in detail.

To export or delete a group of individuals:

1. Create either a report, Ancestor tree, Descendant tree, or Outline Descendant tree containing the group of individuals that you want to export or delete.

    For help with creating trees, see Chapter 8, "Creating and Printing Trees," page 229. Information about creating reports begins on page 275.

2. After you have created your document, look through it to make sure that it contains the correct set of individuals. Be especially careful if you are deleting the individuals from your Family File.

    Note: You don't have to worry about what information appears in the document, because all information associated with the individuals in the document will either be deleted or exported.

3. If you want to export the group of individuals to a new file, from the **File** menu, select **Copy/Export Individuals** and then continue with step 4. If you want to permanently delete the group of individuals, from the **People** menu, select **Delete Selected Individuals**. Family Tree Maker deletes the individuals after you select **Yes** in the confirmation dialog box. In this case, you're done. Skip the remaining steps.

4. In the Copy/Export Individuals dialog box, click the **File format** drop-down list and then select a file format for your new file. See Figure 11-15.

    You can use any available file format; your choice will depend on the type of file you want to create.

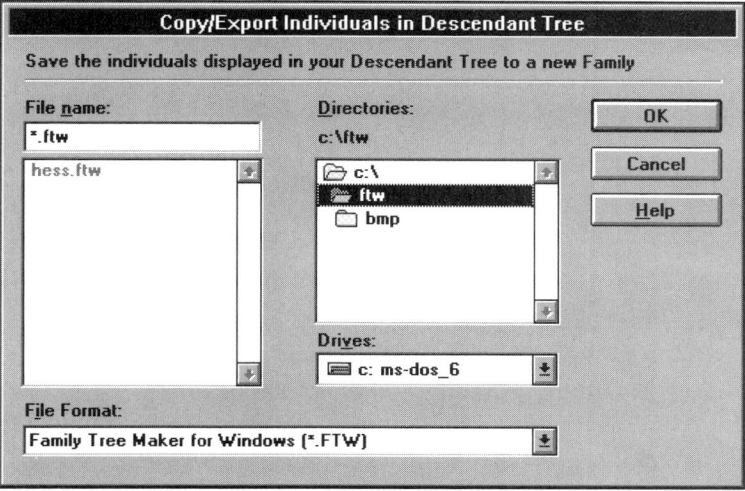

Figure 11-15. The Copy/Export Individuals dialog box

5. Type a name for your new file in the **File name** field.

    The name of your file must be eight letters or less, plus a three letter extension. You should use the extension that corresponds with the file format you selected in step 4.

6. In the **Drives** and **Directories** fields, select the drive letter and the name of the directory where you want Family Tree Maker to create your new file.

7. Click **OK** when you've made your selections.

    Family Tree Maker creates a new file containing a copy of the selected information. Your original Family File has not changed in any way.

FINDING FILES

There may be times when you need to find an existing file to use with Family Tree Maker. You can begin a search from two different locations:

- The Open dialog box, which Family Tree Maker displays when you select **Open** from the **File** menu.

- The Insert Picture dialog box, which Family Tree Maker displays when you select **Insert Picture from File** from the **Picture/Object** menu (only available from the Scrapbook view).

From either of those dialog boxes, take these steps to find your file:

1. Click **Find file**.

   Family Tree Maker displays the Find File dialog box. Now you can tell Family Tree Maker where to look for your file, following steps 2 through 4 below. Your search will take less time if you enter the most exact locations you know.

2. Click the **File name** field and type in a file name if you already know part or all of it.

   You can type in any valid DOS file name, using the asterisk symbol (*) to indicate "any," or a question mark (?) to hold the place of characters if you're unsure of exact spelling but know how long a file name is. For example, you could type **sm?th.*** if you didn't recall whether the Smith Family File used the spelling "Smith" or "Smyth." If you know that the file you're looking for has a name that is six letters long, you can enter **??????.*** to retrieve a list that excludes all shorter and longer titles.

3. Click the **File format** drop-down list and then select a file type.

   The selection of file types will depend on which dialog box you were in when you opened the Find File dialog box. For example, if you were in the Import Picture dialog box, Family Tree Maker lists graphics file formats. If you don't know which file format your file is saved with, select the last format in the list: **All Files (*.*)**.

4. Click the **Search** drop-down list and then select a set of drives for Family Tree Maker to search.

   The list will give you the choice of selecting a single drive or a combination of drives. Your search will take more time if Family Tree Maker has to search in many different locations, so don't include a drive in your search if it's very unlikely that your file is stored there.

5. Once you've made your selections, click **Search**.

   Family Tree Maker searches in the designated areas and lists the matching file paths in the Found files box.

6. If several file names appear in the box, use the scroll bar to scan the list for the file name you're trying to find. To open a file in the list, you can either select the file name and click **Open**, or double-click the name in the list.

   Once you open a file, you can begin working with it.

DELETING FILES

You can use Windows File Manager if you need to delete files. First, find the file you want to delete using the method described in "Finding Files." Then use File Manager's Delete command to delete it. See your Microsoft Windows User's Guide for more information about File Manager.

GETTING INFORMATION ABOUT YOUR ENVIRONMENT

System Information gives you important information, such as the amount of memory available to your computer and the display type. If you call our technical support lines, this is information that technical support may ask for.

To display the System Information dialog box:

1. From the **Help** menu, select **System Information**.

   Family Tree Maker displays the System Information dialog box.

2. If you would like to access standard Windows system editors, click **Run**.

3. When you're finished using this dialog box, click **OK**.

   Family Tree Maker returns you to the previous view.

FAMILY FILE STATUS

To get information about your Family File, such as the number of individuals it contains and its size in kilobytes:

1. From the **Help** menu, select **Family File Status**.

    Family Tree Maker displays the Family File Status dialog box.

2. Click **OK** when you are finished reading the information in the dialog box.

    Family Tree Maker closes the Family File Status dialog box.

APPENDICES

Admiring Easter cakes made by their grandmother's sister, are Jessica Cornette and her brother Justin. This picture was taken at their grandmother's home in Kentucky, when Jessica, one of this manual's editors, was six.

RESEARCHING FAMILIES

This appendix gives you an overview of how to gather information. It includes brief descriptions of the following:

- Note-taking
- Types of forms
- Filing
- Research sources
- Requesting information
- Things to watch for

The CD-ROM version of Family Tree Maker covers all of these and many other topics in-depth. If you have the CD-ROM version, from the **Help** menu, select **Genealogy "How-To" Guide**. If you do not have the CD-ROM version, but are interested in learning more about it, see Chapter 7 and Appendix D.

NOTE-TAKING

As you begin to collect your information, there are several basic note-taking techniques that you should keep in mind.

1. Write everything down. The information you collect will grow rapidly. If you try to rely on your memory, you may easily forget or become confused. This also applies to those who insist that they will "write it down later," which often leads to more errors.

2. Don't use home-spun abbreviations. Abbreviations are often confusing when you go back to review your notes. They also can lead to inaccurate information. Use standard abbreviations such as "b" for "born," "d" for "died," "m" for "married."

3. Record your sources. If you have the name, location, and date searched for each source, you can easily return to that source later. You also know what sources you've already checked. It's helpful to keep a different list of sources for each person (or each last name) in your family tree. Family Tree Maker includes an optional sources/notes field for most dates and events that you record. See "Recording Sources for Your Information" on page 101.

4. Keep a copy of all letters. It's very likely that you'll have to write to relatives or send away for information. Copies act as a record of what information you requested, from whom, payment sent (if any), and date sent. You should also note what you receive back. See "Requesting Information" on page 402 for examples of what to include in your letters.

5. Record each person's name in full. It's especially important to list a woman's maiden name. Be sure to avoid abbreviations here; you may have more than one J. Smith within your family. If a person has a nickname, record it in quotation marks (e.g. "Bud").

6. Most genealogists use a day/month/year date format. The actual format you use is not as important as remembering to spell out the month and to use the complete year. Dates can be ambiguous, you can interpret the date 4/7/76 as April 7 or 4 July 1976 (or 1876, or 1776, etc.). Writing out the month and year reduces the chance of misinterpreting dates no matter what format you use. Family Tree Maker will automatically convert all dates to the style you choose. It will also accept double dates. See "Things To Watch For" on page 402 for an explanation of double dates.

7. Copy information — especially dates, locations, and last names — exactly as you find it. You can interpret your findings later when you have time to review your notes and make comparisons with other information. This is particularly important when copying down last names. Over time they often take on many spellings. In general, never change information to what you think it ought to be.

8. Take notes in such a way that they'll be understandable to you, or anyone else, when reviewed later. The hastily written note often makes sense at the time you write it, but can be confusing when you look at it days later.

Types of Forms

You can make your own forms or print out blank forms from Family Tree Maker. In either case, it's important to keep things simple and consistent enough for anyone to understand.

Standardize the size of the paper you'll be using. Nothing will confuse you faster than trying to find a vital piece of information written on a tiny piece of scrap paper. The most commonly used size is the standard 8.5 by 11 inch 3-hole punch. This size is easy to find and to place into a loose-leaf binder. Binders are preferable to regular wire-bound notebooks because binders are more sturdy, and it's easy to add to or remove paper from them.

An empty ancestor tree form is commonly used for gathering and organizing information. Filling in portions of a tree allows you to see what information you have and what you still need to get. This is helpful when you are doing research and don't have immediate access to your permanent files or to your computer.

Another common form is the family group sheet. It shows an entire family unit at a glance. This sheet lists the dates and locations of births, deaths, and marriages for a husband, wife, and their children. Each of your direct ancestors can appear on one sheet as a child and on another sheet as an adult.

To aid you in your note-taking, Family Tree Maker prints out blank copies of these forms. See "Empty print-outs" in the Index of this manual.

FILING

The two most important things to consider when filing your notes and finished forms are location and order.

Wherever you decide to locate your notes (binders, filing cabinet, etc.) be sure they are easy to get to, orderly, and safe from damage. An old shoe box on the floor is probably not a good idea.

You must decide in what order to file your notes. The most common way is to organize them alphabetically by surname with a folder or section for each individual. This folder will include any family group sheets that you've collected for a particular individual. You can also include any other documentation such as wills, photos, or certificates. For documents that you want to store somewhere else, insert a page into your files noting the name of that document, its content, and current location.

RESEARCH SOURCES

Now that you are familiar with filing and note-taking techniques, you are ready to begin gathering your information. Start with yourself and your family. From memory, write down all you know about your family. Use Family Tree Maker to make an ancestor tree; this will help you see what information you have and what you don't have.

When you've recorded what you know about your family, it's time to question other family members. To save time and energy, ask your relatives if anyone else has done research on your family.

Some information you get may not give definite answers to your questions. Most however, provides clues to direct your search. Many sources in your own home fall into this category. For example, people often refer to births, deaths, and marriages in family bibles, diaries, scrapbooks, photos, letters, newspaper clippings, or legal documents. Elderly relatives carry with them a wealth of information and stories that could be valuable to your search. Recording their stories on a tape recorder can ensure that you don't miss any of the details.

Your family research should give you enough information to decide which side of your family to follow first. It's important to have a clear picture of what research you need to do and to proceed in an orderly manner. The further back you search, the more names and information you'll collect. When you research both sides of your family at the same time, it's easy to confuse names and other information. To avoid this, set goals for your research and keep track of which goals you've achieved.

After searching family documents and talking to relatives, it's time to turn to outside sources. One of the first places to visit is a local library. Your local historical and genealogical societies will know what libraries have genealogy sections, or you can call libraries directly. They can also tell you where to find libraries dedicated entirely to genealogy.

Genealogy sections of libraries can contain family histories, census records, genealogy books, magazines, or other local records. The extent and variety will vary with the library. (Some libraries combine their genealogy and history sections.) At the very least, your local library will provide you with valuable reference books. These can include encyclopedias, almanacs, atlases, and local history books.

Additionally, libraries usually have many books that deal with specific types of research. You can find books on researching specific areas of the country, finding certain types of records, doing foreign research, and researching particular ethnic groups.

Learning local history in the library can give you many clues to direct your search. You may discover that a town or county that was once in your state now belongs to another state. You could also discover that many of the people living in your state moved there from a particular state or country.

Your research will inevitably lead you out of the library and into local, government, and church records. A brief description of some of these sources begins on the next page.

Local Records

Vital Records — These include birth, death, and marriage certificates. These are among the most reliable sources of information. Keep in mind, however, that no type of document is error-proof. You should be skeptical even of these documents, especially if they conflict with other information. You'll find these documents in local and state government offices, or in local or state archives.

Probate Records — Most important of these records is the last will and testament, often an excellent source for finding the names of a person's spouse and children. Locating a will depends on what county and in which court that particular state files these documents. You should call the county clerk's office for more information.

Land Records — Deeds to land or homes can show where a person lived at a particular time. Such deeds often list the spouse of the buyer, as well as the name of the seller (possibly another relative). Older records occasionally list where the person was moving from or to. You'll most likely find these records in the county clerk's office having jurisdiction over that land.

Contact the city where you will be searching and ask for information on their particular filing practices.

Church Records

Vital Records — Churches usually keep records of all births, deaths, and marriages occurring among their members. They also keep track of people entering and leaving the church. This sometimes includes where they were coming from or going to. To find these records, try to locate the particular church your ancestors attended. If it no longer exists, other local churches of the same religion may be able to help you. Occasionally, local libraries have published archives of some of the local church records. Unfortunately, these church records can be some of the most difficult to find.

Cemetery Records — People often bury relatives in parish cemeteries. It's not uncommon to find whole families buried next to one another. Even if the church no longer exists, its cemetery may still be there. If you have difficulty finding the church burial records, you may still be able to locate the gravestone of your ancestor. Inscriptions often contain valuable genealogical information.

REQUESTING INFORMATION

It's likely that you will write letters requesting information for your family tree. The following is a list of guidelines to follow when requesting information.

1. Keep the letter short. There's no need to go into a lengthy explanation of why you are doing your research. You're more likely to get a reply to a short, clearly written letter. This is especially true when sending away for vital records. The clerks working in such offices are very busy and don't have the time or desire to read a long letter.

2. Make your request specific. The easier it is to understand your request, the more likely you are to get a response. Be sure to clearly state the following:

   • the kind of record you want

   • the full name of the person you are searching for

   • the date of the event (birth, death, etc.)

3. Enclose a self-addressed stamped envelope with your letter. The person receiving your request is more likely to respond.

4. Enclose a small payment for any copying costs. Unless there's another specific fee, a check for a few dollars should cover any expenses required to answer your request. You should also offer to pay any additional fees you didn't know about.

5. Remember to say thank you. There is no need to apologize for making your request, but a simple thank you acknowledges that you appreciate the effort someone is making for you.

THINGS TO WATCH FOR

When you research, look out for the following potentially confusing items.

Double Dates

The practice of double dating resulted from the switch from the Julian to the Gregorian calendar. The Julian calendar (named for Julius Caesar) declared March 25 as the first of the year and a solar year to be 365 days and 6 hours long. In 1582 Pope Gregory XIII determined that the Julian calendar was off by 11 minutes and 14 seconds. The new Gregorian calendar resolved the discrepancy and declared January 1 as the first of the year.

Not all countries accepted this calendar at the same time. England and the American colonies didn't accept it until 1752. Before that date, the government observed March 25 as the first of the year, but most of the population observed January 1 as the first of the year. So many people wrote dates falling between January 1 and March 25 with both years, as in the following examples.

Julian or Old Style	Gregorian or New Style	Double Date
December 25, 1718	December 25, 1718	December 25, 1718
January 1, 1718	January 1, 1719	January 1, 1718/19
February 2, 1718	February 2, 1719	February 2, 1718/19
March 20, 1718	March 20, 1719	March 20, 1718/19
March 25, 1719	March 25, 1719	March 25, 1719

Figure A-1. Double dates

By the time England and the colonies adopted the new calendar, the discrepancy between the calendars was eleven days. To resolve the discrepancy, the government ordered that September 2, 1752 be followed by September 14, 1752. Some people also added 11 days to their birth dates (a fact which is **not** noted on their birth certificates).

Marriage Banns

Church records often list the date on which a couple makes the announcement that they intend to marry (the marriage banns). Don't misinterpret this as the actual wedding date.

Death and Burial Dates

Church and cemetery records often contain the date of the funeral in addition to the date of death. Don't confuse the burial date with the date of death.

Incorrect Documents

In the past, people occasionally recorded information incorrectly on vital records, especially for marriage and death certificates. One reason for this was that people often recorded information several days or even weeks after the fact and forgot actual dates and names. People also occasionally altered the facts. This usually occurred with birth dates. (For example, a husband might lie about his birthday in order to appear older than his bride.) By far the most common error was name misspellings. Because many people couldn't read or write, the clerk or official wrote the name down the way it sounded. You can see that no source is totally reliable and you must constantly cross-check your findings.

Location Names and Boundary Changes

Many cities, counties, and states didn't always have the names and boundaries we associate with them today. Some sections of a city were at one time its suburbs. In short, it may be helpful to learn the history of boundary changes in the area where you suspect that a person lived.

THE FINAL PRODUCT

Genealogy is not just finding out how you relate to your ancestors. It's also discovering what these people were like, how they lived, and how that might affect you. Occupation, education, military service, hobbies, and residences are just some of the interesting details you may discover about your ancestors. The trees and forms produced with Family Tree Maker will let you produce many different combinations of this information.

Family Tree Maker offers a practical use for your family tree. The Medical dialog box includes medical information for each person. More and more doctors are using family trees to record medical history patterns in some of their patients. They find that it's often easier for patients to see and understand how a disease runs in a family when they see it presented in the form of a family tree.

Genealogy can be a challenging task requiring patience and good problem-solving skills. But what you learn along the way and the results you produce with Family Tree Maker will be quite rewarding. You will find yourself learning much more than just names and dates. At the very least, you'll gain a better perspective on how you and your family came to be who you are today.

LDS Ordinance Information

If you choose to use the LDS format, some field labels and the Family Group Sheet change to conform to LDS standards. See "Preferences for Field Labels" on page 78 for instructions on selecting the LDS format.

- Five of the Comment/Location field labels in the Facts dialog box change to the following: "Baptism," "Endowment," "Christened," "Buried," and "Seal to Parents."

- The field labels in the More About Marriage — Facts dialog box (see page 146) now ask for the Sealing date and location.

- The location and date fields will accept temple codes and several special date codes. These codes can be spelled out or abbreviated.

BIC (born in the covenant)
Cancelled or CAN
Child or CHI
Cleared or CLE
Completed or COM
DNS (do not seal)
Infant or INF
See notes
Stillborn or STI
Submitted or SUB
Uncleared or UNC

Figure B-1. Special Date Codes

The Family Group Sheet will reflect these changes:

- Ordinance data is now listed along the right hand side of the sheet.

- Last names are printed in capital letters.

- All dates are automatically formatted — Day/Month/Year — with the month abbreviated (10 Sep 1988).

- The Title & Footnote dialog box for Family Group Sheets will provide space for entering the submitter's name, address, stake, and unit number. See "Adding a Title & Footnote" on page 310.

- Space is provided for entering information about proxies.

- Space is provided for entering the relationship of the submitter to the husband or wife.

- The title will change to "Family Group Record."

KODAK PHOTO CD-ROM DISCS

Kodak Photo CDs offer an excellent way to store and preserve your precious family photographs. Up to 100 photographs can be stored on a single Photo CD, and unlike negatives, pictures, and slides, the images on Kodak Photo CDs are not subject to the discoloring effects of time.

Moreover, it is simple to transfer your photographs from film, negatives, and slides onto a Photo CD. You can even transfer old family photos for which you have no negatives. Best of all, once your photographs are transferred to a Photo CD, they can easily be incorporated into Family Tree Maker.

THE BASICS

Creating a Kodak Photo CD is quite simple. In fact, there are only two main steps to follow:

1. Collect the film, photos, negatives, and/or slides that you want to place on the Kodak Photo CD.

2. Take these items to the photo finisher in your area that can create Kodak Photo CDs.

How Do I Transfer Photos onto a Kodak Photo CD?

To transfer your photos onto a Photo CD, take your film, negatives, or slides to a photo finisher offering the Photo CD transfer service. You can also transfer photos for which you do not have film or negatives, but you will have to have your photo finisher make a negative for that picture first. See "Transferring Photographs Without Negatives" on page 411.

Once you have all of your film, negatives, or slides ready, the photo finisher can help you fill out an order form. The order form is similar to the order form that you use when you order a set of reprints.

There are five different kinds of Kodak Photo CD discs. Family Tree Maker supports both the "Photo CD Master Disc" and the "Pro Photo CD Master Disc." With the "Photo CD Master Disc," you can transfer pictures from rolls of undeveloped 35 mm film as well as from 35 mm negatives and slides. Other film sizes can be transferred to the "Pro Photo CD Master Disc." The other three types of Kodak Photo CD discs are professional versions with special purposes. Make sure that you get either a "Photo CD Master Disc" or a "Pro Photo CD Master Disc" when you have your Kodak Photo CD made.

There are a few other things to know:

- Transferring pictures from rolls of film onto a Kodak Photo CD is usually less expensive than transferring from pictures, negatives, or slides that have already been developed.

- The price of the disc is often but not always included in the transfer price. This is important to remember if you already have a Kodak Photo CD to which you want to add more photos. While some photo finishers may charge less because you are providing your own disc, others may still charge the price that includes the cost of the disc.

- Photo finishers that offer the Kodak Photo CD transfer service can also make prints for you. And, just as with normal print developing, most photo finishers will give you a set of negatives so that you can make additional prints in the future.

- The Kodak Photo CD disc, which stores your photographs, can also be used as a "digital negative." That is, you can later have prints made directly from the Kodak Photo CD disc.

Who Can Create a Kodak Photo CD for Me?

There are over 30,000 photo finishers world-wide who can help you create your Kodak Photo CD. To locate photo finishers in your area who offer this service, check your local Yellow Pages. You can also call Kodak's Digital and Applied Imaging Support Center at the following number:

    1-800-CD-KODAK (1-800-235-6325)

This toll-free number is open 24 hours a day. Kodak will give you a list of the Kodak dealers near you which do transfers.

It is a good idea to call a couple of different photo finishers for price quotes before dropping off your film. Be sure to check the difference in price between (1) developing and transferring a new roll of film to a Photo CD, and (2) transferring images from negatives and slides to a Photo CD. You may also want to ask whether the price of the disc is included, how much it costs to also make prints, and how many days the transfer service will require.

Instead of going to a photo finisher, you can also mail your film, negatives, or slides directly to a Kodalux processing center. In some cases, mailing your order may be quicker and less expensive than taking your order to a local photo finisher. However, it is best to call and compare prices. Call the toll-free number of the processing center nearest you to get the price for the services you require. When you call, indicate that you are a consumer, not a business, because most of the calls these centers receive are from photo finishers.

Kodalux Processing Services
3131 Manor Way
Dallas, TX 75235
1-800-345-6971

Kodalux Processing Services
1 Choke Cherry Road
Rockville, MD 20850
1-800-345-6974

Kodalux Processing Services
555 Industrial Park Drive
Manteca, CA 95336
1-800-345-6976

Kodalux Processing Services
16-31 Route 208
Fairlawn, NJ 07410
1-800-345-6973

When you send in your order, you must include both the payment and instructions for what you want to have done to the film. If you are having only a few photographs transferred from previously developed negatives, be sure to indicate the frame numbers of the pictures that you want transferred.

What Types of Pictures Should I Place on a Kodak Photo CD?

What you put on your Kodak Photo CDs is entirely up to you. You should decide if you want to create detailed Scrapbooks for just a few of the individuals in your Family File or if you only want a portrait of each individual. You must remember that the number of Pictures/Objects that you can place into your Scrapbooks is limited by the capabilities of your computer. Realistically, you probably cannot create detailed Scrapbooks for everyone in your Family File.

If you decide to create detailed Scrapbooks for a select group of individuals, you will probably want to include pictures of events such as a first birthday, the first day of school, a prom, a graduation, a wedding, and perhaps some holidays.

How Can I Use a Photo CD with Family Tree Maker?

You can access images on a Kodak Photo CD using a Photo CD-compatible CD-ROM disc drive. Once you have a compatible CD-ROM disc drive, you can import your pictures directly into Family Tree Maker's Scrapbooks.

All major CD-ROM drive manufacturers offer drives which are compatible with Photo CD discs. In fact, most, of the drives currently on the market are compatible with Kodak Photo CD. Usually, authorized manufacturers put the Kodak Photo CD logo on their box if their CD-ROM drive is compatible with Kodak Photo CD discs. If you have an older CD-ROM drive, check with the manufacturer to determine whether it is compatible with Photo CD. In addition, current information on CD-ROM drive compatibility can be obtained by calling Kodak's Digital and Applied Imaging Support Center at 1-800-CD-KODAK.

Those are the basics of creating a Kodak Photo CD. If you would like more detailed information about different aspects of creating a Kodak Photo CD, continue reading below. You can also call Kodak's Digital and Applied Imaging Support Center at 1-800-CD-KODAK (1-800-235-6325) 24 hours a day.

A Few More Tips

Because creating Kodak Photo CDs is a relatively new process, many photo finishers, including those that offer the service, will not be completely familiar with it. If a photo finisher employee is unfamiliar with Kodak Photo CD, ask to speak with someone who may know more.

Most of the time, the transfer of images onto the Photo CD disc is done at a Photo CD processing station rather than on-site. Therefore, many photo finishers that offer the transfer service just send the film to Kodalux and may not know much about the actual process. Just because a photo finisher employee does not know the details of the Photo CD process does not mean the photo finisher cannot have your photos transferred to a Photo CD. By the same token, however, it is wise to shop around for photo finishers with expertise in Kodak Photo CD transfers. If possible, try to get recommendations from others who have transferred their own photos.

GUIDELINES FOR BEST CD TRANSFER

The image that is transferred to the Photo CD will be exactly like that on the original film, negative, or slide. If the original image is not good, the transferred image will not be an improvement. On the other hand, in high resolution, the Photo CD image will be an excellent reproduction of the print image.

Because negatives and slides may become discolored with time, you should have them transferred as soon as possible after the film is developed. You will obtain the best image if you transfer your photos directly from the original roll of film.

If you are transferring negatives or slides that have already been developed, it is a good idea to clean them before you have them transferred to a Photo CD. To clean negatives and slides, you should use a film cleaning solution. You can also re-soak the film and allow it to air dry.

TRANSFERRING PHOTOGRAPHS WITHOUT NEGATIVES

The scanning machine which is used to transfer images to the Photo CD can only scan negatives and slides. If you do not have a negative available for a photo that you want to transfer, you must take a picture of the photograph to create a negative. Most photo finishers will take a picture of a photograph for you, but it can be expensive. However, since the Photo CD image will be exactly like the photo of the original photo, it is usually worthwhile to have the negatives made professionally. If you are not as concerned with the quality of the Photo CD image or if you are confident in your skills as a photographer, you can also take a picture of the photograph yourself.

In order to get the best results when taking a picture of a photograph, you should use a camera with a single-lens reflex, as opposed to a point-and-shoot camera with a view-finder. When you look through a single-lens reflex camera, you see the image which will actually be transferred to the film. This way, you ensure that the final photograph will look just like you want it. Depending on the size of the photograph, you may have to take the picture at a close range. Be sure that your lens is capable of taking close-up shots. For best results, you should use the finest grain film available. For taking pictures of color film, it is best to use Royal Gold 25 (or another film with a low ASA). For black and white photos, use black and white film such as T-MAX 100 or T-MAX 400. Unless you are in bright light, however, these slow-speed films may necessitate the use of a tripod, which is recommended in any case. If you take the picture indoors using diffused incandescent lighting, you will get the best result if you also use an 80 A or B filter. You can also use tungsten film (available for slides only) if you are taking the picture indoors with incandescent lighting.

Be sure that the photograph is mounted on a flat surface and that the plane of the photograph is parallel to the plane of the film in the camera. In other words, take the picture from a location that is directly in front of the photograph and at the same level as the photograph. It is a good idea to mount the photograph on a gray posterboard which can be hung on a wall. If part of the background appears in the final photo, a gray background is best because a white background may cause the final photo to be underexposed, while a black background may cause the photo to be overexposed.

To ensure that there is no glare on the photograph, use diffuse lighting. If you take the picture outside, the most diffuse lighting would be on an overcast day. If it is sunny, it is recommended that you be near white walls which can diffuse the sunlight. Avoid areas which are shaded by trees, because the photograph will appear slightly green due to the green light that is diffused by the tree leaves. If you are indoors, take the photo in a well-lit place. You can use diffuse incandescent lighting or a flash if there is no daylight. If you are using a flash, do not point it directly at the photograph. Otherwise, you may get a glare on the final photograph.

TECHNICAL SPECIFICATIONS

The images on Photo CD Master Disc are saved in five resolutions so that you may choose which best suits your purposes. These resolutions, in order from least to highest resolution, are as follows: BASE/16 (128 x 192 pixels), BASE/4 (256 x 384 pixels), BASE (512 x 768 pixels), 4 BASE (1024 x 1536 pixels), and 16 BASE (2048 x 3072 pixels). For each image, there is thus an "Image Pac" of five resolutions, and there is the potential for 100 "Image Pacs" on each Photo CD Master Disc.

In addition to the Photo CD Master Disc with five levels of resolution, Kodak offers a Pro Photo CD Master Disc with an additional sixth level of resolution (4096 x 6144 pixels). More expensive than the regular Photo CD Master Discs, these Pro Discs are generally used by professional photographers. In addition to 35 mm film, larger film formats, such as 120, 70 mm, and 4 x 5-inch, can be transferred to the Pro Disc. It is usually also possible to transfer other unique film sizes, like those of older film formats, to the Pro disc. Although Family Tree Maker supports the Photo CD Master Disc, at this time you cannot use the sixth level of resolution with Family Tree Maker.

RESOURCES FOR MORE INFORMATION

Further assistance with the Kodak Photo CD System is available by calling Kodak's Digital and Applied Imaging Support Center at 1-800-CD-KODAK. Information is also available in the Kodak Forum on CompuServe under the keyword, "Go Kodak".

PICTURE SIZE AND YOUR COMPUTER

Family Tree Maker cannot import a Kodak Photo CD picture file that is larger than the amount of **physical** RAM or hard disk space available on your machine. Physical RAM refers to the size of the memory chips that are in your computer. Keep in mind that once Windows is running, some of your computer's physical RAM is already in use and is not available for importing pictures.

The higher the resolution of a particular picture, the larger the picture file will be. If your machine is unable to handle a picture at a higher resolution, try importing it at a lower resolution. Please note that the compression that you choose for a picture does not affect whether or not Family Tree Maker can import it. This is because compression takes place after a picture has been imported.

The table below should give you an idea of approximate picture sizes before compression. For example, if you wanted to import a picture at the 1024 x 1536 resolution, you would need 4.7 MB of physical RAM available, no matter what compression you chose for the picture. Please keep this limitation of your computer hardware in mind when you work with Kodak Photo CD pictures.

Photo CD Picture Resolution	Approximate Required Physical RAM or Hard Disk Space
64 x 96 (thumbnail)	36K
128 x 192	73K
256 x 384 (recommended)	295K
512 x 768	1.2 MB
1024 x 1536	4.7 MB
2048 x 3072	18.9 MB

Figure C-1. Approximate physical RAM or hard disk space required to import pictures at different resolutions

ACCESSORIES

You can purchase the accessories described below by sending in the order card in the back of this manual or by calling Brøderbund Customer Support at (415) 382-4770. If you would like to be notified of any new programs, services, or accessories, be sure that we have your current address. Send in your registration card or the change of address card located in the back of this manual.

In addition to the items listed below, we direct the World Family Tree Project, to which you can submit your Family File. For information about the World Family Tree Project, see page 362.

THE FAMILY TREE MAKER DELUXE EDITION

If you have Family Tree Maker for Windows, you may want to upgrade to the Deluxe CD-ROM Edition. In addition to organizing family information, it contains features to help you find your relatives. It can also read *Family Archive CDs*, which contain genealogical records, including the World Family Tree. For a complete description of *Family Archive CDs* and the Deluxe Edition, see Chapter 7 (page 193). For a description of the World Family Tree, see page 362.

BIOGRAPHY MAKER

This clever program makes it easy and fun to write biographies about your relatives or autobiographies about yourself. *Biography Maker* quickly and easily creates a customized list of writing ideas for each individual you write about.

For example, if you are writing about someone who was a teen during the Roaring Twenties, *Biography Maker* gives you writing ideas that capture the spirit of those times. It reminds you of the invention of radio, the reign of Al Capone, Prohibition, and much more. With the research done for you, you can concentrate on the most important part of your biography: telling the story.

The program contains more than 5,500 writing ideas that fall into over 80 different topic categories. All of the important topics of the typical human life are covered, such as Ancestry and Marriage. There are also hundreds of detailed writing ideas about the historical events that may have shaped individuals' lives, such as World War II and The Great Depression. A special, built-in word processor displays pertinent writing ideas on-screen while you write.

With customized writing ideas to guide you along, you won't forget to include anything. You can use it to do an overview of a relative's whole life or just concentrate on some of the major events. It's up to you! *Biography Maker* is the perfect tool for helping you capture all of those family stories that you want your grandchildren to enjoy. See the last page of this manual for even more details about this extraordinary program.

PARCHMENT PAPER

We offer antique-finish parchment paper that you can use to print your trees. The paper is for use with tractor-feed printers or laser printers. See the order card at the back of this manual for details.

OTHER PRODUCTS

For more information about any of the following products or to order, call Brøderbund Customer Support at (415) 382-4770 or write to Brøderbund Customer Support at PO Box 6125 Novato, CA 94948-6125.

Family Tree Maker DOS Version

Family Tree Maker is available for DOS users, too. A veteran member of the Family Tree Maker product line and always a best-seller, the DOS version of Family Tree Maker was first released in 1989. By July of 1995, over 250,000 copies had been sold. Respected by users for its high quality and ease of use, the DOS version of Family Tree Maker comes with a number of distinct features. For information about the differences between the Windows and DOS versions of Family Tree Maker, contact Brøderbund Customer Support.

Uncle Sam's Budget Balancer

Uncle Sam's Budget Balancer makes it easy for ordinary citizens to try their hand at balancing the federal budget. Users can modify the President's budget with over 300 options researched and documented by the Congressional Budget Office. Options for spending and revenue changes are described, including the pros and cons of implementing each one. Print out your budget plan to discuss with others or send it to your congressperson or senator. The program also contains educational information about the budget process.

Org Plus

Org Plus automatically draws organization charts and tree diagrams. Also use it to generate reports such as phone lists or salary summaries directly from your charts. Available for DOS, Windows, and Mac, it's an indispensable tool for managers in all types of businesses. In fact, over 400 of the Fortune 500 companies use *Org Plus*!

TROUBLESHOOTING

Although we hope you never have any problems while using Family Tree Maker, sometimes things just go wrong. If you do have a problem, first try to locate the solution in this chapter. The table below will help you.

For this type of problem...	See page...
Installation problems	419
Printing problems	421
Error messages	425
Display problems	426
Computer problems	427
CD-ROM problems	428
Problems playing videos	431
Print setup problems	432

Figure E-1. Troubleshooting sections

Another place to look for information is in Family Tree Maker's README file. This file contains last-minute information that couldn't be included in the manual. To see the README file, go to Program Manager and double-click the **FTW ReadMe** icon.

If you have tried all of the suggestions and none of them solved the problem, contact Brøderbund's Banner Blue Division Technical Support for further assistance. The Banner Blue Technical Support phone number is 510-794-6850. You can speak directly to a technical support representative Monday through Friday, 8:00 AM to 5:00 PM, Pacific time. Be sure you are in front of your computer with Windows running when you call.

In addition, Banner Blue's Technical Support Department now has an **interactive automated help system**, which consists of pre-recorded voice instructions and the ability to fax back written instructions. It is available 24 hours a day, seven days a week by calling 510-794-6850.

SYSTEM REQUIREMENTS

Family Tree Maker requires an IBM PC or compatible, a 386 CPU (486 or higher recommended), Windows 3.1 or higher running in enhanced mode, a hard disk with *at least* 9 megabytes of free space, *at least* 4 megabytes of physical RAM (8 megabytes highly recommended), a VGA or better monitor running in at least 16 colors, and a Microsoft compatible mouse. In addition, if you install Family Tree Maker to a drive other than the drive where Microsoft Windows is installed, that drive must have at least 1.2 MB of free space on it. (This is for the Windows OLE 2.0 DLLs which are required to run FTW.)

Note: If your system does not meet these minimum requirements, *we cannot guarantee that the program will function correctly.* You will need to upgrade your system to meet these requirements if you wish to use Family Tree Maker.

Please realize that these are the minimum requirements — the more family information you enter, the more free hard disk space and available RAM you will need. If you plan to include many pictures, sounds, and videos in your Family Tree Maker Scrapbooks, you will need a substantial amount of hard disk space. In addition, a scanner, a Kodak Photo CD-compatible CD-ROM drive, a sound card, and a video capture card are optional.

The Deluxe Edition of Family Tree maker has the same system requirements, with the addition of a CD-ROM drive. The CD-ROM drive does not need to be Kodak compatible unless you want to insert Kodak Photo CD pictures into your Family Tree Maker Scrapbooks. Again, if your system does not meet these minimum requirements, we cannot guarantee that the program will function correctly.

To run Family Tree Maker under Windows 95, you must have Windows 95 and 8 megabytes of RAM.

INSTALLATION PROBLEMS

Read through the bolded items below to find your particular problem. The possible solutions are listed below each problem.

Your system locks up during installation.

- Something on your system may be interfering. See "Doing a Clean Boot" on page 434.

A message appears saying "Unable to install temporary files in Windows directory."

- You may be out of space on your hard disk. You will have to remove other files or programs to free up disk space.

- You may be trying to install Family Tree Maker from File Manager. Exit File Manager and install Family Tree Maker through the Program Manager.

- You may be running a Program Manager substitute, such as Norton Commander or Hewlett-Packard Dashboard. Try installing directly from Program Manager.

- If you are installing Family Tree Maker from diskettes, create a temporary directory on your hard drive, such as FTWTEMP, copy all files from the diskettes into that directory, and run the setup program from that directory. Using the "Installing a Diskette Version of Family Tree Maker" instructions on page 14, you would skip step 2 and type **c:\ftwtemp\setup.exe** in step four. Do *not* try this if you are installing a CD-ROM version of Family Tree Maker.

- If you have virus protection software on your system, it may have interfered with the installation process. Temporarily disable the virus protection software. For instructions, call your computer manufacturer or retailer. Then, re-install Family Tree Maker.

- Check your hard disk for problems. Close all running programs and then exit Windows. At the DOS prompt (usually C:\>), type **CHKDSK /F** and press **Enter**. If CHKDSK reports any errors, type **Y** and press **Enter**. At this point, try installing Family Tree Maker.

A message appears indicating that the drive from which you are installing is read-only.

- If you have virus protection software on your system, it may be interfering with the installation process. Temporarily disable the virus protection software. For instructions, call your computer manufacturer or retailer. Then, re-install Family Tree Maker.

A message appears saying "Cannot find a:setup (or one of its components). Check to be sure the path and filename are correct and that all required libraries are available."

- You may have entered something other than **a:setup** in the Command Line field. Check what was entered.

- You may have entered **a:setup**, but put the diskette in your b: diskette drive. Try typing **b:setup** or putting the diskette in the a: diskette drive.

- If you are installing a CD-ROM version of Family Tree Maker, make sure you type the correct letter for your CD-ROM drive. Often, d: represents the CD-ROM drive, in which case you would type **d:setup**.

- Your diskette drive may not be able to read high density diskettes. See "Disk Type" on page 428.

- The diskette may be damaged. Contact Banner Blue Technical Support for assistance.

A message appears saying that you don't have enough disk space to install the program.

- You may be out of space on the drive you're attempting to install to. See "Disk Space" on page 429.

- If the drive you are installing to has plenty of space, check the drive where Windows is installed. If it is a different drive letter than the one you are installing Family Tree Maker to, you will need at least 1.2 MB of free space on it. (This is for the Windows OLE 2.0 DLLs which are required to run Family Tree Maker.)

- Check your temporary directory. (See "Disk Space" on page 429.) If there are several files there, delete any unnecessary files to free up disk space.

A "CDR 101" error message appears.

- There may be fingerprints or dust on your CD. Remove the CD from your CD-ROM drive and gently wipe the shiny side with a clean towel. Do not wipe in a circular motion around the CD. Instead, wipe from the inside edge to the outside edge.

- You may be using an old version of MSCDEX. Exit both Family Tree Maker and Windows and type **mscdex** at the DOS prompt (usually C:\>). Then, press **Enter**. The screen will show you which version of MSCDEX you are using. You must have at least version 2.22 or later. If not, call your CD-ROM driver manufacturer for an update.

- You may be using an old CD-ROM driver. Call your CD-ROM manufacturer to make sure that you have the latest version of the driver.

A message appears saying "Access to specified device or file is denied."

- If you have virus protection software on your system, it may have interfered with the installation process. Temporarily disable the virus protection software. For instructions, call your computer manufacturer or retailer. Then, re-install Family Tree Maker.

PRINTING PROBLEMS

Read through the bolded items below to find your particular problem. The possible solutions are listed below each problem.

Family Tree Maker is printing slowly.

- Printing from Windows, especially when printing graphics, can be slow. If you want it to print faster, you can try printing at lower quality, but the output won't look as nice.

- Windows Print Manager may be slowing it down. To disable Print Manager, see your Microsoft Windows User's Guide.

- Your computer may be running low on memory or resources. You must have at least 50% free resources while printing. See "Memory and Resources" on page 430.

The letters are replaced with symbols.

- You may be using a symbol font, such as Fences or Wingdings. Try switching to a TrueType font such as Arial.

- You may be using the wrong printer driver. See "Print Setup" on page 432.

The boxes are printing without text.

- Your printer's memory may have been corrupted during the last print job. Reset your printer by turning it off and then on again.

- Check the Items to Include dialog box (on the **Contents** menu) to make sure that you have chosen to include items in your boxes.

- Make sure you haven't selected the "Print empty" option in the Print dialog box (on the **File** menu).

- You may be using the wrong printer driver. See "Print Setup" on page 432.

- Windows Print Manager may be interfering. To disable Print Manager, see your Microsoft Windows User's Guide.

- Your computer may be running low on memory or resources. You must have at least 50% free resources while printing. See "Memory and Resources" on page 430.

The text is printing without boxes.

- Your printer's memory may have been corrupted during the last print job. Reset your printer by turning it off and then on again.

- Family Tree Maker provides the option to print trees without boxes. Check the Box, Line, & Border Styles dialog box (on the **Format** menu).

- You may be using the wrong printer driver. See "Print Setup" on page 432.

- Windows Print Manager may be interfering. To disable Print Manager, see your Microsoft Windows User's Guide.

- Your computer may be running low on memory or resources. You must have at least 50% free resources while printing. See "Memory and Resources" on page 430.

The pictures are not printing clearly.

- The brightness setting may be too dark. In the view from which you are printing, open the Print Setup dialog box (on the **File** menu), click **Brightness**, and choose a lighter setting. See "Print Setup" on page 266.

- Image quality may have deteriorated during import. Try importing again using a lower compression setting. See "Controlling Picture Resolution and Compression" on page 178.

- You may be using the wrong printer driver. See "Print Setup" on page 432.

- Windows Print Manager may be interfering. To disable Print Manager, see your Microsoft Windows User's Guide.

- Start a word processor on your machine, such as Notepad, and open the FTW.INI file. This file is in the same directory as your Family Tree Maker program (usually C:\FTW). In the [OPTIONS] section of the FTW.INI, insert a new line and type **PrintColorImage=True**   If there is not an [OPTIONS] section, you can create one at the bottom of the file by pressing **Enter** once and then typing **[OPTIONS]**

- The image may have been of poor quality to begin with. If possible, get a better quality image.

Absolutely nothing prints at all.

- Your printer may not be hooked up correctly. Check to see if it's turned on, online, and connected to the computer.

- You may have incorrect Print Setup settings. See "Print Setup" on page 432.

- You may be using the wrong printer driver. See "Print Setup" on page 432.

- Your computer may be running low on memory or resources. You must have at least 50% free resources while printing. See "Memory and Resources" on page 430.

- Your printer may not be able to handle all the information being sent to it. Check for error messages on the printer and consult your printer manual for possible solutions.

Text is printing outside boxes.

- You may be using the wrong printer driver. See "Print Setup" on page 432.

- Your printer may be using the wrong character spacing. Set up your printer so that the software is in control of what size character is printed, instead of having the printer set to only do one size.

- You may be using a font that is not scaling correctly. Try using a TrueType font such as Arial.

- Your computer may be running low on memory or resources. You must have at least 50% free resources while printing. See "Memory and Resources" on page 430.

Garbage characters are printing.

- Your printer's memory may have been corrupted during the last print job. Reset the printer by turning it off and then on again.

- You may be using the wrong printer driver. See "Print Setup" on page 432.

- If you are printing to a serial printer, you may have incorrect port, baud rate, or parity settings in Print Setup. See "Print Setup" on page 432.

- You may have a bad cable. Try using a new one.

- Your computer may be running low on memory or resources. You must have at least 50% free resources while printing. See "Memory and Resources" on page 432.

- Your printer may not be able to handle all the information being sent to it. Check for error messages on the printer and consult your printer manual for possible solutions.

You cannot get a printer file to print.

- Be sure that you are typing the correct command at the DOS prompt. For example, you could type **copy /b c:\ftw\mytree.prn lpt1** where "mytree.prn" is the file name, "c:\ftw" are the drive and directory where the file is located, and the printer was connected to LPT1.

- When you create the printer file, make sure that the printer listed at the top of the Print dialog box is the printer to which you will eventually print the file.

Other

- See the README file for information about specific printers.

ERROR MESSAGES

Read through the bolded items below to find your particular error message. The possible solutions are listed below each message.

A message appears saying that you need to load "share."

- VSHARE.386 has not been loaded. Try restarting Windows.

- The [386 ENH] section of your SYSTEM.INI file may not contain the line "device=vshare.386". Add this line, then restart Windows. For more information about share and vshare, see "Working with Share" on page 438.

A message appears saying that one of the library files needed to run Family Tree Maker needs to be reinstalled.

- One of the nine DLL files that Family Tree Maker uses may be corrupted. Reinstall the DLLs and then restart Family Tree Maker using the instructions in "Reinstalling DLLs" on page 431.

- Install Microsoft Windows into a *new* directory on your hard drive and start that copy of Windows. Then, reinstall Family Tree Maker.

An item in the Scrapbook does not play as you expect, or gives a message that the server couldn't be found.

- Server applications must "register" themselves with Windows. Your server may not be registered or may not be installed properly. Try reinstalling the server application or consulting the server's manufacturer.

A message appears saying that Family Tree Maker cannot find a font of appropriate size for this display.

- Appropriate fonts may not be installed on your machine. From Program Manager, double-click the **Control Panel** icon, and then double-click the **Fonts** icon. In the Fonts dialog box, check to see that both Arial (TrueType) and MS Sans Serif are installed. If you need to install them, see your Microsoft Windows User's manual. In addition, click the **TrueType** button in the Fonts dialog box and make sure that the **Enable TrueType Fonts** check box is selected in the TrueType dialog box.

- Your video driver may be incompatible with Family Tree Maker or you may need a new video driver. Try using the Standard Windows VGA driver (see your Microsoft Windows User's manual) or contact your video driver manufacturer to see if they have a newer version.

A message appears saying that Family Tree Maker has detected a possible problem with your file.

- Click **Yes** to try to open your file. If the same or another error message appears after you click "Yes," try opening the backup file instead. See "Opening Backup Files" on page 378.

A message appears saying that you don't have enough disk space to save or to run.

- You may be out of space on the drive Windows is installed on, the drive you're attempting to save to, or the drive your temporary directory is on. See "Disk Space" on page 429.

DISPLAY PROBLEMS

Read through the bolded items below to find your particular problem. The possible solutions are listed below each problem.

The tabs along the right side of the Family Page have garbage characters on them or the text is not vertical.

- Appropriate fonts may not be installed. From Program Manager, double-click the **Control Panel** icon, and then double-click the **Fonts** icon. In the Fonts dialog box, check to see that both Arial (TrueType) and MS Sans Serif are installed. If you need to install them, see your Microsoft Windows User's manual.

- Your video driver may be incompatible with Family Tree Maker or you may need a new video driver. Try using the Standard Windows VGA driver (see your Microsoft Windows User's manual).

Images are not displayed clearly.

- Your system may not be using enough colors to display the image. Check the documentation that came with your computer for instructions on how to get more colors. (A video driver with 256 colors is the normal amount of colors required to display images clearly.)

- Image quality may have deteriorated during import. Try importing again using a lower compression setting. See "Controlling Picture Resolution and Compression" on page 178.

- The image may have been of poor quality to begin with. If possible, get a better quality image.

COMPUTER PROBLEMS

Read through the bolded items below to find your particular problem. The possible solutions are listed below each problem.

Your system locks when running, generates a General Protection Fault, or generates an Application Error.

- Write down the exact error message before doing anything else.

- If the error message contains ".drv", contact the manufacturers of your video and printer drivers to make sure that you have the latest versions of them.

- Your computer may be running low on memory or resources. See "Memory and Resources" on page 430.

- Check your hard disk for problems. Close all running programs and then exit Windows. At the DOS prompt (usually C:\>), type **CHKDSK /F** and press **Enter**. If CHKDSK reports any errors, type **Y** and press **Enter**. At this point, you should reinstall Family Tree Maker.

- Something on your system may be interfering. See "Doing a Clean Boot" on page 434.

The computer freezes when adding or searching through a Photo CD.

- You may be using Smart Drive, Microsoft's disk caching software. This may occur as you read the last image on a Photo CD-ROM disc. Try disabling Smart Drive or disable read caching on your CD-ROM drive. Consult your Windows manual for instructions.

Family Tree Maker is running very slowly.

- If you are working in a view with images or OLE objects, this may be normal. You can improve performance by increasing the amount of memory (RAM) on your machine. If you plan to include *many* images or OLE objects, then we highly recommend you use a 486 or higher CPU and 8 to 16 MB of physical RAM.

- Your computer may be running low on memory or resources. See "Memory and Resources" on page 430.

- Try increasing the size of Family Tree Maker's cache. See "Startup Preferences" on page 26.

- You may need to clean up your hard drive. Try defragmenting it with a commercial defragmenting tool, such as PC Tools or Norton Disk Doctor. If you have DOS version 6.0 and higher or Windows 95, you already have a defragmenting tool called DEFRAG.EXE.

- If you are using a "disk doubling" utility such as Stacker®, Family Tree Maker may run faster if you install it on the uncompressed portion of your hard disk. Both DOS 6.0 and higher and Windows 95 have disk doublers.

- Check your hard disk for problems. Close all running programs and then close Windows. At the DOS prompt (usually C:\>), type **CHKDSK /F** and press **Enter**. If CHKDSK reports any errors, type **Y** and press **Enter**. At this point your should reinstall Family Tree Maker.

CD-ROM PROBLEMS

You're having trouble accessing a CD.

- There may be fingerprints or dust on your CD. Remove the CD from your CD-ROM drive and gently wipe the shiny side with a clean towel. Do not wipe in a circular motion around the CD. Instead, wipe from the inside edge to the outside edge.

- You may be using Smart Drive, Microsoft's disk caching software. Try disabling Smart Drive or disable read caching on your CD-ROM drive. Consult your Windows manual for instructions.

- You may be using an old version of MSCDEX. Exit both Family Tree Maker and Windows and type **mscdex** at the DOS prompt (usually C:\>). Then, press **Enter**. The screen will display what version of MSCDEX you are using. You must have at least version 2.22 or later. If not, call your CD-ROM driver manufacturer for an update.

- You may be using an old driver. Call your CD-ROM manufacturer and make sure that you have the latest version of the driver.

DISK TYPE

Family Tree Maker is shipped on high density (Double Sided High Density), 1.44 megabyte 3.5" diskettes. Please note that 5.25" high density diskettes, 5.25" low density diskettes, and 3.5" low density diskettes are *not* available. In addition, the CD-ROM version of Family Tree Maker is not available on diskettes.

DISK SPACE

In Windows programs, many operations such as printing and saving require disk space. If a warning message tells you that you don't have enough disk space, you should check the following:

- Disk space available on the drive where Windows is installed. You need to have at least 1.2 MB free disk space available on the drive where Windows is installed. In addition, Windows needs at least 1 MB of free disk space to run properly, after Family Tree Maker has been installed. You may encounter problems if you have less.

- Disk space available on the drive where Family Tree Maker is saving your Family File. You generally need to have 3 times the size of your file available because of the way many Windows programs (including Family Tree Maker) save files. For example, if your file is 400,000 bytes, you actually need 1,200,000 bytes (1.2 MB) available to save it.

- The existence of a directory on your hard drive for temporary files. You can check this by exiting to DOS and typing **set**. There should be a line that says something like **set temp = c:\temp**. If you don't have such a line, then you should set up a temp directory for Windows to use. See "Using the TEMP Environment Variable" in your Windows 3.1 manual for information about doing this.

MEMORY AND RESOURCES

If either your available memory or available resources falls too low, then your computer may behave unpredictably. To check your available memory and resources, from the **Help** menu, select **System Information**. Family Tree Maker displays the System Information dialog box. The most important items on it are Memory and System Resources. If you are unable to get into Family Tree Maker, then from the **Help** menu on your Windows Program Manager screen, select **About Program Manager**.

Family Tree Maker requires that you have at least 4 megabytes (4000 KB) of physical memory and 3 megabytes (3000 KB) of virtual memory to run. Family Tree Maker also requires that you run Windows in 386 enhanced mode. (See your Microsoft Windows manual.) If the number displayed next to "Memory" is less than 7,000, you will need to free up more memory. You may be able to do this by closing other programs.

If all other programs have been closed and you still don't have enough memory available, you should try doing a clean boot. See "Doing a Clean Boot" on page 434. If you have less than 3 megabytes of memory free after doing a clean boot, then you don't have enough memory available to run Family Tree Maker. Try consulting your DOS and Windows manuals for details about making more memory available, or consider buying more memory for your computer.

Microsoft Windows requires that your system resources be at least 40% just to run Windows alone. Each program you are running takes up some of your resources. So, the more programs you want to run at one time, the more resources you need. If you are running Family Tree Maker and your resources are less than 50%, you don't have enough. You can free up more resources by closing other programs or doing a clean boot, described on page 434. If you have tried this and still are low on resources, contact Microsoft for information on how to get more resources.

PLAYING VIDEOS IN SCRAPBOOKS

If you place videos into your Scrapbooks and then move your Family Tree Maker software and Family File to another computer, you may not be able to play your videos.

To play a video on another computer, that computer must have all of the hardware and software that is required by the OLE server that you used to create the video files. Depending on the type of OLE server, the required items may even include the video capture board.

To eliminate having to move all of the hardware and software that the OLE server requires, use the most generic video compression available when you create your video files. Check with the manufacturer of your video capture hardware and software. They should be able to tell you which of the available compression methods is the most generic and which elements are required to play a video.

In addition, when you move your Family File, you must also move any .AVI (video) files that are included in your Scrapbooks. This is because the .AVI files are linked to, not embedded, in your Family File.

REINSTALLING DLLs

Family Tree Maker copies the following DLL (Dynamic Link Library) files to your hard drive when you install the software.

COMPOBJ.DLL	OLE2PROX.DLL	OLE2NLS.DLL
CTL3DV2.DLL	OLE2CONV.DLL	STORAGE.DLL
OLE2.DLL	OLE2DISP.DLL	TYPELIB.DLL

Figure E-2. Family Tree Maker DLLs

If these files are corrupted, Family Tree Maker cannot function normally, so you need to install fresh copies into the Windows System directory. You can do this by reinstalling Family Tree Maker. However, because Family Tree Maker will not overwrite existing DLLs, you first need to rename the existing DLL files. Instructions begin on the next page.

To rename the files:

1. Exit Windows if it is running.

2. At the DOS prompt, change to the drive in which Windows is installed by typing the drive letter followed by a colon.

   For example, you would type **c:** if Windows is installed on your c: drive.

3. Change to the Windows System Directory (normally c:\windows\system) by typing **cd\windows\system**

4. Type **rename <oldname> <newname>** and then press **Enter**, where **oldname** is the old name of the DLL and **newname** is what you are renaming it. For example, to rename COMPOBJ.DLL, you would type **rename compobj.dll compobj.old**

5. Repeat step 4 for every file listed in Figure E-2.

6. Restart Windows and reinstall Family Tree Maker.

   Installation places fresh copies of all nine files in the Windows System directory. You can delete all the old DLL files, but be aware that DLL files are shared by other Windows applications. Make sure that all other Windows applications are functioning normally before you delete the old DLL files.

PRINT SETUP

One of the nicest things about Windows is that it handles all printing. You don't have to install your printer over and over again in different programs — once your printer is installed in Windows, it should work with all Windows programs. If you're having trouble printing from Family Tree Maker, it probably is because of an incorrect setting in your print setup.

1. Make sure that your selection in print setup *exactly* matches the kind of printer you have. To check this, from the **File** menu in Family Tree Maker, select **Print Setup**. Using a driver other than the one specifically designed to work with your printer can cause unpredictable results. If you don't have the correct printer driver, contact your printer manufacturer or Microsoft for information on how to get one.

2. Family Tree Maker allows you to have different settings in print setup for each view. For example, you could choose legal-size paper and one-inch margins for your Ancestor trees, but letter-size paper and half-inch margins

for your Descendant trees. You could also select completely different printers for each tree! If you find that you can print correctly from one view, but not from another, compare the settings in Print Setup for each view to determine what is different between the two.

3. Try printing from another Windows program, such as Write or Notepad. If you experience the same problem, then the problem lies somewhere in either your printer or Windows setup. Contact Microsoft or your printer manufacturer for assistance.

4. Check your settings in Program Manager's Control Panel to verify that they match your system. You should have a Control Panel icon in your Main group in Program Manager. If you don't, from the **File** menu in Program Manager, select **Run**. Type `control` in the Command Line field and click **OK**. This will bring up the Control Panel. Double click the **Printers** icon to access printer information.

   The Printers dialog box will tell you which port Windows is printing to. (A port is a place on your computer that the printer can plug into.) Check the documentation that came with your computer to find out which port your printer is connected to. This port should be the one shown in the Printers dialog box.

   In particular, if you are printing through a COM port (e.g. COM1), make sure that the settings for baud rate, parity, and stop bits match those set on your printer. If you aren't sure what they should be set to, consult your printer manual. You may also want to try decreasing the baud rate. Sometimes there's simply too much going on for Windows to talk to your printer at a high speed. Decreasing the speed will usually solve the problem.

5. Make sure you're using the most current driver available for your printer. You can check the version by going to the **File** menu in Family Tree Maker and selecting **Print Setup**. Click **Options** in the Print Setup dialog box. This will bring up a screen specific to your printer. There is usually an "About" button which gives information about the driver, including the version. If there isn't a button, then the version number may appear somewhere else in the dialog box. Check with your printer manufacturer to see if you have the latest version of the driver. (They can also tell you how to find out which version you have, if you aren't sure.) Also, make sure that the printer driver is for the version of Windows you're using. A driver from Windows 3.0 probably won't work correctly in Windows 3.1.

Doing a Clean Boot

A "clean boot" is a way of starting up Windows using only the essential files that the machine needs to run. It's usually something you do only when the computer is having memory problems or is experiencing frequent errors.

Note: Do not attempt a clean boot unless you have experience with computers. You need to understand what you are doing in order to avoid making mistakes from which it is difficult to recover. In addition, you should only attempt a clean boot if you are using Windows version 3.1.

To prepare your system for the clean boot, first make backup copies of your CONFIG.SYS, AUTOEXEC.BAT, WIN.INI, and SYSTEM.INI files. You can place copies of these files in a different directory on your hard disk or copy them onto a floppy diskette.

After creating backup copies of these files, you first need to edit your WIN.INI, CONFIG.SYS and AUTOEXEC.BAT files. The editing steps outlined here assume that you do not have any TSR (Terminate & Stay Resident) programs installed that your system needs in order to function properly. A disk-doubling program would be an example of such a TSR. If you are using a TSR, you will need to identify which lines belong to the TSR in your AUTOEXEC.BAT, CONFIG.SYS, and WIN.INI files and make sure that you do *not* modify these lines. Before editing, refer to the documentation provided by your TSR programs to find out which lines to avoid. If you aren't sure about a certain line, don't change it.

Important: Have some scratch paper handy so you can write down the changes you make to the CONFIG.SYS and AUTOEXEC.BAT files. You might later need to change back to the original commands.

Before editing your files, you should create a bootable floppy disk that contains the MS-DOS system files and any other files that are required to make the system operational, such as disk-compression utilities (for example, Stacker®), disk partitioning drivers (for example, Disk Manager) and other third-party device drivers. If your computer does not start up properly after making changes to your files, insert this "boot disk" into your A: drive and restart your computer. This will allow you to get your computer up and running again.

The files listed in the following table are examples of drivers that *should not* be removed from your AUTOEXEC.BAT and CONFIG.SYS files. Please note that this is not a complete list, but it does contain most of the commonly used drivers:

Hard Disk Drivers:	SQY55.SYS, SSTBIO.SYS, SSTDRIVE.SYS, AH1544.SYS, ILIM386.SYS, ASPI4DOS.SYS, SCSIHA.SYS, SCSIDSK.EXE, SKYDRVI.SYS, ATDOSXL.SYS, NONSTD.SYS
Disk Partitioners:	DMDRVR.BIN, SSTOR.SYS, HARDRIVE.SYS, EDVR.SYS, FIXT_DRV.SYS, LDRIVE.SYS, ENHDISK.SYS
Disk Compression Utilities:	STACKER.COM, SSWAP.COM, SSTOR.EXE, DEVSWAP.COM, DBLSPACE.SYS
CD-ROM Drivers:	SLCD.SYS, SBCD.SYS, TEAC_CDA.SYS, TSLCDR.SYS

Figure E-3. Sample drivers that should not be removed

If the purpose of a device driver or program is unknown, **DO NOT** remove it. Most device drivers and programs will display a message describing their purpose when they are initialized.

Editing Your Files

1. From Windows, display Program Manager.

2. From Program Manager's **File** menu, select **Run**.

   Program Manager displays the Run dialog box.

3. Click the **Command Line** field and type **sysedit**, then click **OK**.

   Program Manager displays a group of windows that you use to edit your system setup.

4. Select the window titled AUTOEXEC.BAT by clicking its title bar.

5. Type **rem** at the beginning of each line in the AUTOEXEC.BAT file, *except* for the lines that start with the following words:

   path
   prompt
   set temp
   share (Note: Your own AUTOEXEC.BAT file may not include a "share" line.)

Typing "rem" at the beginning of a line (or "**remming-out**" a command) temporarily prevents the computer from reading and running that line. Figure E-4 shows an AUTOEXEC.BAT file that has been edited.

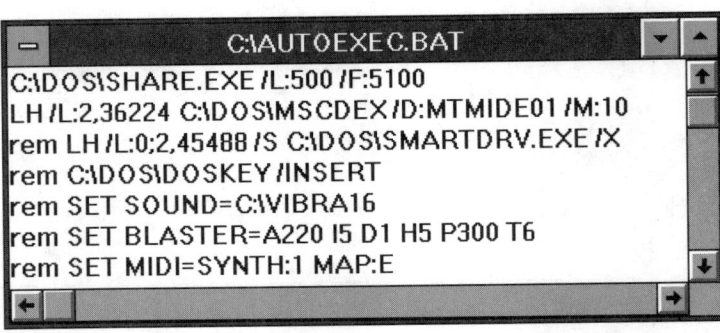

Figure E-4. Sample AUTOEXEC.BAT file

6. After typing "rem" at the beginning of the appropriate lines, select the window titled CONFIG.SYS by clicking its title bar.

7. Type **rem** at the beginning of each line of the CONFIG.SYS file, *except* for the lines which start with the following words:

   files=
   buffers=
   stacks=
   device=<third-party disk compression driver>
   device=<third-party disk partitioner>
   device=<third-party CD ROM driver>
   device=<other third-party driver>
   device=<path>himem.sys

As with the AUTOEXEC.BAT file, typing "rem" at the beginning of a line temporarily prevents the computer from reading and running that line. Figure E-5, on the next page shows a CONFIG.SYS file that has been edited.

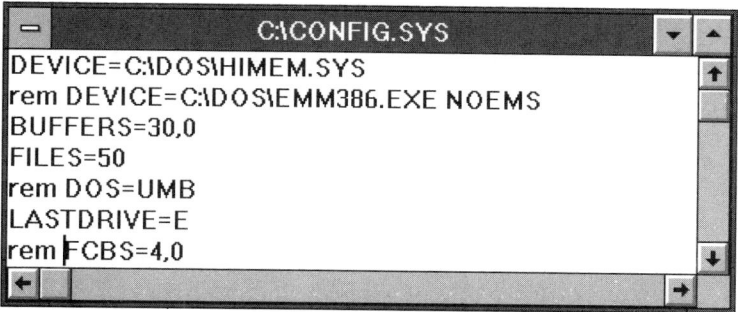

Figure E-5. Sample CONFIG.SYS file

8. After typing "rem" at the beginning of the appropriate lines, select the window titled WIN.INI by clicking its title bar.

9. Type **rem** at the beginning of *all* lines in the WIN.INI file that start with either of the following words:

run=
load=

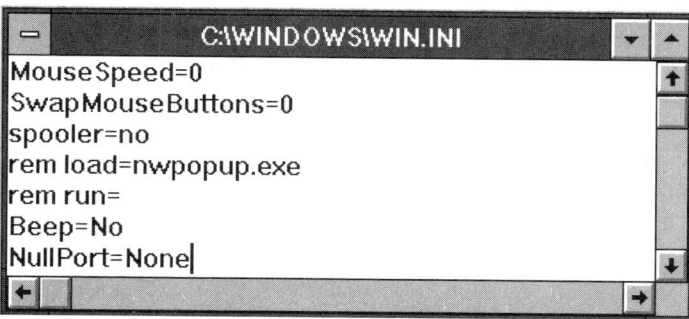

Figure E-6. Sample WIN.INI file

10. From the **File** menu, select **Save**.

The System Configuration Editor saves the changes you have made.

11. Exit Windows.

12. Restart your computer.

    By restarting your computer after editing the AUTOEXEC.BAT, CONFIG.SYS, and WIN.INI files, you are doing a "clean boot."

13. Start Windows. Hold down the **Shift** key when you see the Windows startup screen, to prevent any programs in the Startup Program Group from loading.

    Note: If Windows usually starts automatically when you turn your computer on, but it doesn't automatically start now, you can start it by typing **win** at the C:\> prompt and then pressing **Enter**.

14. Start Family Tree Maker and open one of your Family Files to make sure the system is working properly again.

If your computer functions properly after you do a clean boot, then you know that one of the items you "remmed out" of your AUTOEXEC.BAT, CONFIG.SYS or WIN.INI file was causing the problem. If this is the case, you can try to isolate which line it was by running Sysedit again, removing one "rem" (to add that item back in), restarting your computer and trying again. Once you isolate which line was causing the problem, contact the manufacturer of that program to see if there is an updated version available that is more compatible with your computer.

If the clean boot did not solve your problem, there is a good chance that the problem you are experiencing is being caused by your computer hardware or an error in Family Tree Maker. Please call Banner Blue's Technical Support department for further assistance.

WORKING WITH SHARE

Applications like Family Tree Maker that support object linking and embedding (OLE) 2.0 require that you run either SHARE.EXE or VSHARE.386. When you install Family Tree Maker, VSHARE.386 is automatically installed.

If you have both SHARE.EXE and VSHARE.386, you can remove one of them (instructions are on the next page). SHARE.EXE is an MS-DOS application that is loaded into the conventional memory area, so it competes with other programs that use conventional memory. Also, SHARE.EXE requires a small amount of memory to store information. VSHARE.386 does not impact other applications.

Removing SHARE.EXE

To remove SHARE.EXE:

1. From the **Help** menu, select **System Information.**

   Family Tree Maker displays the System Information dialog box.

2. Click the **Run** field and select **System Editor**.

   Family Tree Maker displays the System Configuration Editor dialog box.

3. Click on the window titled "C:\AUTOEXEC.BAT."

4. Remove the line that says "share.exe."

5. From the **File** menu of the System Configuration Editor, select **Exit**.

6. Click **Yes** when it asks if you want to save.

7. Click **OK** to close the System Information dialog box in Family Tree Maker.

Removing VSHARE.386

To remove VSHARE.386:

1. From the **Help** menu, select **System Information.**

   Family Tree Maker displays the System Information dialog box.

2. Click the **Run** field and select **System Editor**.

   Family Tree Maker displays the System Configuration Editor dialog box.

3. Click on the window titled "C:\WINDOWS\SYSTEM.INI."

4. Use the arrow keys to scroll down to the [386 ENH] section of the file.

5. Remove the line that says "device=vshare.386."

6. From the **File** menu of the System Configuration Editor, select **Exit**.

7. Click **Yes** when it asks if you want to save.

8. Click **OK** to close the System Information dialog box in Family Tree Maker.

INDEX

Accessories, 415-16
Add Unrelated Individual, 100
Adding
    data from FamilyFinder, 210-13, 217
    individuals to a Family File, 77-100
    individuals to groups, 283-90, 324-30, 339-45
    information from other files, 379-87
    other parents, 113-16
    other spouses, 110-12
Address dialog box, 132-33
Address fields, 132-33
Address inheritance, 295
Address labels
    See Labels and cards
Address reports
    creating, 275-78
    See also Reports
Adoptive relationships
    entering information about, 94, 113-16, 136
    excluding from Kinship reports, 292
    excluding from trees, 136
Age
    including in calendars, 331
    possible mistakes in, 79, 275-78, 367-75
Ahnentafel numbering
    creating, 251
    defined, 245-46
    including in trees, 248
aka
    entering, 85, 134-35
    in Index of Individuals, 118
    including in calendars, 331
    including in reports, 297
    including in trees, 247-48
    including on labels and cards, 297-300
Alphabetizing
    labels and cards, 318
    reports, 318
    Scrapbooks, 171
    the Index of Individuals, 120

Ancestor trees
    characteristics, 231
    creating, 237
    creating and printing, 229-67
    Custom, 230
    customizing, 239-40
    defined, 229-30
    example of, 5, 230
    Fit to Page, 229, 231
    print setup, 266-67
    printing, 263-67
    printing (in Tutorial), 66-71
    See also Trees
Anniversaries
    including in calendars, 331
Annulments
    recording, 145
Antique-finish parchment paper, 416
Appending
    all information, 387
    destination file defined, 379
    files, 379-87
    mapping information between
        files, 380-81
    merging with confirmation, 385-86
    source file defined, 379
    viewing Merge reports, 384
    World Family Tree pedigrees, 217
Application error, 427
Arranging
    individuals in a batch print, 339
    labels and cards, 318
    reports, 318
    Scrapbooks, 171, 318
    the Index of Individuals, 120
ASCII
    exporting from Notes, 144
    importing into Notes, 143
Attaching
    children to correct parents, 188-89
    spouse to correct spouse, 189-90

Aunts
    entering information about, 99
Automatic backup defaults, 26-27
Automatic error checking, 77, 79, 275-78,
    367-75
Automatically filling fields, 90-91

Backups
    defaults for automatic backups, 26-27
    making, 376-77
    opening, 378
    retrieving, 378
Banner Blue products, 415-16
Banner Blue/Brøderbund
    address, 10
    fax number, 10
    phone number, 10
    technical support, 9
Batch print
    page numbering, 346
    print settings, 346
    selecting individuals to print, 339-45
    selecting the document type, 338
    sorting individuals, 339
    uses for, 347
Beginning status field, 93
Biography Maker, 415
Birth date
    entering, 87
    including in calendars, 331
    including in reports, 293
    including in trees, 243-46
    possible mistakes in, 79, 275-78, 367-75
Birthday reports
    creating, 275-78
    See Calendars
    See also Reports
Blank
    rows in labels and cards, 316
    rows in trees, 244
    rows to make room for photos, 244
Borders
    styles for calendars, 333
    styles for labels and cards, 313-14
    styles for reports, 313-14
    styles for Scrapbooks, 313-14
    styles for trees, 254

Boxes
    connections between, 255-56
    location of Picture/Objects in, 247-50
    making the same size, 255-56
    printing without text inside, 422
    styles for calendars, 333
    styles for labels and cards, 313-14
    styles for Picture/Objects in
        Scrapbooks, 313-14
    styles for trees, 254
    varying sizes, 255-56
    width in trees, 258
Branches
    adding empty, 259
Brightness of Picture/Objects, 177-78
Brøderbund/Banner Blue
    address, 10
    fax number, 10
    phone number, 10
    technical support, 9
Bubble Help
    choosing where it appears, 28-29
    disabling, 25
    preferences for, 28-29
    resetting, 28-29
    using, 25
Burial
    entering, 130-31

Cache, 26-27
Calendars
    borders, 333
    colors, 333
    creating, 323-24
    customizing, 324-33
    date range of, 331
    example of, 7
    excluding individuals from, 136
    font, 332
    formatting text, 332
    including ages in, 331
    including anniversaries in, 331
    including birthdays in, 331
    individuals to include, 324-30
    page lines, 323-24
    print setup, 266-67
    print to file, 334

printing, 333-34
selecting border styles, 333
selecting info to include, 331
selecting items to include, 331
subtitle and footnote, 332
viewing, 323-24
zooming on, 323
Canon law, 276
Captions
creating for Picture/Objects, 164-66
Cards
See Labels and cards
Categories
creating for Picture/Objects, 164-66
CD-ROM,
problems with, 428
See also Family Archives
See also Family Tree Maker Deluxe Edition
See also Kodak Photo CD
See also World Family Tree
Census records, 193
Centering
trees, 255-56
Centering text
See Formatting
Check box
using, 24
Check marks
in Family Archives, 205
in the FamilyFinder Index, 205
in the World Family Tree, 205
Children
adding, 94-97
adopted, 94
attaching to correct parents, 188-89
deleting, 185
detaching from wrong parents, 186
displaying Family Page of, 108
entering information about, 94-97
foster, 94
inserting in a Children list, 98
moving in Children list, 98
rearranging, 98-99
removing, 186
sorting, 99
step, 94
with multiple sets of parents, 113-16
with wrong parents, 186

Choosing
a printer, 266
individuals to print in a batch
print, 339-45
individuals to print in
calendars, 324-30
individuals to print in
reports, 283-90
individuals to print on labels and
cards, 283-90
info to print in Family Group
Sheets, 293-96
info to print in calendars, 331
info to print in reports, 293-96
info to print in trees, 243-46
info to print on labels and
cards, 293-96
info to print on Scrapbook
pages, 293-96
Christening
entering, 130-31
City field, 132
Civil law, 276
Clean boot, 434-38
Clipboard
copying to, 81, 162-63, 180, 348
cutting to, 81, 180-81
defined (in Tutorial), 57
pasting from, 162-63, 180
Color
printing, 264, 320, 334, 336,
337, 346
selecting, 253, 254, 309, 313,
332, 333
Column labels
including in trees, 259
Columns
width in reports, 315
Combining files, 217, 379-87
Companion products, 415
Compression
of Picture/Objects, 152, 178-79
Contents pages
example of, 197
in Family Archives, 197
in the FamilyFinder Index, 197

Copying
    Family Archive info to a Family
        File, 210-13, 217
    Family Files, 389
    Family Tree Maker items for
        Scrapbooks, 348
    index entries, 205-6
    individuals into another file, 390-91
    items to other applications, 348
    Picture/Objects between
        Scrapbooks, 180
    text, 81, 83
    text from one Notes dialog box to
        another, 140
    text in the Notes dialog box, 81
    text into Notes from another
        program, 142
Copyright abuse, 224
Country field, 132-33
Cousins
    entering information about, 99
    including in Kinship reports, 292
    intermarriage of, 100
Creating
    additional parents, 113-15
    additional spouses, 110-11
    Address reports, 275-78
    Ancestor trees, 229-67
    ASCII files from Notes, 144
    Birthday reports, 275-78
    calendars, 323-24
    Custom reports, 275-78
    Data Errors reports, 275-78
    Descendant trees, 229-67
    Direct Descendant trees, 229-67
    family books, 338-47, 348
    Family Group Sheets, 273-74
    Incomplete Individual Ordinances
        reports, 275-78
    Incomplete Marriage Sealings
        reports, 275-78
    Kinship reports, 275-78
    labels and cards, 272-73
    Medical Information reports, 275-78
    new Family File, 18-19, 351
    new Family File from DOS file, 19
    new Family File from GEDCOM
        file, 339-44
    new Family File from PAF
        file, 338-39
    Outline Descendant trees, 229-67
    Outline Direct Descendant
        tree, 229-67
    Parentage reports, 275-78
    reports, 275-78
    Scrapbook pages, 147, 278-80
    Scrapbook presentations, 170-71
Cropping
    Picture/Objects, 175-76
Cue Cards
    choosing where they appear, 28-29
    disabling, 25
    preferences for, 28-29
    resetting, 28-29
    using, 25
Cursor movement, 80, 139
Custom Ancestor trees
    characteristics, 231
    defined, 230
    See also Trees
Custom reports
    See Reports
Customer assistance
    how to get, 9
Customer registration, 10
Customizing Family Tree Maker, 25-29,
    78, 79, 86, 88, 91, 152, 202
Cutting
    Picture/Objects in the Scrapbook, 181
    text, 81, 83
    text in the Notes dialog box, 56-7, 81

Data
    checking for errors, 77, 79, 275-78,
        367-75
Data entry checking
    preferences for, 79
    using, 79, 367-75
Data Errors reports
    creating, 275-78
    defined, 367
    explanation of messages, 371-75
    See also Reports
Date field(s), 87-89
Date range
    of a calendar, 331

Date(s)
    changing format of, 88
    default format, 87
    different formats, 87-89
    double, 88
    entering, 87-89
    estimated, 87
    finding and fixing mistakes in, 77, 79,
        275-78, 367-75
    preferences, 88
    printing format in trees, 247-52
    printing format on labels and
        cards, 297-308
    private, 87, 88
    searching for, 123-25
    uncertain, 87
Death of spouse
    recording, 145
Delay
    between played Picture/Objects, 171
Deleting
    Fastfield words, 92
    files, 393
    groups of individuals, 390-91
    individuals, 185
    individuals (in Tutorial), 49
    individuals incorrectly, 95
    information, 83, 92
    Picture/Objects from Scrapbooks, 181
Deluxe Edition, 6, 193, 415
Descendant trees
    characteristics, 236
    creating, 238
    creating and printing, 229-67
    customizing, 239-40
    defined, 232
    example of, 5, 233
    people included in, 232
    print setup, 266-67
    printing, 263-67
    viewing, 238
    See also Trees
Destination file
    defined, 379
Detach
    child from wrong parents, 186
    spouse from wrong spouse, 187

Direct Descendant trees
    defined, 232
    people included in, 232
    See also Descendant trees
    See also Trees
Disease(s)
    recording, 133-34
Disk space
    not enough, 426, 429
    required, 8
Divorces
    recording, 93, 145
DLLs
    problems with, 425
    reinstalling, 431-32
Domestic partners, 93
DOS file
    appending, 379-87
    opening, 19, 351-52
Double date
    changing cutoff year, 88
    defined, 88, 402
    entering, 88
    example of, 402
    shutting off, 88
Dr.
    entering, 134
Drop-down list
    using, 24
Duplicate individuals
    defined, 387
    deleting one, 387-89
    merging, 387-89

Editing
    Fastfields, 92
    in the Notes dialog box, 140
    information, 81-83
    Picture/Objects in Scrapbooks, 172-76
Empty branches
    in ancestor trees, 259
Empty print-outs
    calendars, 334
    Family Group Sheets, 320
    Family Pages, 336
    More About dialog boxes, 337
    trees, 264

English units of measure
    using, 88-9
Entering
    addresses, 132-33
    comments, 130-31
    dates, 87-89
    double dates, 88
    estimated dates, 87
    events, 130-31
    facts, 130-31
    info about children, 94-97
    info about other relatives, 99
    info about Picture/Objects, 164-66
    info in fields, 77
    info in More About dialog boxes, 129-46
    info in More About dialog boxes (in
        Tutorial), 50-58
    info in Scrapbooks, 154-63
    info in the Family Page, 75-102
    info in the Family Page (in
        Tutorial), 36-39
    intermarriages, 100
    last names with suffixes, 85
    locations, 89-90
    marriage information, 93, 145-46
    medical information, 133-34
    missing last names, 85
    multiple marriages, 110-12
    multiple parents, 113-16
    names, 84-85
    nicknames, 85, 134
    Notes, 137-44
    parentage, 134-36
    phone numbers, 133
    Picture/Objects, 154-63
    reference numbers, 134-36
    Roman numerals with names, 85
    sources, 101-2
    stories about a marriage, 145-46
    stories about an individual, 137-44
    unrelated individuals, 100
    unusual last names, 85
Erasing files, 393
Error messages, 417-39, 425-26
Errors
    correcting typos, 83
    finding and fixing, 79, 275-78, 367-75
    ignored, 79, 370
    with relationships, 185-90

Events
    recording, 130-31
Ex-husband
    status field, 145
Ex-wife
    status field, 145
Excluding
    individuals from calendars, 136
    individuals from Kinship
        reports, 136, 292
    individuals from labels and
        cards, 283-90
    individuals from reports, 283-90
    individuals from trees, 136
    Picture/Objects when playing
        Scrapbooks, 170
Exiting
    Family Tree Maker, 72, 376
    the More About dialog boxes, 130
    World Family Tree mode, 217
Exporting
    Family Files, 389
    GEDCOM files, 359-62
    individuals into another file, 390-91
    text from Notes, 144

Facts dialog box, 130-31
Fair Use law, 223-24
Family Archives
    abusive use of, 224
    changing image size in, 212
    check marks, 205
    Contents page, 197
    copying info from into Family
        Files, 210-13, 217
    defined, 6, 193
    getting details about, 206
    Index page, 198-99
    Information page, 200-201
    Introduction page, 196
    legal use, 223-25
    magnifying glass in, 208-9
    merging info to your Family File, 217
    opening, 197, 198, 207
    printing images from, 213
    printing multiple index entries, 205
    problems locating names in, 218
    purchasing, 204, 206, 219

questions about legal use, 223-25
scrolling through an index, 199
searching in, 208-9, 214-15
selecting index entries for printing or
 copying, 205
turning to information in, 197, 198, 217
types, 194
using, 193-219
See also World Family Tree
Family File
 adding World Family Tree info to, 217
 adding Family Archive info to, 210-13
 appending another file to, 379-87
 backing up, 376-77
 combining with another file, 379-87
 copying, 389
 copying Family Archive info to, 210-13, 217
 creating new, 18, 351
 creating with GEDCOM import, 353-58
 creating with PAF import, 352-53
 defined, 75
 deleting, 393
 exporting, 389
 finding, 392-93
 merging with another file, 379-87
 opening, 351-52
 saving, 72
 searching for errors in, 367-75
 status, 393
 submitting to the World Family Tree
  Project, 362-67
Family Group Sheets
 batch printing, 338-47
 customizing, 274
 defined, 273
 entering preparer information, 310
 example of, 7
 font, 298
 formatting items in, 297-308
 formatting text in, 308-9
 including Picture/Objects on, 296
 items to include, 293-96
 page lines, 281
 page numbers, 310-11
 print setup, 266-67
 printing, 273-74, 319-20
 printing format, 316
 titles, 310
 zooming on, 280

Family Page
 child's, 108
 defined, 21-22, 76
 entering information on, 77-102
 example of, 3
 filling out (in Tutorial), 36-40
 finding, 122-25
 garbage characters on, 426
 in World Family Tree mode, 216
 More buttons, 129
 moving from one to another, 105-25
 other parents', 113-16
 other spouse's, 110-12
 parents', 107, 113-16
 print setup, 266-67
 print to file, 336
 printing, 335-36
 sample, 35, 76
 searching for, 122-25
 siblings, 108-9
 Spouses buttons, 110
 tabs on right side of, 105
Family Tree Maker
 Deluxe Edition, 6, 193
 DOS Version, 416
 installing, 13-16
 running slowly, 427-28
 starting, 17-18
Family Tree Maker for DOS file
 appending to Family File, 379-87
 combining with Family File, 379-87
 opening, 351-52
FamilyFinder Index
 check marks, 205
 Contents page, 197
 copying index entries, 205
 defined, 6, 193-94
 Index page, 198-99
 Information page, 200-201
 Introduction page, 196
 magnifying glass in, 203
 opening, 195
 opening Family Archives from, 207
 printing multiple index entries, 206
 problems locating names in, 218
 scrolling through, 199
 searching in, 203-4
 selecting index entries for printing or
  copying, 205
 using, 193-217

FamilyFinder view
   defined, 193
Fastfields
   defined, 90-91
   deleting words from, 92
   preferences for, 91
   turning off or on, 91
Field label(s)
   changing, 78
   defined, 77
   preferences, 78
   printing in trees, 247-52
   printing on labels and cards, 297-98
Field(s)
   beginning status, 93
   changing labels, 78
   children, 84, 94-97
   comment/location, 130-31
   copying from Family
     Archives, 210-11, 217
   date, 87-89
   defined, 77
   divorce, 93, 145
   editing, 81-83
   ending status, 93
   Fastfields, 90-92
   filling automatically, 90-92
   husband, 84, 93
   labels, 77
   location, 89-91
   marriage, 93
   merging, 217, 379-89
   name, 84
   reference number, 135, 146
   sex, 94
   source, 101-2
   wife, 84
File formats
   for pictures in Scrapbooks, 157
   that Family Tree Maker can open, 351
File name format, 7, 18, 19, 351
File(s)
   appending, 379-87
   backing up, 376-77
   combining, 217, 379-87
   copying part of, 390-91
   damaged, 378
   deleting, 393
   destination file defined, 379

   finding, 392-93
   Family Tree Maker for DOS, 351-52
   GEDCOM, 353
   importing into Notes, 143
   in temp directory, 429
   merging, 217, 379-87
   new, 351
   opening, 351-52
   PAF, 352-53
   printing to, 263
   source file defined, 379
   See also Family Files
Filing
   genealogical data, 399
Find and Include button, 288, 329, 344
Find and Remove button, 288, 329, 344
Find Individual
   searching tips, 124-25
   using, 122-25
Find Name
   in the Index of Individuals, 119
Finding
   a picture on a Photo CD, 155
   errors automatically, 77, 79, 275-78,
     367-75
   files, 392-93
   individuals, 122
   individuals in reports, 291
   information, 122
   names in Family
     Archives, 202-4, 208-9
   names in the FamilyFinder
     Index, 202-4
   names in the World Family
     Tree, 214-15
   Picture/Objects in the
     Scrapbook, 167
   someone in your Family
     File, 122, 203-4, 208-9, 214-15
   someone not in your Family
     File, 203-4, 208-9, 214-15
   text in the Notes dialog box, 141
Fit to Page Ancestor trees
   characteristics, 231
   creating and printing, 229-67
   defined, 229
   people included in, 229
   See also Ancestor Trees
   See also Trees

Fixing relationship mistakes, 185-90
Flipping
    Picture/Objects, 174-75
Floating menu, 20
Fonts
    changing in calendars, 332
    changing in Family Group Sheets, 308-9
    changing in labels and cards, 308-9
    changing in Notes, 142
    changing in reports, 308-9
    changing in Scrapbook pages, 308-9
    changing in trees, 253
Footnote
    See Title and Footnote
Formatting
    items in Family Group Sheets, 297-98
    items in reports, 297-98
    items in trees, 247-52
    items on labels and cards, 297-98
    text in calendars, 332
    text in Family Group Sheets, 308-9
    text in Notes, 142
    text in reports, 308-9
    text in trees, 253
    text on labels and cards, 308-9
    text on Scrapbook pages, 308-9
Foster relationships
    entering information about, 94, 113-16, 136
    excluding from trees, 136
    excluding from Kinship reports, 136, 292
Friend
    status field, 93
Full-size
    viewing Picture/Objects at, 168
    See also Zooming

Garbage characters
    printer printing, 424
GEDCOM
    about, 353
    exporting, 359-62
    importing, 353-58
    tag table, 357-58
    tags defined, 355
GEDCOM file
    appending to Family File, 379-87
    merging with Family File, 379-87
Genealogy "How-To" Guide, 6, 25, 220-22

General Protection Fault, 427
Generations
    choosing the number of for Kinship
      reports, 292
    choosing the number of for trees, 242
Go To Page command, 201
Graduation
    entering, 130-31
Grandchildren
    entering information about, 99
Grandparents
    entering information about, 99
Great aunts and uncles
    entering information about, 99
Great-grandparents
    entering information about, 99

Hard disk
    installing Family Tree Maker
      on, 13-16
Height
    of tree, 261
Height of individual, 133
Help
    preferences for, 28-29
    resetting, 28-29
    using Bubble Help, 25
    using Cue Cards, 25
    using the Help System, 25
Highlighting text, 81, 140
Household printing format
    for labels and cards, 316-17
Husband(s)
    entering information about, 84
    multiple, 110-12
    with wrong wife/children, 187
Husband field
    changing label of, 78
    finding mistakes in, 79, 275-78,
      367-75

Icons
    displaying in Scrapbooks, 159, 163
ID number
    See Reference number
Ignored errors, 79, 370
Illogical dates
    in Family File, 367-75

Images
  changing size in Family Archives, 212
  copying from Family Archives to
      Family Files, 210-13
  printing from Family Archives, 213
  See also Picture/Objects
  See also Scrapbooks
Importing
  Family Tree Maker for DOS files, 351-52
  GEDCOM files, 353-58
  info from Family Archives, 210-13, 217
  items into Scrapbooks, 153-63
  PAF files, 352-53
  text into Notes, 143
Inches and feet
  using, 88-9
Include All button, 287, 328, 343
Include button, 28, 244-45, 286, 327, 342
Incomplete Individual Ordinances reports
  creating, 275-78
  See also Reports
Incomplete Marriage Sealings reports
  creating, 275-78
  See also Reports
Incorrect
  child, 186
  documents, 364
  drive, 420
  individual, 185
  information in Family File, 79, 275-78,
      367-75
  spouse, 186-87
Index of Individuals
  alphabetizing, 120
  defined, 117
  example of, 117
  Find Name, 119
  navigating in, 118-19
  opening, 117-18
  printing, 118
  Quick Search, 118
  sorting, 120
  using, 117-21
Index pages
  example of, 198
  in Family Archives, 198-99
  in the Family Finder Index, 198-99
Indexes
  scrolling through, 199

Individual printing format
  for labels and cards, 316
Individual titles (Mr., Dr.)
  See Titles
Individuals
  copying groups to another
      file, 376-77
  deleting groups, 390-91
  excluding from calendars, 136
  excluding from Kinship
      reports, 136, 292
  excluding from trees, 136
  merging duplicates, 387-89
Individuals to Include
  in a batch print, 339-45
  in calendars, 324-30
  in reports, 283-90
  on labels and cards, 283-90
Information
  checking for errors, 77, 79, 275-78,
      367-75
  copying from Family Archives to
      Family Files, 210-13, 217
  editing, 81-83
  entering, 75-102, 129-39, 143-46,
      154-63
  entering sources for, 101-2
  finding, 122-25, 167, 193-217
  merging, 217, 379-89
  possible mistakes in, 79, 275-78,
      367-75
  printing, 204-205, 213, 217 229-67,
      271-320, 323-48
  saving, 72, 376-77
  viewing, 4
Information pages
  example of, 200
  in Family Archives, 200-201
  scrolling through, 201
  types of, 200-201
Inherited addresses, 132
Inserting
  children in a Children list, 98
  OLE objects, 159-62
  Photo CD pictures, 154-56
  pictures from files, 157-58
  text, 81
  See also Picture/Objects

Installing
    CD-ROM version of Family Tree
        Maker, 15
    Family Tree Maker, 13-16
    problems with, 419-21
Intermarriages
    affect on Kinship reports and
        trees, 100
    recording, 100
Introduction pages
    example of, 196
    in Family Archives, 196
    in the FamilyFinder Index, 196
Items to Include
    formatting, 247-52, 297-308
    in calendars, 331
    in Family Group Sheets, 293-94
    in labels and cards, 293-94
    in reports, 293-94
    in Scrapbooks, 293-94
    in trees, 243-46

Jr.
    entering, 85

Kinship reports
    creating, 275-78
    defined, 276
    excluding individuals from, 136
    intermarriage's effect on, 100
    number of generations in, 292
    See also Reports
Kodak Photo CD
    all about, 407-13
    creating, 407
    defined, 149
    guidelines for transferring
        photos, 410-11
    inserting pictures into
        Scrapbooks, 153-56
    Kodak dealer telephone
        numbers, 408-9
    picture compression and
        resolution, 178-79
    picture file size, 413
    transferring photos to, 407
    using with Family Tree Maker, 153-56, 409

Label(s)
    changing, 78
    field, 77
    preferences, 78
    printing for empty fields, 307
Labels and cards
    address inheritance, 132, 295
    alphabetizing, 318
    border styles, 313
    customizing, 273
    default titles for individuals, 86
    entering addresses for, 132-33
    font, 298
    formatting items in, 297-98
    formatting text in, 308-9
    including Picture/Objects
        on, 295, 300-302
    including sources on, 303
    individuals to include, 283-90
    items to include, 293-96
    line styles, 313
    location of Picture/Objects on, 301
    missing Picture/Objects, 302
    page lines, 281
    print setup, 282-83
    printing, 272-73, 319-20
    printing for households or
        individuals, 316-17
    selecting individuals to
        include, 283-90
    selecting the size, 282-83
    sorting, 318
    titles for individuals (Mr., Dr.), 134
    using mouse in, 281
    width of Picture/Objects, 314
    zooming on, 280
Land records, 401
Large trees
    printing on plotters, 265
    reducing size of, 261-62
Last name(s)
    entering, 84-85
    missing, 85
    multiple-word, 85
    with suffixes, 85
Layout
    for box-style trees, 255-56
    for outline-style trees, 256-58
    in printed Scrapbooks, 312

LDS
    ordinance information, 405-6
    using LDS date codes, 88
    using LDS format, 78, 405
Libraries, 400
Lineage dialog box
    individual titles (Mr., Dr.), 134
    Reference number field, 134-35
    recording special parent/child
        relationships in, 134-36
    using, 134-36
Lines
    in boxes, 244
    page, 241, 281, 323-24
    styles for labels and cards, 313
    styles for reports, 313
    styles for Scrapbooks, 313
    styles for trees, 254
Local records, 401
Location(s)
    entering, 89-91
    fields, 89
    names and boundary changes, 404
    selecting printing format, 247-52, 297-98
    using Fastfields, 90-92

M.D.
    entering, 85
Magnifying glass
    in Family Archives, 208-9
    in the FamilyFinder Index, 203
    in the World Family Tree, 214
Maiden names
    when to use, 84
Mailing labels
    See Labels and cards
Mailing lists, 10
Making backups of your Family
    File, 376-77
Margins
    changing, 267
Marriage
    banns, 364
    fields, 93
    intermarriages, 100
    multiple, 110-12
    multiple (in Tutorial), 45-6
    private information, 93, 145

Marriage dialog box
    marriage ending status, 145
    Notes, 146
    reference number, 146
    using, 145-46
Marriage reports
    creating, 275-78
    See also Reports
Marriage Scrapbook
    See Scrapbooks
Married name
    entered instead of maiden name, 372
    including in calendars, 331
    including in reports, 297-98
    including in trees, 248
    including on labels and cards, 297
    See also Name(s)
Medical dialog box
    Cause of death field, 134
    Height field, 133
    Medical Information field, 134
    using, 133-34
    Weight field, 134
Medical information
    recording, 133-34
Medical Information reports
    creating, 275-78
    See also Reports
Memory
    cache, 26-27
    error messages, 430
    physical RAM, 412-13
    required for importing
        pictures, 413
Menu
    pull-down, 77
    secondary mouse button, 20
Menu bar, 35, 77
Merging
    appending all information, 387
    destination file defined, 379
    duplicate individuals, 387-89
    files, 379-87
    mapping information between
        files, 380-81
    merging with confirmation, 385-86
    source file defined, 379
    viewing Merge reports, 384
    World Family Tree pedigrees, 217

Messages
    error messages, 425-26
    on Data Errors Report, 371-75
Metafile
    creating, 348
    defined, 348
Metric units of measure
    using, 88-89
Microsoft Windows, 20-24
Microsoft Windows "95", 8, 13
Missing
    last names, 85
    Picture/Objects in trees, 250
    Picture/Objects on labels and
        cards, 302
Mistakes
    correcting typos, 36, 82
    finding and fixing, 77, 79, 275-78,
        367-75
    finding with auto error checking, 77
    in Family File, 79, 275-78, 367-75
    relationship, 185-90
More About dialog boxes
    Address dialog box, 132-33
    changing labels in, 78
    defined, 129-30
    entering information in (in
        Tutorial), 50-58
    example of, 3
    exiting, 130
    Facts dialog box, 130-31
    Lineage dialog box, 134-36
    Marriage dialog box, 145-46
    Medical dialog box, 133-34
    navigating in, 130
    Notes dialog box, 137-44
    print setup, 266-67
    printing, 307, 336-37
    using, 129-46
    See also Notes dialog box
More About Picture/Object dialog
    box, 164-66
Mouse
    using in labels and cards, 281
    using in reports, 281
    using in Scrapbooks, 168
    using in trees, 241
    using on the Family Page, 77

Moving
    around in a World Family
        Tree, 216-17
    around in Family Archives, 195
    around in Notes dialog box, 139
    around in Scrapbooks, 168-69
    around in the FamilyFinder
        Index, 195
    between Family Pages, 105-25
    between fields, 80
    children in Children list, 98
    in the Index of Individuals, 118-19
    Picture/Objects between
        Scrapbooks, 180
    text between Notes dialog
        boxes, 140
    text in the Notes dialog box, 81
    the cursor, 80
Moving to
    Family Pages of children, 108
    Family Pages of other
        parents, 113-16
    Family Pages of other
        spouses, 110-12
    Family Pages of parents, 107
    Family Pages of siblings, 108-9
    More About dialog boxes, 129
    other Family Pages, 105-25
    Scrapbooks, 148
Multiple
    sets of parents, 113-16
    spouses, 110-12

Name changes, 85
Name(s)
    entering, 84-85
    entering titles, 85
    entering unusual surnames, 85
    finding and fixing mistakes
        in, 77, 79, 275-78, 367-75
    format in calendars, 331
    format in Family Group
        Sheets, 297-98
    format in reports, 297-98
    format in trees, 247-48
    format on labels and cards, 297-98
    hyphenated married, 135
    missing last names, 85

Name(s), *continued*
    nicknames, 134-35
    printing, 84
    printing format in trees, 247-48
    problems locating in Family
        Archives, 218
    searching for, 118, 119, 122-23
    searching for in Family Archives,
        208-9, 214-15
    searching for in reports, 291
    searching for in the FamilyFinder
        Index, 203-4
    selecting printing format, 247-48,
        297-98, 316-17, 331
    using Fastfields, 90-92
    using Roman numerals with, 85
    with suffixes, 85
    See also Titles
Natural parental relationships
    adding, 94, 113-16, 136
    entering information about, 94
    excluding from Kinship reports, 292
    excluding from trees, 136
New Family File
    creating, 18, 351
Nicknames
    entering, 134-35
    entering (in Tutorial), 52-53
    in the Index of Individuals, 118
    including in calendars, 331
    including in trees, 247-48
    including on labels and cards, 297-98
Note-taking, 397-98
Notes, 137-44
Notes dialog box
    batch printing, 338-47
    copying text in, 81
    editing text in, 140
    exporting text to another
        program, 144
    finding text in, 141
    for a marriage, 146
    formatting text in, 142
    importing text from another
        program, 143
    moving around in, 139
    moving text, 140
    pasting text into, 81
    printing (in Tutorial), 58

    printing information from, 336-37
    rearranging text in, 81
    sample of, 137
    undeleting text in, 82
    using, 137-44
    using (in Tutorial), 54-58
    what you can do in, 137
Number(s)
    Ahnentafel, 246, 248, 251
    for generations in Outline trees, 256-57
    of generations in Kinship reports, 292
    of generations in trees, 242
    reference, 134-36, 146
    searching for, 124
    Standard, 246, 248, 251

Object Linking and Embedding
    defined, 150-51
    See also Scrapbooks
OLE objects
    creating a show from, 170-71
    editing, 176
    playing, 170-71
    See also Scrapbooks
Opening
    backups, 378
    Family Archives, 195, 197, 198, 207
    Family Files, 351-52
    Family Tree Maker for DOS
        files, 19, 351-52
    FamilyFinder Index, 195
    GEDCOM files, 353-58
    More About dialog boxes, 129
    new Family File, 351
    PAF files, 352-53
    the Index of Individuals, 117-18
    World Family Tree pedigrees, 216
Option buttons
    using, 24
Ordering
    Family Archives, 204, 206, 219
    products, 10
Org Plus, 416
Other parents, 113-16
Other products
    Biography Maker, 415
    Family Tree Maker Deluxe
        Edition, 415

Family Tree Maker DOS
    Version, 416
    Org Plus, 416
    Uncle Sam's Budget Balancer, 416
Other spouses, 110-12
Other spouses (in Tutorial), 45
Outline Descendant trees
    characteristics, 236
    creating, 238-39
    creating and printing, 229-67
    customizing, 239-40
    defined, 234
    example of, 235
    formatting options, 256-58
    print setup, 266-67
    printing, 263-67
    viewing, 238
    See also Trees
Outline Direct Descendant trees
    defined, 234
    people included in, 234
    See also Outline Descendant trees
    See also Trees
Overlapping pages, 267

PAF file
    combining with Family File, 379-87
    exporting to, 389
    importing, 352-53
Page
    margins, 267
    numbers in a batch print, 346
    numbers in Family Group Sheets, 310
    numbers in Outline Descendant
        Trees, 254-55
    numbers in reports, 310-11
    numbers in Scrapbooks, 310-11
Page lines
    showing, 241, 281, 323-24
Paper
    continuous forms, 267
    orientation, 266
    size, 267
    source, 267
Parchment paper, 416
Parentage reports
    creating, 275-78
    See also Reports

Parents
    age mistakes with, 367-75
    displaying Family Page of, 107
    displaying Family Page of other, 115
    more than two, 113-16
    multiple sets of, 113-16
    selecting preferred, 116
    sharing addresses with, 132
Parents' Family Page
    how to get to, 107
Partner
    status field, 93
Pasting
    items into other applications, 348
    Picture/Objects into the Scrapbook,
        162-63
    text, 81, 83
    text in the Notes dialog box, 57, 81
Pedigree tree
    defined, 4
    from World Family Tree, 214-17
    See also Ancestor trees
Personal titles (Mr., Dr.)
    See Titles
Phone number(s) field, 133
Photo CD
    See Kodak Photo CD
Photo trees
    printing, 244
    See also Picture/Objects
    See also Trees
Physical characteristics
    recording, 133-34
Picture/Objects
    brightness, 177-78
    compression, 178-79
    contrast, 177-78
    copying, 180
    creating in Family Tree Maker, 348
    cropping, 175-76
    defined, 149-51
    deleting from the Scrapbook, 181
    disk space required, 178-79, 413
    displaying icons instead
        of, 159-60, 162-63
    editing, 172-76
    editing OLE objects, 176
    finding, 167
    flipping, 174-75

Picture/Objects, *continued*
    including in Family Group
        Sheets, 293-94
    including in trees, 243-46, 249-50
    including on labels and
        cards, 293-94, 300-2
    mirroring, 174
    missing, 250, 302
    moving, 180
    not displayed clearly, 426
    not printing clearly, 423
    playing, 170, 171
    quality of, 152, 178-79
    resolution, 178-79
    rotating, 174
    selecting to play in show, 170
    selecting to print, 164-66
    time delay between, 171
    troubles with playing, 431
    types, 165
    viewing at larger sizes, 168
    width of in trees, 258
    width of on labels and cards, 314
    See also Scrapbooks
Pictures
    defined, 149
Playing
    Picture/Objects, 170, 171
    Scrapbooks, 170-71
Plotters
    printing trees on, 265
Predefined reports
    See Reports
Preferences
    data entry checking, 79
    dates, 88
    defined, 26
    FamilyFinder, 202
    Fastfields, 91
    field labels, 78
    Help, 28-29
    Scrapbooks, 152
    Search Expert, 202
    startup, 26-27
    titles, 86
    units of measure, 88-89
Preferred parents
    defined, 116
    selecting, 116

Preferred Picture/Objects, 164-66
Preferred spouse
    defined, 112
    selecting, 112
Preparer information
    entering on Family Group Sheets, 310
Primary individual
    changing in labels and cards, 281
    changing in reports, 281
    changing in trees, 241
    defined, 148, 237, 238
    selecting, 237, 238
Print setup
    changing, 266-67
    for all items except labels and
        cards, 266-67
    for labels and cards, 282-83
    problems with, 432-33
Printer
    choosing, 266
    not printing, 423
Printer file
    not printing, 424
Printing
    address labels, 272-73
    adopted children, 134-36
    Ancestor trees, 229-67
    Ancestor trees with photos, 244
    batch printing, 338-47
    blank rows in tree boxes, 244
    calendars, 333-34
    Descendant trees, 229-67
    Descendant trees with photos, 244
    Direct Descendant trees, 229-67
    empty branches, 259
    empty calendars, 334
    empty Family Group Sheets, 320
    empty Family Pages, 336
    empty trees, 264
    Family Group Sheets, 273-74, 319-20
    Family Pages, 335-36
    foster children, 134-36
    from a World Family Tree
        pedigree, 216-17
    garbage characters, 424
    images from Family Archives, 213
    index entries, 205-6
    Index of Individuals, 118
    labels and cards, 272-73, 319-20

lines in tree boxes, 244
mailing labels, 272-73
More About dialog boxes, 307
More About information in
    documents, 336-37
names, 84
Notes, 336-37
on continuous forms, 267
Outline Descendant trees, 229-67
Outline Direct Descendant
    trees, 229-67
Picture/Objects in trees, 243
Picture/Objects on labels and
    cards, 295
print to file, 263, 320
problems with, 421-24
reports, 275-78, 319-20
Scrapbook pages, 278-80, 319-20
selected Family Archive Index
    entries, 205-6
siblings in Ancestor trees, 259
sources in trees, 248
spouse of primary individual, 245
symbols for text, 422
text outside boxes, 424
too slowly, 421
trees, 263-67
trees (in Tutorial), 66-71
trees on plotters, 265
World Family Tree pedigrees, 216-17
Private
    dates, 88
    relationship information, 136
    marriage information, 93, 145
Probate records, 401
Problems
    installing Family Tree Maker, 419-21
    using Family Tree Maker, 417-39
    with a CD-ROM, 428
    with your computer, 427-28
    with your display (monitor), 426
    with print setup, 432-33
    with printing, 421-24
Product support, 9
Products
    purchasing, 10, 219, 415-16
Pull-down menu
    using, 35, 77
    See also Secondary mouse button menu

Purchasing
    Family Archives, 204, 206, 219
    other products, 415-16

Quick Search
    in Index of Individuals, 118
    in reports, 291
    See also Find Individual
Quitting Family Tree Maker, 72, 376

RAM
    requirements, 8, 418
Rearranging
    children, 98-99
    individuals in a batch print, 339
    labels and cards, 318
    Picture/Objects in
        Scrapbooks, 180, 318
    reports, 318
    Scrapbooks, 171
Rearranging the Index of Individuals, 120
Recording sources, 101-2
Record(s)
    accessing with Family Tree
        Maker, 193-220
    cemetery, 401
    census, 193
    church, 401
    copying from Family Archives to
        Family Files, 210-13
    land, 193, 401
    local, 401
    marriage, 193
    probate, 401
    vital, 401
Reference number
    entering, 135, 146
    including in trees, 248
Reference number field, 135, 146
Registration
    customer, 10
Reinstalling DLLs, 431-32
Relationship
    annulment, 145
    beginning status, 93
    death of spouse, 145
    degree, 276
    divorce, 145

Relationship, *continued*
    ending status, 145
    mistakes, 185-90, 371
    private information, 136, 145
    special with children, 113-16, 134-36
Remove All button, 287, 294, 328, 343
Remove button, 28, 244, 286, 294,
    327, 342
Removing
    individual(s) from a file, 185, 390-91
    individuals from groups, 283-90,
        324-30, 339-45
    info from trees, 243-46
    Picture/Objects from Scrapbooks, 181
    siblings, 186
    See also Deleting
Reports
    Address reports, 275-78
    alphabetizing, 318
    Birthday reports, 275-78
    border styles, 313-14
    column width in, 315
    creating, 275-78
    Custom reports, 275-78
    customizing, 278
    Data Errors report, 275-78, 367, 371
    finding individuals in, 291
    formatting items in, 297-308
    formatting names in, 297
    formatting text in, 308-9
    Incomplete Individual Ordinances
        reports, 275-78
    Incomplete Marriage Sealings
        reports, 275-78
    individuals to include, 283-90
    items to include, 293-96
    Kinship reports, 275-78
    line styles, 313-14
    Medical Information reports, 275-78
    page lines, 281
    page numbers, 310-11
    print setup, 266-67
    Parentage reports, 275-78
    printing, 275-78, 319-20
    sorting names in, 318
    spacing between columns in, 315
    titles, 310-11
    using mouse in, 281
    zooming on, 280

Requesting information, 402
Requirements
    system, 8, 418
Research
    sources, 193-222, 399-401
    tips for, 399-401
Resolution
    of Picture/Objects, 152, 178-79
Resources
    problems with, 430
Retrieving
    backups, 378
    Family Files, 351-52
Reverend
    entering, 134
Roman numerals
    using with names, 85
Rotating
    Picture/Objects, 174
Row labels
    including in trees, 259

Saving
    a portion of your file, 390-91
    See also Backups
Scanning
    defined, 150
Scrapbook layout
    defined, 312
Scrapbook Print Preview, 279
Scrapbooks
    alphabetizing, 171, 318
    arranging, 171
    batch printing, 338-47
    borders, 313-14
    brightness, 177-78
    compression, 152, 178
    copying Picture/Objects, 180
    creating, 147-81
    cropping Picture/Objects, 175-76
    customizing, 279
    defined, 129
    deleting Picture/Objects from, 181
    disk space required, 178-79
    displaying icons in, 159, 163
    editing OLE objects, 176
    editing Picture/Objects, 172-76
    example of, 3
    finding Picture/Objects, 167

flipping Picture/Objects, 174
font, 308-9
format, 312
formatting, 279
formatting text in, 308-9
image editing, 172-76
inserting items from Family Tree
    Maker, 348
inserting items from Family Archives, 212
inserting items into, 153-63
inserting OLE objects, 159-61
inserting Photo CD pictures, 154-56
inserting picture files, 157-58
inserting sounds and videos in, 150-51,
    153, 159-60, 160-61
items to include, 293-96
Kodak Photo CD defined, 149
line styles, 313-14
mirroring Picture/Objects, 174
More About Picture/Object dialog
    box, 164-66
moving around in, 168-69
moving Picture/Objects, 180
Object Linking and Embedding
    defined, 150
opening, 148
page lines, 281
page numbers, 310-11
page turning, 168
pasting items from the
    Clipboard, 161-63
pasting OLE objects from the
    Clipboard, 162-63
picture compression, 178-79
picture file formats, 157
picture resolution, 178-79
Picture/Object brightness, 177-78
Picture/Objects defined, 149-51
playing OLE objects, 170, 171
preferences, 152
print setup, 266-67
printed layout, 312
printing, 319-20
printing Picture/Objects, 164-66,
    293-96, 317
rearranging, 171
resolution, 178
resolution of Picture/Objects, 152
rotating Picture/Objects, 174
sample page, 147

scanned images, 150
selecting items in, 168-69
sorting, 171, 318
text, 151
titles, 310-11
troubles with playing, 431
tutorial, 59-66
using, 147-81
viewing pictures at larger sizes, 168,
    170-71
working with Picture/Objects, 164-81
zooming on, 280
Scroll bars
    using, 23
Scroll to name field, 201
Search Expert
    defined, 193
    using, 202-4
Searching
    for a picture on a Photo CD, 155
    for dates, 123-24
    for files, 392-93
    for mistakes in Family File, 367-75
    for names in Family File, 122-23
    for names in Family Archives, 208-9
    for names in the FamilyFinder
        Index, 203-4
    for names in the World Family
        Tree, 214-15
    for other items, 123-24
    for Picture/Objects in a
        Scrapbook, 167
    for someone in your Family
        File, 203-4, 208-9, 214-15
    for someone not in your Family
        File, 203-4, 208-9, 214-15
    for text in the Notes dialog box, 141
    in reports, 291
    in the Index of Individuals, 118-19
    tips, 124-25
    using Soundex codes, 202
Secondary individual
    defined, 238
    selecting, 238
Secondary mouse button menu, 20
Selecting
    date format, 87-89
    index entries, 205
    individuals to print in a batch
        print, 339-48

Selecting, *continued*
    individuals to print in calendars,
        324-30
    individuals to print in reports,
        283-90
    individuals to print on labels and
        cards, 283-90
    info to print in calendars, 331
    info to print in Custom reports,
        293-94
    info to print in Family Group
        Sheets, 293-94
    info to print in trees, 243-46
    info to print on labels and cards,
        293-94
    info to print on Scrapbook pages,
        293-94
    LDS format, 78, 405-6
    number of generations to print
        in Kinship reports, 292
    number of generations to print
        in trees, 242
    text, 81, 140
    the primary individual, 237-38
    the secondary individual, 238
Separations
    recording, 145
Setting up
    Family Tree Maker, 13-16
    printers, 266-67
Sex
    changing, 94
    recording, 94
Share
    deleting, 438-39
    loading, 425, 438
Sharing your Family File, 362-67, 389
Shrinking your tree, 261-62
Siblings
    defined, 108-9
    displaying Family Page of, 108-9
    printing in Ancestor trees, 259
    See also Children
Size
    maximum for trees, 231, 236
    of paper, 267
    of print area, 266-67
    of Picture/Objects in trees, 258
    of your tree, 261-62

Size on screen
    See Zooming
Sorting
    a batch print, 339
    children, 99
    labels and cards, 318
    reports, 318
    Scrapbooks, 171, 318
    the Index of Individuals, 120
Soundex
    defined, 202
Sounds
    inserting in Scrapbooks, 150-51, 153,
        159-61
    playing, 170-171
Source file
    defined, 379
Sources
    entering, 101-2
    genealogical information, 399-401
    including on labels and cards, 303
    recording, 101-2
Spouses
    attaching, 189-90
    creating multiple, 110-11
    creating multiple (in Tutorial), 44-5
    detaching incorrect spouses, 187-88
    including in outline-style
        trees, 246, 260
    more than one, 110-12
    more than one (in Tutorial), 44-5
    printing in same box, 245
    selecting preferred, 112
    sharing addresses with, 132
Spouses buttons, 110
Sr.
    entering, 85
Standard numbers (Ahnentafel), 248
    creating, 251
    defined, 245-46
    including in trees, 248
Starting Family Tree Maker, 17-18
Startup preferences, 26-27
State or province field, 132
Statistics
    printing in trees, 252
Status field
    beginning, 93
    ending, 145

Step- relationships
    entering information about, 94, 113-16, 136
    excluding from Kinship reports,
        136, 292
    excluding from trees, 136, 292
Stories
    entering in Notes, 137-44
Storing your diskette(s), 13
Submitting a file to the World Family
    Tree Project, 362-67
Subtitle and footnote
    See Title and footnote
Suffixes
    on last names, 85
Surname(s)
    See Last name(s)
Symbols
    printing problems with, 422
System locking up, 427
System requirements, 8, 418
System resources
    how to check, 430
    problems with, 430

Tabs
    using on Family Page, 107-9
Technical support, 9
Temp directory, 429
Text
    copying from Family Archives to
        Family Files, 210-11
    cutting, copying, and pasting, 81
    entering in Marriage Notes, 146
    entering in Notes, 137-44
    exporting from Notes, 144
    formatting in the Notes dialog box, 142
    importing into Notes, 143
    in Scrapbooks, 151
    printer printing outside boxes, 424
    printer printing without boxes, 422
    printing incorrectly, 422
Text styles
    selecting for calendars, 332
    selecting for Family Group Sheets, 308-9
    selecting for labels and cards, 308-9
    selecting for reports, 308-9
    selecting for Scrapbook pages, 308-9
    selecting in Notes, 142
    selecting in trees, 253

Thumbnail
    defined, 156, 172
Time delay
    between played Picture/Objects, 171
Title and footnote
    in calendars, 332-33
    in Family Group Sheets, 310-11
    in reports, 310-11
    in trees, 254-55
Title and page numbers
    in Scrapbooks, 310-11
Titles for individuals
    changing, 86, 134
    cutoff age for using, 86
    defaults, 86
    entering, 85
    on labels and cards, 297-98
    preferences for, 86
    special, 134
Toolbar, 77
Transferring data
    from Notes, 144
    from Family Archives to a
        Family File, 210-13, 217
    in ASCII format, 143, 144
    into Notes, 143
    through GEDCOM, 353-62
Trash can button, 92
Tree size
    controlling, 261-62
    limit, 261-62
Trees
    borders, 254
    box connections, 255-56
    box style, 254
    box width, 258
    centering, 255-56
    color, 254, 264
    column labels in, 259
    connecting lines, 254
    copying as Metafiles, 348
    copying to the Clipboard, 348
    customizing, 239-40
    enlarging, 240
    example of, 230, 233
    excluding individuals from, 136
    fitting on one page, 261-62
    font in, 253
    footnotes in, 254-55
    format, 255, 256

Trees, *continued*
    format of names in, 247-48
    including duplicate ancestors, 259
    including duplicate descendants, 259, 260
    including nicknames in, 247-48
    including Picture/Objects in, 249-50
    including reference numbers in, 248
    including row labels, 259
    including siblings, 259
    including sources in, 248
    items to include in, 243-46
    layout for box-style trees, 255-56
    layout for outline-style trees, 256-58
    limit on size, 261-62
    line style, 254
    making boxes the same size, 255-56
    missing Picture/Objects, 250
    multiple page, 261-62
    number of generations, 242
    other printing options, 259-60
    page lines, 241
    Picture/Object width, 258
    print setup, 266-67
    print to file, 263
    printing, 263-64
    printing (in Tutorial), 66-71
    printing color, 264
    printing empty, 264
    printing on plotters, 265
    printing spouse of primary individual, 245
    selecting border styles, 254
    selecting box styles, 254
    selecting items to include in, 243-46
    selecting items to include in (in Tutorial), 69
    selecting line styles, 254
    selecting text styles, 253
    sets of, 264
    size, 261-62
    size limit, 231, 236
    titles in, 254-55
    types of, 229-36
    varying box sizes, 255-56
    World Family Tree, 362-67
    zooming on, 240
Troubleshooting, 417-39
Tutorial, 33-72

Types
    of forms, 398-99
    of trees, 229-36
    selecting for Picture/Objects, 164-66
Typing modes, 26-27

Uncertain dates, 87-8
Uncle Sam's Budget Balancer, 416
Uncles
    entering information about, 99
Undelete, 82-3
Undo, 82-3
Units of measure
    preferences, 88-9
Unknown dates, 87-8
Unrelated individuals
    entering, 100
Upgrade plan, 10

Videos
    inserting in Scrapbooks, 150-51, 153, 159-161
    locating, 431
    playing, 170, 171
    troubles with playing, 431
    watching, 170, 171
Viewing
    pictures at full size, 168
    videos, 170
Views, 4, 67, 76, 121
Vital records
    finding, 401
Vshare
    deleting, 438-39
    loading, 425, 438
    troubleshooting, 438-39

Weight field, 134
Width
    box width in trees, 258
    column width in reports, 315
    of tree, 262
    Picture/Object width in labels and cards, 314
    Picture/Object width in trees, 258

Wife
    entering information about, 84
    multiple, 110-12
    with wrong children/husband, 187
Wife field
    finding mistakes in, 79, 275-78, 367-75
    changing label of, 78
Windows, 20-24
Windows "95"
    installing under, 16
    using, 8, 13
Word wrapping
    in trees, 248, 251
World Family Tree
    check marks, 205
    described, 362
    getting details about, 215
    Information pages, 201
    magnifying glass in, 214
    merging with a Family File, 217
    moving around in, 216-17
    opening a pedigree, 216
    printing multiple index entries, 205, 206
    printing pedigrees from, 216-17
    printing other documents from. 216-17
    privacy issues, 363
    quality of information in, 364
    searching in, 214-15
    selecting index entries for printing or
        copying, 205
    submission instructions, 365-67
    submitter rights, 366-67
    turning to a pedigree, 216-17
    using World Family Tree mode, 216-17
World Family Tree Archives
    See Family Archives
    See also World Family Tree
Wrong parents
    detaching children from, 186
Wrong spouses
    detaching from each other, 187

Zip or postal code field, 132
Zooming
    images in Family Archives, 212
    on calendars, 323
    on Family Group Sheets, 280
    on labels and cards, 280
    on Picture/Objects, 168
    on reports, 280
    on Scrapbook pages, 280
    on Scrapbooks, 280
    on trees, 240

NOTES

NOTES

NOTES

NOTES

Get Your Free CompuServe Introductory Membership Today!

Start connecting with Brøderbund Software and other CompuServe® members by completing and returning this reply card, or call 800-524-3388 and ask for Representative #194. (In the United Kingdom, call 0800 289 378. In Germany, call 0130 37 32. In the rest of Europe, call (+49) (89) 66 55 0-111. Outside the U.S., Canada, and Europe, call 614-529-1349. Be sure to ask for Representative #194.) If you're already a CompuServe member, enter BBFORUM at any ! prompt to access the Brøderbund Software forum on CompuServe.

YES! Send me my Free CompuServe Introductory Membership!

Name: _____

Position: _____

Company: _____

Address: _____

_____

City: _____ State: _____ Zip: _____

Country: _____ Daytime Phone: _____

Please fold in half, tape closed, and return. No postage necessary.

NO POSTAGE
NECESSARY IF
MAILED IN THE
UNITED STATES

BUSINESS REPLY MAIL
FIRST CLASS MAIL   PERMIT NO. 407   COLUMBUS, OHIO

POSTAGE WILL BE PAID BY ADDRESSEE

COMPUSERVE INFORMATION SERVICE
DEPARTMENT 194
5000 ARLINGTON CENTRE BLVD
PO BOX 20212
COLUMBUS OH 43220-9988

I own: ☐ Family Tree Maker for Windows   Serial
☐ Family Tree Maker Deluxe CD-ROM Edition   Number _____

Family Tree Maker™ Accessories Order Form

	PRICE x QTY	DISKETTE	TOTAL
Family Tree Maker Deluxe CD-ROM Edition*			
Full Product (Makes a great gift!)	$44.99 x _____		$_____
Upgrade from Windows or DOS	$29.99 x 1 (only)		$_____
Biography Maker** (DOS)	$29.99 x _____	🖫 or 🖬 (circle one)	$_____
Parchment Paper Pack (75 sheets)	$12.99 x _____		$_____

*Family Tree Maker Deluxe CD-ROM Edition requires a CD-ROM drive. All other system requirements are the same as Family Tree Maker for Windows.

**Biography Maker requires a hard disk, OR any high density drive, OR two 3 ½" disk drives.

Shipping / Handling (allow 7-10 working days) $ __4.00__
Outside Continental US add $5.00 $_____
Subtotal $_____
Sales Tax (AZ, CA, FL, GA, IL, MA, MN, NJ, OH, PA, TX, UT) $_____
Order Total $_____

Name _____
Shipping Address _____
City _____ State _____ Zip _____
Country _____ Daytime Phone _____
☐ Visa   ☐ MC   ☐ AmEx   ☐ Discover   ☐ Check (drawn on a US Bank in US funds ONLY)
Card Number _____ Exp. Date _____
Name on Card _____ Signature _____

Send to: Brøderbund Software, Banner Blue Division, PO Box 6125, Novato, CA 94948-6125
OR Fax: 1-415-382-4419
Orders are generally shipped within 48 hours of receipt (if in stock).   *Thank You For Your Order!*

I own: ☐ Family Tree Maker for Windows   Serial
☐ Family Tree Maker Deluxe CD-ROM Edition   Number _____

Change of Address Card

If you have changed your address, please fill out this card and return it to us. You won't want to miss information on future products and enhancements.

Old Address Information (please print legibly or type)
Name _____
Address _____
City _____ State _____ Zip _____
Country _____ Daytime Phone _____

New Address Information
Name _____
Address _____
City _____ State _____ Zip _____
Country _____ Daytime Phone _____

Send to: Brøderbund Software, Banner Blue Division, PO Box 6125, Novato, CA 94948-6125
OR Fax: 1-415-382-4419
FTW/D

Don't Let Your Family Stories Fade Away!

New Biography Maker™ helps record your family stories the easy way

Biography Maker is the perfect tool for the family history enthusiast who wants to write biographies about relatives or an autobiography about himself. It offers an extensive selection of historical information and personal topics to help you create a collection of your family stories. In fact, you will probably learn much about your relatives just by using the program. There's no better way to help you recall all those wonderful family stories you want to preserve.

Creates custom writing guides fast

Biography Maker is so smart, it creates a customized list of Writing Ideas for each relative you write about. All you have to do is provide the program with a few dates and answer some yes-no questions about the subject of your biography. Then Biography Maker searches through its database to find Writing Ideas that are appropriate to the person you are writing about.

Your own personal research assistant

Since Biography Maker knows that each person is a unique individual, the Writing Ideas it presents for a farmer who lived in the late 1800's will be entirely different than the Writing Ideas it presents for a nurse who lived in the mid 1900's. It's just like having your own research assistant. Both historical and personal Writing Ideas are presented together — in chronological order. So the list of Writing Ideas serves as a ready-made outline for your book. With this kind of help, all you have to concentrate on is telling the story.

Make a family keepsake to last for generations

Whether you want to write a complete overview of a life or just concentrate on a few important events, Biography Maker turns family history into a fun project. And the rewards are great. The biographies you create with Biography Maker are sure to become family treasures.

Just select topics you want to write about...

Then, while you write, you can view the detailed writing ideas of each topic. See the back of this brochure to view some of the writing ideas from the "Family Traditions" topic.

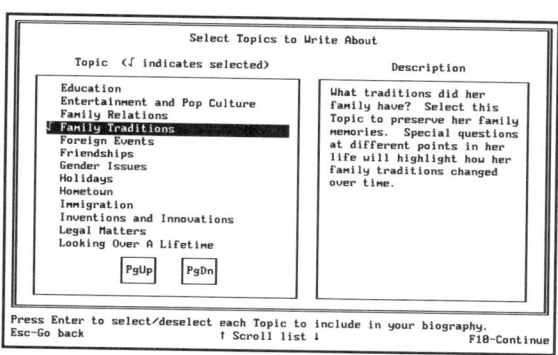

Some of the many topics covered...

Biography Maker takes an in-depth look at the events that shaped your relatives' lives. It includes over 80 topics and more than 5,500 Writing Ideas.

Raising A Family
Marriage
Traveling
Inventions and Innovations
Military Service
Birth of Children
Relationships and Dating
Education
Wall Street Crash
Great Depression
U.S. Expansion
U.S. Exploration
JFK's Assassination
World War I
Foreign Events

Friendships
Recreation
Prohibition Era
Family Traditions
Personal Finances
World War II
Personal Politics
Entertainment
Personality and Values
Religion
Medical History
Ancestry
Natural Disasters
and many more!

Features

- Autobiographies, too!
- Imports text files (in ASCII)
- Exports text files (in ASCII)
- Built-in word processor
- Automatic Table of Contents creation
- Writes scripts for video or audio histories
- Automatic cover page design
- User's Guide that includes writing tips and inspiration

(continued on other side)

How does it work?

Writing Ideas appear on-screen to help you while you write. You can also print lists of Writing Ideas to use as research guides when you're away from your computer.

Since each topic in Biography Maker is so complete, it is hard to show on paper what it's like to browse through the numerous Writing Ideas of a whole topic. But the pictures to the right will give you an idea of how Biography Maker works.

The upper portion of each picture displays a few of the 50 Writing Ideas that make up the topic "Family Traditions." The lower portion of each picture displays a sample biography in progress. Notice how the Writing Ideas helped the writer recapture some special moments in Gayle's life. With so many Writing Ideas right at your fingertips, you'll never be at a loss for words!

Writes scripts for video histories, too!

A video-taped interview of an older relative is a terrific way to pass your family heritage on to future generations. And Biography Maker is ideal for making scripts for a video-taped interview. Just give the program a few facts about the relative, choose some topics, and Biography Maker will print your script.

System requirements

- IBM PC, AT, XT, or compatible
- 512KB RAM
- DOS version 2.1 or higher
- Microsoft compatible mouse (optional)
- Hard disk, OR any high density drive, OR two 3 ½" disk drives

1

Each group of Writing Ideas sparks your creativity and helps you write.

```
 ┌ Writing Idea ─────────────────────────────────────────
 What traditions did she and her family have?  Did they eat special foods on
 special days?  Did they make a point of spending time together on certain
 days?

 ┌ Biography of Gayle Barbara Jansen ────────────────────
 Like most children, Gayle especially loved the days and weeks surrounding
 Christmas.  Gayle's mother was from a big, French-Canadian family, the
 Chamberland clan.  Her father was from a big Norwegian family, the
 Jansens.  That meant there were plenty of relatives around to help
 celebrate the holiday.  And it also meant there was a fantastic collection
 of special Christmas time meals and sweets.

 One of Gayle's favorite memories from her childhood was the making of
 Norwegian rosette cookies.  The cookies were made by dipping a special iron
 into a pot of hot oil...

 └ Normal ──────────────────────────────── Row 11 Col 25 ─
 F9-Menu          Esc-Previous Writing Idea      F10-Next Writing Idea
```

2

```
 ┌ Writing Idea ─────────────────────────────────────────
 Describe her everyday family routines.  Did they always eat together at the
 table?  Did they play games or spend time together in the evenings?  Did these
 later become customs in her own family?

 ┌ Biography of Gayle Barbara Jansen ────────────────────
 Other than French and Norwegian recipes handed down from generation to
 generation, Gayle's family really didn't have many other traditions.  They
 were pretty famous around the neighborhood for being good card players,
 though.  And Gayle was among the best.  Maybe it was the long Minnesota
 winters that made card playing such a popular pastime in the Jansen
 family.  But even in the summer they played cards.  Whenever the lake was
 too cold for swimming or it was raining, there would be Bridge, 500,
 Cribbage, you name it...

 └ Normal ──────────────────────────────── Row 23 Col 25 ─
 F9-Menu          Esc-Previous Writing Idea      F10-Next Writing Idea
```

Use two simple keys to quickly scroll through Writing Ideas.

3

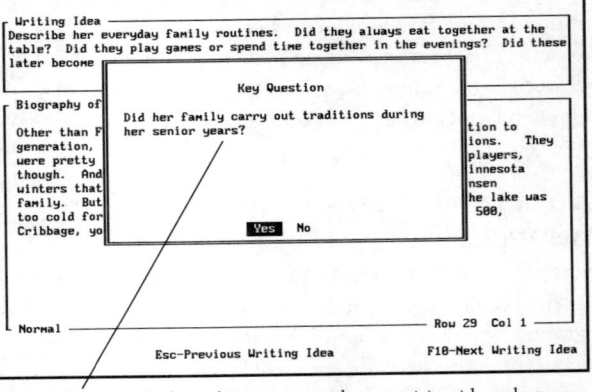

```
 ┌ Writing Idea ─────────────────────────────────────────
 Describe her everyday family routines.  Did they always eat together at the
 table?  Did they play games or spend time together in the evenings?  Did these
 later become

 ┌ Biography of         ┌ Key Question ──────────────────     tion to
 Other than F          Did her family carry out traditions during   ions.  They
 generation,           her senior years?                           players,
 were pretty                                                      innesota
 though.  And                                                     nsen
 winters that                                                  he lake was
 family.  But                                                    500,
 too cold for               ┌ Yes ┐  No                      
 Cribbage, yo               └─────┘
                      └──────────────────────────────────

 └ Normal ──────────────────────────────── Row 29 Col 1 ──
                  Esc-Previous Writing Idea      F10-Next Writing Idea
```

Key Questions help make sure you only see writing ideas that are appropriate for your relative.

WARRANTY

BRØDERBUND 90 DAY SATISFACTION GUARANTEE

If you are not completely satisfied with your purchase, return the product to Brøderbund Software within 90 days of the date of purchase, along with the original sales receipt and the reason for return. Please state whether you would prefer another Brøderbund product of equal or lesser value, or a full refund. Limit 1 per household. Dealers, distributors and their employees are not eligible. Please call Brøderbund Software Direct at 415-382-4745, or return the merchandise to Brøderbund Software, Attention Customer Support, P.O. Box 6125, Novato, CA 94948-6125. If you wish to return the product via U.P.S., please send it to Brøderbund Software, Attention Returns Department, 775 South Point Boulevard, Petaluma, CA 94954.

The Brøderbund 90 Day Satisfaction Guarantee also warrants for a period of 90 days that this copy of Family Tree Maker is free from substantial errors or defects that will materially interfere with the operation of the program as described in the enclosed user documentation. This policy applies to the initial purchaser only.

If you believe you have found any such error or defect in the program during the 90 day period, call Brøderbund's Banner Blue Division Technical Support Department at 510-794-6850 between the hours of 7 AM and 5 PM. (Pacific time), Monday through Friday. Banner Blue Technical personnel will attempt to help you correct or avoid the problem. If any such error or defect cannot be corrected or reasonably avoided, Brøderbund will inform you how to obtain a corrected program disk (or you can inform Brøderbund that you prefer another Brøderbund product of equal or lesser value or a full refund).

RESTRICTIONS

The Software contains copyrighted material, trade secrets and other proprietary material. In order to protect them, and except as permitted by applicable legislation, you may not decompile, reverse engineer, disassemble or otherwise reduce the Software to a human-perceivable form. You may not modify, network, rent, lease, loan, distribute, or create derivative works based upon the Software in whole or in part. You may not electronically transmit the Software from one computer to another or over a network.

EXPORT LAW ASSURANCES

You agree and certify that neither the Software nor any other technical data received from Brøderbund, nor the direct product thereof, will be exported outside the United States except as authorized and as permitted by the laws and regulations of the United States. If the Software has been rightfully obtained by you outside of the United States, you agree that you will not re-export the Software nor any other technical data received from Brøderbund, nor the direct product thereof, except as permitted by the laws and regulations of the United States and the laws and regulations of the jurisdiction in which you obtained the Software.

GOVERNMENT END USERS

If you are acquiring the Software on behalf of any unit or agency of the United States Government, the following provisions apply. The Government agrees:

(i) if the Software are supplied to the Department of Defense (DoD), the Software are classified as "Commercial Computer Software" and the Government is acquiring only "restricted rights" in the Software, and its documentation as that term is defined in Clause 252.227-7013(c)(1) of the DFARS; and

(ii) if the Software are supplied to any unit or agency of the United States Government other than DoD, the Government's rights in the Software, and its documentation will be as defined in Clause 52.227-19(c)(2) of the FAR or, in the case of NASA, in Clause 18-52.227-86(d) of the NASA Supplement to the FAR.

DISCLAIMER OF WARRANTY

You expressly acknowledge and agree that use of the Software is at your sole risk. The Software, and related documentation are provided "AS IS" and without warranty of any kind. If for any reason you are dissatisfied with the software, return the product with your original sales receipt to Brøderbund within 90 days of the date of purchase for a full refund or a replacement product of equal or lesser value. Brøderbund expressly disclaims all warranties, express or implied, including, but not limited to, the implied warranties of merchantability and fitness for a particular purpose. Brøderbund does not warrant that the functions contained in the software will meet your requirements, or that the operation of the software will be uninterrupted or error-free, or that defects in the software and the fonts will be corrected. Furthermore, Brøderbund does not warrant or make representations regarding the use or the results of the use of the software or related documentation in terms of their correctness, accuracy, reliability, or otherwise. No oral or written information or advice given by Brøderbund or a Brøderbund authorized representative shall create a warranty or in any way increase the scope of this warranty. Should the software prove defective, you (and not Brøderbund or a Brøderbund authorized representative) assume the entire cost of all necessary servicing, repair or correction. Some jurisdictions do not allow the exclusion of implied warranties, so the above exclusion may not apply to you.

LIMITATIONS ON WARRANTY

Unauthorized representations: Brøderbund warrants only that the program will perform as described in the user documentation. No other advertising, description or representation, whether made by a Brøderbund dealer, distributor, agent or employee, shall be binding upon Brøderbund or shall change the terms of this warranty.

No consequential damages: Brøderbund shall not be liable for special, incidental, consequential or other damages, even if Brøderbund is advised of or aware of the possibility of such damages. This means that Brøderbund shall not be responsible or liable for lost profits or revenues, or for damages or costs incurred as a result of loss of time, data or use of the software, or from any other cause except the actual cost of the product. In no event shall Brøderbund's liability exceed the purchase price of this product. Some states do not allow the exclusion or limitation of incidental or consequential damages, so the above limitation or exclusion may not apply to you.

You are entitled to use this product for your own use, but may not sell or transfer reproductions of the software or manual to other parties in any way, nor rent or lease the product to others without the prior written permission of Brøderbund. You may use one copy of the product on a single terminal connected to a single computer. You may not network the product or otherwise use it on more than one computer or computer terminal at the same time.

For technical support, on this program, call Brøderbund's Banner Blue Division Technical Support Department at 510-794-6850. For technical support on any other Brøderbund product, call 415-382-4700.